Frontispiece: Anita. See page 102 for instructions.

Title Page: Mary Hoyer and her dolls.

Front Cover: Olga. See page 62 for instructions.

Back Cover: Dolly Madison. See pages 134 and 159 for pattern and instructions.

Mary Hoyer and Her Dolls
Patterns to Crochet, Knit, and Sew

by Mary Hoyer

edited by Virginia Ann Heyerdahl

Published by HOBBY HOUSE PRESS, INC.
Cumberland, Maryland

For The Reader

The Crochet, Knit, and Sewing Patterns fit the 14in (35.6cm) Mary Hoyer Doll. Doll enthusiasts who want the best and authenticate styles from the 1940s through the 1960s will find that these Mary Hoyer Projects will fit (with some minor alterations sometimes necessary): Sweet Sue, Betsy McCall, Toni, Maggie, Alice, Harriet Hubbard Ayer, R & B dolls, Madame Alexander dolls and many others.

© 1982 by Hobby House Press, Inc.
2nd printing, 1986.

All rights reserved. No part of this book may be reproduced or utilized in any form or by any means, electronic or mechanical, including photocopying, recording, or by any information storage and retrieval system, without permission in writing from the publisher. Inquiries should be addressed to Hobby House Press, Inc., 900 Frederick Street, Cumberland, Maryland 21502-1298.

Printed in the United States of America

ISBN: 0-87588-282-X

Table of Contents

Introduction 1
Chapter I: Biographical Sketch 2
Chapter II: The Mary Hoyer Doll
    How It All Began 8
    Advertising 12
    Price Lists 19
    Publicity 33
    Fashion Shows 36

How-To-Section - Knit & Crochet Patterns
Chapter III: *Mary's Dollies* 45

Annabelle page 60   Carol page 123

Goldilocks - Princess Dress and Beret — *Knit* .. 54
Julianna - Ski Suit — *Knit* 56
Arlene - Bathing Ensemble — *Knit* 58
Annabelle - Sport Suit — *Knit* 60
Olga - Skating Outfit — *Crochet* 62
Mayree - Party Frock — *Crochet* 64
The Wavette — *Knit* 66
Judy - Lace Party Dress — *Crochet* 68
May-Belle - The Majorette — *Crochet* 70
Nadine - Red Cross Nurse — *Knit* 72
Sonja - Skiing Costume — *Knit* 74
Lucretta - Skating Costume — *Crochet* 76
Zorina - "Miss Victory" dressed as a Charming Ally — *Crochet* 78
Terry - Little "Miss Victory" and her little Mommy — *Crochet* 80
Sunny - "Miss Victory" is Queen of the Courts — *Knit* 82
Janie - "Miss Victory" is a Modern Cinderella — *Knit* 84
Kathleen - "Miss Victory" — *Knit* 88
Susanna - "Miss Victory" — *Crochet* 90
Patsy - Coat, Hat and Bag — *Crochet* 92
Corine - Queen of the Jungles — *Knit* 94
Paula - Bathing Ensemble — *Crochet* 96
Billie - Riding Habit — *Knit* 98
Jackie - Bare Back Rider — *Crochet* 100

Anita - Skiing Costume — *Knit* 102
Dolores - Skating Costume — *Crochet* 105
Lucille - Roller Skating Outfit — *Knit* 107
The Westerner — *Knit* 109
Peggy - Travel Costume — *Crochet* 111
Greta - A Dutch Treat — *Crochet* 113
Jo-Ann - Swimming Suit — *Knit* 115
Mary Hoyer Twins, Bobby and Betty — *Knit* ... 117
Nancy and Dick - The Cow Boy and Girl — *Knit* 119
Hans and Tina - "The Pond's Sweethearts" — *Knit* 121
Carol - Suit and Hat — *Crochet* 123
Louise - Travel in the Best Circles — *Crochet* 125
Connie - Short and Sweet — *Knit* 127
Nan and Jack - The Ship's In — *Crochet/Knit* 129
Janette - ...in the Spotlight — *Knit* 132
Renee - Crocheted Sun Dress and Cape 135
Isabelle - Knitted Skating Costume 137

How-To-Section-Sewing Patterns
Chapter IV: Original Styles by Mary Hoyer 139

 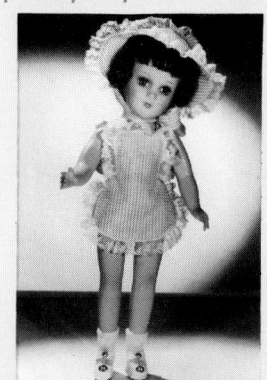

Bride page 139   Sunsuit and Bonnet page 185

Bride Dress and Veil 139
Bridesmaid Dress and Hat 141
Ballerina 145
Southern Belle 148
Alice Blue Dress and Pinafore 150
Terry Cloth Beach Robe 152
Slacks and Shirt 152
Shorts and Halter 152
Sun Bonnet Sue 156
Dolly Madison 159
Scotch Plaid Jumper and Blousette 162
Blouse and Jumper 164
McCall Printed Pattern 1564, ... 166
McCall's Printed Pattern 1891, ... 180

Continued

How-To-Section-Knit & Crochet Patterns
Chapter V: The Best from Mary Hoyer's *Juvenile Styles* 200

Goldilocks page 214

Arlene - Crocheted Hat 201
A Yoke Coat for Dolly and Her Mamma — *Knit* 202
Lace Dress and Hat — *Crochet* 203
Infants Four-Piece Set — *Crochet* 204
Infants Three-Piece Set — *Crochet* 206
Maybelle - Three-Piece Crochet Set — *Crochet* 207
Shoulderette - Three-Piece Infant's Set — *Crochet* 208
Crocheted Blanket 209
Knitted Blanket 210
A Convalescing Jacket Ensemble — *Knit* 211
Royal Highness - Cape and Hood — *Knit* 212
A Sailor's Sweetheart - Crochet Jacket 213
Goldilocks - Little Princess and her dolly — *Knit* 214
Colleen - Jerkin, Socks and Beanie — *Knit* 215
Slumber Time "Florella" Knitted Infants Set .. 216
Snow Set — *Knit* 218
Little Mama...Little Dolly Lace Baby Dresses — *Crochet* 219
"Love at first sight" - Slip-Over and Jerkin — *Knit* 219
"My Sister and I" Are Two-of-A-Kind — *Knit* 220
Teen Team - Boy's and Girl's Vests — *Knit* 221
Smocked Dress — *Knit* 221
Million Dollar Baby — *Knit* 222
Lace Dress and Dutch Cap — *Crochet* 223
Index 224

Color Illustration 1. Ballerina. See page 145 for pattern and instructions.

See several other color illustrations of sewing projects on pages 6 and 7.

Dedication

I would like to dedicate this book with love and gratitude to my husband, William, and my daughter, Arlene, for their untiring efforts and devotion throughout the early years of work in compiling the Mary Hoyer *Juvenile Styles* books and the Mary Hoyer Doll business.

Without their help and understanding this book and the work therein could not have been compiled, written and published.

Introduction

This book relates the story of Mary Hoyer and the famous doll which she designed and Bernard Lipfert sculpted to her specifications. The Mary Hoyer Doll, popular over a span of nearly 40 years, was a unique offering in the doll world. The doll was sold undressed for the most part, to be dressed by the new owner. The doll's creator not only designed a multitude of different knit, crochet and sewing patterns for garments to be completed, but also designed a large line of accessories to go with the doll. In addition, she designed kits containing patterns, material and complete instructions for the doll dressmaker to complete the garment.

The first two chapters provide detailed biographical information on Mary Hoyer and the evolution of the doll itself. Original advertising including price lists are shown as are articles which appeared in newspapers and magazines. Through the recollections of Mary Hoyer herself, the history of the Mary Hoyer Doll and the other members of her "family" are revealed. One will be able to identify and date Mary Hoyer dolls in their collection.

For the first time, all nine volumes of *Mary's Dollies* are reprinted together. These are the books containing knit, crochet and a few sewing patterns designed by Mary Hoyer for the doll. Also included is a selection of the original patterns from the kits and the McCall patterns that were designed for the doll. Not only do all of these patterns fit the Mary Hoyer Doll, but they fit other 14in (35.6cm) slim bodied dolls popular from the 1940s through the 1960s such as *Sweet Sue, Betsy McCall, Toni, Maggie, Alice, Harriet Hubbard Ayer,* R & B dolls, Madame Alexander dolls and many others.

Since Mary Hoyer began her career as a designer of fashions for babies, children, teen-agers and adults, included herewith is a selection of some of the *best* fashions she designed over the years which were published in volumes of *Juvenile Styles*. Several patterns for doll outfits which appeared in *Juvenile Styles* are reprinted as are several matching outfits for a child and the doll. The patterns reprinted here are as popular today as they were when they were first designed.

About this Book

Mary Hoyer, the originator of this famous doll, has utilized her own records and compiled the story of the Mary Hoyer Doll. For those who at one time or another received a Mary Hoyer Doll as a gift, received a handmade doll's outfit from their mother, or for those who are now collecting the Mary Hoyer Doll, this book has been long awaited. Featured are over 200 color and black and white photographs illustrating fine details of both the doll and her clothing.

The background material on Mary Hoyer traces her career which began as a fashion designer in the early 1930s. She designed children's knitwear for several major yarn manufacturers and eventually published her own *Juvenile Styles* pattern books.

From this it was only a quick step to designing knitted and crocheted costumes for dolls. Since the right sized doll was not available, Mary Hoyer designed a doll and took her idea to Bernard Lipfert who sculpted this special doll. The Mary Hoyer Doll was born.

An instant success which remained popular from its introduction in 1937 until the doll was discontinued in the 1970s. The chapter detailing the history of the Mary Hoyer Doll traces its beginning as a double-jointed composition doll down to the final vinyl version known as *Becky*.

Through the years Mary Hoyer designed over 40 knit and crochet patterns which were published by the McCall Pattern Company. Reprinted here, all together for the first time, are all of the knit and crochet patterns which were originally published in *Mary's Dollies*. In addition to the reprint McCall Mary Hoyer patterns, many of the patterns from the dressing kits Mary Hoyer designed are also included.

Since Mary Hoyer started out designing children's clothing, a sampling of these Juvenile Style patterns have also been included. The designs reprinted are those that are as popular today as they were when they were first published. There are also several infant patterns which can be made up for that new grandchild or even perhaps adapted for a baby doll!

After the first printing of this book appeared, Mary Hoyer put her talents to work again and designed a number of costumes for her doll which were re-creations of outfits first appearing in her fashion shows. These were published in the **Doll Reader** magazine and are included here in color as well as in black and white.

Over 100 knitting, crocheting and sewing projects.

I. Biographical Section

Illustration 1. Sallie Whitman, of English ancestry, and her husband, Daniel Sensenig, of Swiss and German extraction, parents of Mary Sensenig Hoyer.

Illustration 2. Mary at the age of one and a half with her sister, Jane, at the age of three.

Illustration 3. Jane and Mary dressed as twins by their mother.

Mary Sensenig Hoyer, the creator and originator of the famous Mary Hoyer dolls, so popular in the 1940s through the 1960s, was born October 21, 1901, in Lancaster County, Pennsylvania. Her parents were Sallie Whitman and Daniel Sensenig and she was the youngest of their 14 children. Mr. Sensenig operated a general store and post office in Lancaster County and one of the heirlooms she still treasurers is the little scale she has on her coffee table that her father used to weigh the mail.

The family moved to Mohnton, Pennsylvania, when Mary was six months old where her father operated a general store on Main Street. When Mary was seven, her parents moved to Reading, Pennsylvania, where she has lived ever since.

Mary's oldest sister, Alice, was a great influence on her life, and, perhaps more than anyone else, encouraged her interest and talents in needlework. Mary remembers that Alice did a great deal of sewing and would sit Mary on the end of her machine while she worked. Alice made beautiful sun bonnets with the stiff brim of the bonnets made of fine straw taken from the bales of straw in which tobacco was shipped.

When Mary was eight she had appendicitis and on the way to the hospital her appendix burst. She was ill for quite a long time. Alice visited her regularly in the hospital and told her to hurry and get well because she would buy her a beautiful doll.

After leaving the hospital, Mary was taken to Mohnton to live with Alice and her daughter until she recovered. When she arrived, Alice had a doll waiting for her! Mary remembers the doll: "I thought it was the most beautiful doll I had ever seen. The doll had a bisque head with long golden finger curls made of human hair. Her eyes were blue and she was smiling, showing her beautiful little teeth. The arms and legs were jointed and she was made in Germany. Alice had made the doll a dress of china blue silk, ruffled from the waist to the hem of her long skirt. The long sleeves were full with a tight band for cuffs. I rarely took her out of the box, but loved to show her off when we had company.

"Years later when I was not at home, my mother gave my doll to one of my little nieces to play with and she let the doll fall on the cement pavement and broke her beautiful head."

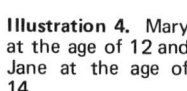

Illustration 4. Mary at the age of 12 and Jane at the age of 14.

During the period of her recuperation, Mary did not attend school. Instead, Alice taught her to knit and crochet and she even experimented with the material left over from Alice's sewing.

Several years later Alice moved to Reading and rented space in Ellis Mills Department Store on Penn Street. She sold yarn, needles and related items and eventually her business expanded so she moved to a large store on South Fifth Street. When Mary was 18 and attending McCanns Business School, she worked for Alice and became very adept at designing and writing knitting instructions.

Mary met William Hoyer around 1923 and they were married in 1926. They drove to Canada on their honeymoon in a model T Ford. Upon returning to Reading, they lived in an apartment until the house they were having built was finished. The house was in Springmont, about three miles from Reading. It was here that their daughter, Arlene, was born.

Illustration 5. Mary at the age of 15.

RIGHT: Illustrations 6A and 6B. William Hoyer and his bride, Mary, in 1926.

Illustration 7. Mary Hoyer with her daughter, Arlene, in 1930.

Illustration 8. William and Mary Hoyer on a buying trip in New York, 1945.

Illustration 10. Arlene, Mary and William Hoyer's daughter.

Illustration 11. Kim Price, grandchild of Mary and William Hoyer.

Illustration 12. Lynne Price, grandchild of Mary and William Hoyer.

Illustration 9. The Hoyer's home on Holly Road, Reading, Pennsylvania, where they lived from 1960 to 1977.

Illustration 13. Kevin Price, grandchild of Mary and William Hoyer.

Illustration 14. Karen Price, grandchild of Mary and William Hoyer.

Upon retirement, the Hoyers purchased a condominium in Florida where they spend the winter months, returning to Reading for the summer. When she was in Florida, Mary found time on her hands and decided to try yet another art form, that of oil painting. She now has nearly 100 paintings to her credit. A small selection of some of her favorite paintings are shown on pages 2 and 3.

Color Illustration 2. Flowers, 1975. 16in x 20in (40.6cm x 50.8cm).

Color Illustration 3. Arlene, 1976. 12in x 16in (30.5cm x 40.6cm). *Courtesy of Arlene Hess.*

Color Illustration 4. House on the Hill, 1976. 12in x 16in (30.5cm x 40.6cm). *Courtesy of Jane Shober.*

Color Illustration 5. The Pond, 1973. 12in x 16in (30.5cm x 40.6cm). *Courtesy of Elizabeth Zug.*

Color Illustration 6. Karen, 6 years old, 1976. 9in x 12in (22.9cm x 30.5cm). *Courtesy of Karen Price.*

RIGHT: Color Illustration 7. Heron in Swamp, 1975. 15in x 6in (38.1cm x 15.2cm). *Courtesy of Arlene Hess.*

Color Illustration 8. Bootsie, Siamese cat, 1974. 12in x 16in (30.5cm x 40.6cm).

Color Illustration 9. Karen, 13 years old, 1975. 9in x 12in (22.9cm x 30.5cm).

5

ABOVE: Color Illustration 10. Southern Belle. See page 148 for pattern and instructions.

RIGHT: Color Illustration 11. Scotch Plaid Jumper and Blousette. See page 162 for pattern and instructions.

RIGHT: Color Illustration 12. Bridesmaid. See page 141 for pattern and instructions.

LOWER LEFT: Color Illustration 13. Blouse and Jumper. See page 164 for pattern and instructions.

LOWER RIGHT: Color Illustration 14. Alice Blue Dress and Pinafore. See page 150 for pattern and instructions.

II. The Mary Hoyer Doll

How It All Began

Mary Hoyer began her career as a designer of knit and crochet fashions for infants and children. It was only natural that her interest would turn to designing the same kind of fashions for dolls.

In Volume I of the *Juvenile Styles* books on page 4 is a photograph of a little girl dressed in a knitted coat and crocheted hat. A doll is also shown wearing a matching coat and hat. The doll belonged to Arlene Hoyer and was a heavy bodied doll of unknown make. While Mrs. Hoyer would have preferred to design an outfit for a slim bodied doll, this 14in (35.6cm) doll was at hand so she made the outfit to fit it. (See Illustration 161, page 202.)

It was at this time that Mrs. Hoyer conceived the idea of having an artist make a doll to her own specifications. She wanted a doll shaped like a little girl and about 14in (35.6cm) tall, a size a child could easily handle. She found a slim bodied doll at the Ideal Novelty and Toy Company. That company liked the idea of marketing a doll with accompanying instruction books for knitting and crocheting garments to fit it. However, a little later the company decided that this doll would not fit into their line of merchandise and offered to sell the doll directly to the Hoyers in large quantities and undressed, for use with the instruction books Mrs. Hoyer proposed to write.

The first doll was 13in (33.0cm) tall and composition with a double jointed body and sleep eyes. The wig was mohair fashioned in curls and came in three different shades. Shown on the back cover of *Juvenile Styles,* Volume 3, the doll sold for $1.50 undressed or $3.00 dressed. She was featured in the first book of doll patterns, *Mary's Dollies,* Volume 5, which was originally published in 1937. Approximately 2,000 of this type of doll were sold before it was discontinued by the Ideal Novelty and Toy Company.

Illustration 16. Another of the first 13in (33.0cm) all-composition dolls wearing the same dress as shown in *Illustration 15*. The dress is the first Mary Hoyer designed for this doll.

"Doll of Tomorrow"

Designed especially for
MARY HOYER

A perfected supple doll, with flexible jointed body, beautiful, graceful and made of the finest "Hard to Break" Composition, with movable eyes and lashes—Real hair, in blond, dark brown and auburn. She is 13 inches tall.

•

Doll's Dress and Bonnet is an original design by
MARY HOYER

•

Send $1.50 for this beautiful Doll, stating the shade of Hair desired and the Doll will be mailed to you Postpaid, together with instructions for making the adorable Lace Bonnet and Dress.
Doll completely dressed as shown on illustration for $3.00. State color of Hair and dress desired.
If you are not more than pleased with your Doll, return it within 10 days and your money will be promptly refunded.

SEND YOUR ORDER DIRECTLY TO:

JUVENILE STYLES PUBLISHING CO.
1008 PENN STREET, READING, PA.

DEALERS—Write for Special Promotional Proposition

Illustration 15. This advertisement shows the first doll purchased by the Hoyers from the Ideal Novelty and Toy Company in 1937. 13in (33.0cm) tall; composition with a double jointed body (note small inserted photograph of undressed doll showing double jointing); sleep eyes; mohair wig in a choice of three shades; no markings. *Juvenile Styles,* Volume 2, Page 34.

Later in 1937 Mary Hoyer had her own doll designed to her specifications and it was sculpted by Mr. Bernard Lipfert, the well-known doll sculptor whose other credits include the *Shirley Temple* doll. Mary Hoyer's doll was produced by the Fiberoid Doll Company in New York while the Hoyers retained ownership of the molds.

These first 14in (35.6cm) dolls were composition. Each piece was molded in two parts - - the head, body, arms and legs - - and then they were glued together. After hand spraying, the parts were hung to dry while the face, including the eyes, was hand painted. Mohair wigs were made by a wig company in New York and came in four shades.

The first run of 1,500 of the 14in (35.6cm) doll was unmarked. After this Mr. Hoyer concluded that it would be a good idea to have a trademark on the doll body. On the next order for 5,000 dolls the mark "THE//MARY HOYER//DOLL" was incorporated into the mold and each doll body carried this mark on the back in raised letters.

The painted-eye composition dolls were featured in *Mary's Dollies,* Volumes 6, 9 and 10. At the time these dolls were made, steel eyes were unobtainable so the doll had painted eyes instead of sleep eyes. When steel eyes became available, they were placed in the composition dolls and these sleep-eyed composition dolls were featured in *Mary's Dollies,* Volumes 11 and 12. Occasionally these dolls

Illustration 18. Enlarged mark on the back of a 14in (35.6cm) composition *Mary Hoyer Doll.*

Illustration 19. Enlarged mark on the back of a 14in (35.6cm) hard plastic *Mary Hoyer Doll.*

Illustration 17. The first 14in (35.6cm) Mary Hoyer Doll designed by Mary Hoyer and sculpted by Mr. Bernard Lipfert. She is all-composition with a mohair wig and painted eyes. The dress is a slightly different version of the dresses seen in *Illustration 15* and *16.*

were costumed as boy dolls and lambs wool or mohair was used for their wigs.

The composition doll was discontinued in 1946 and later the molds were sold to someone in South America without the Hoyer's knowledge or consent. During the period of time between 1937, when the doll was first conceived, and 1946, when it was discontinued, approximately 6,500 of the composition dolls were made and sold.

After the composition doll was discontinued, the Mary Hoyer Doll was duplicated in hard plastic with the mark "ORIGINAL//Mary Hoyer//DOLL" in raised letters inside of a circle on the back of the doll.

A 14in (35.6cm) hard plastic walking doll was produced for a short time. The walking mechanism proved to be troublesome and almost impossible to repair so this doll was discontinued. When the doll was discontinued, the walking mechanism was removed and the heads were used until the stock was depleted. The removal of this mechanism left two slits in the top of the head.

In the early 1950s an 18in (45.7cm) Mary Hoyer Doll was produced and given the name *Gigi.* This doll was marked on the back the same as the 14in (35.6cm) hard plastic Mary Hoyer Dolls. *Gigi* was not photographed or shown in any of the *Mary's Dollies* books but did appear

Illustration 20. Enlarged mark on the back of an 18in (45.7cm) hard plastic *Mary Hoyer Doll* called *Gigi*.

Illustration 21. Mailing label from the Mary Hoyer Doll Manufacturing Company.

in some of the advertising and on the price lists. This doll never quite reached the popularity of the 14in (35.6cm) doll. Only about 2,000 of these dolls were manufactured by the Frisch Doll Company and sold with the Mary Hoyer mark on the back. *Gigi* sold for $5.95 and $6.95 undressed.

About the middle 1950s a 20in (50.8cm) doll was introduced into the line, manufactured by the Ideal Novelty and Toy Company. She had a vinyl head with rooted hair in a pony tail and arched feet for high heeled shoes. Since Mary Hoyer did not have time to design a wardrobe for this doll she was discontinued after only one shipment. She was not shown in any of the *Mary's Dollies* books nor was she photographed to appear on the price lists or in any advertising. She was listed on the price lists for a short period of time and sold for $6.95.

Through advertisements placed in the *McCall's Needlework and Crafts* magazine, the mail order business began. By 1945 Mr. Hoyer found it necessary to leave his position as purchasing agent at the Berkshire Knitting Mills in Wyomissing, Pennsylvania, and take over the mail order business full time. He obtained the building at 1013 Penn Street in Reading, Pennsylvania, where there were rooms for offices, storage areas for stock, wigging rooms with space for professional hairdressers who would glue on the wigs and style them, plus huge shipping rooms. At this time 14 people were employed by the company.

Business continued to expand. In addition to the Mary Hoyer retail shop at 1008 Penn Street in Reading, another shop was opened at 714 Boardwalk in Ocean City, New Jersey.

The distribution of the dolls and kits in shops was discontinued after the first year in the doll business. Undressed dolls with instruction books and kits with enough material or yarn to make the outfits were sold to church organizations and insurance companies for charitable purposes. The rest of the sales were strictly mail order.

In 1957 another new doll was introduced into the Mary Hoyer Doll line. She was *Vicky*, manufactured by the Ideal Novelty and Toy Company. *Vicky* originally came in three sizes: 10½in (26.7cm), 12in (30.5cm) and 14in (35.6cm) but the two larger sizes were discontinued and only the 10½in (26.7cm) size was carried for any length of time. She was all vinyl and was described in the original advertising as having "a perfectly formed body that turns, bends, bows from the waist." The advertising went on to say that she had "realistic eyes that open and close, rooted saran hair!" *Vicky* came dressed in a bra, panties, high heeled sandals and earrings and sold for $2.50 and $2.95.

Vicky's addition to the Mary Hoyer family of dolls was followed in 1958 by *Margie*, a 10in (25.4cm) all-vinyl toddler with rooted hair and sleep eyes. *Margie* was followed in 1961 by *Cathy*, a 10in (25.4cm) all-vinyl infant doll with painted hair and sleep eyes. *Margie* and *Cathy* were manufactured by the Unique Doll Company. An 8in (20.3cm) baby doll *Janie* was also available at this time. *Margie* sold for $2.50, *Cathy* sold for $1.50 and *Janie* cost $1.00 and $1.25.

Instructions for knitting and crocheting garments as well as sewing kits were available for these dolls. Completed costumes could also be purchased.

In 1960 the hard plastic 14in (35.6cm) Mary Hoyer Doll was discontinued. The Fiberoid Doll Company went out of business because plastic was unobtainable. In all, approximately 72,000 of the hard plastic dolls were sold. These were Mary Hoyer's favorites of all the Mary Hoyer Dolls.

Upon the discontinuation of the hard plastic doll, the Hoyers had the doll copied in vinyl. The basic vinyl doll was very similar to the hard plastic Mary Hoyer Doll, but the face was different and the hair was rooted. This doll was called *Becky* and sold for $2.95 and $3.50.

Becky came with a variety of hair styles: long straight hair, long curly hair and upswept hairdos. Her rooted hair could be combed and washed and came in a choice of four shades. This doll was unmarked and did not carry the Mary Hoyer trademark on the back.

At the time *Becky* was introduced she was accepted with as much enthusiasm as the composition and hard plastic Mary Hoyer Dolls.

She was the most popular of the vinyl dolls offered by the Mary Hoyer Doll Manufacturing Company and was discontinued sometime in 1968.

Mary Hoyer was almost as well-known for the custom made garments as she was for her dolls. These garments were sewn by five or more seamstresses employed full time by the Mary Hoyer Doll Manufacturing Company. The sewing requirements were very exacting and great attention was given to detail. These seamstresses did the work in their homes. A professional cutter was also employed and worked from his home. When the seamstresses received their work it was already cut and the trimmings to complete each garment were included. The clothing sold in both retail shops and through mail order, carried the Mary Hoyer label on the completed garments.

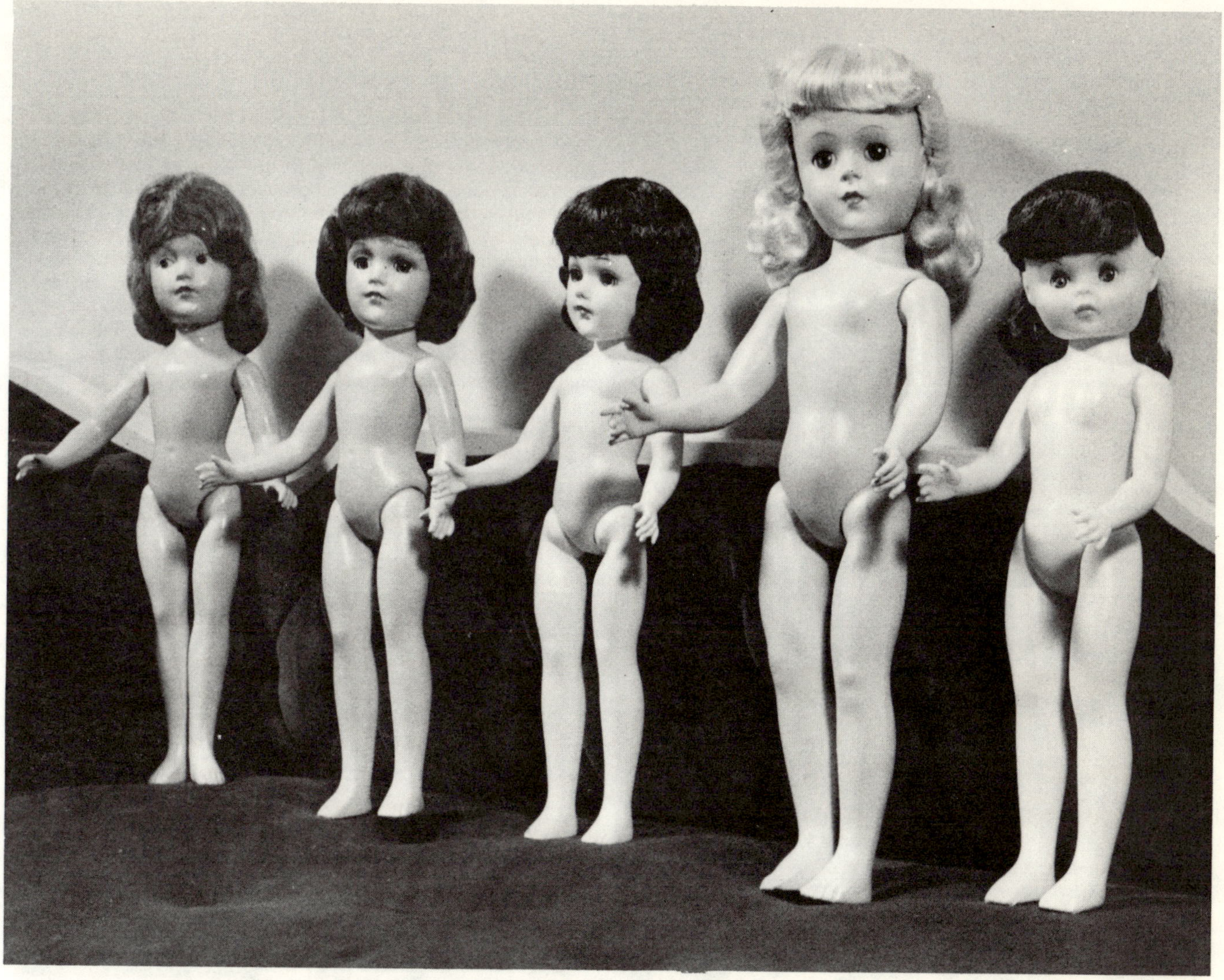

Illustration 22. Mary Hoyer Dolls. Left to right: 14in (35.6cm) composition with painted eyes; 14in (35.6cm) composition with sleep eyes; 14in (35.6cm) hard plastic with sleep eyes; 18in (45.7cm) hard plastic with sleep eyes; 14in (35.6cm) all-vinyl with sleep eyes.

Illustration 23. Enlargement of the woven labels which were sewn into doll clothing made by the Mary Hoyer Doll Manufacturing Company.

Advertising

The Mary Hoyer Doll Manufacturing Company's mail order business grew and expanded rapidly. Much of the success was due not only to the popularity of the dolls themselves and the books and accessories, but also to the fact that much of the advertising was placed in *McCall's Needlework & Crafts* magazine, a publication with a very wide distribution. The impact was fantastic! At first the ads were small, but they gradually increased in size to half and full page ads.

The following pages contain a sampling of the advertising which appeared in the *McCall's Needlework & Crafts* magazine between the years 1943 and 1967.

Illustration 24. *McCall's Needlework & Crafts* magazine, 1943.

Illustration 25. *McCall's Needlework & Crafts* magazine, 1946.

Illustration 26. *McCall's Needlework & Crafts* magazine, 1947.

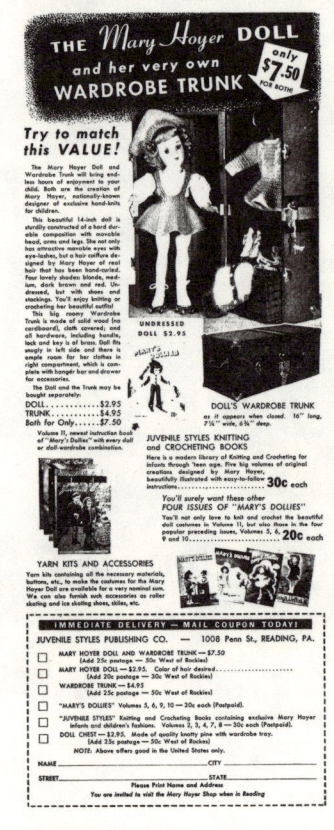

ABOVE LEFT: Illustration 27. *McCall's Needlework & Crafts* magazine, 1948.

ABOVE RIGHT: Illustration 28. *McCall's Needlework & Crafts* magazine, 1949.

RIGHT: Illustration 29. *McCall's Needlework & Crafts* magazine, Winter, 1949-1950.

Illustration 30. *McCall's Needlework & Crafts* magazine, Spring-Summer, 1950.

Illustration 32. *McCall's Needlework & Crafts* magazine, Winter, 1951.

Illustration 31. Full page ad, *McCall's Needlework & Crafts* magazine, Fall-Winter, 1950.

Illustration 33. *McCall's Needlework & Crafts* magazine, Spring-Summer, 1951.

13

Illustration 34. Full page ad, *McCall's Needlework & Crafts* magazine, 1952.

Illustration 36. Full page ad, *McCall's Needlework & Crafts*, Fall-Winter, 1952.

Illustration 35. *McCall's Needlework & Crafts* magazine, Spring-Summer, 1952.

Want to make it a Foursome?...
with the Friendly Mary Hoyer TWINS

MOST BEAUTIFUL DOLLS IN AMERICA!

You and your little girl will find real enjoyment in these famous twin dolls. Your daughter will have endless hours of fun playing with them and you'll enjoy making their costumes—find them easy to knit, crochet and sew for. These lifelike dolls are made of finest durable plastic, are fully jointed and have moving eyes. Girl Doll has DuPont Nylon Washable Wig that can be combed and waved. Shades of Wigs—blond, medium, dark brown and auburn. Boy Doll's hair of curly Lambs Wool dyed in brown or black. BOTH DOLLS COME UNDRESSED, but with shoes and stockings.

BOY $3.50   **GIRL $4.95**

COMPLETE KITS TO MAKE COSTUMES ILLUSTRATED
Kits contain all necessary materials—yarn, slacks or skirt cut to fit, for either boy or girl costume. **$1 ea.**

LARGE MARY HOYER WARDROBE TRUNK
Of sturdy wood construction, cloth covered, lock and key. Has room for two dolls, clothing and accessories. **$5.25**

MARY HOYER DOLLY WAVE SET
Includes shampoo, wave set and curlers to give dolly her hair-do. **49¢**

"MARY'S DOLLIES", Vols. 5, 6, 9, 10, 11, 12, 13, 14, 15—20¢ ea. Books contain simple instructions for Knitting, Crocheting and Sewing many outfits that fit Mary Hoyer Dolls perfectly.

WRITE FOR COMPLETE PRICE LIST OF YARN KITS AND ACCESSORIES

McCall's Pattern No. 1564 Available for sewing a number of costumes which were designed to fit the Mary Hoyer Dolls.

You are invited to visit the Mary Hoyer Shops when in Reading, Pa. or Ocean City, N.J.

```
THE MARY HOYER DOLL MFG. CO.
(Juvenile Styles Publishing Co.)
1013 PENN STREET, READING, PENNA.

□ MARY HOYER GIRL DOLL with DuPont Nylon Washable Wig—$4.95    Color of Hair..........
□ MARY HOYER BOY DOLL with Lambs Wool Wig—$3.50                Color of Hair..........
□ MARY HOYER BOY AND GIRL DOLL (Two Dolls)—$7.95
        (Add 25c postage—40c West of Chicago) for each Doll ordered.
□ COMPLETE KIT TO MAKE  □ GIRL DOLL'S COSTUME—$1.00   □ BOY DOLL'S COSTUME—$1.00
□ MARY HOYER DOLLY WAVE SET—49c (Postpaid)
□ "MARY'S DOLLIES"—Vols. 5, 6, 9, 10, 11, 12, 13, 14, 15—20c each (Postpaid)
□ WARDROBE TRUNK—9" x 9" x 16"—$5.25
        (Add 40c postage—65c West of Chicago) for each Trunk ordered.

NAME......................................... CITY.........................
STREET....................................... STATE........................
    *Canadian Orders Accepted.   *Please Print Name and Address.   *No C.O.D. orders, please!
```

Illustration 37. McCall's Needlework & Crafts magazine, Spring-Summer, 1953.

Save! BUY DIRECT FROM FACTORY!
Mary Hoyer Doll with WASHABLE WIG

ONLY $4.95   *$9.95 VALUE!*

SHE'S 14 INCHES TALL

Comparable with dolls selling in stores at double the price—and more! The Mary Hoyer Doll is made of finest durable plastic, is fully jointed, has lovely moving eyes, and her hair can be washed, combed, waved and curled. Your choice of these shades of wigs—blond, medium, dark brown and auburn. Same doll with hand-curled hair in blond, medium, dark brown and red. Both dolls come undressed, but with shoes and stockings.

Same Doll with hand curled Wig $3.50

MARY HOYER WALKING DOLL is the same large 14-inch doll, but she is so constructed that she can walk. **75¢ ADDITIONAL**

◄ COMPLETE KIT TO MAKE DRESS AND PARASOL
Kit contains all necessary materials cut and fitted ready to sew outfit. Parasol frame and shoes are included. Also instructions. **$2.25**

COSTUME (ready-to-wear) and PARASOL and Shoes exactly as illustrated here. **$3.95**

YARN KITS AND ACCESSORIES
Write for complete Price List and Catalog of sewing, crocheting and knitting kits and accessories.

"MARY'S DOLLIES" Vols. 5-6-9-10-11-12-13-14-15
All the costumes in these nine books are designed to fit the Mary Hoyer Doll perfectly. Simple instructions and illustrations for Knitting, Sewing and Crocheting her many outfits. You'll have fun making these beautiful costumes. **20¢ ea.**

Visit THE MARY HOYER SHOPS when in Reading, Pa. during the Winter, and Ocean City, N.J., during the Summer.

```
THE MARY HOYER DOLL MFG. CO.
(Juvenile Styles Publishing Co.)
1013 PENN STREET, READING, PENNA.

□ MARY HOYER DOLL with Washable Wig—$4.95       Color of Hair..........
     Style of Hair Desired  □ Curled   □ Upsweep   □ Flowing
□ MARY HOYER DOLL with Hand-Curled Wig—$3.50    Color of Hair..........
     □ For MARY HOYER WALKING DOLL—Add 75c for each doll ordered.
     (Add 25c postage—40c West of Chicago) for each Doll ordered.
□ COMPLETE KIT TO MAKE DRESS AND PARASOL—$2.25 (Postpaid)
□ COSTUME (Ready-to-wear) and PARASOL (as illustrated)—$3.95 (Postpaid)
□ "MARY'S DOLLIES"—Vols. 5, 6, 9, 10, 11, 12, 13, 14, 15—20c each (Postpaid)
     *Canadian Orders Accepted    *Please Print Name and Address.

NAME......................................... CITY.........................
STREET....................................... STATE........................
     Note: For Pennsylvania deliveries add 1% Sales Tax
```

Illustration 39. McCall's Needlework & Crafts magazine, Spring-Summer, 1954.

Save 50%! BUY MOST BEAUTIFUL DOLLS IN AMERICA—THE Mary Hoyer Dolls
DIRECT FROM FACTORY!

The 14-inch Mary Hoyer Doll has long been acclaimed the most outstanding doll value on the market—comparable with dolls selling in stores at double the price and even more. Buying direct from our factory saves you the difference! Quality made of finest durable plastic, this perfectly formed Miss has moving eyes, arms, head and legs. She sits and stands easily. Her hair can be washed, combed, waved and curled. NOW—we also offer a big 18-inch companion doll with identical features—same construction—but she's 4 inches taller, and naturally, costs a bit more. Your choice of the following shades of wigs (for either doll)—blond, medium brown, dark brown and auburn—of DuPont Nylon or Dynel, depending on the style of hair-do you select.

Both dolls come undressed, but with shoes and stockings.

$4.95 14-inch doll

$6.95 18-inch doll

Illustrated style book on Knitting, Sewing and Crocheting Kits with each 14-inch doll.

Illustrations of Knitting and Crocheting Kits with each 18-inch doll.

14" Doll With Saran Hand Curled Wig $3.50

Starlight Evening Gown
Here is the most beautiful doll gown you've ever seen, believe us! It has two tiers of sheer Nylon Net over Taffeta and sparkling Silver Metallic Trimming.

COMPLETED GOWN FOR 14" DOLL $3.50   **COMPLETED GOWN FOR 18" DOLL $3.95**

Designed exclusively to fit only the Mary Hoyer Dolls. Ready to wear—as illustrated on unretouched photo above.

New! PARASOL for your Mary Hoyer Dolls!
There's nothing just like it on the market! This patented dolly Parasol of fool-proof all-metal construction, is trimmed with Nylon Lace and is available in a great variety of colors. Comes in two sizes—for 14-inch and 18-inch dolls.

$1.50 each

Beautiful FUR CAPE and HEAD BAND SET
Just like the big girls wear when they step out, this gorgeous Fur Cape and Head Band Set is a "must" for your Mary Hoyer Doll! Two sizes—for 14-inch and 18-inch dolls.

$1.95 SET

McCall Patterns Available
No. 1564 and No. 1891/14 for the 14-inch doll; No. 1891/18 for the 18-inch doll—for sewing a number of costumes which were designed to fit the Mary Hoyer Dolls.

35¢ ea.

"MARY'S DOLLIES" Vols. 5-6-9-10-11-12-13-14-15
All the costumes in these nine books are designed to fit the 14-inch Mary Hoyer Doll perfectly. Simple instructions and illustrations for Knitting, Sewing and Crocheting her many outfits. You'll have fun making these beautiful costumes!

20¢ ea.

FREE PRICE LIST!
Write for complete Price List and Catalog of sewing, crocheting and knitting kits and the most fabulous selection of Doll Accessories in the World!

Visit THE MARY HOYER SHOPS
Mary Hoyer cordially invites you to visit her shops in Reading, Pa. during the Winter; and Ocean City, N.J., during the Summer.

IMMEDIATE DELIVERY — MAIL COUPON TODAY!

```
THE MARY HOYER DOLL MFG. CO.
(Juvenile Styles Publishing Co.)
1013 PENN STREET, READING, PENNA.

□ 14" MARY HOYER DOLL with Saran Washable hand curled wig—$3.50.   Color of Hair..........
□ 14" MARY HOYER DOLL with DuPont Nylon or Dynel Wig—$4.95.        Color of Hair..........
□ 18" MARY HOYER DOLL with Dynel Wig—$6.95.                        Color of Hair..........
     Style of Hair desired  □ Upsweep (Dynel)  □ Curled (Nylon)  □ Flowing (Dynel)
                            □ Side sweep and curls (Dynel)
□ STARLIGHT EVENING GOWN (Ready to Wear) for  □ 14" Doll—$3.50   □ 18" Doll—$3.95
□ FUR CAPE AND HEAD BAND SET—$1.95 Set.  □ 14" Doll   □ 18" Doll
□ PARASOL—$1.50 each.  □ 14" Doll   □ 18" Doll
□ McCALL'S PATTERNS—35c each.  □ No. 1564   □ No. 1891/14—14" Doll;   □ No. 1891/18—18" Doll
□ "MARY'S DOLLIES" for 14" Doll only! Vols. 5,6,9,10,11,12,13,14,15—20c each.
            ALL ITEMS SHIPPED IN THE UNITED STATES POSTPAID.
                    *Please Print Name and Address

NAME......................................... CITY.........................
STREET....................................... STATE........................
            Note: For Pennsylvania deliveries add 1% Sales Tax
```

Illustration 38. McCall's Needlework & Crafts magazine, Winter, 1954.

15

MOST BEAUTIFUL DOLLS IN AMERICA!
Mary Hoyer Dolls

Save 50%
BUY DIRECT FROM OUR FACTORY!

Comparable with dolls selling in stores at double the price, this 14-inch Mary Hoyer Doll is made of finest durable plastic, perfectly formed. She has moving eyes, arms, head and legs, and her hair can be washed, combed, waved and curled. Easy to make her sit or stand. 18-inch Mary Hoyer Doll has identical features—same construction—but she's 4 inches taller. Your choice of following shades of wigs (for either doll)—blond, medium brown, dark brown and auburn—of DuPont Nylon or Dynel, depending on the style of hair-do you select. Both dolls come undressed, but with shoes and stockings.

$4.95 14-inch doll
$6.95 18-inch doll

14" Doll With Saran Hand Curled Wig $3.50

Gorgeous EVENING GOWN
Made of heavy Taffeta with Nylon Tulle Overthrow, trimmed in sparkling metallic thread. Pink or Blue.
Completed Gown for 14" Doll $2.50   Completed Gown for 18" Doll $2.95

Lace Trimmed PARASOL
This patented Parasol of fool-proof all-metal construction is trimmed with Nylon Lace. Pink or Blue to match Evening Gown. For 14" or 18" doll. **$1.50**
Uncovered Parasol Frame available at $1.00 each.

McCall Patterns Available
No. 1564 and No. 1891/14 for 14" doll; No. 1891/18 for 18" doll—for sewing a number of costumes which were designed to fit the Mary Hoyer Dolls. ea. **35c**

"MARY'S DOLLIES"—Vols. 5-6-9-10-11-12-13-14-15
Simple instructions and illustrations for Knitting, Sewing and Crocheting the 14-inch Mary Hoyer Doll's many outfits............................ **20c**

FREE PRICE LIST! Write for complete Price List and Catalog of sewing, crocheting and knitting kits and the most fabulous selection of Doll Accessories in the World!
VISIT THE MARY HOYER SHOPS when in Reading, Pa. during the Winter; and Ocean City, N.J. during the Summer.

IMMEDIATE DELIVERY

MARY HOYER DOLL MFG. CO.
(Juvenile Styles Publishing Co.)
1013 PENN STREET • READING, PENNA.

☐ 14" MARY HOYER DOLL with Saran Washable Wig. $3.50. Color of Hair........
☐ 14" MARY HOYER DOLL with DuPont Nylon or Dynel Wig. $4.95. Color of Hair........
☐ 18" MARY HOYER DOLL with Dynel Wig. $6.95. Color of Hair........
Style of Hair desired ☐ Upsweep ☐ Curled
☐ Flowing ☐ Side sweep and curls
☐ EVENING GOWN (Ready to Wear)
☐ $2.50 ☐ $2.95 ☐ Blue ☐ Pink
☐ PARASOL—$1.50 ☐ Blue ☐ Pink
All items shipped in the U.S. Postpaid!

NAME...
ADDRESS.......................................
CITY..................STATE..................
Note: For Pennsylvania deliveries add 1% Sales Tax

Illustration 40. *McCall's Needlework & Crafts* magazine, Spring-Summer, 1955.

AMERICA'S MOST BEAUTIFUL DOLLS AT LOW, LOW PRICES!
Mary Hoyer Dolls

- MOST PLAYABLE DOLLS!
- PERFECTLY FORMED!
- EASIEST TO DRESS!
- UNBREAKABLE PLASTIC!
- MOVING EYES ARMS, HEAD AND LEGS!
- WASHABLE AND COMBABLE HAIR!

New DOLL STAND at Extra Cost

Completely DRESSED as illustrated
$4.95 14-inch doll
$7.95 18-inch doll

Your choice of following shades of hair (for either doll)—blond, medium brown, dark brown and auburn. Fashionable lace-trimmed coat and hat of high quality felt. In pink or blue. Price also includes shoes, but not dress. Dolls sold to you direct from our factory, hence the Low Prices!

Undressed 14" DOLL... **$3.50**
Undressed 18" DOLL... **$5.95**
Shoes and Stockings included.

SEWING KIT to Make Complete Outfits
Kit contains all necessary materials cut and fitted ready to sew Hat, Coat and Dress pictured above...also Sewing Instructions.
$1.50 For 14" Size   **$1.95** For 18" Size

Catalogue showing numerous other Mary Hoyer Kits and a complete Price List of Accessories included with each order.

Nickel Steel DOLL STAND
Will hold doll firmly—won't tip over! Available for 14" and 18" dolls............. **$1.00**

"MARY'S DOLLIES"
All the costumes in Volume 15 (pictured here) and Vols. 5, 6, 9, 10, 11, 12, 13 and 14 are designed to fit the 14" Mary Hoyer Doll perfectly. Simple instructions and illustrations for Knitting, Sewing and Crocheting her many costumes... **20c** ea.

McCall's Patterns
Available for sewing a number of costumes for 14" and 18" dolls.

VISIT THE MARY HOYER SHOPS when in Reading, Pa. during the Winter; and Ocean City, N.J. during the Summer.

IMMEDIATE DELIVERY

MARY HOYER DOLL MFG. CO.
1013 PENN STREET • READING, PENNA.

☐ Completely Dressed 14" MARY HOYER DOLL............$4.95
 Color of Hair....... Color of Outfit......
☐ Completely Dressed 18" MARY HOYER DOLL............$7.95
 Color of Hair....... Color of Outfit......
☐ Undressed 14" MARY HOYER DOLL.....$3.50
 Color of Hair.......
☐ Undressed 18" MARY HOYER DOLL.....$5.95
 Color of Hair.......
☐ COMPLETE KIT to make Hat, Coat and Dress. Color.........
 ☐ for 14" Doll, $1.50 ☐ for 18" Doll, $1.95
☐ DOLL STAND ☐ for 14" Doll......$1.00
 ☐ for 18" Doll......$1.00
☐ "MARY'S DOLLIES"—Vols. 5, 6, 9, 10, 11, 12, 13, 14, 15..............20c each

POSTPAID ANYWHERE IN THE U.S.A.
Add 3% Pa. Sales Tax if you live in Pennsylvania.

NAME...
ADDRESS.......................................
CITY..................State..................

Illustration 41. *McCall's Needlework & Crafts* magazine, 1956-1957.

16

New! Mary Hoyer VICKY DOLL

This newest member of the Mary Hoyer Doll family is an exquisite 10½" miniature with shapely legs (notice how well she looks in high heels!), a perfectly formed body that turns, bends, bows from the waist. Realistic eyes that open and close, rooted saran hair! She comes to you dressed in bra and panties, high heel sandals—all for **2.95**
Summer cotton dress shown, 1.25

Complete wardrobe available, from sportswear to formals!
You'll find them listed in Free Brochure that comes with your order.

KNITTING & CROCHETING INST. BOOKS VOLS. 5, 6, 9, 10, 11, 12, 13, 14, 15
Always a favorite because she's so easy to dress and play with! 14" MARY HOYER DOLL, in formal gown of nylon sparkle net over woven taffeta.....................**5.95**
See order coupon below for separate prices.
You'll see listed in your free brochure the complete lines of patterns and kits in knitting, crocheting and sewing...plus a fabulous array of accessories.

ORDER COUPON
Postpaid except Canada — add 3% tax in Pa.
Mary Hoyer Doll Mfg. Co.
1013 Penn Street, Reading, Pa.
Summer Shop — Ocean City, N.J.

10½" VICKY DOLL, ☐ Blonde ☐ Dark 2.95........☐
Vicky Doll Dress, 1.25.................................☐
14" DOLL, ☐ blonde ☐ medium brown ☐ auburn ☐ dark 3.50
Kit to make Evening Gown, 1.50...................☐
Dressed Doll without Mink stole, 5.95............☐
Mink stole, 2.95..☐
Knitting and crocheting Instruction Books, ea. 20¢ ☐
                                        plus 5¢ postage

Name...
Address.......................................
City................................State..........

FREE BROCHURE WILL COME TO YOU WITH YOUR ORDER

Illustration 42. *McCall's Needlework & Crafts* magazine, Fall-Winter, 1957-1958.

...Up For Adoption!
THE ORIGINAL Mary Hoyer DOLL and her NEW Sisters Vicky and Margie

ALL PLASTIC 14" DOLL either BOY or GIRL
$3.50 UNDRESSED

EVENING GOWN as illustrated
Gorgeous Nylon dotted net over Taffeta. **$2.95**

MATCHING PARASOL trimmed with same net. **$1.75**

PARASOL FRAMES Uncovered 14", 18" and 20" **75c**

COTTON FROCK as illustrated on 10½" Doll **$1.75** below.

McCall Pattern #1891—14" and 18" size (to fit Mary Hoyer Dolls) **35c**
Doll Display Stand for low heel dolls. **$1.00**

High Heel 14" DOLL in Life-like Vinyl. Including high-heel shoes. Undressed doll. **$3.50**
Doll Stand for 14" dolls with high heels. **75c**

"MARY'S DOLLIES" Knitting & Crocheting Instruction Books...for 14" Dolls only! Vols. 5 - 6 - 9 - 10 - 11 - 12 - 13 - 14 - and 15. **25c ea.**

10½" Vicky DOLL
A perfectly formed all-Vinyl "teenager" doll with High Heels...complete with Earrings, Panties and Bra. **$2.50**

EVENING GOWN
Made of identical materials as on 14" Doll pictured above. **$1.95**

COTTON FROCK as illustrated. **$1.25**
Doll Stand for 10½" Doll—all steel heavy construction. **50c**
Choice of hair: Blonde or Dark.

Baby Margie DOLL
This huggable little Toddler is 10" tall and is made of durable Vinyl. **$2.95**
SUIT as illustrated Either Knit or Crochet
$2.50 COTTON DRESS with Panties. (not illustrated) **$1.25**
Choice of Hair: Blonde or Dark.

INSTRUCTIONS AND YARN WITH EACH DOLL FREE OF EXTRA CHARGE (either Knit or Crochet)

FREE Brochure Price Lists with complete line of clothing and Accessories for ALL MARY HOYER DOLLS
SPECIAL PRICES TO RELIGIOUS & FRATERNAL ORGANIZATIONS
Visit the Mary Hoyer Shops at 1008 Penn St., Reading, Pa. or the Summer Shop at 714 Boardwalk, Ocean City, N.J.
Orders over $5 prepaid ... Under $5, add 25c for postage.
                              Add 3% Sales Tax in Penna.
Send all Orders to:

MARY HOYER DOLL MFG. CO.
P.O. BOX 1538 • READING, PENNSYLVANIA

Illustration 43. *McCall's Needlework & Crafts* magazine, Fall-Winter, 1958-1959.

The PERFECTLY FORMED DOLLS for those who like to make their clothing!

Mary Hoyer Dolls

ALL PLASTIC (Boy or Girl) **14" Doll.. $3.95** UNDRESSED

EVENING GOWN as illustrated **$2.95** Sparkle Net over Taffeta
PRICE INCLUDES TAFFETA STOLE
High Heel Dolls available in 10½", 15", 20" Sizes

McCall Pattern #1891—14" and 18" size (to fit Mary Hoyer Dolls) **35¢**

Doll Display Stand for low heel dolls.... **$1.00**

"MARY'S DOLLIES", Vols. 5, 6, 9, 10, 11, 12, 13, 14, 15—25¢ ea.
Knitting & Crocheting Instruction Books for 14" Dolls only!

10" BABY Margie DOLL $2.95
Made of durable Vinyl
YARN KIT and INSTRUCTIONS FREE of extra charge with Doll—Either Knit or Crochet.
SUIT as illustrated—$2.50

FREE—Brochure Price Lists with complete line of Clothing and Accessories for all Mary Hoyer Dolls—with order!

WRITE FOR QUANTITY PRICES!
You are invited to visit the Mary Hoyer Shops when in Reading, Pa., or Ocean City, N.J.

THE MARY HOYER DOLL MFG. CO.
P. O. BOX 1538 • READING, PENNSYLVANIA

☐ 14" MARY HOYER DOLL (Undressed)—$3.95 ☐ Girl ☐ Boy Hair ☐ Blonde ☐ Red ☐ Dark
☐ EVENING GOWN as illustrated (ready to wear) with STOLE—$2.95
☐ McCALL'S PATTERN #1891—35¢ ☐ for 14" Doll ☐ for 18" Doll
☐ DOLL DISPLAY STAND for low heel Dolls—$1.00
☐ "MARY'S DOLLIES", Vols. 5, 6, 9, 10, 11, 12, 13, 14, 15—25¢ each
☐ BABY MARGIE DOLL (with Kit)—$2.95 Hair ☐ Blonde ☐ Dark ☐ Knit ☐ Crochet
☐ BABY MARGIE'S SUIT as illustrated (ready to wear)—$2.50

Orders over $5 prepaid ... Under $5, add 25¢ for postage.

NAME... CITY.............................
STREET... STATE...........................
Note: For Pennsylvania deliveries add 3½% Sales Tax

Illustration 44. *McCall's Needlework & Crafts* magazine, Fall-Winter, 1959-1960.

It's EASY ... It's FUN to make clothing for these Beautiful, Perfectly Formed

Mary Hoyer Dolls
with Our PATTERNS, KITS and INSTRUCTION BOOKS!

This lovely all-Plastic **14" DOLL... $3.95** UNDRESSED POSTPAID

COMPLETE OUTFIT ... Genuine Leather Jacket and Beret, Belt and Shoes—as illustrated .... **$1.95** POSTPAID

10" MARGIE TODDLER DOLL
... made of durable Vinyl
YARN KIT and INSTRUCTIONS FREE of extra charge with Doll—Either Knit or Crochet. **$2.95** POSTPAID

10" CATHY DOLL $1.50 UNDRESSED POSTPAID
KIT To Make Christening Outfit **$1.00** POSTPAID

"MARY'S DOLLIES"
Vols. 5, 6, 9, 10, 11, 12, 13, 14, 15. **30¢ ea.**
Knitting and Crocheting Books for 14" Dolls only!
FREE Brochure Price List with complete line of Accessories; Sewing, Knitting, Crocheting Kits—with every order!
VISIT THE MARY HOYER SHOP at 1008 Penn St., Reading, Pa., and in Summer, our shop at 714 Boardwalk, Ocean City, N.J.

WRITE FOR QUANTITY PRICES FOR BAZAAR PURPOSES!

THE MARY HOYER DOLL MFG. CO.
P. O. BOX 1538 • READING, PENNSYLVANIA

☐ 14" MARY HOYER DOLL (Undressed)—$3.95 Hair ☐ Blonde ☐ Medium ☐ Auburn ☐ Dark
☐ COMPLETE OUTFIT for 14" Doll, as illustrated (ready to wear)—$1.95
☐ 10" MARGIE TODDLER DOLL (with Kit)—$2.95 Hair ☐ Blonde ☐ Dark ☐ Knit ☐ Crochet
☐ 10" CATHY DOLL $1.50 ☐ KIT $1.00
☐ "MARY'S DOLLIES", Vols. 5, 6, 9, 10, 11, 12, 13, 14, 15—30¢ each

NAME... CITY.............................
STREET... STATE...........................
Add 4% Sales Tax in Penna. and any other Taxes levied in your State.

Illustration 46. *McCall's Needlework & Crafts* magazine, 1961.

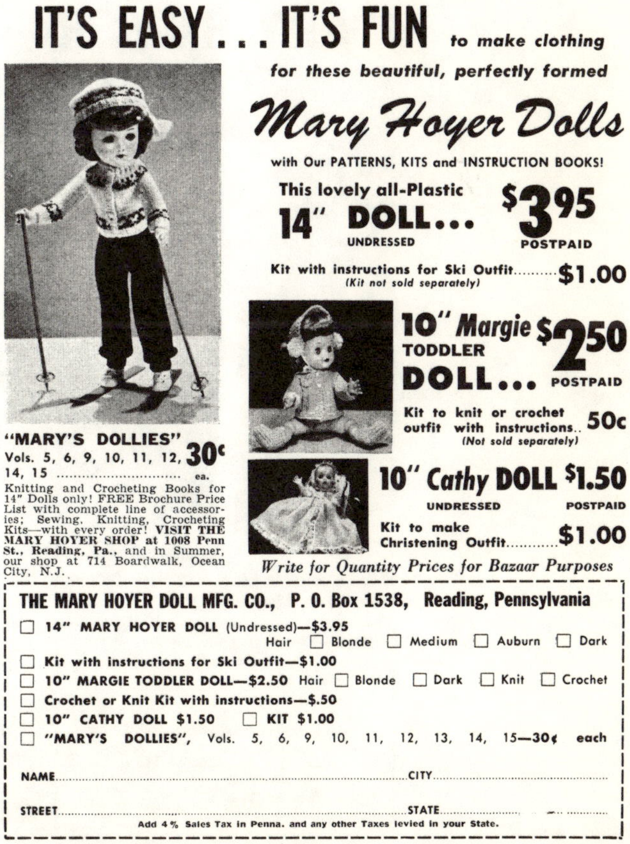

It's EASY ... It's FUN to make clothing for these Beautiful, Perfectly Formed

Mary Hoyer Dolls
with Our PATTERNS, KITS and INSTRUCTION BOOKS!

This lovely all-Plastic **14" DOLL... $3.95** UNDRESSED POSTPAID

COMPLETE OUTFIT ... Genuine Leather Jacket and Beret, Belt and Shoes—as illustrated .... **$1.95** POSTPAID

10" MARGIE TODDLER DOLL
... made of durable Vinyl
YARN KIT and INSTRUCTIONS FREE of extra charge with Doll—Either Knit or Crochet. **$2.95** POSTPAID

10" CATHY INFANT DOLL
Complete with SEWING KIT to make SUN SUIT OUTFIT as illustrated. Rattle included. **$1.95** POSTPAID

"MARY'S DOLLIES"
Vols. 5, 6, 9, 10, 11, 12, 13, 14, 15. **30¢ ea.**
Knitting and Crocheting Books for 14" Dolls only!
FREE Brochure Price List with complete line of Accessories; Sewing, Knitting, Crocheting Kits—with every order!
VISIT THE MARY HOYER SHOP at 1008 Penn St., Reading, Pa., and in Summer, our shop at 714 Boardwalk, Ocean City, N.J.

WRITE FOR QUANTITY PRICES FOR BAZAAR PURPOSES!

THE MARY HOYER DOLL MFG. CO.
P. O. BOX 1538 • READING, PENNSYLVANIA

☐ 14" MARY HOYER DOLL (Undressed)—$3.95 Hair ☐ Blonde ☐ Medium ☐ Auburn ☐ Dark
☐ COMPLETE OUTFIT for 14" Doll, as illustrated (ready to wear)—$1.95
☐ 10" MARGIE TODDLER DOLL (with Kit)—$2.95 Hair ☐ Blonde ☐ Dark ☐ Knit ☐ Crochet
☐ 10" CATHY INFANT DOLL (with Kit)—$1.95
☐ "MARY'S DOLLIES", Vols. 5, 6, 9, 10, 11, 12, 13, 14, 15—30¢ each

NAME... CITY.............................
STREET... STATE...........................
Add 4% Sales Tax in Penna. and any other Taxes levied in your State.

Illustration 45. *McCall's Needlework & Crafts* magazine, 1960.

IT'S EASY ... IT'S FUN to make clothing
for these beautiful, perfectly formed

Mary Hoyer Dolls
with Our PATTERNS, KITS and INSTRUCTION BOOKS!

This lovely all-Plastic **14" DOLL... $3.95** UNDRESSED POSTPAID

Kit with instructions for Ski Outfit............**$1.00**
(Kit not sold separately)

10" Margie TODDLER DOLL... $2.50 POSTPAID

Kit to knit or crochet outfit with instructions.... **50¢**
(Not sold separately)

10" Cathy DOLL $1.50 UNDRESSED POSTPAID

Kit to make Christening Outfit............**$1.00**

"MARY'S DOLLIES"
Vols. 5, 6, 9, 10, 11, 12, 14, 15 **30¢** ea.
Knitting and Crocheting Books for 14" Dolls only! FREE Brochure Price List with complete line of accessories; Sewing, Knitting, Crocheting Kits—with every order! VISIT THE MARY HOYER SHOP at 1008 Penn St., Reading, Pa., and in Summer, our shop at 714 Boardwalk, Ocean City, N.J.

Write for Quantity Prices for Bazaar Purposes

THE MARY HOYER DOLL MFG. CO., P. O. Box 1538, Reading, Pennsylvania

☐ 14" MARY HOYER DOLL (Undressed)—$3.95
  Hair ☐ Blonde ☐ Medium ☐ Auburn ☐ Dark
☐ Kit with instructions for Ski Outfit—$1.00
☐ 10" MARGIE TODDLER DOLL—$2.50 Hair ☐ Blonde ☐ Dark ☐ Knit ☐ Crochet
☐ Crochet or Knit Kit with instructions—$.50
☐ 10" CATHY DOLL $1.50 ☐ KIT $1.00
☐ "MARY'S DOLLIES", Vols. 5, 6, 9, 10, 11, 12, 13, 14, 15—30¢ each

NAME... CITY.............................
STREET... STATE...........................
Add 4% Sales Tax in Penna. and any other Taxes levied in your State.

Illustration 47. *McCall's Needlework & Crafts* magazine, 1962.

Knit, Crochet and Sew for the

mary hoyer doll
america's best dressed doll

10" cathy infant doll — undressed — $1.50 plus postage
Kit to make this cute christening outfit (shipped only with doll) $1.00

The lovely, all-plastic, fully-jointed 14" doll — undressed — $3.95 plus postage
Easy-to-knit mohair coat, dress, hat kit (shipped only with doll) $2.00

Patterns! Kits! Instruction Books!

10" margie undressed toddler doll $2.50 plus postage
Knit or crochet 3-piece outfit kit (shipped only with doll) $.50

DOLL STAND for all Mary Hoyer dolls $1.25
"MARY'S DOLLIES" knitting & crochet instruction books for 14" dolls only—Vols. 5, 6, 9, 10, 11, 12, 13, 14. each $.30
Complete brochure price list of accessories enclosed with each order. Visit the Mary Hoyer Shop at 1008 Penn Street, Reading, Pa., for our complete display.

QUANTITY PRICES FURNISHED TO ORGANIZATIONS ON REQUEST

The Mary Hoyer Doll Mfg. Co. 1008 Penn St., Reading, Pennsylvania

☐ 14" Doll (undressed), $3.95 Hair: ☐ Blonde ☐ Medium ☐ Auburn ☐ Dark
☐ Easy-to-knit Kit, $2.00
☐ 10" Margie Toddler Doll (undressed), $2.50 Hair: ☐ Blonde ☐ Auburn ☐ Dark
☐ 3-Piece Outfit, $.50
☐ 10" Cathy Infant Doll (undressed), $1.50
☐ Christening Outfit Kit, $1.00
☐ Doll Stand, $1.25
☐ "Mary's Dollies", Vols. 5, 6, 9, 10, 11, 12, 13, 14, 30¢ each

NAME.........
ADDRESS.........
CITY......... STATE.........
Add 5% sales tax in Penna. and any other taxes levied in your state.
POSTAGE—50¢ EAST, 75¢ WEST PER ORDER

Illustration 48. *McCall's Needlework & Crafts* magazine, Fall-Winter, 1964-1965.

---

knit, crochet and sew for

MARY HOYER DOLLS

◀ BECKY
14" doll with shoes and panties...... $2.95
Kit to make costume shown, including parasol frame......... $2.95
Display stand of rustproof steel.... $1.25
Instruction Books to knit and crochet Becky outfits. (Volumes 5, 6, 9, 10, 11, 12, 13, and 14) ... $.30 each incl. postage

CATHY ▶
10" doll with shoes and socks....... $1.50
Kit to make christening outfit shown.. $1.00
All Prices Plus Postage

Write for complete list of Mary Hoyer Dolls and special prices on quantity orders.

The Mary Hoyer Doll Mfg. Co.
1008 Penn St., Reading, Pa.

☐ 14" Becky Doll, $2.95
   Hair: ☐ Blonde ☐ Auburn ☐ Dark
☐ Becky Costume, $2.95
☐ Display Stand (14" doll only), $1.25
☐ Becky Instruction Books, $.30 incl. postage Volumes 5, 6, 9, 10, 11, 12, 13, 14
☐ 10" Cathy Doll, $1.50
☐ Cathy Outfit Kit, $1.00

NAME.........
ADDRESS.........
CITY......... STATE.........
Add 5% sales tax in Pa. and any other taxes levied in your state. POSTAGE: $.50 East, $.75 West—per order

Illustration 51. *McCall's Needlework & Crafts* magazine, Spring, 1967.

knit, crochet, and sew for America's best-dressed doll!...

MARY HOYER DOLL
Patterns! Kits! Instruction Books!

$3.95 - 14"
mary
full jointed, all plastic. Easy-to-knit mohair coat, dress, hat kit $2.

$1.95 - 12"
vicky
including kit and instructions to make outfit shown.

$2.50 - 10"
margie
toddler doll: including kit and instructions to knit or crochet 3-pc. outfit.

$1.50 - 10"
cathy
infant doll. Christening outfit kit—$1.

☞(All dolls shipped undressed—all prices plus postage).

DOLL STAND for Mary Hoyer dolls, $1.25 (14" only).
MARY'S DOLLIES, knit and crochet instruction books for 14" dolls only. Vols. 5, 6, 9, 10, 11, 12, 13, 14, ea. 30¢.
COMPLETE BROCHURE and price list of accessories enclosed with each order.
VISIT the Mary Hoyer Shop, 1008 Penn St., Reading, Pa.

sell mary hoyer dolls to make money for your organization!
Write for special prices on quantity purchases.

The Mary Hoyer Doll Mfg. Co.
1008 Penn St., Reading, Pennsylvania

☐ 14" Doll (undressed), $3.95 Hair:
   ☐ Blonde ☐ Medium ☐ Auburn ☐ Dark
☐ Easy-to-knit Kit, $2.00
☐ "Mary's Dollies", Vols. 5, 6, 9, 10, 11, 12, 13, 14, 30¢ each
☐ Mary Hoyer Doll Stand, $1.25—for 14" doll only
☐ 10" Margie Toddler Doll (undressed), complete with kit and instructions—$2.50 Hair: ☐ Blonde ☐ Auburn ☐ Dark
☐ 10" Cathy Infant Doll (undressed), $1.50
☐ Christening Outfit Kit, $1.00
☐ 12" Vicky Doll (undressed), complete with kit and instructions—$1.95

NAME_____
ADDRESS_____
CITY_____
Add 5% sales tax in Penna. and any other taxes levied in your state.
POSTAGE—50¢ EAST, 75¢ WEST, PER ORDER

Illustration 49. *McCall's Needlework & Crafts* magazine, 1965.

knit, crochet and sew for AMERICA'S BEST-DRESSED DOLLS

the original

MARY HOYER DOLL

"a collector's item"

ALL-PLASTIC FULLY-JOINTED 14"—$3.95

Pattern for series of Mary Hoyer Doll costumes (sold only with doll). $.35
Steel Parasol Frame with kit and instructions to cover, lace to trim. $1.00
Display Stand of rustproof steel for 14" Mary Hoyer Doll. $1.25
Knit and Crochet Instruction Books for 14" Mary Hoyer Doll — vols. 5, 6, 9, 10, 11, 12, 13, 14. $.30 ea. incl. postage

VICKI DOLLS
12" doll with kit and instructions to knit outfit shown. $1.95
15" doll with kit and instructions to crochet outfit shown. $2.95

MARGIE
10" toddler doll with shoes. Includes kit and instructions to knit or crochet 3-piece outfit shown. $2.50

CATHY
Infant doll with kit and instructions to make christening outfit shown.
8" doll $1.95   10" doll $2.50

Complete Accessory Brochure and Price List enclosed with each order. All dolls shipped undressed... all prices plus postage.

VISIT The Mary Hoyer Shop
1008 Penn St., Reading, Pa.

▷ SELL MARY HOYER DOLLS to make money for your organization. Write for special prices on quantity purchases.

The Mary Hoyer Doll Mfg. Co.
1008 Penn St., Reading, Pa.

☐ 14" Mary Hoyer Doll, $3.95
   Hair: ☐ Blonde ☐ Auburn
         ☐ Medium ☐ Dark
☐ Mary Hoyer Pattern, $.35
☐ Parasol Kit, $1
☐ Display Stand (14" doll only), $1.25
☐ Instruction Books, vols. 5, 6, 9, 10, 11, 12, 13, 14, $.30 each including postage
☐ 12" Vicky Doll, $1.95
☐ 15" Vicky Doll, $2.95
☐ 10" Margie Doll, $2.50
   ☐ Knit   ☐ Crochet
   Hair: ☐ Blonde ☐ Auburn ☐ Dark
☐ 8" Cathy Doll, $1.95
☐ 10" Cathy Doll, $2.50

NAME_____
ADDRESS_____
CITY_____ STATE_____
Add 5% sales tax in Pa. and any other taxes levied in your state.
POSTAGE: $.50 EAST ... $.75 WEST—per order

Illustration 50. *McCall's Needlework & Crafts* magazine, Fall-Winter, 1966-1967.

Price Lists

The price list for the Mary Hoyer Doll began as one page advertising the doll, the books, a few accessories and the yarn kits. As the popularity of the doll increased, the Hoyers decided to expand their line of accessories. A trip to New York resulted in more doll toys made to Mary Hoyer's specific designs and manufactured by the S. B. Novelty Company in New York.

The Mary Hoyer Doll had everything! There were Western riding boots, a two gun holster, belts, English riding boots, majorette and snow boots, shoes in every conceivable color, roller skates, ice skates, slippers in pastel satin, school bags, gold and silver evening bags, travel suits with handbags and luggage to match, skis, tennis rackets and even a golf bag with three clubs. You name it, this doll had it! She had hosiery and gloves which were imported from Taiwan and handmade hats and bags from the Bahamas. A chest of drawers, a table and chair set and a four poster bed, all made in two shades of wood, were included in the line of accessories. Two different wooden sleds were also included.

The skis and poles were made in Reading by a blind man and then the shoes were glued on separately. The unique steel doll stands were designed by Mary Hoyer and made locally by a tool and die maker.

Illustration 53A. The Mary Hoyer Doll shown with her wardrobe trunk.

Illustration 52. The sled shown here with the doll in it is one of the many accessories offered by the Mary Hoyer Doll Manufacturing Company. This wooden sled is the same as the one shown on the cover of *Mary's Dollies*, Volume 9. *Juvenile Styles*, Volume 8, Page 14.

Illustration 53B. *Mary's Dollies*, Volume 9, back page.

19

The *Mary Hoyer* DOLL
and her very own WARDROBE TRUNK

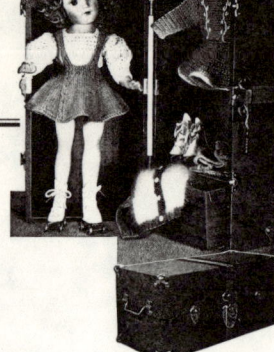

This big roomy wardrobe trunk is of metal-covered wood construction, with lock and key. Doll fits snugly in left side and there is ample room for her clothes in right compartment, which is complete with hanger bar and drawer for accessories.

$4.95 Size 16" x 9½" x 8½"
Plus Postage

The *Mary Hoyer* Doll and Her Twin Brother

Here are two of the most outstanding doll values ever offered. These beautiful 14-inch brother and sister dolls, creations of Mary Hoyer, are sturdily constructed of the finest plastic with movable head, arms, legs and movable eyes. Yes, both of these durable dolls have combable-hair. Sister's coiffure has been hand curled. Four lovely shades: blonde, medium, dark brown, and auburn. Brother has a head of well-groomed hair—medium brown only. Both dolls come undressed, but with shoes.

As Advertised in McCall's Needlework Magazine

Yarn kits containing all the necessary materials, buttons, etc., to make the costumes for the Mary Hoyer Brother and Sister Dolls are available for a very nominal sum. We can also furnish such accessories as roller skating and ice skating shoes, skis, holsters and guns, school bags, etc. WRITE FOR COMPLETE PRICE LIST!

POSTAGE MUST ACCOMPANY ALL ORDERS: Dolls—East 50¢, West 75¢. Wardrobes—East 75¢, West $1.25.

America's Biggest Doll Values!
BROTHER DOLL OR SISTER DOLL
$3.95 each
Plus Postage
UNDRESSED, but with Shoes

Mary Hoyer Doll Mfg. Co.
1008 PENN STREET IN READING, PENNSYLVANIA

Illustration 53C. *Mary's Dollies*, Volume 10, back page.

The *Mary Hoyer* DOLL
and her very own WARDROBE TRUNK

This big roomy wardrobe trunk is of wood construction, with lock and key. Doll fits snugly in left side and there is ample room for her clothes in right compartment, which is complete with hanger bar and drawer for accessories.

$4.95 for Size 16" x 7¼" x 6¾"
Plus Postage
LARGE ENOUGH FOR ONE DOLL AND ACCESSORIES

$5.25 for Size 16" x 9" x 9"
Plus Postage
LARGE ENOUGH FOR TWO DOLLS AND ACCESSORIES.

The *Mary Hoyer* Doll and Her Twin Brother

Here are two of the most outstanding doll values ever offered. These beautiful 14-inch brother and sister dolls, creations of Mary Hoyer, are sturdily constructed of the finest plastic with movable head, arms, legs and movable eyes. Yes, both of these durable dolls have real hair. Sister's coiffure has been hand curled. Four lovely shades: blonde, medium, dark brown, and red. Brother has a head of well-groomed hair—your choice of medium brown or dark brown. Both dolls come undressed, but with shoes and stockings.

As Advertised in McCall's Needlework Magazine

Yarn kits containing all the necessary materials, buttons, etc., to make the costumes for the Mary Hoyer Brother and Sister Dolls are available for a very nominal sum. We can also furnish such accessories as roller skating and ice skating shoes, skis, holsters and guns, school bags, etc. WRITE FOR COMPLETE PRICE LIST!

POSTAGE MUST ACCOMPANY ALL ORDERS: Mary Hoyer Doll (or two dolls) and Wardrobe Trunk—30¢; 50¢ West of Chicago. One Doll—20¢; 30¢ West of Chicago. Two Dolls—30¢; 50¢ West of Chicago. Wardrobe Trunk—25¢; 50¢ West of Chicago.

America's Biggest Doll Values!
BROTHER DOLL OR SISTER DOLL
$3.50 each
Plus Postage
UNDRESSED, but with Shoes and Stockings

Juvenile Styles Publishing Co.
1013 PENN STREET IN READING, PENNSYLVANIA

Illustration 53D. *Mary's Dollies*, Volume 11, back page.

When Mary Hoyer designed a dress called "Dolly Madison" she thought a parasol would complete the costume. After she found someone who could make the parasol frame, a tool and die maker in Reading was able to manufacture the parasol frame to her specifications. It was very intricately made and the parts were assembled by hand. It opened and closed like a real parasol. These were made in sizes to fit both the 14in (35.6cm) and 18in (45.7cm) dolls.

Even the wardrobe trunks were specially designed by Mary Hoyer. These also came in two sizes to fit both the 14in (35.6cm) and 18in (45.7cm) dolls.

The price lists expanded over the years to include new items, but remarkably, very little increase was seen in the cost of the dolls themselves and the accessories.

The *Mary Hoyer* DOLL
and her very own WARDROBE TRUNK

This big roomy wardrobe trunk is of metal-covered wood construction, with lock and key. Doll fits snugly in left side and there is ample room for her clothes in right compartment, which is complete with hanger bar and drawer for accessories.

$4.95 for Size 16" x 9½" x 8½"
Plus Postage
LARGE ENOUGH FOR TWO DOLLS AND ACCESSORIES

The *Mary Hoyer* Doll and Her Twin Brother

Here are two of the most outstanding doll values ever offered. These beautiful 14-inch brother and sister dolls, creations of Mary Hoyer, are sturdily constructed of the finest plastic with movable head, arms, legs and movable eyes. Yes, both of these durable dolls have combable-hair. Sister's coiffure has been hand curled. Four lovely shades: blonde, medium, dark brown, and auburn. Brother has a head of well-groomed hair—medium brown only. Both dolls come undressed, but with shoes.

As Advertised in McCall's Needlework Magazine

Yarn kits containing all the necessary materials, buttons, etc., to make the costumes for the Mary Hoyer Brother and Sister Dolls are available for a very nominal sum. We can also furnish such accessories as roller skating and ice skating shoes, skis, holsters and guns, school bags, etc. WRITE FOR COMPLETE PRICE LIST!

POSTAGE MUST ACCOMPANY ALL ORDERS: Dolls—East 50¢, West 75¢. Wardrobes—East 75¢, West $1.25.

America's Biggest Doll Values!
BROTHER DOLL OR SISTER DOLL
$3.95 each
Plus Postage
UNDRESSED, but with Shoes

Mary Hoyer Doll Mfg. Co.
1008 PENN STREET IN READING, PENNSYLVANIA

Illustration 53E. *Mary's Dollies*, Volume 13, back page.

PRICE LIST AND ORDER BLANK
JUVENILE STYLES PUBLISHING COMPANY
1008 PENN STREET, READING, PENNSYLVANIA

DOLLIES AND YARN KITS
Specially Designed by MARY HOYER

Quantity	Please ship me the items checked below—	Amount
	"MISS VICTORY" DOLL—POSTPAID	$2.25
	(including Shoes and Stockings) Blonde___ Medium___ Dark Wig___	
	Yarn Kits for costumes in Volume No. 5 of Mary's Dollies	
	Goldilocks	$ .85
	Julianna	.65
	Arlene	.50
	Annabelle	.85
	Olga (Angora Trimmed)	1.25
	Moyree (Angora Trimmed)	1.25
	Yarn Kits for costumes in Volume No. 6 of Mary's Dollies	
	Wavette	.85
	Maybelle	.85
	Nadine	.65
	Sonja (Angora Trimmed)	1.25
	Lucretta (Angora Trimmed)	1.25
	Yarn Kits for costumes in Volume No. 9 of Mary's Dollies	
	Zorina	1.25
	Zorina (Angora for robe)	1.00
	Terry	.65
	Sunny	.65
	Janie, Tinsel Crepe for Jacket & Fascinator	.65
	Kathleen (Angora for Jacket)	1.00
	Kathleen (Angora for Snood)	.30
	Susanna	.65
	Toys, to fit Doll in all books	
	Tennis Racket Sets	.25
	Skees and Poles	.35
	Golf Bag and 3 clubs	.35
	Skating Shoes—White	.35
	Majorette Boots	.25
	Russian Boots	.25
	Shoes and Stockings—White	.20
	Extra Wigs___ Blonde___ Med___ Dark___	1.00
	Style Books, Mary's Dollies	
	Volume No. 5—includes postage	.15
	Volume No. 6	.15
	Volume No. 9—Free with "Miss Victory Doll" (Not Sold Separately)	

MAYFAIR YARNS
Finest Quality by MARY HOYER

Mayfair Yarns were used on all styles illustrated in Mary Hoyer's Juvenile Styles Books.
Be sure to use same quality and weight to insure the exact results illustrated.

Quantity		Amount
	Knitting Worsted—4 ply—4 oz. skeins	$1.00
	Sports Yarn —3 ply—2 oz. balls or skeins	.65
	Baby Yarn —3 ply—1 oz. balls (White—Blue—Pink)	.50
	Sweater Yarn —3 ply—1 oz. balls (All shades)	.50
	Kahki —4 ply Knitting Worsted (For Army Sweaters)	1.00
	Kahki —3 ply Sports Yarn (For Army Sweaters)	.65
	100% PURE ANGORA All You Want White - Pink - Blue	$1 the Ball

Style Books, Juvenile Styles
Volume No. 2—includes postage		.30
Volume No. 3	" "	.30
Volume No. 4	" "	.30
Volume No. 7	" "	.30
Volume No. 8	" "	.30

Total Amount enclosed $ _____

NOTE: Color Cards will not be available for the duration. Please do not request them.

Name _____
Address _____
City _____

Send Orders to JUVENILE STYLES PUBLISHING COMPANY
1008 Penn Street, Reading, Pa.

(Send 10¢ to cover postage on all orders except those on which postage is included —15¢ West of Rockies)

Illustration 54. One of the first price lists and order blanks advertising the "Miss Victory" doll, the yarn kits and the books.

Illustration 55. An early ad for the Mary Hoyer "Miss Victory" Doll as well as the *Mary's Dollies* and *Juvenile Styles* books.

PRICE LIST AND ORDER BLANK
Mary Hoyer's Doll and Yarn Kits

Quantity		Amount
	COMPLETELY DRESSED BRIDE DOLL $5.00	
	DOLLS....Blonde....Medium....Dark Wig	
	Undressed, But Including Shoes & Stockings....$2.50	

Yarn Kits for Costumes in Vol. No. 5 of Mary's Dollies
	Olga (Angora Trimmed)	$1.25
	Mayree (Angora Trimmed)	1.25
	Annabelle	.85
	Goldilocks	.85
	Julianna	.85
	Arlene	.60

Yarn Kits for Costumes in Volume No. 6 of Mary's Dollies
	Sonja (Angora Trimmed)	1.25
	Lucretta (Angora Trimmed)	1.25
	Wavette	.85
	Maybelle	.85
	Nadine	.85

Yarn Kits for Costumes in Volume No. 9 of Mary's Dollies
	Zorina	1.25
	Zorina (Angora for Robe)	1.00
	Kathleen (Angora for Jacket)	1.00
	Kathleen (Angora for Snood)	1.00
	Terry	.65
	Sunny	.65
	Janie, Tinsel Crepe for Jacket & Fascinator	.65
	Susanna	.65
	Patsy	1.25
	Jackie	1.25
	Paula	.55
	Corine	1.25 1.00
	Billie	1.00
	Bride Kit	1.50

Toys, to fit Doll in all books
	Tennis Racket Sets	.25
	Skees and Poles	.50 .35
	Golf Bag and 3 Clubs	.35
	Skating Shoes—White	.35
	Marjorette Boots	.25
	Russian Boots	.25
	Riding Boots	.25
	Sled (shipped only with other items)	1.00
	Shoes and Stockings—White	.20
	Extra Wigs....Blonde....Med....Dark	1.00

Style Books, Mary's Dollies
	Volume No. 5—includes postage	.15
	Volume No. 6 " "	.15
	Volume No. 9 " "	.15
	Volume No. 10—Free With Doll—Separately	.20

MARY HOYER'S YARNS
FINEST QUALITY

Mary Hoyer's own yarns were used on all styles illustrated in Juvenile Styles Books. Be sure to use same quality and weight to insure the exact results illustrated.

Quantity			Amount
	Knitting Worsted	—4 ply—4 oz. skeins	$1.00
	Sports Yarn	—3 ply—2 oz. balls or skeins	.65
	Baby Yarn	—3 ply—1 oz. balls	.50
		(White, Blue, Pink, Peach)	
	Sweater Yarn	—3 ply—1 oz. balls	.50
		(All shades)	

Soft Pure Wool, with a rayon thread. Mary Hoyer's own choice for Baby Blankets, Sweaters, etc. (White, Pink, Blue, Deep Pink) 2 oz. skein .... .85

MARY HOYER'S ANGORA—100% pure rabbit hair; white, pink, blue, aqua — $1 per Ball

JUVENILE STYLES INSTRUCTION BOOKS
	Volume No. 2—includes postage	.30
	Volume No. 3— " "	.30
	Volume No. 4— " "	.30
	Volume No. 7— " "	.30
	Volume No. 8— " "	.30

Total Amount Enclosed $ _____

Name ....

Address ....

City ....

PLEASE PRINT YOUR NAME AND ADDRESS

Send Orders to
JUVENILE STYLES PUBLISHING COMPANY
1008 Penn Street, Reading, Pa.

PLEASE NOTE: Add 15c to cover postage on all orders except those on which postage is included—20c West of Rockies

August 1st, 1946—This list supersedes all previous lists.

Illustration 56. Price list dated August 1, 1946, from Juvenile Styles Publishing Company.

MARY HOYER DOLL AND YARN KITS

WITH

Custom-Built Wardrobe Trunk

As Advertised in McCall's Needlework Magazine

PRICE LIST AND ORDER BLANK

For Your Knitting and Crocheting Pleasure
DURING
1948

Illustration 57A. Price list dated October 1, 1948.

THE MARY HOYER DOLL

Quantity		Amount
	DRESSED BRIDE DOLL, Movable Eyes	$5.95
	DRESSED BRIDE'S MAID DOLL With Hat and Panties	$6.45
	DOLLS, 14" Tall, With Movable Eyes Undressed, But Including Shoes & Stockings Blonde......Medium......Dark......Red Wig	$2.95

PLEASE NOTE: Add 20c to cover postage on each doll---30c west of Chicago.

| | DOLL'S WARDROBE TRUNK 16x7¼x6¾ in. wood, cloth covered; brass hardware | $4.95 |
| | DOLL'S KNOTTY PINE CHEST 17x7x5¼ in. | $2.95 |

NOTE: Add 25c for Postage on each Trunk or Chest; 50c West of Chicago.

Yarn Kits for Costumes in Vol. No. 5 of Mary's Dollies

	Olga (Angora Trimmed)	$1.25
	Mayree (Angora Trimmed)	1.25
	Annabelle	.85
	Goldilocks	.60
	Julianna	.85
	Arlene	.60

Yarn Kits for Costumes in Volume No. 6 of Mary's Dollies

	Sonja (Angora Trimmed)	1.25
	Lucretta (Angora Trimmed)	1.25
	Wavette	.85
	Maybelle	.85
	Nadine	.85

Yarn Kits for Costumes in Volume No. 9 of Mary's Dollies

	Zorina	1.25
	Zorina (Angora for Robe)	.75
	Kathleen (Angora for Jacket)	.75
	Kathleen (Angora for Snood)	.65
	Terry	.65
	Sunny	.65
	Janie, Crepe for Jacket & Fascinator	.65
	Susanna	.85

Yarn Kits for Costumes in Vol. No. 10 of Mary's Dollies

	Patsy	1.25
	Jackie	1.25
	Corine	1.00
	Billie	.55
	Paula	.55
	Bride Kit	1.50

Yarn Kits for Costumes in Vol. 11 of Mary's Dollies

	Lucille	1.25
	Dolores (Angora Trimmed)	1.25
	Bride's Maid Kit	1.75
	Anita (Angora Trimmed)	1.25

Toys, to fit Doll in all books

	Tennis Racket Sets	.25
	Tennis Shoes—Brown	.20
	Skees and Poles	.50

Toys, to fit Doll in all books (continued)

	Sled (as illustrated in Vol. No. 7)	1.00
	Skating Shoes—White	.35
	Majorette Boots	.25
	Russian Boots	.25
	Riding Boots	.25
	Shoes and Stockings—White	.25
	Extra Wigs ....Blonde....Med....Dark....Red	1.00
	Plastic Doll Clothes Hangers—6 for	.25
	Two-Way-Stretch Girdles	.25
	Miniature Child's Bible, Catholic or Protestant	.25
	Ballet Slippers, gold, pink, red, black suede, pr.	.25
	White Roller Skates, pr.	.25
	Doll Stand	.75
	Doll Purse with Metal Chain	.50

NOTE: Add 20c for postage; 30c west of Chicago on complete Order for Items above.

Style Books, Mary's Dollies

	Volume No. 5—includes postage	.20
	Volume No. 6 " "	.20
	Volume No. 9 " "	.20
	Volume No. 10 " "	.20
	Volume No. 11—Free With Doll (Separately)	.20

MARY HOYER'S YARNS

Use Mary Hoyer's Fine Yarns for exact results illustrated in style books

Quantity		Amount
	Knitting Worsted —4 ply—4 oz. skeins	$1.00
	Sports Yarn —3 ply—2 oz. balls or skeins	.75
	Baby Yarn —3 ply—1 oz. balls (White, Blue, Pink, Peach)	.50
	Sweater Yarn —3 ply—1 oz. balls (All shades)	.50
	Soft Pure Wool, with a rayon thread, (White, Pink, Blue, Deep Pink) 2 oz. skein	.75
	Crepelane (All Colors) 2 oz. Ball	1.00
	MARY HOYER'S ANGORA—100% pure rabbit hair: white, pink, blue, aqua	75c per Ball

NOTE: Add 20c for postage; 30c west of Chicago on complete Order for items above.

JUVENILE STYLES INSTRUCTION BOOKS

	Volume No. 2—includes postage	.35
	Volume No. 3— " "	.35
	Volume No. 4— " "	.35
	Volume No. 7— " "	.35
	Volume No. 8	.35

Total Amount Enclosed $_____

Name _____

Address _____

City _____

PLEASE PRINT YOUR NAME AND ADDRESS
October 1, 1948—This list supersedes all previous lists.

Illustration 57B. Price list dated October 1, 1948.

Mary's Dollies

AND

YARN KITS

WITH

CUSTOM-BUILT WARDROBE TRUNK

As Advertised in McCall's Needlework Magazine

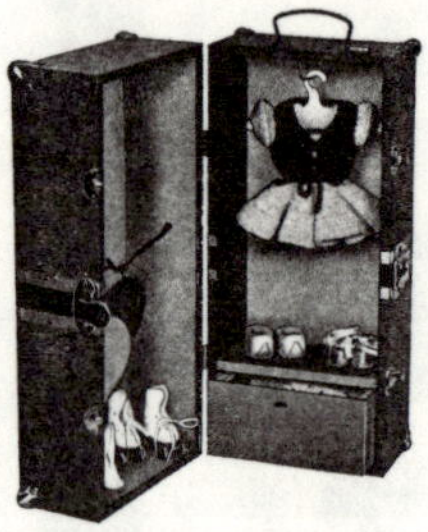

Illustration 58A. Price list and order blank dated September 1, 1950.

★ *For Your Knitting and Crocheting Pleasure during* 1950

PRICE LIST AND ORDER BLANK

MARY HOYER TWIN DOLLS
(Made of Finest Quality Plastic)

	GIRL DOLL, 14" Tall, With Movable Eyes, Undressed, But Including Shoes and Stockings. Blonde......Medium......Dark......Red Wig	$3.25

PLEASE NOTE: Add 20c to cover postage on each doll---30c west of Chicago.

| | BOY DOLL, 14" Tall, With Movable Eyes, Undressed, But Including Shoes and Stockings only ......Medium...... and ......Dark Wig | $3.25 |

NOTE: Add 20c to cover postage on each doll---30c west of Chicago.

| | GIRL DOLL, with Nylon Wig ......Blonde and ......Dark Wig | $4.75 |

NOTE: Add 20c to cover postage on each doll---30c west of Chicago.

| | DOLL'S WARDROBE TRUNK for one Doll, size 16x7¼x6¾ cloth covered, Brass Hardware, Washable. Postage on each 25c---50c west of Chicago | $4.95 |
| | DOLL'S WARDROBE TRUNK for two Dolls, size 16x9x9, Wood, Brass Hardware, Washable. Postage on each 25c---50c west of Chicago | $5.25 |

Yarn Kits for Costumes in Vol. No. 5 of Mary's Dollies

	Olga (Angora Trimmed)	$1.25
	Mayree (Angora Trimmed)	1.25
	Annabelle	.85
	Goldilocks	.85
	Julianna	.85
	Arlene	.60

Yarn Kits for Costumes in Vol. No. 6 of Mary's Dollies

	Sonja (Angora Trimmed)	1.25
	Lucretta (Angora Trimmed)	1.25
	Wavette	.85
	Maybelle	.85
	Nadine	.85

Yarn Kits for Costumes in Vol. No. 9 of Mary's Dollies

	Zorina	1.25
	Zorina (Angora for Robe)	.75
	Kathleen (Angora for Jacket)	.75
	Kathleen (Angora for Snood)	.65
	Terry	.65
	Sunny	.65
	Janie, Crepe for Jacket & Fascinator	.65
	Susanna	.85

Yarn Kits for Costumes in Vol. No. 10 of Mary's Dollies

	Patsy	1.25
	Jackie	1.25
	Corine	1.25
	Billie	1.00
	Paula	.55
	Bride Kit	1.50

Illustration 58B. Price list and order blank dated September 1, 1950.

Yarn Kits for Costumes in Vol. 11 of Mary's Dollies

	Lucille	1.25
	Dolores (Angora Trimmed)	1.25
	Bride's Maid Kit	1.75
	Anita (Angora Trimmed)	1.25

Yarn Kits for Costumes in Vol. 12 of Mary's Dollies

	Greta	.75
	Jo-Ann	.25
	Westerner, including Belt	1.00
	Peggy (Angora Trimmed)	1.25
	Ballet Kit	1.25

Yarn Kits for Costumes in Vol. 13 of Mary's Dollies

	Mary Hoyer Twins - Bobby	.75
	Mary Hoyer Twins - Betty	.75
	Cow Girl, Nancy, Including 2-Gun Holster Belt	1.00
	Cow Boy, Dick, Including 2-Gun Holster Belt	1.00
	Sweethearts, Hans	1.00
	Sweethearts, Tina	1.00
	Crocheted Suit, Carol	1.25

Completed Costumes for Mary's Dollies

	Bride with Veil and Panties	2.95
	Bride's Maid with Hat and Panties	3.50
	Ballerina (Taffeta and Nylon Net) See Vol. No. 13	2.50
	Ballet (See Vol. No. 12)	1.95
	Centennial Queen	2.50
	Nylon Pajamas	1.25
	Nightie with Bootees (Brushed Rayon Trimmed in Lace)	1.50
	Plaid Rain Cape & Hood (Plastic Cover)	1.50
	Rayon Lace Trimmed Panties	.35
	Rayon Lace Trimmed Half Slips	.45
	(the two items above in a matching set)	.75
	Two-way Stretch Girdle	.25
	Bathing Suit, Satin Lastex	.59
	Rayon Beach Coat	.85
	The two above items in matching set	1.35

Accessories, to fit Doll in all books

	Leather Hand Bag, plaid trimming	.59
	Red Rubber Bathing Cap with Chin Strap	.35
	Snap Shoes and Stockings, white	.20
	Black Lace Shoes & Black Stockings	.20
	Imported Straw Hat, hand embroidered	1.00
	Tennis Racket Sets	.25
	Tennis Shoes—Brown	.20
	Skees and Poles	.50
	Dutch Wooden Shoes	.35
	Ice Skating Shoes—White	.35
	Majorette Boots	.25
	White Boots	.25
	Riding Boots	.25
	Sandals, Gold and Silver	.25
	Bedroom Slippers, White, Pink, Blue	.25

NOTE: Add 20c for postage; 30c west of Chicago on complete Order for items above.

Accessories - Continued

	Western Boots with Spurs	.35
	Belt with Western Buckle	.20
	Belt with 2 Gun Holsters	.25
	Western Felt Hat	.75
	Real Hair Wigs ....Blonde....Medium....Dark Red	1.00
	Nylon Wigs....Medium....Blonde—only	2.50
	Plastic Doll Clothes Hangers—6 for	.25
	Plastic Hanger with Clips, each	.10
	Miniature Child's Bible, Cath or Prot	.25
	Ballet Slippers, gold, pink, red, blue satin, black suede, pr.	.25
	Miniature Suit Case	.35
	Miniature School Bag	.25
	White Roller Skates, pr.	.35
	Doll Stand	.75
	Doll Purse with Metal Chain	.50
	Golf Bag with Golf Sticks	.39
	Black Patent Leather Shoes	.25

Style Books, Mary's Dollies

	Volume No. 5—includes postage	.20
	Volume No. 6 " "	.20
	Volume No. 9 " "	.20
	Volume No. 10 " "	.20
	Volume No. 11 " "	.20
	Volume No. 12 " "	.20
	Volume No. 13—Free With Doll (separately)	.20

MARY HOYER'S ANGORA
100% pure rabbit hair: white, pink, blue, aqua **75c per Ball**

NOTE: Add 20c for postage; 30c west of Chicago on complete Order for items above.

JUVENILE STYLES INSTRUCTION BOOKS

	Volume No. 2—includes postage	.30
	Volume No. 3— " "	.30
	Volume No. 4— " "	.30
	Volume No. 7— " "	.30
	Volume No. 8	.30

Total Amount Enclosed $_____

Name _____

Address _____

City _____

PLEASE PRINT YOUR NAME AND ADDRESS
September 1, 1950 - This list supersedes all previous lists.

Send Orders to

JUVENILE STYLES PUBLISHING CO.

1013 Penn Street, Reading, Pa.

Illustration 59A. Booklet advertising the Mary Hoyer Doll and costumes and kits that were available.

Illustration 59B. Booklet advertising the Mary Hoyer Doll and costumes and kits that were available.

Illustration 59C. Booklet advertising the Mary Hoyer Doll and costumes and kits that were available.

Illustration 59D. Booklet advertising the Mary Hoyer Doll and costumes and kits that were available.

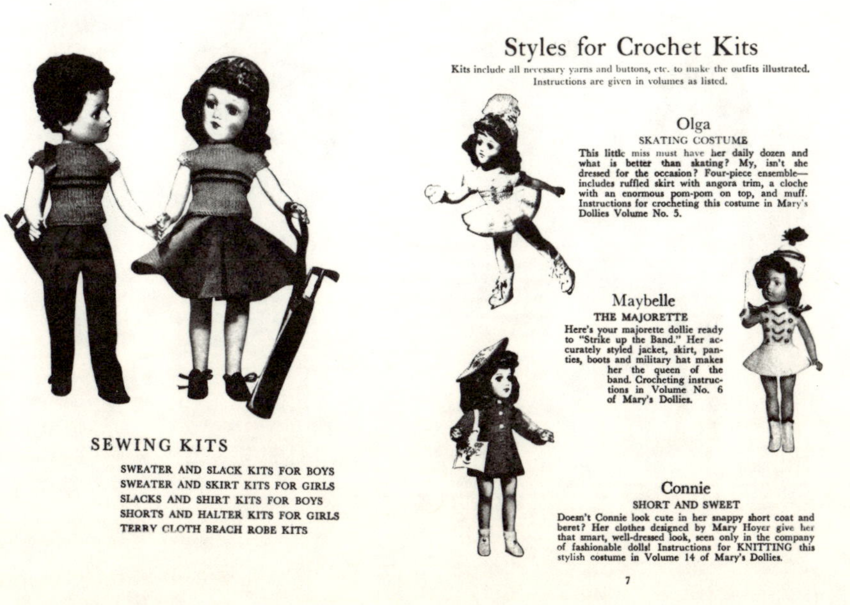

STYLES FOR CROCHET KITS

Dolores
SKATING COSTUME

Somewhat bashful looking, but can she skate! See how warm she is dressed in her one piece dress, cap and mitts. Her full skirt is perfect for figure skating. Crocheting Instructions in Volume No. 11 of Mary's Dollies.

Greta
A DUTCH TREAT

How did Holland get into the picture? That's because Mary Hoyer remembers little girls from every corner of the earth. The wooden shoes are an exact replica of the little girls' shoes of Holland. Crocheting Instructions in Vol. 12 of Mary's Dollies.

Carol
A STYLISH MISS

Who have we here? Carol surely looks the part of the well-dressed adult. The upward sweep of her bonnet adds an inexplainable charm to her looks. Note the perfection of detail. Crocheting Instructions in Volume No. 13.

8

STYLES FOR CROCHET KITS

Louise
PARTY DRESS AND HAT

Where is Louise going? If to a party, her ensemble will be the envy of all the dolls present. Those large dark eyes are magnified by the flare of her skirt, straw picture hat and delicate footwear. Hat and shoes are included in this kit. Crocheting Instructions in Volume No. 14.

Renee
CROCHETED DRESS AND CAPE

Look at that ensemble! Also the flare of that skirt—scalloped edges and drape over the shoulders. Can an adult wear anything finer and nicer looking? Skirt just right for walking and sitting. Extra cape to ensemble or a separate one for extra strapless gowns. Crocheting Instructions in Volume No. 15.

9

Illustration 59E. Booklet advertising the Mary Hoyer Doll and costumes and kits that were available.

Styles for Knitting Kits

Kits include all yarns and buttons, etc. to make the outfits illustrated. Instructions are given in the volumes listed.

Arlene
BATHING ENSEMBLE

Here's Arlene in her 4-piece ensemble all togged out for her visit to the shore. At Ocean City, she'll surely be the center of attraction all along the beach. That's because she wears clothing designed by Mary Hoyer. Knitting Instructions in Vol. 5.

Billie
A RIDING HABIT

Billie is all dressed for the occasion, but, where is her horse? It is a sure bet, that with this lovely riding habit, she won't have any trouble securing one. Knitting Instructions in Volume No. 10.

Anita
SKIING COSTUME

When Anita goes skiing, she is properly and warmly dressed. Her ensemble will be the talk of the ski run and many will copy her style. Skis are available with the poles. Knitting Instructions in Volume No. 11.

10

STYLES FOR KNITTING KITS

Nadine
RED CROSS NURSE

This little "Angel of Mercy" is ready to care for anything that ails you. Who wouldn't get well under her spell? Knitting Instructions in Vol. 6.

Lucille
ROLLER SKATING OUTFIT

Well, here we have Lucille in her specially designed skating outfit. She may not have won any medals, but she will surely win you. Very cute. Knitting Instructions in Vol. No. 11.

Nancy and Dick
COWBOY AND COWGIRL COSTUMES

Is this Roy Rogers or Gene Autrey? Watch out Nancy, for that lariat! Dick is real tricky with the rope. Those two costumes will intrigue the most exacting little girl. Knitting Instructions in Volume No. 13.

11

Illustration 59F. Booklet advertising the Mary Hoyer Doll and costumes and kits that were available.

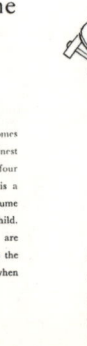

Ballet Costume

THE PETITE SHORT BALLET

This beautiful costume comes completed only. Made of finest quality tissue taffeta and four rows of nylon tulle. This is a truly delightful doll costume that will delight any child. Matching ballet slippers are available. Be sure to tell us the color of your doll's wig when ordering this one.

ANOTHER MARY HOYER TRIUMPH

Mary Hoyer's artistry is eloquently expressed in this expertly designed masterpiece. Its elegance and gossamer qualities will fairly take your breath away. Order this fine costume today with the ballet slippers and enjoy its charm.

Illustration 59G. Booklet advertising the Mary Hoyer Doll and costumes and kits that were available.

Shoes, Boots and Slippers

The doll footwear listed below is accurate in every detail and the size is perfect for the Mary Hoyer Doll. Each one has been carefully designed to compliment the costumes illustrated in this booklet and all the volumes of Mary's Dollies. Only the finest workmanship is used throughout.

Smart Footwear for Beautiful Mary Hoyer Dolls!

Majorette Boots, white with gold tassels; including baton.
Russian Boots—white trim at top.
Brown Riding Boots.
Tan Western Boots with spurs.
Ballet Slippers, in gold, silver, pink, red and blue satin; black suede.
Bridal Slippers with silk bows.
Cinderella Slippers with buckles.
Felt Bedroom Slippers with pompoms in white, pink and blue.
Black Shoes with lacers complete with black stockings.
White Shoes with lacers and white stockings.
Black Patent Leather Shoes with Lacers.

Black Patent Leather Shoes with buckle.
Dutch Wooden Shoes.
Ice Skating Shoes with lacers; white or gold.
Roller Skates with lacers, white or gold.
White Snap Shoes with white stockings.
Brown Tennis Shoes.
Mules of Satin with elastic in white, pink or blue.
Sandals with snaps in gold foil or silver foil.
Saddle Shoes with eyelets in two-tone brown and white; also red and white.
Mary Jane Anklet Shoes in white, pink, blue, black patent leather.

Be Sure to Include Several Pairs of Shoes with your Doll's Wardrobe!

13

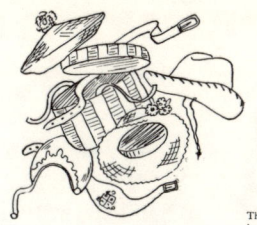

Hats, Hat Boxes, Bags, etc.

•

The following items are always in stock and can be purchased and shipped to you anytime.

Lovely Accessories for Lovely Dolls!

Western Felt Hats for the Western Costumes.
Imported Straw Hat, hand embroidered from Jamaica—natural straw only.
French Straw Poke Bonnet—untrimmed.
Same Poke Bonnet beautifully trimmed with flowers and appropriate ribbons.
French Straw Picture Hats—untrimmed.
Same Picture Hat trimmed with flowers and ribbons.
Small size Poke—untrimmed
Same Poke trimmed with flowers and ribbons.
Colors available: White, Pink, Blue and Yellow.

•

Red Rubber Bathing Caps with a chin strap.
Black Patent Leather Belts.
Contour Belts in black patent leather, red and gold.
Refer to our price list for dozens of other costume accessories.

14

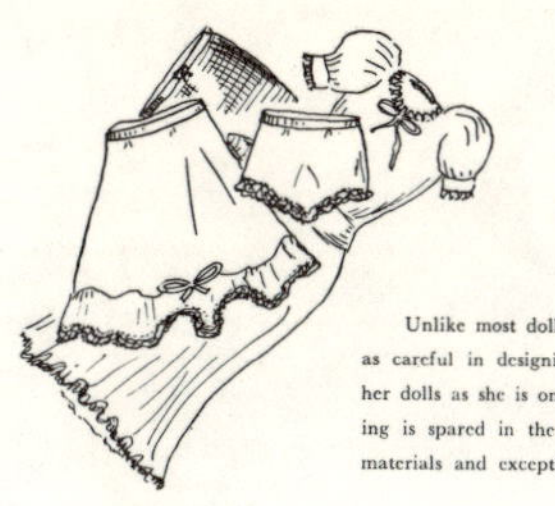

Dainty Lingerie

•

Unlike most dolls, Mary Hoyer is just as careful in designing undergarments for her dolls as she is on outergarments. Nothing is spared in the furnishing of quality materials and exceptional handicraft.

Quality Lingerie for Dolls of Quality!

•

Lace Trimmed Nylon Panties with elastic top.
Lace Trimmed Nylon Half Slips with elastic top.
Heavy Weight Nylon Nities with lace tops—either white or black.
Nylon Pajamas.
Two-way Stretch Girdles.
Satin Lastex Bathing Suits.
Nylon Beach Coat.
Terry Cloth Beach Robe.

All of these undergarments are made of nylon. They may be easily washed and will dry quickly. Order a complete set!

15

Illustration 59H. Booklet advertising the Mary Hoyer Doll and costumes and kits that were available.

DOLL PARTS AND WIGS

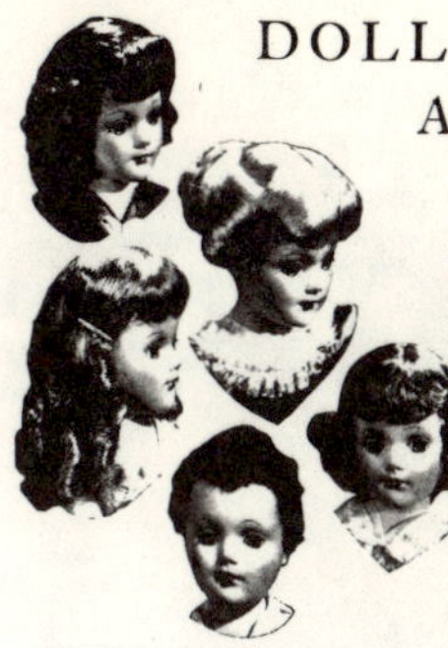

When a doll is purchased from Mary Hoyer, the sale does not stop there. No indeed! If your little Miss, at some time, should be unfortunate in breaking a leg or an arm, or any other part of her doll, don't worry. Just write Mary Hoyer and a new part will be mailed promptly. New parts are simple to install.

LIST OF NEW PARTS AND WIGS

•

Head without Wig
Left Leg — Body — Right Leg
Left Arm — Joiners — Right Arm
Wigs of DuPont Nylon—Rolled Bangs
Up-Sweep Wig with Bustle Back
Alice Flowing Wig with Permanent Wave
Curled Wig with Straight Bangs
Boy's Wool Wig

We hope you have enjoyed looking through this booklet. Start making some of the Mary Hoyer Doll Clothes today.

Mary Hoyer Doll Manufacturing Company
1013 Penn Street — Reading, Pa.

16

Illustration 59I. Booklet advertising the Mary Hoyer Doll and costumes and kits that were available.

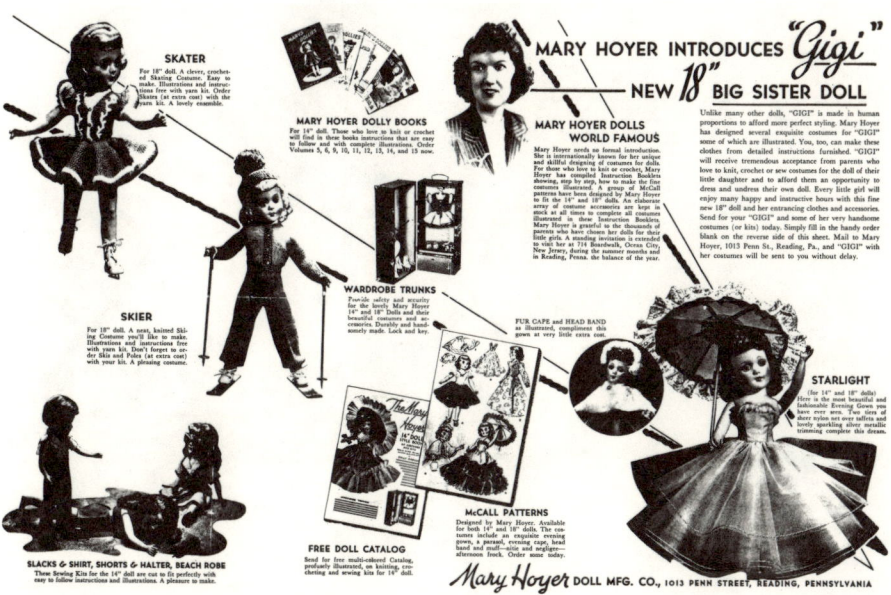

Illustration 60A. Price list and order blank dated June 1, 1954.

Illustration 60B. Price list and order blank dated June 1, 1954.

MARY HOYER 14" DOLLS

GIRL DOLL, with curled, washable, SARAN wig. Blonde, Medium Brown, Dark Brown, Auburn.	$3.50
BOY DOLL, with lamb's wool wig, mohair combed wig, fur wig.	$3.50
GIRL DOLL, with curled, washable DuPONT NYLON wig. Can be combed, curled and waved. Blonde, Medium Brown, Dk. Brown, Auburn.	$4.95
GIRL DOLL: side-sweep, up-sweep, Alice flowing, curled with straight bangs; comb, curl and wave these washable DYNEL wigs. Blonde, Medium Brown, Dark Brown, Auburn.	$4.95
DOLL'S WARDROBE TRUNK for 1 doll, approx. size 16x7x7 inches, washable covering, brass hardware.	$4.95
DOLL'S WARDROBE TRUNK for 2 dolls, approx. size 16x9x9 inches, washable covering, brass hardware.	$5.25
Yarn Kits for Costumes, Vol. 5, Mary's Dollies	
Olga (angora trimmed)	$1.25
Mayree (angora trimmed)	1.25
Annabelle	.75
Goldilocks	.75
Julianna	.85
Arlene	.65
Yarn Kits for Costumes, Vol. 6, Mary's Dollies	
Sonja (angora trimmed)	1.00
Lucretta (angora trimmed)	1.25
Wavette	.85
Maybelle	.85
Nadine	.85
Yarn Kits for Costumes, Vol. 9, Mary's Dollies	
Zorina (angora trimmed)	1.25
Zorina (angora for robe)	.69
Kathleen (angora for jacket)	.69
Kathleen (angora for snood)	.69
Terry	1.00
Sunny	.75
Janie, crepe for jacket & fascinator	1.00
Susanna	1.00
Yarn Kits for Costumes, Vol. 10, Mary's Dollies	
Patsy (angora trimmed)	1.25
Jackie (angora trimmed)	1.25
Corine	1.25
Billie	1.00
Paula	.55
Yarn Kits for Costumes, Vol. 11, Mary's Dollies	
Lucille	1.00
Dolores (angora trimmed)	1.25
Anita (angora trimmed)	1.25
Yarn Kits for Costumes, Vol. 12, Mary's Dollies	
Greta	.75
Jo-Ann	.35
Westerner, including belt	1.25
Peggy (angora trimmed)	1.25
Yarn Kits for Costumes, Vol. 13, Mary's Dollies	
Mary Hoyer Twins - Bobby	.85
Mary Hoyer Twins - Betty	.85
Cow Girl, Nancy, w.2 gun hol. belt	1.25
Cow Boy, Dick, with 2 gun hol. belt	1.25
Sweethearts, Hans	1.00
Sweethearts, Tina	1.00
Crocheted Suit, Carol	1.25
Yarn Kits for Costumes, Vol. 14, Mary's Dollies	
Louise (incl. hat and sandals)	1.25
Connie	.75
Nan	1.00
Jack	.85
Jeanette	.85
arn Kits for Costumes, Vol. 15, Mary's Dollies	
Renee	1.50
Isabelle	1.25

Completed Costumes for Mary's 14" Dollies	
Starlight Eve. Gown, pink or blue	3.50
Short Taffeta Print Dress w. parasol	3.95
Dolly Madison w. parasol, vol. 15	5.95
Alice Blue Pinafore, w. blue matching shoes	2.95
Bride, w. veil & panties (nylon net)	2.95
Bridegroom with top hat and shoes	4.95
Bride's Maid w. hat & panties	2.95
Ballet (short) all colors	2.50
Ballerina (long) pink & blue	2.25
Scotch Plaid Costume, w. miniature hand bag & shoes	3.95
Scotch Plaid Child's Matching Hand Bag	1.00
Southern Belle Costume, w. shoes & parasol	4.50
Nylon Pajamas	1.00
White Nightie, nylon—lace trimmed	1.00
Black Nightie, nylon—lace trimmed	1.00
Rain Cape & hood, plastic cov.	1.25
Nylon Scibbies	.25
Rayon Lace Trimmed Panties	.35
Rayon Lace Trimmed Half Slip	.50
(two items above in a matching set)	.75
Two-way Stretch Girdle	.35
Bathing Suit, Lastex, trimmed	.85
Bathing Suit, Satin Lastex, untrim.	.50
Nylon Beach Coat	.75
Sun Bonnet Sue	1.50
Slack Set with Belt	1.50
Terry Cloth Beach Robe	1.00
Shorts and Halter	1.00
Fur Cape with Head Band	1.95
Woolen Coat, Dress and Hat	3.95
Short Cotton Playtime Dress	2.25
Sewing Kits—All Material Cut to Fit (14")	
Dolly Madison with parasol frame	3.25
Alice Blue Pinafore Kit, w. blue matching shoes	1.50
Bride's Maid Kit (with nylon net)	1.50
Bride Kit, (with nylon net)	1.50
Ballerina Kit, (with nylon net)	1.25
Sweater and Slack Kit for Boy	1.00
Sweater and Dress Kit for Girl	1.00
Scotch Plaid Kit	1.95
Southern Belle Kit, w. shoes and parasol frame	2.95
Sun Bonnet Sue	.75
Terry Beach Robe	.60
Shorts and Halter	.50
Slacks and Shirt with Belt	.85
Woolen Coat, Dress and Hat	2.25
Short Taffeta Print Dress & parasol	2.25
Accessories to fit Doll in all Books	
Accessories—Dolly's Bags and Purses (14")	
Silk Purse with Metal Chain	.50
Dolly Hand Bag, Scotch plaid trim.	.50
Gold Finish Purses with metal chain	.50
Golf Bag with Sticks	.35
Miniature School Bag	.25
Over-Nite Zipper Bag, plastic	.39
Plastic Shoulder Bag	.25
Mesh Hand Bag, gold finish	1.00
Accessories—Boots, Slippers and Shoes (14")	
Majorette Boots, with Baton	.35
Russian Boots	.25
Riding Boots	.25
Western Boots with Spurs	.35
Ballet Slippers, (gold, silver, pink, red, blue satin, black suede) pr.	.25
Bridal Slippers with Silk Bows	.25
Cinderella Slippers	.35
Felt Bedroom Slippers,wh.,pink,blue	.25
Black Lace Shoes & black stockings	.25
White Lace Shoes and stockings	.25
Black Patent Leather Shoes w. laces	.25
Black Patent L'ther Shoes w. buckle	.25
Dutch Wooden Shoes	.35
Ice Skating Shoes, white or gold	.35
Roller Skates, white or gold, pr.	.35
Snap Shoes and stockings, white	.25

Tennis Shoes, brown	.25
Mules, (white, pink or blue)	.25
Sandals, (gold and silver color)	.25
Saddle Shoes (brown and white)	.25
Saddle Shoes (red and white)	.25
Mary Jane Shoes (white, pink, blue, black patent leather)	.25
Scotch Kilties	.25
Beach Shoes	.25
Accessories—Hats and Caps (14")	
Imported Straw Hat, hand embroid.	.75
Western Felt Hat	.75
Red Rubber Bath. Cap w. chin strap	.35
Poke Bonnet, trim., French Straw	.75
Poke Bonnet, untrim., French Straw	.50
Picture Hat, trimmed, Fr. Straw	.75
Picture Hat, untrimmed, Fr. Straw	.50
Straw Hat Box	.59
Off-face Felt Hat	.50
Accessories—Toys and Miscellaneous Items (14")	
Belt with Western Buckle	.20
Belt with 2 Gun Holsters	.25
Black Patent Leather Belt	.15
Contour Belt, blk. patent, red, gold	.25
Hair Net, blonde, medium, dark	.10
Sparkle Hair Net, silver or gold	.15
Min. Child's Bible, Cath. or Prot.	.25
Miniature Suit Case	.25
Miniature Silk Fans	.25
Parasol With Frilling	1.50
Parasol Frames, uncovered	1.00
Skis and Poles	.50
Sun Glasses	.25
Tennis Racket Set	.25
Doll Stand	.75
Doll Stand w. dress expander (pat.)	1.50
Plastic Doll Clothes Hangers, 6 for	.25
Plastic Hanger with Clips, each	.10
Beautiful Gold Plated Dress Hanger	.10
Plastic Garment Bag, with zipper and hanger bar	1.00
Dress Rack	.59
Miniature Camera	.69
Pearl Neckace	.25
Doll Stockings (14")	
Long Nylon Stockings, elastic tops	.25
Rayon Stockings, white or black, pr.	.05
Bridal Garters, Nylon: lace trim, pr.	.30
Parts for the Mary Hoyer 14" Dolls	
New Head	1.25
New Leg	.50
New Arm	.50
New Body	.50
New Rubber Joiner	.25
DuPont Nylon Curled Wigs, wash. blonde, med.brown, dk.brown, auburn	2.50
Alice Wig, washable blonde, med.brown, dk.brown, auburn	2.25
Saran Curled Wig	1.50
Side-Sweep Wig with Curls	2.50
Up-Sweep Wig with Bustle Back blonde, med.brown, dk.brown, auburn	2.50
Boy's Wig, mohair, wool or fur	1.25
STYLE BOOKS—MARY'S DOLLIES	
Knitting & Crocheting Costumes for 14" Doll	
Volume No. 5, includes postage	.20
Volume No. 6, " "	.20
Volume No. 9, " "	.20
Volume No. 10, " "	.20
Volume No. 11, " "	.20
Volume No. 12, " "	.20
Volume No. 13, " "	.20
Volume No. 14, " "	.20
Volume No. 15, " "	.20
McCall Patterns for Sewing (14")	
Pattern No. 1564	.35
Pattern No. 1891	.35
Wash and Wave Kits	
For all Mary Hoyer Washable Wigs	.49

"GIGI" NEW BIG 18" DOLL

By MARY HOYER

SLIM GIRL DOLL, 18" — with the perfect figure for costuming. DYNEL Wigs can be combed and washed. Platinum, Blonde, Dark, Med.Brown. Wig Styles: Up-Sweep with Bustle Back, Curled with Cut Bangs, Long Flowing with Permanent Waves, Side Sweep with Curls, Cut Bangs. Doll undressed w. shoes.	$6.95
DOLL'S WARDROBE TRUNK approx. size 10½x10½x20. NEW; handsomely styled with rounded edges and fine hardware—lock and key.	$7.50
Completed Costumes for New 18" Doll	
Starlight Evening Gown, metallic trim. Pink or Blue	$3.95
Nylon Nitie, nylon lace trimmed	1.25
Panties, lace trimmed	.40
Nylon Scibbies	.30
Two-Way Stretch Girdle	.45
Lastex Bathing Suit, nylon trim	1.00
Fur Cape with Head Band	1.95
Short Cotton Play-Time Dress	2.50
Custom Built Shoes for New 18" Doll	
Majorette Boots with Baton	.40
Western Boots with Spurs	.40
Ballet Slippers, gold, silver, pink, red, blue satin	.30
Bridal Slippers	.30
Felt Bedroom Slippers, white, pink, blue	.30
Ice Skates, high shoes	.70
Roller Skates, high shoes	.40
Snap Shoes and Socks	.30
Mules, white, pink, blue	.30
Evening Sandals, gold or silver	.30
Saddle Shoes, brown and white or red and white	.30
Mary Jane Blk. Pat. Leather Shoes	.30
Skis with Poles	.60
Hats for New 18" Doll	
Picture Hat, French Straw, untrim.	.50
Picture Hat, French Straw, trimmed with flowers and ribbon	1.00
Straw Hat Box	1.00
Doll Stockings for New 18" Doll	
Long Nylon Stockings, elastic tops	.25
Bridal Garters, Nylon: lace trim, pr.	.30
Accessories for New 18" Doll	
Parasol, nylon lace trimmed	1.50
Parasol Frame w. pattern for cover.	1.00
Belt with gun & holster	.30
Contour Belts, blk. pat., red, gold	.25
Hair Net, blonde, medium, dark	.10
Sparkle Hair Net, silver or gold	.15
Min. Child's Bible, Cath. or Prot.	.25
Miniature Suit Case	.25
Miniature Silk Fans	.25
Sun Glasses	.25
Tennis Racket Set	.25
Miniature Camera	.69
Pearl Neckace	.25
NEW Doll Display Stand with dress expander. (metal base with positive leg lock	1.50
Plastic Doll Clothes Hangers, 6 for	.25
Plastic Hanger with Clips, each	.10
Beautiful Gold Plated Dress Hanger	.10

Accessories—Doll's Bags and Purses for New 18" Doll	
Silk Purse with Metal Chain	.50
Dolly Hand Bag, Scotch plaid trim.	.50
Gold Finish Purses with metal chain	.50
Golf Bag with Sticks	.35
Miniature School Bag	.25
Over-Nite Zipper Bag, plastic	.39
Plastic Shoulder Bag	.25
Mesh Hand Bag, gold finish	1.00
Parts for New 18" Doll	
New Head without wig	1.50
New Leg, either left or right	.60
New Arm, either left or right	.60
New Body	.60
Joiner	.25
Washable Wigs for the New 18" Doll	
Curled with cut bangs	2.00
Long Flowing w. permanent waves	2.50
Up-Sweep with bustle back	3.00
Side Sweep with curls	3.00
Patterns & Knit & Crocheted Kits for the New 18" Doll (to make your own costumes)	
McCall Pattern No. 1891-18	.35
Gigi Skating Kit, crocheted, angora trim	1.50
Gigi Ski Suit, knit, angora trim (kits incl. illustrations & instructions)	1.25
Wash and Wave Kits	
For all Mary Hoyer Washable Wigs	.49
Mary Hoyer's Angora — 100% pure rabbit hair; white, pink, blue and aqua, per ball	60c
JUVENILE STYLES INSTRUCTION BOOKS	
Knitted and Crocheted Garments for Infants and Children	
Volume No. 2, includes postage	.30
Volume No. 3, " "	.30
Volume No. 4, " "	.30
Volume No. 7, " "	.30
Volume No. 8, " "	.30
Total	$
PA. SALES TAX	$
Postage (if any)	$
Total Amount Enclosed	$

PA. RESIDENTS! Add to total remittance, Sales Tax of one cent for every dollar or part of a dollar!

POSTAGE: ALL ORDERS $5.00 or over PREPAID. Under $5.00, add 25c for postage & handling (except west of Chicago, add 50c).

Name ____________________

Address ____________________

City ____________________

Please Print Your Name and Address

June 1, 1954—This list supercedes all previous lists.

Send Orders to

MARY HOYER DOLL MFG. CO.
JUVENILE STYLES PUBLISHING CO.
1013 Penn Street, Reading, Pa.

The MARY HOYER DOLL
STYLE BOOK
OF COSTUMES AND KITS
For Knitting, Crocheting and Sewing

• **DOLLY MADISON**
Kits and Completed Costumes for the 14" and 18" Dolls. With matching parasol. Isn't she a beauty? Mary Hoyer's latest creation will endear her to the heartstrings of little girls everywhere. Exquisite satin with dotted sheer nylon trim. She's lovely.

WARDROBE TRUNKS
This durable wardrobe trunk, with brass corners, lock and key, is available in several sizes. It has a large hanger bar providing ample space for her wardrobe. Also drawer is perfect for storing her many accessories.
Sizes for 14" and 18" Dolls.

Illustration 61A. Booklet advertising the Mary Hoyer Doll and costumes and kits that were available.

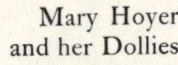

Mary Hoyer and her Dollies

The name "Mary Hoyer" today, is of national prominence, and all because of her unique and exclusive designing of clothes and costumes for dolls. Her original, fascinating designs attract mothers from all over the country and bring happiness to thousands and thousands of little girls.

She has designed the perfect doll for those who love to knit, crochet and sew. The slim body has been beautifully made of finest unbreakable plastic; has moving eyes, arms, head and legs. She sits and stands easily. She is 14" tall.

See the three beautiful hair styles on page 16. These wigs are made of DuPont Nylon and may be washed, combed and waved. Your child may re-set the hair in any style she chooses. The Mary Hoyer Doll is one of the very few dolls on the market that comes to you with DuPont Nylon Wigs.

You will have many hours of pleasure in making complete wardrobes for your Mary Hoyer Doll, from the kits illustrated in this booklet and the other Style and Instruction Booklets entitled "Mary's Dollies." There are over 100 costumes to select from; more original designs have been designed for her than for any other doll in the world. Then, too, your child will have endless hours of enjoyment dressing and undressing her Mary Hoyer Doll in the costumes you have made for her.

When ordering completed costumes or kits, please tell us the color of the doll's wig, so that we can give you the proper contrasting costume.

A complete group of costume accessories, such as shoes in many styles; hats, belts, purses, etc. are always in stock to complete all costumes illustrated in all instruction books. These are "Mary's Dollies," Volumes Nos. 5, 6, 9, 10, 11, 12, 13, 14, 15.

Mary Hoyer is grateful to the many parents who have centered their choice on her dolls and extends an invitation to visit her when in Ocean City, N. J. for a summer vacation, or Reading, Pa. in the winter.

MARY HOYER DOLL MFG. CO.
1013 Penn St., Reading, Pa.

Illustration 61B. Booklet advertising the Mary Hoyer Doll and costumes and kits that were available.

Sewing Kits
All materials in these Kits are of the highest quality and are cut to fit the Mary Hoyer Doll perfectly. When instructions are followed closely, the finished costumes will be exactly as illustrated.

Bride's Kit
Lovely to look at! Silks and satins with sheer dotted nylon net, such as you have never seen before. Complete with veil and panties.
Kit for 14" Doll only. Completed Costumes for 14" and 18" Dolls.

Bride's Maid Kit
In keeping with the bride, is the Bride's Maid with her demure picture hat. Taffeta with sheer nylon net. Hat illustrated is included.
Kit and Completed Costume for 14" doll only.

Ballerina Kit
The orchestra appears and the house lights are lowered—when the petite Ballerina comes into view. She wears crisp taffeta with full over-throw of sequined nylon net.
Kit for 14" Doll only. Completed Costumes for 14" and 18" Dolls.

Sewing Kits

Southern Belle Kit
Every little girl loves a parasol. It is cut with 8 gores, finished with a lace frill. Opens and closes. Dress has matching insertion, taped with satin ribbon. Made of finest quality dotted swiss. Includes special shoes.
Kit and Completed Costume for 14" Doll only.

Alice Blue Pinafore Kit
A cute cotton dress with separate pinafore that can be worn with other dresses. Lace trimmed, includes matching shoes.
Kits and Completed Costumes; 14" and 18" Dolls.

Sun Bonnet Sue Kit
This little model reflects all the vivaciousness of Spring. It is designed and charted so simply that a child can make it.
Kit and Completed Costume for 14" Doll only.

Sewing Kits

Polly Prim Kit
Coat is soft wool with contrasting silk lining. Dress is made of same silk with drop shoulders and inverted unpressed pleats in skirt. Patent leather belt and shoes, also hat are included in this kit.
Kit and Completed Costume for 14" Doll only.

Scotch Plaid Kit
Bonnie Lassie is a complete costume or kit with matching hand-bag for dollie and her little "mother." The child's hand-bag is made of matching scotch plaid trimming and includes a coin dispenser, comb, mirror and separate compartment for other necessities.
Kits and Completed Costumes; 14" and 18" Dolls.

Illustration 61C. Booklet advertising the Mary Hoyer Doll and costumes and kits that were available.

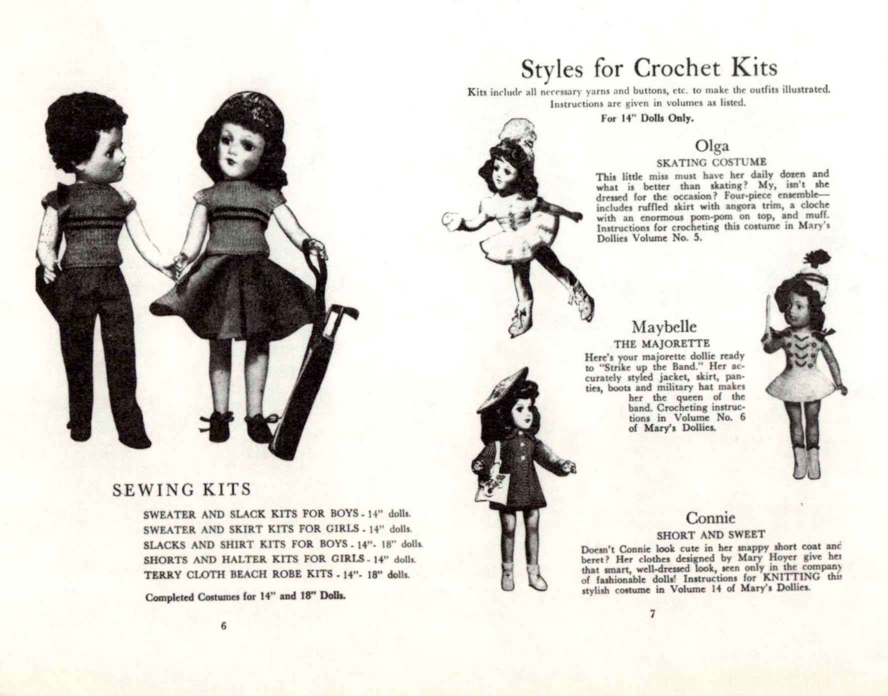

SEWING KITS
SWEATER AND SLACK KITS FOR BOYS - 14" dolls.
SWEATER AND SKIRT KITS FOR GIRLS - 14" dolls.
SLACKS AND SHIRT KITS FOR BOYS - 14"- 18" dolls.
SHORTS AND HALTER KITS FOR GIRLS - 14" dolls.
TERRY CLOTH BEACH ROBE KITS - 14"- 18" dolls.

Completed Costumes for 14" and 18" Dolls.

Styles for Crochet Kits
Kits include all necessary yarns and buttons, etc. to make the outfits illustrated. Instructions are given in volumes as listed.
For 14" Dolls Only.

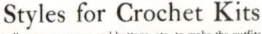

Olga
SKATING COSTUME
This little miss must have her daily dozen and what is better than skating? My, isn't she dressed for the occasion? Four-piece ensemble—includes ruffled skirt with angora trim, a cloche with an enormous pom-pom on top, and muff. Instructions for crocheting this costume in Mary's Dollies Volume No. 5.

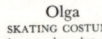

Maybelle
THE MAJORETTE
Here's your majorette dollie ready to "Strike up the Band." Her accurately styled jacket, skirt, panties, boots and military hat makes her the queen of the band. Crocheting instructions in Volume No. 6 of Mary's Dollies.

Connie
SHORT AND SWEET
Doesn't Connie look cute in her snappy short coat and beret? Her clothes designed by Mary Hoyer give her that smart, well-dressed look, seen only in the company of fashionable dolls! Instructions for KNITTING this stylish costume in Volume 14 of Mary's Dollies.

Illustration 61D. Booklet advertising the Mary Hoyer Doll and costumes and kits that were available.

STYLES FOR CROCHET KITS
For 14" Dolls Only.

Dolores
SKATING COSTUME
Somewhat bashful looking, but can she skate! See how warm she is dressed in her one piece dress, cap and mitts. Her full skirt is perfect for figure skating. Crocheting Instructions in Volume No. 11 of Mary's Dollies.

Greta
A DUTCH TREAT
How did Holland get into the picture? That's because Mary Hoyer remembers little girls from every corner of the earth. The wooden shoes are an exact replica of the little girls' shoes of Holland. Crocheting Instructions in Vol. 12 of Mary's Dollies.

Carol
A STYLISH MISS
Who have we here? Carol surely looks the part of the well-dressed adult. The upward sweep of her bonnet adds an inexplainable charm to her looks. Note the perfection of detail. Crocheting Instructions in Volume No. 13.

STYLES FOR CROCHET KITS
For 14" Dolls Only.

Louise
PARTY DRESS AND HAT
Where is Louise going? If to a party, her ensemble will be the envy of all the dolls present. Those large dark eyes are magnified by the flare of her skirt, straw picture hat and delicate footwear. Hat and shoes are included in this kit. Crocheting Instructions in Volume No. 14.

Renee
CROCHETED DRESS AND CAPE
Look at that ensemble! Also the flare of that skirt—scalloped edges and drape over the shoulders. Can an adult wear anything finer and nicer looking? Skirt just right for walking and sitting. Extra cape to ensemble or a separate one for extra strapless gowns. Crocheting Instructions in Volume No. 15.

Illustration 61E. Booklet advertising the Mary Hoyer Doll and costumes and kits that were available.

Styles for Knitting Kits
Kits include all yarns and buttons, etc. to make the outfits illustrated. Instructions are given in the volumes listed.
For 14" Dolls Only.

Arlene
BATHING ENSEMBLE
Here's Arlene in her 4-piece ensemble all togged out for her visit to the shore. At Ocean City, she'll surely be the center of attraction all along the beach. That's because she wears clothing designed by Mary Hoyer. Knitting Instructions in Vol. 5.

Billie
A RIDING HABIT
Billie is all dressed for the occasion, but, where is her horse? It is a sure bet, that with this lovely riding habit, she won't have any trouble securing one. Knitting Instructions in Volume No. 10.

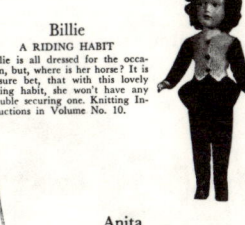

Anita
SKIING COSTUME
When Anita goes skiing, she is properly and warmly dressed. Her ensemble will be the talk of the ski run and many will copy her style. Skis are available with the poles. Knitting Instructions in Volume No. 11.

Illustration 61F. Booklet advertising the Mary Hoyer Doll and costumes and kits that were available.

STYLES FOR KNITTING KITS
For 14" Dolls Only.

Nadine
RED CROSS NURSE
This little "Angel of Mercy" is ready to care for anything that ails you. Who wouldn't get well under her spell? Knitting Instructions in Vol. 6.

Lucille
ROLLER SKATING OUTFIT
Well, here we have Lucille in her specially designed skating outfit. She may not have won any medals, but she will surely win you. Very cute. Knitting Instructions in Vol. No. 11.

Nancy and Dick
COWBOY AND COWGIRL COSTUMES
Is this Roy Rogers or Gene Autrey? Watch out Nancy, for that lariat! Dick is real tricky with the rope. Those two costumes will intrigue the most exacting little girl. Knitting Instructions in Volume No. 13.

Ballet Costume

•

THE PETITE
SHORT BALLET

•

This beautiful costume comes completed only. Made of finest quality tissue taffeta and four rows of nylon tulle. This is a truly delightful doll costume that will delight any child. Matching ballet slippers are available. Be sure to tell us the color of your doll's wig when ordering this one.

•

ANOTHER
MARY HOYER
TRIUMPH

•

Mary Hoyer's artistry is eloquently expressed in this expertly designed masterpiece. Its elegance and gossamer qualities will easily take your breath away. Order this fine costume today with the ballet slippers and enjoy its charm.
For 14" Doll Only.

Shoes, Boots and Slippers

The doll footwear listed below is accurate in every detail and the size is perfect for the Mary Hoyer Doll. Each one has been carefully designed to compliment the costumes illustrated in this booklet and all the volumes of Mary's Dollies. Only the finest workmanship is used throughout.

Smart Footwear for Beautiful Mary Hoyer Dolls!

Majorette Boots, white with gold tassels: including baton.
Russian Boots—white trim at top.
Brown Riding Boots.
Tan Western Boots with spurs.
Ballet Slippers, in gold, silver, pink, red and blue satin; black suede.
Bridal Slippers with silk bows.
Cinderella Slippers with buckles.
Felt Bedroom Slippers with pompoms in white, pink and blue.
Black Shoes with lacers complete with black stockings.
White Shoes with lacers and white stockings.
Black Patent Leather Shoes with Lacers.

Black Patent Leather Shoes with buckle.
Dutch Wooden Shoes.
Ice Skating Shoes with lacers: white or gold.
Roller Skates with lacers, white or gold.
White Snap Shoes with white stockings.
Brown Tennis Shoes.
Mules of Satin with elastic in white, pink or blue.
Sandals with snaps in gold foil or silver foil.
Saddle Shoes with eyelets in two-tone brown and white; also red and white.
Mary Jane Anklet Shoes in white, pink, blue, black patent leather.

Be Sure to Include Several Pairs of Shoes with your Doll's Wardrobe!

Illustration 61G. Booklet advertising the Mary Hoyer Doll and costumes and kits that were available.

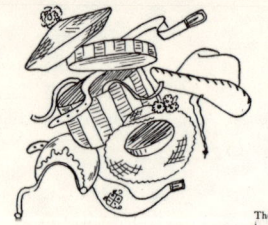

Hats, Hat Boxes, Bags, etc.

The following items are always in stock and can be purchased and shipped to you anytime.

Lovely Accessories for Lovely Dolls!

Western Felt Hats for the Western Costumes.
Imported Straw Hat, hand embroidered from Jamaica—natural straw only.
French Straw Poke Bonnet—untrimmed.
Same Poke Bonnet beautifully trimmed with flowers and appropriate ribbons.
French Straw Picture Hats—untrimmed.
Same Picture Hat trimmed with flowers and ribbons.
Small size Poke—untrimmed
Same Poke trimmed with flowers and ribbons
Colors available: White, Pink, Blue and Yellow.

Red Rubber Bathing Caps with a chin strap.
Black Patent Leather Belts.
Contour Belts in black patent leather, red and gold.
Refer to our price list for dozens of other costume accessories.

14

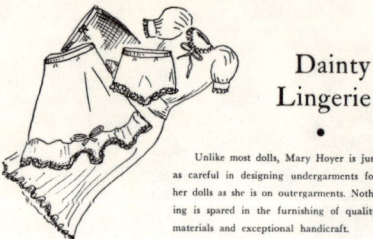

Dainty Lingerie

Unlike most dolls, Mary Hoyer is just as careful in designing undergarments for her dolls as she is on outergarments. Nothing is spared in the furnishing of quality materials and exceptional handicraft.

Quality Lingerie for Dolls of Quality!

Lace Trimmed Nylon Panties with elastic top.
Lace Trimmed Nylon Half Slips with elastic top.
Heavy Weight Nylon Nities with lace tops—either white or black.
Nylon Pajamas.
Two-way Stretch Girdles.
Satin Lastex Bathing Suits.
Nylon Beach Coat.
Terry Cloth Beach Robe.

All of these undergarments are made of nylon. They may be easily washed and will dry quickly. Order a complete set!

15

DOLL PARTS AND WIGS

When a doll is purchased from Mary Hoyer, the sale does not stop there. No indeed! If your little Miss, at some time, should be unfortunate in breaking a leg or an arm, or any other part of her doll, don't worry. Just write Mary Hoyer and a new part will be mailed promptly. New parts are simple to install.

LIST OF NEW PARTS AND WIGS

Head without Wig
Left Leg   Body   Right Leg
Left Arm   Joiners   Right Arm
Wigs of DuPont Nylon—Rolled Bangs
Up-Sweep Wig with Bustle Back
Alice Flowing Wig with Permanent Wave
Curled Wig with Straight Bangs
Boy's Wool Wig

We hope you have enjoyed looking through this booklet. Start making some of the Mary Hoyer Doll Clothes today.

Mary Hoyer Doll Manufacturing Company
1013 Penn Street   Reading, Pa.

Illustration 61H. Booklet advertising the Mary Hoyer Doll and costumes and kits that were available.

Illustration 61I. Booklet advertising the Mary Hoyer Doll and costumes and kits that were available.

Illustration 62A. Price list and order blank dated October 1, 1956.

Illustration 62B. Price list and order blank dated October 1956.

28

MARY HOYER'S RETAIL SHOP · 1008 PENN STREET · READING · PENNSYLVANIA

Illustrations 63A, B and C. Price list and order blank dated June 1, 1962.

THE MOST BEAUTIFUL DOLLS IN THE WORLD—WITH COMPLETE ACCESSORY GROUP!

MARY HOYER'S DOLLS

Made of Durable PLASTIC—Fully Jointed—Movable Eyes. Complete with Shoes, Washable and Combable Wigs.

ALL DOLLS 14" TALL.

GIRL DOLL, curled Saran wig only	$3.95
BOY DOLL, Fur wig, medium brown	$3.95
GIRL DOLL, Dynel wig in the following styles—Side Sweep with Curls, Long Alice Flowing wig and Pony Tail in Blonde, Medium Brown, Auburn and Dark	$4.50
DOLL'S WARDROBE TRUNK — Metal Covering. Size 9x9x16 inches	$4.95

ADD for POSTAGE on DOLL, East .50, West .75.
ADD for POSTAGE on TRUNK, East .50, West 1.00.

COMPLETED COSTUMES
UNDERWEAR AND NIGHTWEAR DEPT.

Nylon Briefs	.25
Nylon Lace Trimmed Panties	.35
Two-Way Stretch Girdle	.35
Nylon Half Slip, short, stiff	.65
Crinoline Long Slips, double nylon	1.25
Lounging Pajamas with Belt	1.25
Pajamas, cotton crepe	1.25
Nitie, black lace trimmed nylon	1.00
Nitie, white lace trimmed nylon	1.00
Nitie and Negligee combination, nylon	4.95

SPORT CLOTHES

Sport Shirt, short sleeves	.85
Blouse, full sleeves	.85
Slacks	1.00
Jodhpurs	1.50
Bermuda Shorts	.75
Shorts and Halter Set (two pieces)	1.00
3 Piece, Skirt, Shorts and Blouse Set	2.25
Bathing Suit, Lastex one piece, nylon shirring	.85
New Bathing Suit, Terry Cloth, one piece	.85
Beach Robe, Terry Cloth, to match suit	1.00
Hand Knitted Slip Over Sweater	1.25
Hand Knitted Cardigan with Sleeves	1.75
Hand Knitted Skating Costume	4.95
Hand Knitted Ski Costume	4.95
Leotards—Helenca	.35
Matching Turtle Neck Shirt	.50
Matching Tights	.35
Nylon Party Dress with Lace Trim	1.95
Cotton Party Dress, Lace Trim (wash and wear)	1.75
Jumper, lace trimmed	1.25
Skirt	1.00
Strapless Sun Dress, cotton print	1.00
Cotton Frock, Square Dance Costume	2.75
Cotton Frock with collar	1.25
Afternoon Cotton Dress, Sun Bonnet and Panties	1.50
LEATHER JACKET with BELT and BERET	1.95
TAFFETA DRESS for use with JACKET	1.25

BRIDAL PARTIES

Bridal Gown, Panties and Veil, dotted nylon and taffeta	2.95
Bridal Gown, Panties and Veil, (illustrated)	3.95
Bridal Gown, Panties and Veil, nylon trim	4.95
Bride's Maid with Panties and Hat	2.95
Bridegroom, Top Hat, Patent Leather Shoes	4.95
Bridal Garters, shirred nylon with lace trim	.30
Bible trimmed with flowers and ribbons	1.00

EVENING CLOTHES

Taffeta Evening Gown, lace trim	3.95
Dolly Madison with parasol, satin (on cover)	5.95
Southern Belle with parasol, dotted swiss	4.95
Strapless Gown, dotted net over taffeta	2.95

TRAVEL CLOTHES

Felt Coat and Hat	1.95
Short Taffeta, woven print, matching Parasol	3.95
Velvet Coat, Hat and matching Purse	4.50
Corduroy Coat and Hat with Purse	3.95

NEW HAWAIIAN ENSEMBLES

Bathing Suit with reversible Jacket for Boy	2.50
Bathing Suit with reversible Jacket for Girl	2.50
Culotte with matching Beach Coat	2.25
Mu-Mu Tropical Print with flower lei	1.50
Hula Skirt and Halter with flowers	1.75
Tropical Shirt, short sleeves for boy or girl	.85

MISCELLANEOUS COSTUMES

Alice Blue Pinafore	2.95
Rain Cape with Boots	1.25
Ballet, short with 4 tiers of nylon tulle	2.50
Scotch Plaid Jumper Blouse, Beret and Bag	3.95
Pennsylvania Dutch Costume	1.00

PURSES and BAGS, For Mary Hoyer Costumes

Pearl Hand Bag	.50
Plastic Shoulder Bag	.25
Scotch Plaid Hand Bag	.50
Imported Straw Bag	.25
Velvet Purse	.50
Corduroy Bag	.50
Beach Bag	.35

JEWELRY DEPARTMENT

Wrist Watch, hands move	.10
Single Pearl Choker	.15
Double Pearl Choker	.25
Single Pearl Necklace	.15
Pearl Bracelet	.10
Pearl Tiara	.25
Gold Choker	.15
Gold Necklace with Heart, (gift boxed)	.30
Rhinestone Bracelet, (gift boxed)	.35
Rhinestone Necklace (gift boxed)	.50
Ear Rings for vinal dolls only	.15
Rhinestone Rings for vinal dolls only	.10
Clustered Pearl Hair Spray Comb	.35

HOSIERY DEPARTMENT

Full Length Nylon Stockings, elastic top, beige or white	.25
Rayon Socks, white or black	.10

MILLINERY DEPARTMENT

Beach Hat, hand embroidered, imported	.75
Western Fur Felt Hat, untrimmed	.50
Off-Face Felt Hat, untrimmed	.35
Picture Hat, French straw, untrimmed	.50
Picture Hat, French straw, trimmed	.75
Open Crown Straw Hat, untrimmed	.29
Jockey Hat with Visor	.25
Summer Hat	.50

SHOES, Custom Built, Mary Hoyer Dolls only

Black Shoes with Laces	.25
White Snap Shoes	.25
Black Patent Leather Snap Shoes	.25
Black Patent Leather Shoes with Laces	.25
White Shoes with Laces	.25
Beach Shoes to match Bathing Suit	.25
Saddle Shoes, black and white	.25
Evening Sandals, silver, gold, black suede or blue	.25
Mules, white, pink or blue	.25
Bed Room Slippers, white, pink or blue	.25
Black Patent Leather Shoes with Buckle	.25
Bridal Slippers with Silk Bows	.25
Ballet Slippers, gold, silver, pink, red, blue or black	.25
Tennis Shoes, brown	.25
Mary Jane Shoes, black patent, white, pink or blue	.25
Roller Skates, white or gold	.35
Ice Skates, white or gold	.35
Dutch Wooden Shoes	.35
Majorette Boots with Baton	.35
Circus Boots	.25
Rain Boots	.25
Riding Boots, brown	.25
Western Boots with Spurs	.35
Skis and Pole Set	.50
HIGH HEEL SHOES, flex. lasts, white, gold, pink, blue	.39

MISCELLANEOUS ACCESSORIES

Doll Stand with nickel steel base, not plastic	1.00
Plastic Clothes Hangers, 6 for	.20
Plastic Hanger with dress clip	.10
STEEL PARASOL FRAME, uncovered, 14" or 18"	1.00
STEEL PARASOL, covered with frilling, 14" or 18"	1.75
Garment Bag, plastic, with hanger bar, side zipper	1.00
Black Patent Leather Belt	.10
Gold Belt, non-tarnishable	.10
Belt with Western Buckle	.15
Belt with 2 gun holsters	.25
Miniature Bible, Catholic or Protestant	.25
Sun Glasses	.25
Golf Bag with Clubs	.35
Tennis Racquet Set	.25
Miniature Suit Case	.25
Miniature School Bag	.25
Miniature Fan	.10
Sparkle Hair Nets	.10
Hair Nets, either light or dark	.10
Nylon Gloves, black, white, pink or blue	.35
Nylon Long Gauntlets, black, white, pink or blue	.50

WIGS—Washable and Combable

Pony Tail	2.00
DuPont Nylon, curled only, medium brown only	2.00
Dynel Side Sweep with Curls	2.00
Alice Long Flowing	2.00
Saran with Curls, choice of ☐ blonde, ☐ medium brown, ☐ auburn or ☐ dark brown	1.50
Boy's Fur Wigs, medium shade only	1.25
Wash and Wave Kits to wash all wigs	.39
Doll cleaner for either plastic or vinal dolls	.25

REPLACEMENT PARTS

Replace Eyes	1.00
Leg, specify either left or right	.50
Arm, specify either left or right	.50
Body	.50
Rubber Joiner with Hook	.25

SEWING KITS—All Materials Cut to Fit

Bridal Gown, Veil and Panties	1.50
Dolly Madison, with Parasol Frame	3.25
Southern Belle, with Parasol Frame	2.95
Party Taffeta Dress, with Parasol Frame	1.95
Alice Pinafore, with Shoes and Panties	1.50
Scotch Plaid Jumper with Blouse and Beret	1.95
Sport Shirt with Slacks	.85
Sun-Bonnet Costume with Panties	.75
Shorts and Halter	.50
Sweater and Skirt for Girl Doll	1.00
Sweater and Slacks for Boy Doll	1.00
Long Ballerina with Panties	1.25
Felt Coat and Hat Set	1.50
Evening Gown of sparkle net	1.50
Terry Cloth Beach Robe	.60

McCALL PATTERNS FOR SEWING — MARY HOYER DOLLS

Includes Cotton Dress, Evening Gown, Parasol, Nitie Negligee, instructions for knit Cape	.35

SUPPLIED ONLY WITH PURCHASE OF DOLL

MARY'S DOLLIES INSTRUCTION BOOKS FOR KNITTING AND CROCHETING COSTUMES FOR THE 14" DOLL

With Illustrations. Check Books Desired.

Vol. No. 5 .20 ☐	Vol. No. 12 .20 ☐
Vol. No. 6 .20 ☐	Vol. No. 13 .20 ☐
Vol. No. 9 .20 ☐	Vol. No. 14 .20 ☐
Vol. No. 10 .20 ☐	Vol. No. 15 .20 ☐
Vol. No. 11 .20 ☐	

____ Books at .20 each ____
Add .10 per volume for Postage ____

YARN KITS FOR COSTUMES ILLUSTRATED IN MARY'S DOLLIES INSTRUCTION BOOKS (14")

Yarn Kits for Costumes, Vol. 5, Mary's Dollies

Olga, crocheted skating outfit	1.25
Mayree, crocheted jacket, bonnet and skirt	1.25
Annabelle, knitted golf skirt and jacket	.75
Goldilocks, crocheted dress and beret	.75
Julianna, knitted ski suit	.85
Arlene, knitted bathing suit	.65

Yarn Kits for Costumes, Vol. 6, Mary's Dollies

Sonja, knitted ski costume	1.00
Lucretta, crocheted skating costume	1.25
Wavette, knitted "Wave" suit	.85
Maybelle, crocheted Majorette suit	.85
Nadine, knitted Red Cross Nurse	.85

Yarn Kits for Costumes, Vol. 9, Mary's Dollies

Zorina, crocheted Russian costume	1.25
Kathleen, knitted Angora jacket and beret	.75
Terry, crocheted dress and bonnet	1.00
Sunny, knitted tennis costume	.75
Janie, knitted jacket and snood	1.00
Susanna, crocheted skirt and hat	1.00

Yarn Kits for Costumes, Vol. 10, Mary's Dollies

Patsy, crocheted coat and bag	1.25
Jackie, crocheted riding outfit	1.25
Corine, knitted dress and cap	1.25
Billie, knitted riding habit	1.00
Paula, crocheted bathing suit	.55

Yarn Kits for Costumes, Vol. 11, Mary's Dollies

Lucille, knitted roller skater	1.00
Dolores, crocheted ice skater	1.25
Anita, knitted Angora ski suit	1.25

Yarn Kits for Costumes, Vol. 12, Mary's Dollies

Greta, crocheted Dutch costume	.75
Jo-Ann, knitted bathing suit	.35
Westerner, knitted cow-girl outfit	1.25
Peggy, crocheted coat and hat	1.25

Yarn Kits for Costumes, Vol. 13, Mary's Dollies

Mary Hoyer's Twins, boy Bobby, knitted	.85
Mary Hoyer's Twins, girl Betty, knitted	.85
Cow-Girl, Nancy, knitted	1.25
Cow-Boy, Dick, knitted	1.25
Hans, Dutch boy, knitted	1.00
Tina, Dutch girl, knitted	1.00
Carol, crocheted suit and bonnet	1.25

Yarn Kits for Costumes, Vol. 14, Mary's Dollies

Louise, crocheted dress	1.25
Connie, knitted coat and beret	.75
Nan, crocheted sailor suit, girl	1.00
Jack, crocheted sailor suit, boy	.85
Jeannette, knitted ice skating suit	.85

Yarn Kits for Costumes, Vol. 15, Mary's Dollies

Renee, crocheted sun dress and cape	1.50
Isabelle, knitted ice skater	1.25

ANGORA, 100% IMPORT. FRENCH, ball 75c ____

JUVENILE STYLES INSTRUCTION BOOKS

Knitted and Crocheted Garments for Infants and Children
Check Books Desired.

Vol. No. 3 .30 ☐	Vol. No. 7 .35 ☐
Vol. No. 4 .30 ☐	Vol. No. 8 .35 ☐

____ Books at .30 each ____
____ Books at .35 each ____
Add .15 per volume for Postage ____

Place total purchases here	$
Postage or Service Charge	$
Pa. Resident 4% Sales Tax	$
Total amount enclosed	$

PA. RESIDENTS—Add 4% Sales Tax in space provided above.
Orders under 5.00 Add .25 Service Chg. Except on dolls, trunks, books

Name ____

Address ____

City ____

Please Print Your Name and Address

June 1, 1962—This list supercedes all previous lists.

Send Orders to

MARY HOYER DOLL MFG. CO.
P. O. Box 1538, Reading, Pa.

Custom Built WARDROBE TRUNKS AND A FULL LINE OF ACCESSORIES

MARY'S DOLLIES

WITH INSTRUCTION KITS FOR KNITTING, CROCHETING AND SEWING A COMPLETE DOLLY WARDROBE

PRICE LIST & ORDER BLANK

BECKY, 14" undressed $2.95
PATTERN KIT, with Parasol Frame
Contains all material already cut to fit. $2.95

CATHY, 10" undressed $1.50
PATTERN KIT, with all materials cut to fit $1.00

NEW BECKY DOLL $2.95
(undressed, with Long Straight Hair)
NEW PATTERN KIT for BLOUSE and JUMPER $1.00
Rust-proof STEEL DISPLAY STANDARD $1.25

SEE THE
Full Displays
at the
Mary Hoyer Shop
1008 Penn Street
Reading, Pa.

ORDER SOME OF THESE • • • • •
INSTRUCTION BOOKS and KITS
There is a complete yarn kit available for each style illustrated in these instruction books.
Volumes 5, 6, 9, 10, 11, 12, 13, 14
30¢ each postpaid

SEE INSIDE THIS BROCHURE FOR LIST OF SEWING PATTERN KITS
All materials furnished already cut to fit in each Kit.

MOHAIR COAT, BERET, to MATCH
with KNITTED DRESS,
COMPLETE KIT $1.75

Illustrations 64A, B and C. Price list and order blank from the 1960s after *Becky* was added to the line.

ORDER THE BEAUTIFUL "MARY HOYER" DOLLS FOR FUN AND PROFIT.

NEW BECKY DOLL 14" TALL $2.95
Fully Jointed with Movable Eyes
Shoes Included - Washable and Combable Hair
Colors of Hair: Auburn, Blond and Dark
Specify Hair Style: Waved Pony Tail, Teased High Style,
Curled with Side Part, Long Straight Ironed Hair

CUTE CATHY 10" INFANT DOLL $1.50
(including shoes and socks - undressed)
Kit with materials cut to fit to make Christening
Costume (illustrated on cover) $1.00

THE NEW JANIE BABY 8" DOLL $1.00
Kit with materials cut to fit to make Christening
Costume (illustrated on cover) $1.00

DOLL'S WARDROBE TRUNK - Wooden Construction, Size 9x9x16 inches $4.95

FOLLOWING COSTUMES ARE ONLY FOR BECKY 14" DOLL
COMPLETED COSTUMES
UNDERWEAR AND NIGHTWEAR DEPT.
Nylon Briefs .... .25
Nylon Lace Trimmed Panties .... .35
Soft Nylon—Lace Trimmed Slips .... .50
Crinoline Long Slips 1.25
Pajamas, cotton Wash & Wear 1.25
Nitie, black lace trimmed nylon 1.00
Nitie, white lace trimmed nylon 1.00
Nitie and Negligee combination, nylon (Beautiful) 5.95

SPORT CLOTHES
Sport Shirt, short sleeves .... .85
Blouse .... .85
Slacks 1.00
Jodhpurs 1.25
Bermuda Shorts .... .75
Shorts and Halter Set (two pieces) 1.00
Bathing Suit, Lastex one piece, nylon shirring .... .85
New Bathing Suit, Terry Cloth, one piece .... .85
Beach Robe, Terry Cloth, to match suit 1.00
Leotards - Helenca, red or white .... .35
Matching Turtle Neck Shirt, red or white .... .50
Matching Tights, red or white .... .35
Nylon Party Dress With Lace Trim 1.50
Cotton Party Dress, Lace Trim (wash and wear) 1.75
Jumper, lace trimmed, cotton 1.25
Skirt 1.00
New Corduroy Jumper 1.50
Cotton Dress with collar 1.25
Afternoon Cotton Dress, Sun Bonnet 1.50
Cotton Dress 1.50

BRIDAL PARTIES
Bridal Gown and Veil, nylon and taffeta 2.95
Dolly Madison with parasol, satin 3.95
Bridal Gown and Veil 3.95
Bridal Gown and Veil, nylon trim 4.95
Bridal Garters, shirred nylon with lace trim .... .30
Bible trimmed with flowers and ribbons 1.00

EVENING CLOTHES
Taffeta Evening Gown, lace trim 3.95
Dolly Madison with parasol, satin 5.95
Southern Belle with parasol, dotted swiss 5.95
Lawn Party Gown with parasol 5.95

TRAVEL CLOTHES
Felt Coat and Hat 1.95
Short Taffeta, woven print, matching Parasol 3.95
Velvet Coat and Hat 3.95
Corduroy Coat and Hat 3.50

NEW HAWAIIAN ENSEMBLES
Bathing Suit with reversible Jacket for Boy 2.50
Bathing Suit with reversible Jacket for Girl 2.50
Mu-Mu Tropical Print with flower lei 1.95
Hula Skirt and Halter with flowers 1.75
Tropical Shirt, short sleeves for boy or girl .... .85

MISCELLANEOUS COSTUMES
Alice Blue Pinafore 2.50
Rain Cape with Boots 1.50
Ballet, short with 4 tiers of nylon tulle 2.50
Red Riding-Hood Dress-Cape with Hood 4.50

PURSES and BAGS, For Mary Hoyer Costumes
Pearl Hand Bag .... .50
Scotch Plaid Hand Bag .... .35
Imported Straw Bag .... .25
Beach Bag .... .35

JEWELRY DEPARTMENT
Wrist Watch, hands move .... .10
Single Pearl Choker .... .15
Pearl Bracelet .... .10
Pearl and Rhinestone Tiara .... .75
Rhinestone Bracelet, (gift boxed) .... .35
Rhinestone Necklace (gift boxed) .... .50
Ear Rings for vinal dolls only .... .15
Rhinestone Rings for vinal dolls only .... .10

HOSIERY DEPARTMENT
Full Length Nylon Stockings, elastic top, beige or white .... .25
Socks, white or black .... .10

MILLINERY DEPARTMENT
Beach Hat, hand embroidered, imported .... .50
Western Fur Felt Hat, untrimmed .... .25
Off-Face Felt Hat, untrimmed .... .35
Jockey Hat with visor, straw .... .25
Summer Hat .... .50
Black Top Hat .... .25

SHOES, Custom Built, Mary Hoyer Dolls only
Black Shoes with Laces .... .25
Black Patent Leather Shoes with Laces .... .25
White Shoes with Laces .... .25
Beach Shoes to match Bathing Suit .... .25
Evening Sandals, silver, gold .... .25
Mules, white, pink or blue .... .25
Bed Room Slippers, white, pink or blue .... .25
Bridal Slippers .... .25
Ballet Slippers, silver, red, gold .... .25
Tennis Shoes, brown .... .25
Mary Jane Shoes, black patent, white .... .25
Roller Skates, white .... .35
Ice Skates, white .... .35
Majorette Boots with Baton .... .85
Rain Boots .... .25
Riding Boots, brown .... .85
Skis and Pole Set .... .50

MISCELLANEOUS ACCESSORIES
Doll Stand with steel base, (not plastic) 1.25
Plastic Clothes Hangers, 6 for .... .20
Plastic Hanger with dress clip .... .10
STEEL PARASOL FRAME, uncovered, 14" or 18" 1.00
STEEL PARASOL, covered with frilling, 14" or 18" 1.75
Garment Bag, plastic, with hanger bar, side zipper 1.00
Black Patent Leather Belt .... .10
Gold Belt, non-tarnishable .... .15
Belt with Western Buckle .... .25
Belt with 2 gun holsters .... .25
Miniature Bible, Catholic or Protestant .... .25
Sun Glasses .... .25
Golf Bag with Clubs .... .25
Tennis Racquet Set .... .25
Miniature Suit Case .... .25
Miniature School Bag .... .25
Sparkle Hair Nets .... .25
Hair Nets, either light or dark .... .10
Nylon Gloves, black, white, pink or blue .... .35

WIGS—Washable and Combable
Pony Tail 2.00
DuPont Nylon, curled only, medium brown only 2.00
Alice Long Flowing 2.00
Saran with Curls, choice of ☐ blonde, ☐ medium brown,
  ☐ auburn or ☐ dark brown 1.75
Boy's Mohair Wigs, medium shade only 1.25

REPLACEMENT PARTS
Replace Eyes 1.00
Leg, specify either left or right .... .50
Arm, specify either left or right .... .50
Body .... .50
Rubber Joiner with Hook .... .25

PATTERN KITS—All Materials Cut to Fit
Bridal Gown, Veil and Panties 1.50
Dolly Madison, with Parasol Frame 3.25
Southern Belle, with Parasol Frame 3.25
Lawn Party Gown with Parasol 2.95
Corduroy Jumper and Blouse 1.00
Party Taffeta Dress, with Parasol Frame 1.95
Alice Pinafore, Blue 1.00
Sport Shirt with Slacks 1.50
Sun-Bonnet Costume .... .85
Shorts and Halter .... .75
Sweater and Skirt for Girl Doll 1.00
Long Ballerina with Panties 1.25
Felt Coat and Hat Set 1.50
Evening Gown of sparkle net 1.50
Terry Cloth Beach Robe .... .60

PATTERN KITS, KNITTING—FOR BECKY DOLL
KNITTED COAT, BERET & DRESS KIT — Advertised in McCall's 1.75
NEW SCANDINAVIAN SKI KIT, illus. in Special Leaflet 1.00

MARY'S DOLLIES INSTRUCTION BOOKS FOR KNITTING AND CROCHETING COSTUMES FOR THE 14" DOLL
With Illustrations.   Check Books Desired.
Vol. No. 5 .20 ☐   Vol. No. 12 .20 ☐
Vol. No. 6 .20 ☐   Vol. No. 13 .20 ☐
Vol. No. 9 .20 ☐   Vol. No. 14 .20 ☐
Vol. No. 10 .20 ☐
Vol. No. 11 .20 ☐
Books at .20 each, add .10 per volume for Postage

YARN KITS FOR COSTUMES ILLUSTRATED IN MARY'S DOLLIES INSTRUCTION BOOKS (14")
Yarn Kits for Costumes, Vol. 5, Mary's Dollies
Olga, crocheted skating outfit 1.25
Mayree, crocheted jacket, bonnet and skirt 1.25
Annabelle, knitted golf skirt and jacket .... .75
Goldilocks, knitted dress and beret .... .75
Julianna, knitted ski suit .... .85
Arlene, knitted bathing suit .... .65

Yarn Kits for Costumes, Vol. 6, Mary's Dollies
Sonja, knitted ski costume 1.00
Lucretta, crocheted skating costume 1.25
Wavette, knitted "Wave" suit .... .85
Maybelle, crocheted Majorette suit .... .85
Nadine, knitted Red Cross Nurse .... .85

Yarn Kits for Costumes, Vol. 9, Mary's Dollies
Zorina, crocheted Russian costume 1.25
Kathleen, knitted Angora jacket and beret 1.00
Terry, crocheted dress and bonnet 1.00
Sunny, knitted tennis costume .... .75
Janie, knitted jacket and mood 1.00
Susanna, crocheted skirt and hat 1.00

Yarn Kits for Costumes, Vol. 10, Mary's Dollies
Patsy, crocheted coat and bag 1.25
Jackie, crocheted riding outfit 1.00
Corine, knitted dress and cap 1.25
Billie, knitted riding habit 1.00
Paula, knitted bathing suit .... .55

Yarn Kits for Costumes, Vol. 11, Mary's Dollies
Lucille, knitted roller skater 1.00
Dolores, crocheted ice skater 1.25
Anita, knitted Angora ski suit 1.25

Yarn Kits for Costumes, Vol. 12, Mary's Dollies
Greta, crocheted Dutch costume .... .75
Jo-Ann, knitted bathing suit .... .35
Westerner, knitted cow-girl outfit 1.00
Peggy, crocheted coat and bonnet 1.25

Yarn Kits for Costumes, Vol. 13, Mary's Dollies
Mary Hoyer's Twins, boy Bobby, knitted .... .85
Mary Hoyer's Twins, girl Betty, knitted .... .85
Cow-Girl, Nancy, knitted 1.00
Cow-Boy, Dick, knitted .... .85
Carol, crocheted suit and bonnet 1.00

Yarn Kits for Costumes, Vol. 14, Mary's Dollies
Louise, crocheted dress 1.25
Connie, knitted coat and beret .... .75
Nan, crocheted sailor suit, girl 1.00
Jack, crocheted sailor suit, boy .... .85
Jeannette, knitted ice skating suit .... .85

ANGORA, 100% IMPORT. FRENCH, ball .... .85

JUVENILE STYLES INSTRUCTION BOOKS
Knitted and Crocheted Garments for Infants and Children
Vol. No. 3   Vol. No. 4   Vol. No. 7
Set of Three Post Paid 1.50

Place total purchases here .... $ _____
Postage or Service Charge .... $ _____
Pa. Resident 5% Sales Tax .... $ _____
Total amount enclosed .... $ _____

PA. RESIDENTS—Add. 5% Sales Tax in space provided above
ADD .50 per DOLL for POSTAGE ANYWHERE IN THE U.S.
ADD .75 per TRUNK in EAST - 1.50 in WEST

Name _____
Address _____
City _____

Please Print Your Name and Address
Send Orders to
MARY HOYER DOLL CO.
1008 Penn St., Reading, Pa.
P. O. BOX 925, READING, PA. 19603
WRITE FOR WHOLESALE QUANTITY PRICES

Custom Built WARDROBE TRUNKS
AND A FULL LINE OF ACCESSORIES

MARY'S DOLLIES
WITH INSTRUCTION KITS FOR KNITTING, CROCHETING AND SEWING A COMPLETE DOLLY WARDROBE

PRICE LIST & ORDER BLANK

BECKY, 14" undressed $2.95

PATTERN KIT, with Parasol Frame
Contains all material already cut to fit. $2.95

CATHY, 10" undressed $1.50
PATTERN KIT, with all materials cut to fit $1.00

Illustration 65. Cover for a price list and order blank from the 1960s showing *Becky* in a different pose and with an upswept hairdo.

31

Mary Hoyer DOLLS

with Instruction Kits for Knitting, Crocheting and Sewing a Complete Doll Wardrobe

Custom built Wardrobe trunks and a full line of accessories

MARGIE 10" undressed with shoes & socks $2.50
Kit, with Yarn, Buttons & Instructions .50

BECKY 14" undressed with shoes $3.50
Kit with Yarn, Buttons & Instructions 1.25

CATHY 10" Infant, undressed with shoes & socks $1.50
Kit, with materials, cut to fit and instructions to sew $1.00

PRICE LIST and ORDER BLANK

Mohair Coat, Beret and Knitted dress Complete Kit with instructions & Buttons 1.75

Becky Doll, Long Straight Hair $3.50
Pattern Kit for Blouse & Jumper 1.25
Rust Proof Steel Display Stand 1.50

Becky Doll with short Hair 3.50
Pattern Kit for Maxie Coat with buttons, Yarn & Instructions for Baret & Scarf 3.00

Instruction books—for Knitting & crochet Volumes #6, 9, 10, 12, 13, 14 each postpaid .50
Yarn Kits available for each style illustrated in these books.

See inside this brochure for sewing pattern kits. All materials furnished, already cut to fit.

See Full Displays at the **Mary Hoyer SHOP**
1008 Penn St., Reading, Pa.

Illustrations 66A, B and C. One of the last price lists and order blanks from the 1960s.

ORDER THE BEAUTIFUL "MARY HOYER" DOLLS FOR FUN AND PROFIT

NEW BECKY DOLL 14" TALL $3.50
Shoes included - Washable & Combable Hair
Fully Jointed with Movable eyes
Colors of Hair:
Blonde
Dark
Auburn
Styles of hair: Short, side part, Waved Pony tail, Long
Long straight ironed hair

CATHY 10" INFANT TYPE DOLL $1.50
Painted head—no hair, Shoes and white socks included.
Kit to make christening outfit $1.00

MARGY 10" TODDLER $2.50
(with Pony Tail only)
Colors of Hair:
Blonde
Dark
Auburn
Shoes & white socks included.
Hair is washable and combable
Kit to make outfit illustrated on cover $.50

JANIE 8" BABY TYPE DOLL $1.25
Painted head—no hair, shoes & Panties included
Kit to make christening outfit $1.00

WARDROBE TRUNK—Wooden frame $4.95

The following completed costumes are only for the 14" Becky doll:—

UNDERWEAR AND NIGHTWEAR DEPARTMENT
Nylon Briefs .25
Nylon Lace Trimmed Panties .35
Nylon Lace Trimmed Slips .65
Crinoline Long Slips 1.25
Pajamas, Cotton Wash & Wear 1.50
White Nylon Nitie Lace Trimmed 1.25
Nylon Nitie & Negligee Combination (Beautiful) 6.95

SPORT CLOTHES
Sport Shirt, Short Sleeves .85
Blouse .85
Slacks 1.25
Jodphurs 1.25
Bermuda Shorts .75
Shorts & Halter Set (2 piece) 1.00
Lastex Bathing Suit .85
Beach Robe 1.00
Bikini Beach Set 1.00
Helenca Tights — Red or White .35
Matching Turtle Neck Sweater .50
Party Dress, Cotton Wash & Wear 1.75
Nylon Party Dress, Lace 1.00
Skirt 1.00
Corduroy Jumper 1.50
School Dress with Collar 1.50
Afternoon Dress with Sun Bonnet 1.75
Cotton Summer Dress 1.25

BRIDAL PARTIES
Luscious Bridal Gown with Veil 4.95
Bridal Garters, per pair .30
Catholic Prayer Books trimmed with Flowers & Ribbon 1.25

EVENING CLOTHES
Taffeta Evening Gown 3.95
Short Taffeta Print Dress 1.75
Velvet Coat, Baret & Dress (Beautiful) 6.95
Corduroy Coat & Baret 3.95

MISCELLANEOUS COSTUMES
Alice Blue Pinafore 2.95
New Raincape & Boots 2.00
New Short Ballet with Lace 3.00
Red Riding Hood Dress — Cape with Hood 4.95

PURSES and BAGS
Pearl Hand Bag .50
Scotch Plaid Hand Bag .35
Imported Straw Bag .25
Beach Bag — Straw .25

JEWELRY DEPARTMENT
Wrist Watch .10
Single Pearl Choker .15
Pearl Bracelet .10
Rhinestone Bracelet & Necklace (Gift Boxed) 1.00
Ear Rings .15

HOSIERY DEPARTMENT
Socks, Black or White .10
Full Length Nylon Hose, White or Beige .25
(NEW) Lace Pantie Hose, White .35

MILLINARY DEPARTMENT
Beach Hat, Hand Embroidered (imported from Jamaica) .75
Western Fur Felt, untrimmed .50
Off-face Felt Hat .35
Jockey Hat with Visor, Straw .25
Black Top Hat .35

SHOES (Custom made, for 14" Dolls only)
Black Patent Leather with lacers .30
White Shoes with lacers .30
Colorful Beach Shoes .30
Evening Sandals, Gold or Silver .30
Mules, White, Pink or Blue .30
Bed-room Slippers, White, Pink or Blue .30
Satin Bridal Slippers .30
Ballet Slippers, Silver, Gold or Red .30
Tennis Shoes, two tone .30
Mary Jane Black Patent Leather .50
Roller Skates, White .50
Ice Skates, White .50
Majorette Boots with Baton .40
Rain Boots .30
Riding Boots, Brown .50
Ski & Pole Set, beautifully hand made 1.00

MISCELLANEOUS ACCESSORIES
Doll Stand, improved rust-proof steel 1.50
Plastic Doll Hangers, 6 in package .20
Plastic Hanger with Dress Clips .10
Garment Bag, with Side Zipper 1.00
Black Patent Leather Belt .10
Gold Belt, non-tarnishable .10
Sun Glasses, improved .25
Golf Bag with Clubs .25
Tennis Racquet and Ball .25
Sparkle Hair Net .10
Hair Nets, either black or blonde .10
Nylon Gloves, White, Black, Pink or Blue .35

REPLACEMENT PARTS for ORIGINAL DOLL
Rubber Joiner .25
DuPont Nylon Wig for 14" Plastic Dolls 2.00
Saran Curled Wigs (state colors) 2.50
Replace eyes for plastic dolls 1.00
Arms or Legs for Plastic 14" Dolls .50

PATTERN KITS for 14" DOLLS, materials cut to fit
Bridal Gown, Veil 1.75
Corduroy Jumper & Blouse 1.25
Alice Pinafore 1.75
Sport Shirt and Slacks 1.00
Sun Bonnet Costume 1.00
Shorts and Halter .50
Long Ballerina with Panties 1.25
Evening Gown with Sparkle Net 1.50
(NEW) Maxicoat—including Buttons & Yarn 3.00

KNITTING KITS for BECKY DOLL
Knitted Coat, Beret & Dress (Mohair) 1.75
Scandinavian Ski Kit 1.25
Ski Kit (as illustrated on cover) 1.25

MARY'S DOLLIES INSTRUCTION BOOKS FOR KNITTING AND CROCHETING FOR THE BECKY DOLL
With Illustrations. Check Books Desired
Volume No. 6 ☐ Volume No. 12 ☐
Volume No. 9 ☐ Volume No. 13 ☐
Volume No. 10 ☐ Volume No. 14 ☐
Books at .50 each Post Paid

Yarn Kits for Costumes, Vol. 6, Mary's Dollies
Sonja, knitted ski costume 1.00
Lucretta, crocheted skating costume 1.25
Wavette, knitted "Wave" suit .85
Maybelle, crocheted Majorette suit .85
Nadine, knitted Red Cross Nurse .85

Yarn Kits for Costumes, Vol. 9, Mary's Dollies
Zorina, crocheted Russian costume 1.25
Kathleen, knitted Angora jacket and beret .85
Terry, crocheted dress and bonnet 1.25
Sunny knitted tennis costume .75
Janie, knitted jacket and snood 1.00
Susanna, crocheted skirt and hat 1.00

Yarn Kits for Costumes, Vol. 10, Mary's Dollies
Patsy, crocheted coat and bag 1.25
Jackie, crocheted riding outfit 1.25
Corine, knitted dress and cap 1.25
Billie, knitted riding habit 1.00
Paula, crocheted bathing suit .55

Yarn Kits for Costumes, Vol. 12, Mary's Dollies
Greta, crocheted Dutch costume 1.00
Jo-Ann, knitted bathing suit .50
Westerner, knitted cow-girl outfit 1.25
Peggy, crocheted coat and hat 1.25

Yarn Kits for Costumes, Vol. 13, Mary's Dollies
Mary Hoyer's Twins, boy Bobby, knitted .85
Mary Hoyer's Twins, girl Betty, knitted .85
Cow-Girl, Nancy, knitted 1.25
Cow-Boy, Dick, knitted 1.25
Carol, crocheted suit and bonnet 1.25

Yarn Kits for Costumes, Vol. 14, Mary's Dollies
Louise, crocheted dress 1.25
Connie, knitted coat and beret 1.00
Nan, crocheted sailor suit, girl 1.00
Jack, crocheted sailor suit, boy 1.00
Jeannette, knitted ice skating suit 1.00
ANGORA, 100% IMPORT, FRENCH, ball .85

JUVENILE STYLES INSTRUCTION BOOKS
Knitted and Crocheted Garments for Infants and Children
Vol. No. 3   Vol. No. 4   Vol. No. 7
Set of Three Post Paid 1.80

Place total of purchases here $
Postage or Service Charge $
Pa. Resident 6% Sales Tax $
Total amount enclosed $

PA. RESIDENTS—Add 6% Sales Tax in space provided above.
ADD .50 per DOLL for POSTAGE ANYWHERE IN THE U.S.A.
ADD 1.00 per TRUNK in EAST — 2.00 in WEST

Name
Address
City

Please Print Your Name and Address

Send Orders to
MARY HOYER DOLL CO.
1008 Penn St., Reading, Pa.
P. O. BOX 925, READING, PA. 19603
WRITE FOR WHOLESALE QUANTITY PRICES

Publicity

Over the years Mary Hoyer and her dolls have received wide publicity. The following articles are a few of the many that have been written about her and range from the local papers in Reading, Pennsylvania, to the *Christian Science Monitor* in Boston, Massachusetts.

Mary Hoyer Has an Idea That Clicks

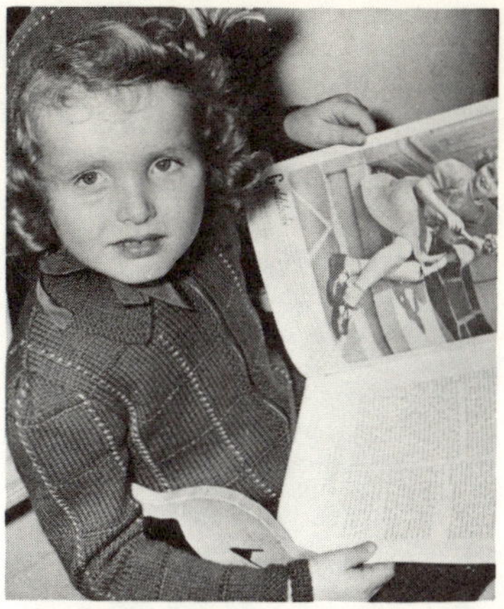

So Do Needles As Mothers Knit One, Purl One

By J. FRANK TRAGLE

FROM an idea and no capital to a circulation of 50,000 copies a year is the story of Mary Hoyer's magazine, "Juvenile Styles."

Mrs. Hoyer, the wife of William A. Hoyer, 41 Wilson Ave., West Lawn, was leafing through the trade magazines that come to her Reading yarn shop when the idea struck her that perhaps people would be interested in a magazine that would illustrate and give instructions for the knitting of garments for children.

Had Convincing Argument

That was five years ago. The publication of a magazine is an expensive proposition, especially if it is liberally illustrated. Mrs. Hoyer hadn't the capital. But she had ability, a convincing argument and a wealth of vitality. She found a printer to whom the project sounded worthwhile and several months later Volume 1 rolled from the presses. Today she has distributors in New York, Chicago, Philadelphia and Boston, sells 50,000 copies a year at 25 cents a copy, and has readers in Alaska and South America.

The magazine is a Berks County product. Mrs. Hoyer writes the copy, makes the designs. Reading photographers make her pictures, Berks County children model the garments, and Mrs. Hoyer's staff of workers knit each garment three times to be sure that the instructions in the magazine are correct.

And now, encouraged by the success of "Juvenile Styles," Mrs. Hoyer has published another magazine, "Mary's Dollies," which is devoted to doll clothes. What's more, Mrs. Hoyer also has patented "The Mary Hoyer Doll," which she employs to model the creations, every bit as chic as those she has designed for the children who carry the dolls.

Doll Clothes

An introduction to "Mary's Dollies" outlines the purpose of the magazine: "As a companion piece to Mrs. Hoyer's 'Juvenile Styles' this publication is issued to offer suggestions to keep the hands busy with flying needles. Little sister's dolls will need some fall and winter clothes for that trip to the summer or winter resorts. On these pages will be the pictures and directions for appropriate clothes that will follow the seasons—from California to Florida, thence to the Adirondacks, to the shimmering ice of Lake Placid, to the beach at Atlantic City. We sincerely hope that all of these doll clothes will help keep your favorite doll the best dressed in the neighborhood."

Judging from the illustrations in both magazines, sister-dolly combinations will be the thing this season. One of Mrs. Hoyer's attractive models is five-year-old Lois Ann Lenstrohm, daughter of Mr. and Mrs. John W. Lenstrohm, 1875 Grand Blvd., Wyomissing, whose photograph, in one of Mrs. Hoyer's smart creations, appears on the cover of "Juvenile Styles" and in the inside pages of "Mary's Dollies."

Costumes for skiing, golfing, bathing, skating and dancing not only are available for boys and girls, but for the dolls as well in identical creations. Similarly, it is possible for mother and daughter to attire themselves in matching ensembles. And the family that wants to indicate careful planning in dress will arrange a matching ensemble for mother, daughter and doll. The possibilities, one gathers from the magazines, are legion.

Mrs. Hoyer publishes but one volume of each magazine a year. In the first place, there is sufficient material in one magazine to keep a knitter busy for months, and in the second place it takes Mrs. Hoyer about seven months to prepare her copy, which includes the designing of styles, and knitting them.

By the way, it is possible to buy skates, skis and golfing paraphernalia for the dolls, indicating that the success of her magazine hasn't caused Mrs. Hoyer to rest on her oars.

Five-year-old Lois Ann Lenstrohm, of Wyomissing, one of the models for Mary Hoyer's magazine, "Juvenile Styles," examines a photograph for which she posed. Below, Mrs. Hoyer dresses her dolls in the chic costumes she creates, and which are exhibited in her magazine, "Mary's Dollies."—Times Staff Photos.

Illustration 67. Write-up about Mary Hoyer and her *Juvenile Styles* and *Mary's Dollies* books. *Reading Times*, Reading, Pennsylvania; Tuesday, September 30, 1941.

Face-Lifting Improves Yarn Shop Business

Typically Cluttered Yarn Shop Gets a Thorough Going-Over by Store Display Experts to Make It a Pleasure to Shop in. Customers Now Find Merchandise Dramatically and Tastefully Displayed in Clean, Modern and Well-Illuminated Surroundings.

A little over a year ago the Mary Hoyer Yarn Shop, otherwise known as the Juvenile Styles Publishing Company, was a typically cluttered and uninviting retail yarn shop at 1008 Penn Street, Reading, Pa.

Counters, shelves, bins and space on top of the wall cabinets were filled with a miscellany of disarranged merchandise in musty cartons, boxes, etc. Also, there was no relationship in the design of the various store fixtures and the entire area was poorly illuminated. The long narrow space was not particularly inviting to the prospective customer and business went haphazardly along.

Probably most distressing of all was the front of the store, a relic of the early thirties. Here, ill-lighted and uncoordinated windows greeted the passerby with an appearance that was anything but enticing.

It was that picture a field engineer for The Displayers, Inc., an outfit that makes a specialty of renovating stores, found when he made his first inspection of the premises more than a year ago. Through no direct fault of proprietor Mary Hoyer, the store had, through inertia, "degenerated" into that condition through the years.

The Picture Changes

But today the Mary Hoyer store presents an entirely new picture. The visitor to this newly renovated yarn shop is presented with a delightful and very attractive interior which immediately invites closer inspection of the entire line of merchandise, now dramatically and tastefully displayed.

After the preliminary report of the field engineer, dimensions were taken, and designs prepared suggesting an entirely new layout for the store front and interior. All of the display cabinets, counters and other fixtures were prefabricated in The Displayers' New York shop. The structural changes and treatment were handled in Reading by a local contractor carrying out the designs, and supervised by a local architect.

The illumination was tremendously improved by a system of indirect fluorescent lighting. Display cases, built into the wall are well illuminated for better display of a line of dolls—a line the Hoyer store is well-known for. These are protected by sliding glass doors and are kept in an immaculate condition. The same cases, of course, are ideal for displaying finished art needlework models or novelty yarns, as the case may be.

Modern Yarn Displays

Modern counters partially constructed of thick plexiglas provide a streamlined surface for the display and demonstration of merchandise. Skeins of wool are displayed in showcases constructed with diamond-shape egg-crate design similar to that employed in storing fine wines.

These are also protected by sliding glass doors and the customer is able to select from a complete visible arrangement of colors. This is far superior to the former system of storing skeins in drawers which did not permit color selection without handling merchandise. Mary Hoyer has discovered that customers like this set up because they are assured of clean, unhandled merchandise at all times. The store likes it, too, for it eliminates soilage—not a small item in any store.

At the extreme rear end of the store is an elevated platform upon which the latest fashions are displayed on a life sized mannequin. The background behind the mannequin, which also forms a separator between the front and the rear working space, is a curved surface of natural wood.

Large plate glass mirrors are freely used to effectively increase the limited width of the store.

A serpentine arrangement of fluorescent lighted showcases presents a line of jewelry—another source of income for the store—with a mirror for examination of earrings. The jewelry collection is a good-will builder for the store because women who pass the counters for yarns, usually wind up buying a bauble or two. Above these counters is a continuous arrangement of additional narrow showcases mounted against the wall. These also have sliding glass doors for easy access to the merchandise displayed there.

Above the display cases is a long line of illustrations of the latest fashions. These are set on the wall between two horizontal mouldings which are grooved for easy changeability of the pictures.

That this was truly a transformation—not only physically, but financially, as well, was stressed by Mary Hoyer. "Our business," she said, "over the first year has definitely improved and we are attracting a more select clientele. Visitors from all over the country, who are attracted to our shop due to our national advertising, have commented on the beauty of design and color scheme. It addition to a better year in volume of sales, it is a great pleasure to serve our customers in such attractive surroundings."

Comparing the two large photos with the smaller one (right) tells graphically how The Displayers completely changed the face of this ill-lighted, musty establishment. The face-lifting, which was completed about a year ago, has attracted a wider, more select clientele to the yarn shop.

Before . . . Front of the Mary Hoyer store as it looked before the renovation.

And after . . . The front of the Hoyer store, after a startling renovation, becomes a well-lighted, modern entrance inviting customers.

Illustration 68. Article appearing in a trade magazine describing the renovation of the Mary Hoyer Yarn Shop. Note how the dolls are more readily displayed in the remodeled store. *Art Needlework*, June 1949.

Mary Hoyer

invites you most cordially
to attend the re-opening of her modern

Yarn and Gift Shop

on

Saturday, November 29th to Saturday, December 6th
nineteen hundred forty-seven
9.30 a. m. to 6.00 p. m.

at

1008 Penn Street, Reading, Pennsylvania

The Ocean City New Jersey Store is located at 1106 Boardwalk

Illustration 69. Invitation extended after the remodeling of the Mary Hoyer shop in Reading, Pennsylvania, in 1947.

Illustration 70. A little girl dressed as a Mary Hoyer Doll on a float in the Baby Parade on the boardwalk in Ocean City, New Jersey, in the middle 1950s. The dolls shown were on loan from the Mary Hoyer shop, which was the third building from the corner.

RIGHT: Illustration 71. This photograph appeared on the cover of the *Reading Automobile Club Magazine,* Reading, Pennsylvania; April 1950, Volume 28, Number 2, and the write-up appeared on page 19.

BELOW: Illustration 72. Write-up on Mary Hoyer and her dolls from *The Christian Science Monitor,* Boston, Massachusetts; Friday, August 12, 1955. Reprinted by permission from The Christian Science Monitor, © 1955, The Christian Science Publishing Society, all rights reserved.

READING-AUTOMOBILE-CLUB MAGAZINE

APRIL, 1950 VOL. 28 NO. 2

OFFICIAL READING AAA AUTO CLUB PUBLICATION

Drive Carefully and Save LIVES

Our Cover

Meet Mary's Dollies.

Our cute models this week are the creations of Mary Hoyer's Yarn Shop, Penn St., Reading. They remind us that the gardening season is at hand and we'd better get out the spades and hoes — and liniment for the back.

Mary's Dollies are famous throughout the nation. They're made in New York and then shipped to Reading where the wig is donned. The yarn shop sells the dolls with yarn and a booklet of instructions on how to knit the doll's clothing.

The hat on the doll at left was made in South America.

Cliff Yeich, a lad who never has been further South than South of Penn, set up this cute scene on top of a card table, and then photographed it.

Model Dollies Step Out

By Carolyn L. Posey
Written for The Christian Science Monitor

"Look at the beautiful dolls. Aren't they out of this world!"

"Out of this world" and similar comments from summer shoppers at her Ocean City, N.J., store were the source of new ideas that Mrs. Mary Hoyer, designer, and originator of the Mary Hoyer doll, quickly translated into form.

Asked to put on a fashion show—a sideline for her business—she found the theme in these comments. The title of the fashion show? "Dolls From Out of This World"!

The new styles for the prettiest dolls on earth were presented, but the costumes for their charming sisters from Venus, Mars, and faraway Pluto were the high light of the show.

Gradual Start

"Planet dolls," fashion shows, two busy stores, doll patterns that appear in a leading woman's magazine—all these are facets of Mrs. Hoyer's business. Talking with her in her home studio, where she was surrounded with models of her dolls and many yards of interesting materials (such as red silk interwoven with metallic thread, that came from a hand loom in Syria), we learned how she began her work.

"At first I designed knitted clothes for children and sold them to yarn manufacturers on a free-lance basis," Mrs. Hoyer explained. "Soon I began to publish my own knitting books, which were called 'Juvenile Styles.'"

Then, about 16 years ago, she expanded her field to include costumes for dolls, and here she found unrestricted opportunity to express her talents. Unlike those young women who put aside their affection for dolls when they lay them aside, Mrs. Hoyer has always retained a love for dolls.

"A doll had to be found that would wear clothes to advantage," she continued. "Most dolls at that time had chubby childish figures. What I needed was a slim doll—one that war fairly tall but dainty."

Displaying the ingenuity that has characterized all her activities, she designed her own doll. Today, her business well established, Mrs. Hoyer is using this same model. Reflecting the improvement in materials over the years, today's doll is made of plastic instead of composition, and the hair may be combed, washed and waved.

The first dresses for the Mary Hoyer doll were knitted and crocheted, but the line was soon enlarged. Her wardrobe now includes washable cotton dresses, a knitted skating costume complete with tiny ice skates), a bridal gown, and trousseau, ball gowns of nylon net and taffeta, slacks, shorts, a "Dolly Madison" dress, skiing outfit, to name a few.

Kits Sold, Too

Variety, one soon sees, has not been achieved at the expense of style. Each costume shows definite thought and skill behind it: a skirt flowing into graceful fullness, an edging of lace along a blouse, a miniature picture hat trimmed with ribbons and tiny flowers, a parasol that matches a gown.

A mother who likes to sew or knit may buy a sewing kit, which contains pattern and dress materials, and complete an outfit herself. Recently, Mrs. Hoyer even introduced a child's sewing kit.

Instructions are given for the ten-year-old. The "Sun Bonnet Sue Outfit," pretty enough to light up any little girl's eyes, consists of a cotton dress and bonnet, simple in lines, so that small, untutored hands can stitch the seams.

In addition to her shop in Ocean City which is open during the summer, Mrs. Hoyer has her headquarters in Reading, Pa., where the doll clothes are manufactured. A large mail-order business is also carried on from here, and she sends the Mary Hoyer doll to many parts of the United States.

There are many details to be attended to; such as assembling the tiny accessories that go with the different costumes—boots, slippers, toys, tennis rackets, even a miniature camera. Mrs. Hoyer is glad to leave this work in the capable hands of her husband, William Hoyer, who devotes his entire time to the business. With his assistance, she is free to develop new ideas.

Mary Hoyer Doll Wardrobes Now Include Complete Bridal Party Styles

Mrs. Hoyer's abilities are as varied as her dolls' wardrobes. While preparing for a fashion show one year, she noticed that the metal stands holding the dolls in an upright position were cumbersome, interfering with the costumes because they supported the dolls at the waist. Promptly, a new stand that clamped the doll firmly at its feet, leaving the dress to fall free, was designed by Mrs. Hoyer.

Again, when background music and songs are needed for a fashion show, gay melodies are likely to come tumbling from her piano. Modestly, she will admit that she writes the words for the songs, too.

Puts on Shows

The fashion shows that Mrs. Hoyer gives periodically are requested by church groups, women's organizations, fine arts' clubs. She adapts each program to the size and type of audience expected.

At one show, she presented a fairyland series. Little Bo-Peep, Cinderella, and Miss Muffet took their bows for gay costumes, along with Snow-White and her Seven Dwarfs. The climax of that show was the appearance of the Queen, exquisitely gowned in white lace over a tulle skirt that contained 50 yards of material.

The costumes for the planet dolls in her most recent fashion show, "Dolls From Out of This World," highlight her artistry. For example, Miss Mars looked regal in her flowing costume of red silk. In Miss Pluto, a saucy young lady from a land of frozen scenes and constant twilight, the designer captured a snow-maiden in an ice-blue gown and white coat that swirled into angora along its edges.

With affection, care, and artistry, Mrs. Hoyer goes about her work. It is no small wonder that visitors standing before her windows exclaim, "What beautiful dolls . . . !"

Doll Trousseau Has Special Trunk

They remember...
People still want Hoyer dolls

By JOAN B. GILBERT
Staff Writer

The letters still come, about one a day, said Mary Hoyer. Although her dolls are out of production 10 years now, people are still attempting to buy them. And they're still searching for the many accessory items Mrs. Hoyer designed to adorn her dolls.

NOT ALL of the letters to her Reading home, though, are orders from people unaware that Mrs. Hoyer has retired from the doll business.

Some are fan letters. And many are from doll collectors enthusing over their latest Mary Hoyer find on the antique market.

MRS. HOYER is a gracious lady, still fascinated with dolls, still awed somewhat by her personal successes, and very willing to talk about them, humbly, yet without reservations.

Her career in the doll business evolved from her work in knitting and crocheting. She gave instructions in both forms of needlework in her first little yarn shop on N. 9th Street. But more, she started to put her ideas for designs down on paper.

Basically, the patterns she created were for children and, without much selling on her part, they were incorporated into instruction books bearing her name.

MODELING MANY of the styles was her daughter, Arlene, who would be posed with a doll wearing matching clothes.

The idea was catching, said Mrs. Hoyer, who recalled that there was one big problem with the dolls available then. They all had protruding tummies and in no way resembled the young children they would twin.

That led Mrs. Hoyer and her husband, William A., a former Berkshire International employe until he was needed in the doll business, to New York. There, they sought out a firm which would mold the slim doll Mrs. Hoyer had designed to wear her miniature clothes.

"IT WON'T sell," she was told repeatedly by jobbers. Nonetheless, she was persistent and so was born the forerunner of slim dolls such as Barbie, which were to follow several years later.

Mrs. Hoyer was also a pioneer in doll accessory items. From instructions in her juvenile books, she branched out to kits containing pre-cut fabrics for gowns, dresses, swim suits and various other sportswear items.

Next it was parasols, sleds, skis, ice skates, roller skates and boats, all doll sized.

As her business grew, Mrs. Hoyer moved her shop to larger quarters at 1008 Penn St., where her daughter — of pattern book fame — still runs a women's apparel shop.

Because of her love for the New Jersey seashore, she eventually expanded to a shop on the Ocean City boardwalk.

BY THEN, her business had grown to necessitate a mail order warehouse, at 10th and Penn, too, to handle the battery of requests her books and dolls were producing.

It's a memory now for Mrs. Hoyer. So are the doll fashion shows she'd elaborately stage for the benefit of various community civic organizations and churches.

They're pleasant memories, she says, but she can dismiss them easily to keep up with the relaxing and peaceful demands of her life today, which she divides between Reading and Sarasota, Fla.

TUCKED AWAY with those memories are stacks of memorabilia. She has books and kits and such. Regretfully, though, she has very few of the dolls she fashioned.

"I never kept one of each of the dolls myself, but I guess I should have," she mused.

Illustration 73. 14in (35.6cm) hard plastic Mary Hoyer Doll costumed as a nun. This doll was brought into Mary Hoyer's shop by a customer who made the outfit in the 1950s.

Illustration 74. Publicity for one of the many fashion shows Mary Hoyer gave over the years. Note the bride and groom in the center and Snow White on the right surrounded by her seven "dwarfs." The "dwarfs" all carry a Steiff tag. *Reading Eagle,* Reading, Pennsylvania; Monday, July 22, 1963.

A DOLL AND CHILDREN'S FASHION SHOW has been arranged for Wednesday night, July 31 at the Antietam Valley Recreation and Community Center sponsored by the Women's Guild of the center. Committee members with a variety of dolls shown above include from left, Mrs. J. Bayard Kelly, co-chairman of the ways and means committee; Mrs. Mary Hoyer who made the dolls; Robin Kelly one of the models and Mrs. Jean B. Price, chairman of the ways and means committee.—Eagle Photo.

All dolled up

Photographer: Richard J. Patrick

Owning a Mary Hoyer Doll has brightened the lives of many little (and some big) girls for over 30 years. The world-famous doll empire was founded in Reading and makes its headquarters at 1008 Penn St. Mrs. Mary Hoyer, the originator, at top, displays some of the many dolls. Above, she shows how new outfits can be made for them. At left, a doll models a contemporary maxicoat ensemble, while at right, a complete wardrobe and doll are admired by Karen Price, 11, Mrs. Hoyer's granddaughter.

Illustration 75. These are the last photographs taken in Mary Hoyer's shop showing the dolls on display. The dolls shown here are the all-vinyl dolls with the exception of the one Mrs. Hoyer is holding which is the hard plastic version. *Reading Times,* Reading, Pennsylvania; Monday, January 12, 1970.

Right:
The dolls which made Mary Hoyer of Reading famous are out of production for 10 years, now, but she still receives requests for them. Mrs. Hoyer pioneered the slim doll.

Illustration 76. Write-up about Mary Hoyer and her dolls. *Reading Times,* Reading, Pennsylvania; Monday, June 6, 1977.

Reading's "Doll Lady" is Lovingly Rembered All Year Long

Mary Hoyer, Reading's "Doll Lady", whose shop on Penn St. has been a familiar sight since 1932, has spent much of her life creating the playthings of which little girls' dreams are made. Many Berks Co. residents, as well as people across the country and around the world, remember with joy the Mary Hoyer doll found under the tree on a Christmas morning, or on some other special occasion.

Fashion design was actually the beginning of Mary Hoyer's doll business. In the early 1930s she designed children's knitwear for several major yarn manufacturers, and, with her husband, instituted her own publishing company under the well-known name "Juvenile Styles."

Pictures which often accompanied the instructions in her booklets, and advertisements in *McCall's Art Needlework* magazine created a growing demand for Mrs. Hoyer's designs. An international mail-order business grew out of the "Juvenile Styles" publications.

Through her designing efforts, Mrs. Hoyer realized that dolls which could then be bought were not clothed like little girls. Rather, they looked, and were dressed, like plump babies. Mrs. Hoyer set out to make a doll that would look like, and could be attired like a child, not an infant.

Original Mary Hoyer dolls were sold undressed, with materials and instructions for creating their wardrobes. The workmanship involved in the construction of these dolls was of exceptional quality. The dolls had hand-painted faces and hand-sewn wigs.

Each of the outfits designed for Mary Hoyer dolls was given a name and made available in kits which included such novel miniature accessories as boots, skis, and purses. Kits could be ordered by mail and many local residents were employed by "Mary's Dollies" which advertised nationally.

Mrs. Hoyer, in addition to creating these marvelous playthings, spent many hours giving charity doll fashion shows featuring brides, storybook characters, and "Dollies Out of This World". One such show, a Miss America pageant, included a doll representative from every state.

Today, Mary Hoyer dolls are deservedly treasured. The sale of the original doll was discontinued about 6 yeas ago, and the Mary Hoyer Shop now sells fine women's clothing, but the Mary Hoyer doll fan club and the thousands of people to whom Mary Hoyer dolls brought joy maintain interest in these toys of quality and beauty.

Mrs. Hoyer has often been honored for her creations. She was recently a special guest at the opening of John Wannamaker's annual doll display.

Mary Hoyer, the "Doll Lady", and one of her lovely creations.

Illustration 77. Article appearing in *This Month In Reading*, December 1979, Vol. XVI, No. 12.

Fashion Shows

Over the years Mrs. Hoyer gave quite a number of doll fashion shows in the eastern Pennsylvania area featuring her dolls and costumes. The shows were usually given for church affairs, service associations, benefit groups, charitable organizations and sometimes just for entertainment!

The fashion shows were written with a particular theme in mind. Mrs. Hoyer would design the gowns and each design was executed by a special seamstress, Mrs. Grace Pehlman, who made all the gowns individually for every doll which was to appear in the show. At a later date some of these special designs were incorporated into the regular line of Mary Hoyer clothes for the dolls.

The versatile Mary Hoyer not only designed all of the costumes for the dolls, but also wrote the script and composed the words and music to accompany each show. Her daughter, Arlene, displayed the dolls, assisted by a pianist, Maybelle Clemenson, and a commentator who accompanied them to the shows.

Two of the fashion shows are presented here. The first is the "Miss America Pageant" featuring dolls representing each of the 50 United States, the District of Columbia and a special doll representing our neighbor to the north, Canada. The second fashion show is actually three in one. The first dolls portray various characters from "Fairyland." Then the "Miss Universe Contestants" are introduced, representing the planets in our solar system. Finally, a complete wedding party is presented just before the winner of the Miss Universe contest is announced.

> You and your friends
> are cordially invited to attend
>
> ## A Mary Hoyer Doll Fashion Review
>
> Women's Club
> 140 North 5th Street, Reading, Pa.
>
> Saturday afternoon, December 4th, 1954 - 2:00 to 3:30 o'clock
>
> ## Mary Hoyer Shops
>
> 1008 Penn Street   714 Boardwalk
> Reading, Pa.   Ocean City, N. J.

Illustration 78. Invitation to a Mary Hoyer Doll Fashion Review. This one was given in 1954.

Words and Music by Mary Hoyer — "Here Comes Miss America"

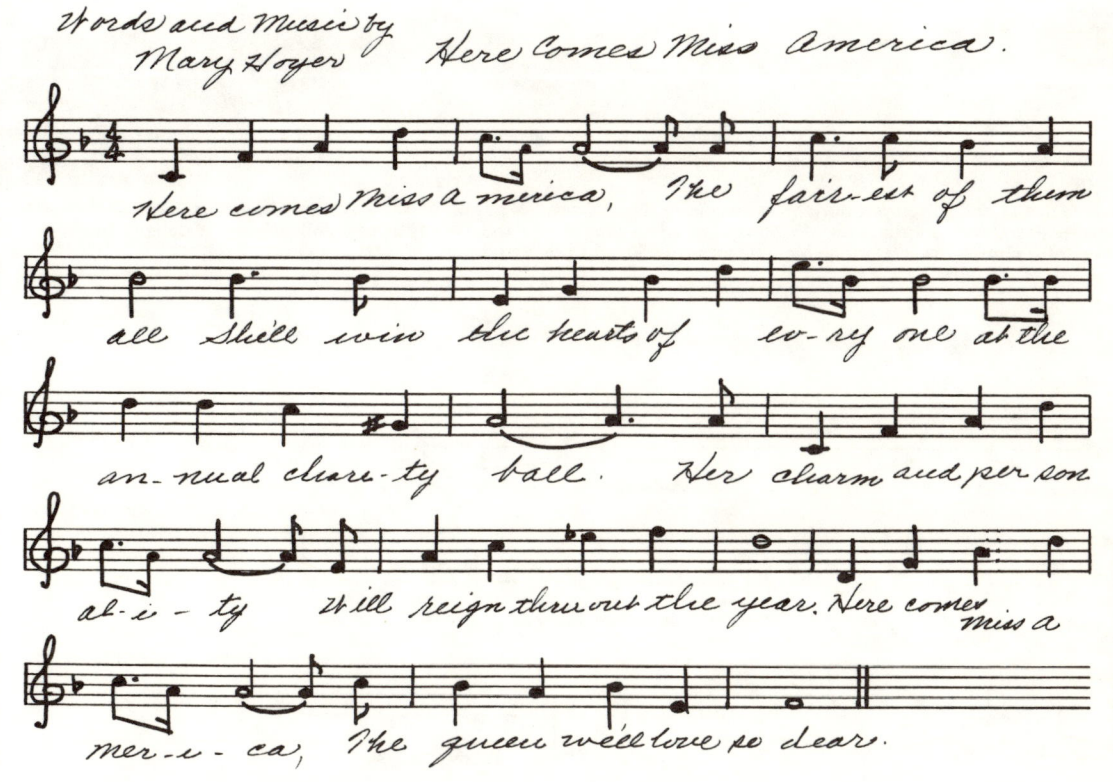

Here comes Miss America, The fairest of them all shall win the hearts of ev-ry one at the an-nual chari-ty ball. Her charm and person-al-i-ty will reign thru-out the year. Here comes miss a-mer-i-ca, The queen we'll love so dear.

Illustration 79. The words and music to "Here Comes Miss America," composed by Mary Hoyer especially for her Miss America Pageant featuring her dolls dressed in her original design gowns.

MISS AMERICA PAGEANT

Good evening ladies and gentlemen and welcome to all the little people here, too.

I would like to introduce myself. I am Bonnie Borelli, your commentator today.

I will bet you have always thought that the Miss America Pageant took place each year only in Atlantic City. Surprise! We are bringing it to you - - the entire drama of the Miss America Pageant - - in this auditorium. All of the famous beauties from Miss Alaska to Miss Wyoming are here tonight for your pleasure.

Without further ado, I am ready to introduce each of our beautiful contestants.

First, are the judges ready? Let us light up the runway, strike up the band and get on with the show. Here is our first contestant.

MISS ALABAMA: White tulle over crisp white taffeta is trimmed with lurex. The bodice is tight fitting and molded to her petite form. With shoestring straps and bursts of frothy white tulle in a skirt that is full to overflowing, the gown has a dramatic drape on the left hip. An Elizabethan red bow is attached, outlining the hip. She is wearing a rhinestone necklace and bracelet. Anyone could fall deeply in love with this little lovely from the Deep South.

MISS ALASKA is a breathtaking beauty queen from our cold most northern state, but I am sure she will melt the hearts of all the judges. Her dress is tulip pink under a coat of white nylon net trimmed with white fur.

MISS ARIZONA is wearing a strapless gown of jewel box blue. Her full skirt boasts a wide ruffle of white dotted nylon net on the bottom. The net is repeated in a narrow

Illustration 80. These are some of the dolls displayed during the various doll fashion shows put on by Mary Hoyer. The center "Queen" doll and the two dolls in the upper right-hand corner are the 18in (45.7cm) dolls while the rest are the 14in (35.6cm) dolls. Note the dolls in the upper left-hand corner wearing some of the clothes made from the McCall pattern 1564, which is also shown.

Illustration 81. The words and music to "I Am A Mary Hoyer Doll," composed by Mary Hoyer for one of her doll fashion reviews.

ruffle on the edge of her bodice. Miss Arizona is wearing long white sheer gloves to complete this lovely gown.

MISS ARKANSAS: Blossom pink with five rows of black lace can only come out one way - - perfect. The most wanted colors combine to show off a full circular skirt in pink paper taffeta. The five rows of sheer black nylon lace encircle it completely. There is also a lace edging on the bib front in the sweetheart shaped neckline.

MISS CALIFORNIA is dressed in pink parfait and it looks good enough to eat. Skinner's satin is under a full skirt of soft nylon net.

MISS CANADA: A northern Canadian sky is the inspiration for this color of blue here under a drift of gold. A ballerina bodice is held in control with flyaway panels down to the floor. Her blonde side swept hair style is another original by Mary Hoyer.

MISS COLORADO: It seems that gold dust was spilled into tiny teardrops on the nylon net. The expressive sweetheart neckline adds charm. The fabric is Skinner's satin with an off-white color making it more glamourous for candlelight hours. The white satin is repeated in huge butterfly bows beginning at her dropped torso bodice in the back.

MISS CONNECTICUT: A nile green satin skirt is under a full skirt of sheer clouds of stardust. The sheer fabric is repeated in the collar, over the shoulders and in the bodice. An addition of mitts looks charming, don't you agree?

MISS DELAWARE: A willowy skirt of nylon sprinkled with stardust is fashioned over Dior blue taffeta. The left hipline is dropped slightly while the right shoulder is raised just enough to point out interest. The edging of silver sequins really focuses attention to the fabulous glamour in this creation. You must recognize the upswept hair style as it is a copy of a recent prize winning style, high and heavenly.

MISS DISTRICT OF COLUMBIA: Her winter white crisp taffeta skirt has a luscious peplum overskirt that is scalloped and edged in bugle beads. It temporarily holds down billowing frothy white net under the peplum. The little strapless bodice is jeweled in pearls and bugle beads. Miss District of Columbia looks as if she stepped out of the President's Ball. And check her stunning rhinestone jewelry. The only thing to make her lovelier would be "Moonlight on the Potomac."

MISS FLORIDA: Six tiers of net and tiny ruffles ripple over a bouffant white net skirt topped off with a silver thread. Her wasp-like waist leads to a shirred ruffle in the bosom line and it slopes to an exciting low back. The land of sunshine proves that Mother Nature has proper ideas for "sunkist" beauty.

MISS GEORGIA: A Georgia Peach!!! She is wearing two petal-like skirts in sheer nylon net of permanent pleating. Lurex metallic thread edges all of the ruffling and the petals. Any southern gentleman would be proud indeed to show off this Georgia Peach.

Here is **MISS HAWAII:** A captivating beauty wearing a Hawaiian print under mauve chiffon. A blue rhinestone necklace and clip in her high styled hairdo and dainty mitts complete her ensemble.

MISS IDAHO: Extravagantly covered with pink sheer nylon net, a bouffant skirt is encircled at the bottom with a wide ruffle and then finished off in tiny pink satin ribbon. A "V" neckline draws attention to the cream puff sleeves. Rhinestone jewels are to be seen also in her side swept hairdo.

MISS ILLINOIS is wearing a powder blue satin gown under sheer blue net. The net is repeated in the bodice and a full ruffle on the scoop neckline. A wide ruffle is repeated on the bottom of her full net skirt.

MISS INDIANA: She starts with a stiff petticoat, covers it with sheer taffeta, then adds nylon net on top. Put the three together and you get a beautiful dress with an overdrape of wide sheer permanent pleated ruffle. It is edged on both the top and bottom with lurex thread. Very full tiny ruffles hold a draped stole over her shoulders and they end in two huge loops. Gloves are a MUST for Miss Indiana.

MISS IOWA: Blue and silver cloth are combined to sparkle in a gown that has a waist cincher bodice. The tiny revers reveal silver straps sloping to the low back and the bodice itself releases petal-like scallops over silver cloth. Mitts climax the glistening appearance.

MISS KANSAS: Green in a multitude of tones is the color; it is ombre taffeta in the bodice all covered with flowered lace and embroidered in silver thread. The same silver metallic finds its way to the shoestring shoulder straps. Cascading through the skirt we discover three luscious ruffles, each touched off with more lurex thread. Kansas captured a charmer when they presented this dolly.

MISS KENTUCKY: Blue Skinner's satin is spotlighted with a coating of exquisite Chantilly lace. The bottom of the bouffant skirt boasts a pleated net ruffle so popular a few years back and the longer you look the more you see. A daughter of an Ol' Southern Colonel!

MISS LOUISIANA: We like the looks of pink taffeta under cobwebby black nylon. The dust ruffle of permanent pleated nylon is edged in lurex. Topped off with sheer black Venetian lace, the unusual décolleté neckline is crisscrossed to form straps and a "V" back. Notice her long gloves. Only a lady of fashion would show them off.

MISS MAINE: Avocado colored slipper satin is gathered under a skirt of black Chantilly lace. The lace is continued to the high jeweled neckline over a strapless bodice. Long pushed up sleeves accent the covered up look. Her lovely blonde hair is combed into a chignon carefully set on top of her head. Tiny rhinestones encircle her tiny wrist.

MISS MARYLAND is wearing a white circular cut gown with taffeta beneath soft clouds of shimmering net with silver lurex added. Piping in American beauty red is exciting. Little shoulder straps and a dainty sash complete the dramatic effect. The trim is repeated in the skirt.

MISS MASSACHUSETTS: Watermelon red is the color; chiffon is the fabric. Shell pink taffeta is under the billowing chiffon. The plunging neckline leads off to dropped shoulder loveliness. Rhinestones in a sculptured spray over clusters of curls set the pace for new styles of 1958. Even the Pilgrims of Plymouth Rock would approve of this beauty.

MISS MICHIGAN's gown portrays the look of 1958. The uneven hemline is swept to the back. The fabric is embossed with gold and it is on cotton backed satin. The full skirt bursts into unpressed pleats. Notice the plunging "V" neckline. Her shoulders are cloaked in mink.

MISS MINNESOTA: Flocked nylon! Completely different! The skirt is transparent over pink taffeta. Her bodice is tight fitting. A low square neckline is repeated in the back. Old rose velvet completes this demure costume, almost; finally, the mitts, so petite, add the finished look.

MISS MISSISSIPPI: Our blonde Southern Belle wears a three layer creation: shimmering pink nylon in ruffles over crisp woven taffeta over a nylon and buckram petticoat. The detailed designing defines clearly the high straight neckline, finished off with narrow net straps. Our blonde beauty has a personalized hair style: finger curls pulled back, clustered at the nape of the neck and topped with an old rose velvet bow.

MISS MISSOURI: The embroidered influence is back again! Nylon in coral pink is worked into flower designs over blue satin. Matching blue is repeated in rich draping at the neckline. Finally, a sash develops into a butterfly bow on the left hip. The Missouri Miss will be in the running for all of the prizes.

MISS MONTANA: Blue silver cloth is fashioned into a slim fitting bodice and then releases sunbursts of pleats in the skirt. This is the refreshing approach to a new design. A tailored bow is placed just right for second glances. The strapless gown is held up better because of the halter necklace of rhinestones. The Paris designers could learn a thing or two from our Mary Hoyer creations.

MISS NEBRASKA: White pure silk twill satin in a sunburst of pleats cascades from the waistline. Pretty indeed is the bosom design. Four rows of bugle beads are handsewn on the neckline. The luxurious back is covered with two powder puff poofs which show off a train flowing into place around the hemline. Nebraska presents a dolly that is "delightful and delovely."

MISS NEVADA: The new look for dollies: a high neckline, a form fitting bodice and a roulette skirt in black nylon tulle that has been finished with a trio of silver threads, carefully spaced. Notice how the silver is repeated in the bodice and a metallic rose adds the perfect touch to her waist. The accent is "jewely" - - brilliant and dainty.

MISS NEW HAMPSHIRE: The jewel tone of the emerald has always been regarded as a strong color. Here it is in taffeta with an overskirt of nylon net with three tiers of net ruffles. The ruffles are interrupted by double rows of lurex thread. Check the regal look in the dipped back. Maybe this miss will wear the crown of the Queen tonight - - then she will wear emeralds to match her gown.

MISS NEW JERSEY: Turquoise satin cut into a circular skirt glistens through sheer star-studded tricot. The bodice - - long torso type - - ends up above a tulip skirt. Star-studded butterfly bows are found in back, complementing the gorgeous gown. She is wearing long nylon gloves.

MISS NEW MEXICO: A red hot success is this rustling red taffeta under a bouffant skirt of white nylon. The "V" neckline is featured by a display of cotton Irish lace, calling attention to the forward look. A bold red taffeta bow is fashioned at the center front of the gown. Catchy, cute and clever, these Mexican beauties.

MISS NEW YORK: A sumptuous skirt of delicate black Chantilly lace is over candle-white taffeta. Underneath there is a horsehair petticoat. The little bodice is created with Grecian influence. The left shoulder is covered and the right is bared. Two red roses are decorative accessories on the right hip. Her blonde upswept locks also feature two red roses in her hair.

MISS NORTH CAROLINA: Hibiscus pink means you are heading South. We head you off with sheer nylon over a self-matched petticoat. Her bodice releases a full-blown pair of sleeves topped with candy blue roses. A whole streamer of roses is the eye-catcher here on the skirt. The roses start at the left side of her waist and go to the right side at the bottom of her long skirt.

MISS NORTH DAKOTA: Monaco, the home of Princesses, is proud to present their own color, Monaco blue, in a gathering of taffeta under serene metallic and flowered lace. The bodice ends in petal points showing a facing of the taffeta. A trim and tailored bow leads into a necklace strap to complete the top glamour. A sash in back features an oversize bow. North Dakota is just the state to produce a Belle like this one!

MISS OHIO: Pink brocade highlighted with silver metallic threads provides the starting point for this little gem. Her tiny waist releases tiny pleats around the entire skirt and an inverted pleat formed at center front. A sweetheart neckline is outlined with cerise sequins, so darling and shiny, but most important of all she covers her bare shoulders with mink! This is not just ordinary mink, but emba mink, one of the finest mutations in the world.

MISS OKLAHOMA: She looks enchanting in her full circular crisp taffeta skirt under black nylon, dotted with velvet leaves. A matching broad ruffle shirred on the taffeta shows a black velvet band encircling the topmost tier. Her strapless fitted bodice is fashioned with a turn down cuff. Milady wears matching gauntlets to complete her ensemble.

MISS OREGON: The note of this gown is simplicity. There is crisp nile green taffeta under sheer net. The full wide skirt is scalloped with wide Venetian lace. The lace is repeated in the strapless bodice. A side swept hairdo is drawn back into soft curls and the finishing touch is a pearl tiara worn on the top of her head. She is carrying an angora stole and her long gauntlets are a MUST.

MISS PENNSYLVANIA: She looks like an American beauty in her flowered metallic tulle overskirt. The unpressed pleats gently cover the satin skirt beneath. Her gown is strapless and a soft white fur stole caresses her bared shoulders. Our home state can be proud of *our* product of beauty.

MISS RHODE ISLAND: Here we have Monaco blue draped in soft clouds of dyed-to-match net with Skinner's satin shimmering through! The poof drapes are held in place with a trio of pink and blue rosebuds. The bodice, cut in a "V" neckline is embroidered with butterflies and to finish the dressy look, the shoulders are covered with a draped net stole. Little ol' Rhode Island has more than its share of fancy dressed females.

MISS SOUTH CAROLINA: A symphony in lace and net! The palest rosebud satin bursts from the waistline in lace and clouds of net. Tulip petals topping the bodice point to bared shoulders for this strapless gown. "Nothing could be finer than to be in Carolina in the morning" - - especially if this pretty girl met you at the station.

MISS SOUTH DAKOTA: Newer than tomorrow morning's sunrise is the "Dutch" bell skirt. Here it is in frosted gold fabric ending abruptly in a tulip bosom. A chain of imported rosebuds is draped over her bare shoulders. This dolly can steal your heart away when she shows up wearing such a lovely Mary Hoyer creation.

MISS TENNESSEE: A trio of sheer nylon net in permanent pinched pleating is graduated from the smallest waist to the fullest sweeping bottom. Ruffled edging explodes in lurex thread for the frothy frill treatment. The trim is repeated around the neck. Even the "Tennessee Waltz" would be a pleasure with this sweet dancing dolly.

MISS TEXAS: Our yellow rose of Texas is dressed in sunny yellow satin. According to the Texan, everything is bigger and better in Texas, but they have nothing to compare with this doll's skirt. It is oversized more than a little. Four yellow roses with centers of chiffon are chained together to be draped across the front portion of her skirt. The soft cowl neckline is very appropriate. Texas never had a rose as sweet as this one.

MISS UTAH: The sophisticated miss from Utah boasts one of the newer than new harem skirts. A long torso sets off the fireworks in fashion. Her low cut back leads to the "V" front and the drapes that caress her soft shoulders. Her hair is done in a bun of curls, and to hold the attention to that spot, she wears a spray of rhinestones.

MISS VERMONT: Aqua paper taffeta under a skirt of nylon net is fashioned with a bold dust ruffle that has an edging of lace. A bowed front releases two straps over her tiny shoulders. Coming from the northern state of Vermont, this dolly can warm your heart anytime.

MISS VIRGINIA: Our little miss looks as if she just stepped off the showboat with her pretty powder puff pink woven taffeta under the delicate pink tulle. The top tier of her engaging costume is shirred. Matching ruffles and flower bouquets peek through the scallops. There is a ruffle treatment repeated over dropped shoulders.

MISS WASHINGTON: A drift of pink sheer over woven taffeta makes the dress start with simplicity but an applique of the velvet leaves studded with rhinestones complements her strapless bodice. The leaves are repeated in the upswept hairdo. The shaping actually creates a velvet hat hugging her hairline. Each contestant wears her Mary Hoyer original like a professional model.

MISS WEST VIRGINIA: Pink woven taffeta is under a shower of ribbed nylon tricot. The huge parasol skirt is finished in a net frill and repeated on the outline of the square neckline. Her wasp waist boasts a huge powder puff baby doll sleeve. The upswept hairdo sets off Miss West Virginia's royal glow.

MISS WISCONSIN: Kelly green satin under ecru embroidered lace looks so right with a full wide sweeping hemline finished in matching velvet. The velvet finds its way to the top of her tight bodice. Her lace gauntlets are also topped with velvet trim.

MISS WYOMING: Sunny yellow satin is used under clouds of white sheer nylon dotted with gold pennies. That is the start. The eyes are caught by the sheer fabric manipulated in a stole draped from the right hip over the left shoulder. The flowing ends go to the back of the gown. A cluster of topaz and pearls makes a fabulous trim at the waist. Intrigue is created with the last swirl of the stole draped over her curls.

Miss Wyoming is the last dolly in the Miss America Pageant. It is now up to our judges to pick a winner. Our judges are Misses Kathleen Clemenson, Sharon Clemenson, Margaret Gardner and Kathleen Wertz, all of West Reading High School. I am glad I am not one of the judges. It is a difficult task to choose a queen from all of these lovely dollies. Each one seemed more beautiful than the other. Don't you agree?

Now while the judges are choosing a winner, I would like to present Mrs. Hoyer's daughter, Arlene, who displayed all of these dollies so beautifully and our pianist, Maybelle Clemenson, who helps to make our fashion shows a success with her incomparable music. I would also like you to meet another person who was a very important part of all these dollies, Mrs. Grace Pehlman, who made all of the special gowns for the Miss America Pageant. They are incredibly beautiful.

Now if the judges are ready, I would like the envelope, please, with the name of the winner who will reign over all the dollies for the coming year.

Our winner is Miss Alaska. Arlene will display Miss Alaska for everyone to see and Sharon Lightcap will sing "Here comes Miss America," an original song with words and music by Mary Hoyer, especially written for the show.

This concludes our Dolly Fashion Show and we hope you have enjoyed all of the dollies.

Now I would like to present Mary Hoyer, creator of the Mary Hoyer Doll and designer of her fabulous wardrobe.

MARY HOYER PRESENTS..........
HER ORIGINAL DOLL AND FASHIONS

INTRODUCTION: Hello, everyone! I am Bonnie Borelli, your commentator for this very special occasion. I am ready to escort you through "The Wonderful World of MARY HOYER DOLLS" where we will meet all the fabulous storybook characters from "Fairyland." We also have a Fairy Princess that will take us out of this world to visit all of the planets.

Tonight we introduce some new dollies into the Mary Hoyer Doll family. We also add a touch of elegance with a "Gala Wedding Party" complete with the bride's trousseau.

The Mary Hoyer Doll was created 25 years ago and we thought it would be fun to invite all of you to her Birthday Party! Here is our BIRTHDAY DOLL! She is a dark haired beauty dressed in pale blue organza, trimmed with Venetian lace and tiny rosebuds. The Mary Hoyer Doll invited all her friends from "Fairyland" to her Birthday Party.

Miss Sharon Lightcap will take you through "Fairyland" in a song by the same name.

Mary was anxiously awaiting the arrival of her guests, when she heard a knock on the door. Her first guests to arrive were CINDERELLA and PRINCE CHARMING. Cinderella's party dress boasts a snug waistline releasing a bouffant skirt of sheer lavendar silk over woven taffeta. The bodice and panels are frilled in narrow turquoise tulle. The frill is repeated on the bottom of her skirt. Her pearled tiara gives her that little princess look.

PRINCE CHARMING looks romantic in his gold cloth cape with white elasticized satin pants and brocaded green jacket. His plum colored hat is topped off with a

Illustration 82. Photograph taken after one of the doll fashion shows. Left to right: a doll in a special gown, the Fairy Godmother and Dolly Madison with her parasol.

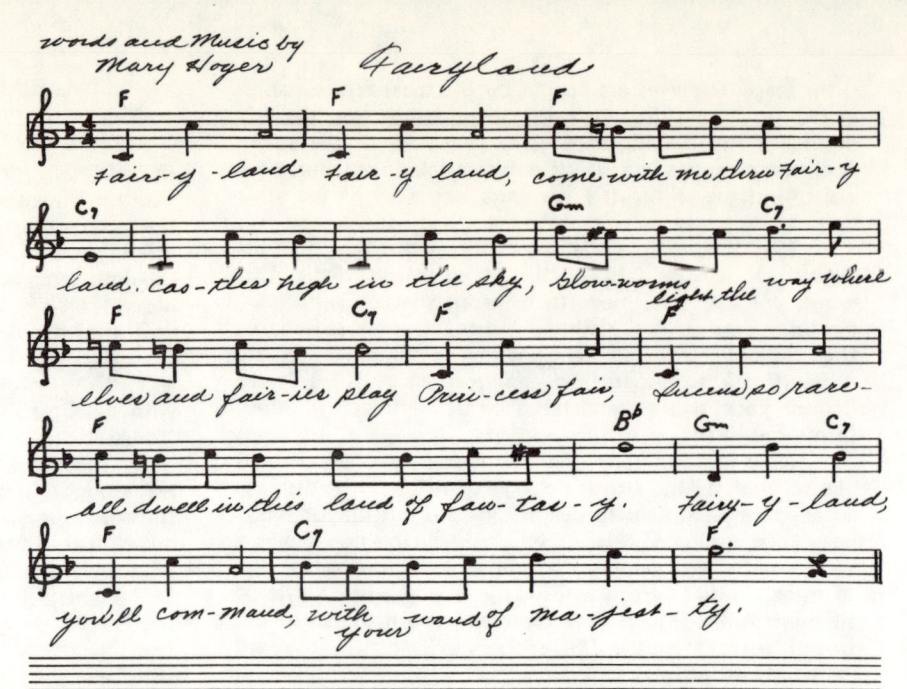

Illustration 83. The words and music to "Fairyland," composed by Mary Hoyer for one of her doll fashion reviews.

white plume. I am sure all the little girls will be thrilled to have him at the party.

The FAIRY GODMOTHER was a darling to come along and she looks enchanting in her pointed bewitching hat, studded with rhinestones and flowing veil. Her full circular black skirt has two white nylon tiers. A full black and white nylon ruffle encircles the top tier. The detail is finished in silver thread. She is staying close by Cinderella's side to keep her beautiful, no matter how late the night becomes.

The next guest to arrive is MISS BO-PEEP carrying her two pet sheep. She never suspected that they were following her until she was near her destination and there was nothing to do but take them with her. Miss Bo-Peep looks crisp and fresh in her pink taffeta frock with blue peplum edged in nylon lace. Her curls are tied with narrow blue ribbon at the nape of her neck.

Here is ALICE IN WONDERLAND. Her long blonde tresses look windblown from falling through the rabbit hole into Wonderland. Her Alice blue taffeta dress has full puff sleeves and a bouffant skirt. The pinafore is made of white eyelet embroidered nylon and trimmed with nylon lace.

LITTLE RED RIDING HOOD came tripping through the woods with her little basket filled with flowers. Her dress is made of crisp white taffeta and her full red taffeta cape and hood, completely lined in white taffeta, keep her safely from the big bad wolf.

Here are HANSEL and GRETEL. Gretel looks darling in her full skirt and full puffed sleeves. Her Tyrolean skirt band and straps are woven in bright colors.

Hansel is wearing knee length pants with suspender straps to match Gretel's. His matching jacket is worn over a white shirt.

Little MISS MUFFET is dressed demurely in crisp pink taffeta. Her dress and pantaloons are trimmed in nylon lace. Miss Muffet made friends with her spider and brought it with her to the party.

Here is SNOW WHITE, accompanied by the seven little dwarfs. Her bodice is blue taffeta under sparkling net and releases a full circular skirt of yellow taffeta under pale blue net. The tiny puffed sleeves and collar are trimmed in yellow. Snow White is wearing her hair in a large bun on the top of her head and tied with a tiny blue ribbon.

The dwarfs only intended to take her to the door, but all of the dollies out of "Fairyland" insisted they stay for the Birthday Party and that made them very very happy.

Now would all of you children like to sing "Happy Birthday" to the Mary Hoyer Dollie? Here is Sharon to help you sing it.

Out of nowhere appears a beautiful FAIRY PRINCESS, wearing a white taffeta gown under soft clouds of net and a shimmering tiara. With her magic wand, she whisks all of the dollies out of "Fairyland" to the planet Mars, where all the planets are participating in a beauty pageant.

The first to appear is lovely MISS VENUS wearing a Grecian gown of nylon permanent pleating over shimmering satin. Her sheer cape completes her costume. The planet Venus is the brightest star in the heavens.

The next contestant is exotic MISS MARS. Her gown is a magnificent combination of pure silk and metallic thread, handwoven in Syria. The drapery used over the left shoulder and the skirt is important, but much of the story is left untold in design so it can be told better in the fabric.

Here is JUPITER'S DARLING. Her gown is nylon net over pink taffeta. The nylon net skirt is draped over a full ruffle encircling the bottom of her gown and fastened with tiny handmade rosebuds, imported from France. Jupiter is the largest planet and has 12 moons.

MISS SATURN is wearing a metallic blue gown with two white nylon tiers. Brilliant sequins encircle the top tier, resembling the rings around the planet Saturn. Her hairdo has been styled especially for her gown by our hairdresser. Outside the rings of the planet Saturn are nine moons.

From the planet Uranus comes this luscious dark haired beauty, MISS URANUS. Her gown is nylon net over rustling metallic cloth completely encircled with yards and yards of nylon net stitched with metallic thread. The ruffle is repeated around the low neckline and the frill falls gracefully over the shoulders.

From the planet Neptune came this captivating beauty, MISS NEPTUNE, looking like the goddess of the sea. Her tight bodice releases a cascade of soft fullness of satin and tulle. The tulle is smocked with small iridescent sea shells. A froth of tulle covers her hair and sea shells frame her face.

MISS PLUTO came from the planet farthest from the sun. A land of ice and snow but I am sure she will melt the heart of every little girl. This lovely "Snow Queen's" gown is made of shimmering satin and her full circular coat of white nylon net is trimmed in white fur.

Here is our MISS EARTH in a pink satin gown. The tight fitting bodice accents a Grecian influence and a soft drape caresses her right shoulder. Her wasp waist releases a full circular skirt with soft pink tulle shirred inside the scallops on the right side. Over the skirt on the same side are huge folds of pink tulle.

Here is Miss Sharon Lightcap to sing "Dollies From Out Of This World."

We are going to select a Miss Universe and crown her Queen of all the dolls at the end of the show and here are our judges: Misses Debby Edmonds, Robin Kelly and Lynne Price. While we leave our dolls and judges in exotic Mars, we take you back to earth and introduce some other members of the Mary Hoyer Doll family.

The 14 inch Mary Hoyer Doll is made of unbreakable plastic and all wigs can be washed and combed. The undressed dolls with shoes and stockings are either $3.50 or $4.50 depending on the style of the wig. The next group of dollies' costumes we are going to show you may be purchased completed or in a kit, containing all the materials cut for you to sew.

This is *Cathy,* Mary Hoyer's cuddly infant. She is wearing her christening dress and slip of organdy, edged with nylon lace. She is made of soft vinyl that is almost identical to real baby skin. So light in weight for a tiny tot's first doll. She is washable, opens and closes her eyes and drinks and wets. Now here comes the big surprise: she costs only $1.50 undressed.

Next we have the Mary Hoyer toddler doll, for the kindergarten group. Her name is *Margie* and she is molded of hard vinyl with jointed arms and legs and a turning head. Her lashed eyes go to sleep. She has rooted saran hair set in pony tail or short hair styles. *Margie* and *Cathy* have extensive wardrobes styled by Mary Hoyer and made of the finest fabrics. *Margie* costs $2.50 undressed. The yarn kit to knit or crochet (with the instructions) costs only 60¢. The little hand-knit suit costs $2.95.

This doll is brand new and we named her *Vicky.* She is a 12 inch teen-age doll with an extensive wardrobe. *Vicky* is wearing a beautiful ballerina costume. The bodice is tight fitting and the skirt has four tiers of sheer net.

Now Miss Sharon will entertain you for a brief intermission, singing "I Am A Mary Hoyer Doll."

We would now like to present the "Wedding of the Mary Hoyer Doll." While the mothers of the bride and groom walked down the aisle, a hush fell over the chapel and the soloist was heard singing "I Love You Truly." The mothers' gowns are sheer organza over lavender taffeta. The bodices are trimmed with tiny rhinestones.

The Bridesmaids wear blossom pink net over crisp taffeta. The ruffle on the bottom of the full skirt is made in sheer net and lace. The lace and net are repeated in the bodice.

The Maid of Honor looks lovely in pale green with her luscious red hair.

The adorable little flower girls in blossom pink taffeta under pink net are carrying orange blossoms in their little hand-crocheted baskets.

Here comes the Bride wearing a sheer chantilly lace over white taffeta. Her bodice is snug fitting and her skirt is full to overflowing. The veil is full length of all-over matching lace. Our Bride is carrying a white Bible trimmed with orange blossoms and streamers of satin ribbon.

Here comes the Groom, wearing formal clothes. His white dress shirt is studded with rhinestones.

After the wedding reception, our Bride and Groom flew by jet plane to Los Angeles. The Bride wore a red

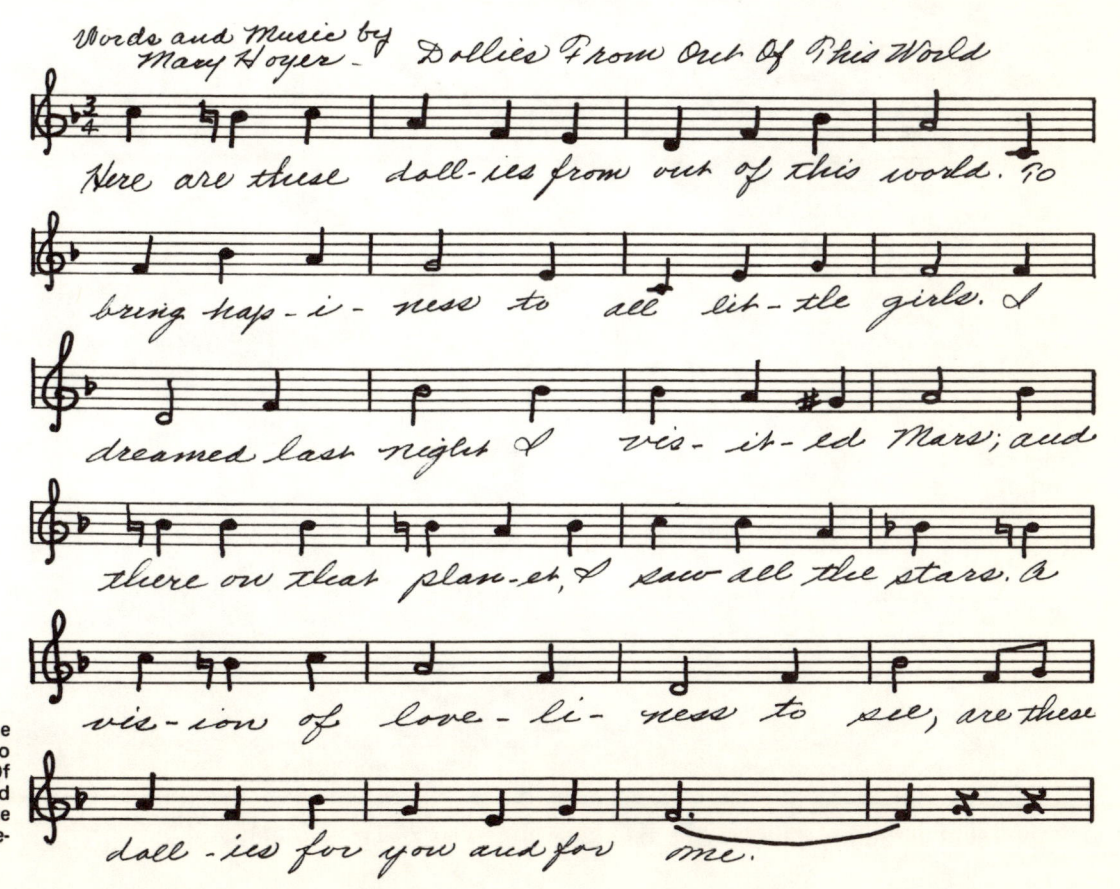

Illustration 84. The words and music to "Dollies From Out Of This World," composed by Mary Hoyer for one of her doll fashion reviews.

velvet fitted coat and hat, over a crisp white taffeta dress. After they arrive in Los Angeles, they will leave by ship, bound for the beautiful exotic isles of Hawaii.

Here is her wardrobe trunk. This is a completely new idea for storing the Mary Hoyer Doll and her extensive wardrobe. It is strongly constructed of wood with a washable covering and has brass hardware, including lock and key. The price is $4.95. Dolly fits snugly in the left side and there is ample room for her clothes in the right compartment, which is complete with hanger bar and a drawer for accessories.

"Our First Nighter" is the name we give to this demure, sheer all nylon nightie and contrasting négligé. The nightie has a fitted bodice with tiny ribbon straps over her shoulders and a full permanent pleated skirt. A full skirt is repeated in the negligee, and the pointed yoke and puffed sleeves are finished with nylon lace and tulle.

This completes our "Wedding Party" and the "Bride's Trousseau." Our Fairy Princess waves her magic wand and takes us back to the planet Mars, where we left our dollies and our judges to pick a winner - - a Miss Universe - - to reign over all the planets for the next year.

I am glad I am not the judge of these beauties from all of the planets. Now, if the judges are ready, may I have the envelope for the winner, please.

The winner is - - - - MISS PLUTO!

Arlene will crown Miss Pluto and escort her down the runway for everyone to see, while our little songstress, Sharon, sings our Miss Universe Song.

Thanks for being a wonderful audience. I hope you have enjoyed our doll fashion show. I surely enjoyed bringing it to you. If you care to see the dolls at a closer range, please feel free to do so. We should be glad to help you with any information you would like to have.

I would like to thank all of the people who helped make the Doll Fashion Show a success: Maybelle Clemenson, our pianist; our judges, Debby Edmonds, Robin Kelly, Lynne Price; Arlene Price who displayed all of the dolls and our little songstress, Sharon Lightcap.

Illustration 85. "Dollies from out of this World" featured in a doll fashion show. Top, left to right: MISS VENUS, MISS MARS, JUPITER'S DARLING, MISS SATURN and MISS URANUS. Front, left to right: MISS EARTH, MISS NEPTUNE and MISS PLUTO. These are all the 18in (45.7cm) Mary Hoyer Dolls.

III. Mary's Dollies

Knit and crochet patterns and instructions from the original books designed exclusively for the Mary Hoyer Doll

Mary Hoyer published nine volumes of *Mary's Dollies* containing over 40 of her exclusive designs for knit and crochet fashions for her 14in (35.6cm) doll. The outfits she designed covered every activity from sports to evening wear and even included several selections for her boy dolls.

Mrs. Hoyer sketched in the backgrounds for many of the photographs appearing in her *Mary's Dollies* books and sometimes she used actual twigs or other material to create the proper scene. The narrative in the books was written by Beaumont, Heller and Sperling Advertising Agency in Reading. This firm also did some of the layout and art work with the remainder being done by Ritter Advertising Agency in Allentown, Pennsylvania.

This chapter includes *all* of the knit and crochet patterns that appeared in *Mary's Dollies* as well as a sewing pattern for two evening gowns.

The following illustrations show some of the different second and third pages that appeared in *Mary's Dollies* books. Sometimes the same page was used in several volumes.

Illustration 86. A view of the Mary Hoyer store at 1008 Penn Street, Reading, Pennsylvania, which appeared in many of the doll pattern books.

As a Companion piece to Miss Hoyer's "Juvenile Styles", this publication is issued to offer suggestions to keep the hands busy with flying needles. Little sister's dolls will need some Fall and Winter clothes for that trip to the summer or winter resorts. On these pages will be the pictures and directions for appropriate clothes that will follow the seasons—from California to Florida—thence to the Adirondacks—to the shimmering ice of Lake Placid, to the Beach at Atlantic City. We sincerely hope that all of these doll clothes will help keep YOUR FAVORITE DOLL the best dressed in the neighborhood.

Sincerely,

Mary Hoyer

Illustration 87. *Mary's Dollies,* Volume 5, Page 2.

VOLUME 5

Mary's Dollies

by

MARY HOYER

Editor and Designer of Juvenile Styles

Price 10c

If you are unable to obtain the exact doll illustrated in the booklet write direct to

JUVENILE STYLES PUBLISHING CO.
1008 PENN STREET · READING, PENNSYLVANIA

Illustration 88. *Mary's Dollies,* Volume 5, Page 3.

VOLUME 6
THE
Mary Hoyer
Doll

by MARY HOYER

Editor and Designer of Juvenile Styles

JUVENILE STYLES PUBLISHING COMPANY

1008 PENN STREET IN READING, PENNSYLVANIA

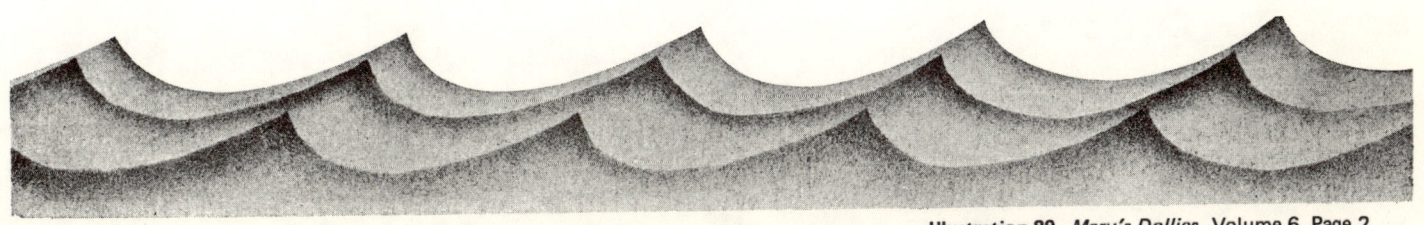

Illustration 89. *Mary's Dollies,* Volume 6, Page 2.

Miss Peteté

This is a story that's fun to do,
    So follow Miss Peteté all the way through.
She went to the circus one day in May,
    Dressed in a knitted ensemble they say,
Her coat was a style that fit just right
    And her hat a creation not too small or too tight.

As she stopped by the box where the tickets were sold,
    Folks all turned their heads and glances stole
For never before had they seen the like—
    A knitted ensemble that fitted just right.

Her ticket in hand she went in to the show
    To see the elephants march by in a row.
The jeweled lady, the clowns and the seals were there.
    As they paraded by without sign of a care.

Then into the ringside the horses came,
    Pranced up and down then back again.
With the ballet dancers on their back astride,
    Twisting and turning away they would ride.

Next came the beauties in bathing suits rare,
    All knitted and purled to make folks stare.
On their float they reclined as they rolled along,
    Smiling and nodding to the happy throng.

Dressed in her habit to ride, Miss Peteté
    Looked so lovely, so quaint and really quite sweet,
She attracted the attention of the bride cross the street
    Who was dressed in white from her head to her feet.

They talked for a minute of knitting and purling,
    And if hair should be straight or slightly curling.
Then both agreed that clothes fitting best
    Were done with two needles, for they stood the test.

Copyrighted 1946 by Mary Hoyer
Printed in U. S. A. by Juvenile Styles Publishing Co.

Illustration 90. *Mary's Dollies,* Volume 10, Page 2.

VOLUME 10

The
"MARY HOYER"
DOLL

by MARY HOYER
Editor and Designer of Juvenile Styles

MARY HOYER DOLL MFG. CO.

1008 PENN STREET IN READING, PENNSYLVANIA

Illustration 91. *Mary's Dollies,* Volume 10, Page 3.

VOLUME 11
Mary's Dollies
by MARY HOYER
Editor and Designer of Juvenile Styles

Juvenile Styles Publishing Company
1013 PENN STREET · READING, PENNSYLVANIA

Illustration 92. *Mary's Dollies,* Volume 11, Page 3.

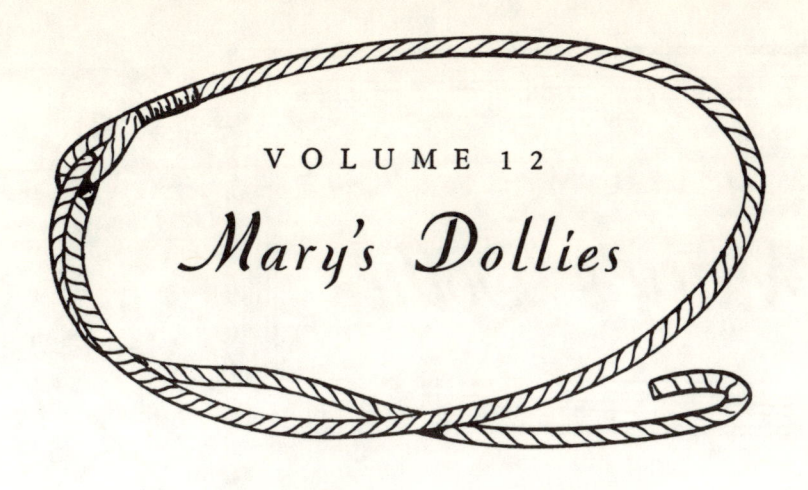

VOLUME 12
Mary's Dollies

by MARY HOYER

Editor and Designer of Juvenile Styles

Juvenile Styles Publishing Company
1008 PENN STREET IN READING, PENNSYLVANIA

Illustration 93. *Mary's Dollies*, Volume 12, Page 3.

VOLUME 13
Mary's Dollies

by MARY HOYER

Editor and Designer of Juvenile Styles

In the past, all of you have found delight in knitting, crocheting and sewing for the Mary Hoyer Doll, and it is with great pride that I introduce the new beautiful plastic twin dolls. They are the exact size in every detail, as the original Mary Hoyer Doll. The little companion for the girl doll, is a handsome, honest-to-goodness boy doll that will not only appeal to the little girls in the family, but will attract the fellows too. He isn't that sissy that most lads associate with girl dolls, but he has boy appeal, and will help teach him how to dress and undress himself, the same as little girls have been taught for generations.

Mary Hoyer

Juvenile Styles Publishing Company
1008 PENN STREET IN READING, PENNSYLVANIA

Illustration 94. *Mary's Dollies*, Volume 13, Page 3.

VOLUME 14
Mary's Dollies

by
MARY HOYER
Editor and Designer of Juvenile Styles

Juvenile Styles Publishing Company
1013 PENN STREET IN READING, PENNSYLVANIA

Illustration 95. *Mary's Dollies,* Volume 14, Page 3.

ABBREVIATIONS USED IN KNITTING AND CROCHET INSTRUCTIONS

The following abbreviations are used throughout the book:

K—Knit	CC—Contrasting Color
P—Purl	L.K.—Lovers Knot
ch—Chain	tr cr—Triple crochet
h d c—Half double crochet	S c—Single crochet
cr—Crochet	d c—Double crochet
sl st—Slip stitch	tog—Together
rnd—Round	st—Stitch
beg—Beginning	sts—Stitches
MC—Main Color	y o—Yarn over
	p—Picot

(asterisk). When this symbol appears, continue working until instructions refer you back to this symbol.

Even means that a row must be worked without increasing or decreasing.

Work means to continue with the stitch as described.

Half Double Crochet—Yarn over, draw up a loop in st, yarn over and draw through all 3 loops on hook.

Slip Stitch—Insert hook in next st, yarn over and draw through both loops on hook.

Blocking—With damp cloth press lightly on right side.

Needle Gauge—When making a garment—work a swatch, using the needles called for to determine whether or not your work measures the same number of stitches to the inch as given in the scale. Change size of needles accordingly.

Illustration 96. This chart shows all the abbreviations used in the following knit and crochet patterns. *Mary's Dollies,* Volume 13, Page 14.

Mary's Dollies

20¢

Illustration 97. Cover for *Mary's Dollies*, Volume 5.

VOLUME No. 5

Goldilocks

... (and her Mother) have decided upon a tour of the U.S.A. (which is really the thing to do this season) so she wears a Princess line dress, just like her mother's, to go shopping for the yarn for the rest of her wardrobe. Princess dress has a Sailor collar with a red, white and blue trim and a Beanie to match. The dress fastens with tiny buttons up the front and will be just the thing to wear on the train when she makes up her mind JUST where she is going.

Illustration 98. No. 750. *Mary's Dollies*, Volume 5, Page 4.

No. 750

Princess Dress and Beret

NEEDLES—1 pair No. 3 bone.
MATERIAL—1 ounce Kashmire Sports, 5 small pearl buttons.
GAUGE—7½ sts to 1 inch.

DRESS

Back—Cast on 50 sts, K 3 rows. Next row, P 16, K 1, P 16, K 1, P 16. K back. Repeat these 2 rows for 7 more rows. Next K row, K 2 tog, K 10, K 2 tog, K 5, K 2 tog, K 8, K 2 tog, K 5, K 2 tog, K 10, K 2 tog. Work 3 rows even. Make 4 more decreased rows, every 4th row (20 sts), having decreases come directly above those of previous row. Work even until piece measures 3 inches from beginning. Bind off 2 sts at beg of the next 2 rows. Work even for 1¼ inches (12 rows). Bind off 2 sts at beg of the next 4 rows, bind off remaining 8 sts for back of neck.

Right Front—Cast on 26 sts, K 3 rows. Next row, P 12, K 1, P 10, K 3 (border). K back. P 1 row, K 1 row for 7 rows, always keeping last 3 sts K on purled rows, for border. Make decreases as follows: K 9, K 2 tog, K 5, K 2 tog, K 6, K 2 tog. Work 3 rows even. Make decreases in same manner 3 more times, having decreases come directly above those of previous rows. (14 sts). Work even until piece measures 3 inches from beginning. Bind off 2 sts at underarm. Discontinue to K 1 st on Purled side. Work even for 12 rows. Bind off 3 sts at neck edge, K 2 tog at beg and end of every row at neck edge until you have 7 sts. Bind off 2 sts at beg of the next 2 rows at shoulder and continue to K 2 tog at beg and end at neck edge. Work left front to correspond. Sew shoulder seams.

Collar—Skip 2 sts, on wrong side, with white yarn, pick up 29 sts around neck to within 2 sts on other side. K 2, P back, K last 2 sts. Next row, *K 2, inc 1 st, repeat from *across row. K 1 row, P 1 row, always knitting first and last 2 sts on purled rows for border, for 4 rows, K 3 rows, bind off loosely.

Sleeves—Pick up 14 center sts, P back. Pick up 2 sts, K 1 row, P 1 row picking up 2 sts, at end of every row, until all sts are picked up (26 sts), P back. K 1 row, P 1 row. On next row, dec 7 sts spaced at equal distances apart, K 3 rows, bind off. Overcast collar with red, break thread. With blue begin at end of red and overcast in same manner. Sew on 5 tiny pearl buttons, buttons are pushed thru border on right side for buttonholes. Sew up side seams and sleeves.

PANTIES

Cast on 22 sts, K 1, P 1 for 4 rows. K 1 row increasing 5 sts, P 1 row, K 1 row for 1¼ inches. Bind off 4 sts at beg of the next 6 rows. On center 3 sts, K 1 row, P 1 row for 4 rows. Cast on 4 sts at beginning of the next 6 rows (27 sts). K 1 row, P 1 row, for 1¼ inches. Dec 5 sts, K 1, P 1 for 4 rows, bind off. Sew up panties. With embroidering needle tape yarn thru top of panties and tie. S c around pantie legs.

DOLL BERET

Ch 4, join, work 6 s c in ring, work 2 s c in each st, until you have 21 sts. Inc in every 7th st, until you have 49 sts. Work even until you have 11 rows. Work 1 row with white, one row with red, one row with white. Pin to wig of Doll.

Reprinted from *Mary's Dollies*, Volume 5, Page 5.

Julianna

. . . has decided on a little skiing at Sun Valley and is wearing this very smart Ski Suit and cap to match. The vest carries out the Norwegian motif and adds a dash of color. The wrists and ankles are snug fitting and the cap is snug fitting so it won't blow off while she is doing a Christiana down the mountainside.

56   Illustration 99. No. 751. *Mary's Dollies*, Volume 5, Page 6.

No. 751

Ski Suit

NEEDLES—1 set No. 4 or 3¾ Double Pointed Needles, American Standard.

MATERIAL—1 two ounce skein Knitting Worsted, 2 yards of Contrasting Shades for Embroidering, 10 small pearl buttons.

GAUGE—6 sts to 1 inch.

SKI PANTS

Cast on 32 sts, 10 sts on 1st needle, 10 sts on 2nd needle, 12 sts on 3rd needle. K 2, P 2 for 1 inch. Inc 8 sts, about every 4th st, 40 sts. K plain for 1¼ inches. Put 20 sts on st holder, cast on 8 sts for crotch; on these 28 sts, K 4¾ inches. Cuff: K 2 sts tog until you have 16 sts, K 2, P 2 for 1 inch. Put 20 sts on 3 needles, pick up 8 sts on crotch, work to correspond to other leg.

JACKET

Cast on 16 sts (tightly) for back, P 1 row, K 1 row, for 1¼ inches, increasing 2 sts on each side. Bind off 2 sts on each side for underarm (16 sts), work even for 1 inch. On next Purled row, P 5, bind off 6 sts, P 5. Put 5 sts on st holder, on other 5 sts, K 1 row, P 1 row for 5 rows. Cast on 10 sts at neck edge, work 1 inch even. Cast on 2 sts for underarm. Work even for 1¼ inches decreasing 2 sts ½ inch apart at seam end. On next row, at seam end, bind off 4 sts, K across row. At beginning of next row, bind off 3 sts. K 2 sts tog at beginning and end of every row, until 2 sts remain, draw together and work in end. Pick up 5 sts at other shoulder and K 1 row, P 1 row for 4 rows. At neck edge cast on 3 sts. Work even for 1 inch. Cast on 2 sts for underarm. Work 1¼ inches even, decreasing 2 sts at seam end, ½ inch apart. Bind off tightly. Band at neck: Skip 3 sts from wide end and pick up 24 sts, K 2, P 2 for 4 rows, bind off. Chain 3 sts at front of neck band for buttonhole. Sleeves: Pick up 3 center sts, P back, pick up 1 st, turn, K 1, inc 1 st in each of the next 3 sts, pick up 1 st. Pick up 1 st at end of each row (20 sts). Now K 1 row, P 1 row ½ inch, dec 1 st on each side. Work 1 inch even, dec 1 st on each side. Work even until sleeve measures 2½ inches from underarm (16 sts). K 2, P 2 for 5 rows, bind off.

HOOD

Cast on 36 sts, K 1 row, P 1 row for 1½ inches. Bind off 11 sts on each side, on center 14 sts, K for 1 inch. On next row, dec 4 sts, work ½ inch even. Bind off tightly. Pick up 36 sts on front of hood, on wrong side and K back. P 1 row, K 1 row for 6 rows. Bind off. Sew up seams. Embroider as shown on illustration. Sew on buttons. Buttons are pushed thru knitted sts. Sew up seams in back of hood and embroider back of hood to match front of jacket. Make a small bow of green satin ribbon and sew at bottom of hood. Pin to hair on each side of front.

Arlene

... WELL!!!! The ball must have landed on the beach at some seaside resort—and whether it be Atlantic City, Asbury Park or Newport your doll will be the best dressed there in this four piece ensemble. Beach Hat and Cape fairly out-do themselves to say nothing of the two button Bra TOP and sleek panties. King Neptune will come right out of the briny deep to see just what is making all the mermaids so discontented. Here, truly, is a PICTURE for DAVY JONES' LOCKER.

58 Illustration 100. No. 752. *Mary's Dollies*, Volume 5, Page 8.

No. 752

Bathing Ensemble

NEEDLES—1 pair American Standard No. 3.
MATERIAL—1 one ounce ball of 3 fold Saxony, 2 small pearl buttons.
GAUGE—7½ sts to 1 inch.

PANTIES

Cast on 24 sts, K 1, P 1 for 4 rows. K 1 row increasing 5 sts, P 1 row, K 1 row for 1½ inches. Bind off 4 sts at beginning of the next 6 rows. On Center 5 sts, K 1 row, P 1 row for 6 rows. Cast on 4 sts at beginning of the next 6 rows (29 sts). K 1 row, P 1 row, for 1½ inches. On next K row, dec 5 sts. K 1, P 1 for 4 rows, bind off. Sew up sides of panties and work 1 row of s c around each leg.

BRA

Cast on 18 sts, K 3 rows. Cast on 4 sts, K 4, P back. Cast on 4 sts. K 1 row, P 1 row, always keeping first and last 4 sts K on P side (sleeve). Work even until piece has 18 rows (9 ribs) at sleeve edges. On right side, K 7, bind off 12, K 7. Work on these 7 sts for 12 rows (6 ribs). Now inc 1 st at neck edge at beg of every row until you have 15 sts. Work even and K first 2 sts on Purled rows for border. When you have 6 rows (3 ribs) from neck edge, bind off 4 sts (sleeve) K 3 rows, bind off. Work other shoulder and front to correspond. Work 1 row of s c around neck. Sew tog at underarms. Sew on buttons; push thru knitted sts.

CAPE

Cast on 32 sts, K 2 rows. Row 3—K 5, *inc 1 st, K 1, repeat from *across row to within last 5 sts, K 5 sts. Row 4—K 1 row even. Row 5—K 3, *Y O, K 2 tog, repeat from *across, ending with K 2. Row 6—K back. Repeat these 6 rows, 2 more times. On last row of open pattern end row with K 3 instead of K2. K 2 rows. K 14, inc 1 st in each of the next 13 sts, K 28, inc 1 st in each of the next 13 sts, K 14 sts. Now K 1 row, P 1 row for 3 inches, always knitting first and last 3 sts on purled rows, increasing every 6th row each side on 4th st. K 6 rows (3 ribs), bind off on wrong side.

HOOD

Cast on 22 sts, K 1 row, P 1 row, always knitting last 3 sts on purled rows for border, until work measures 3½ inches (25 ridges). On next P row, P 17, turn. K back. P 15, turn (always K back), P 13, P 11, P 9, P 7, P 5, P 3. On next row, starting at back, P 4, K back. P 6 (always K back), P 8, P 10, P 12, P 14, P 16, K back. P across row, ending with K 3. K 1 row, P 1 row, for 3½ inches, bind off. Fold and sew seam up back. Sew hood to cape gathering a little. Make a chain about 8 inches, tie thru cape at front. With embroidering needle tape a piece of yarn thru top of panties and tie at back.

Reprinted from *Mary's Dollies*, Volume 5, Page 9.

Annabelle

... Warmer climates beckon and now we find our lady of fashion on the Miami Golf Course (after a brief stay at Pinehurst, N. C. where she won a trophy). She is wearing a two-piece suit, skirt and jacket and if you notice the jacket buttons down the front and has short sleeves that give plenty of elbow room for that stance and swing. Keep your eye on the Ball!

Illustration 101. No. 753. *Mary's Dollies,* Volume 5, Page 10.

No. 753

Sport Suit

NEEDLES—1 pair American Standard No. 3.

MATERIAL—1 two-ounce ball Sport yarn.

GAUGE—7 sts to 1 inch.

BLOUSE

Cast on 20 sts, K 1, P 1, for 5 rows. K 1 row, increasing 6 sts at equal distances apart. P 1 row, K 1 row, until piece measures 1½ inches from start. Bind off 2 sts on each side for underarm. Work even for 1 inch. K 5 sts (put on safety pin) bind off 12 sts for back of neck, K 5. On these 5 sts, work 5 rows for shoulder, cast on 8 sts for front, K back. On purled rows always K last 3 sts for border at front. Work even for 1 inch. At armhole edge cast on 3 sts, work even for 1¼ inches. On next K row dec 3 sts. K 1, P 1, for 5 rows, bind off. Work other side to correspond.

SLEEVES

On right side, pick up 6 center sts, P back, pick up 2 sts, turn, K 2, inc 1 st in each of the next 6 sts, pick up 2 sts. Pick up 2 sts at end of each row (30 sts). K 1 row, P 1 row for 2 rows. On next K row dec 6 sts. K 1, P 1 for 4 rows, bind off.

NECK BAND

Pick up 34 sts, K 1, P 1 for 4 rows, bind off.

SKIRT

With No. 3 needles, cast on 110 sts, K 3 rows. P 1 row, K 1 row for 3 rows. Next row, *K 8, K 2 tog, repeat from *across row. Work 3 rows even. K 7, K 2 tog. Now dec every 4th row, having 1 st less between each dec, until you have 44 sts. Work 4 rows even. K 1, P 1 for 5 rows, bind off.

PANTS

Cast on 24 sts, K 1, P 1 for 4 rows. K 1 row increasing 5 sts, P 1 row, K 1 row for 1½ inches. Bind off 4 sts at beg of the next 6 rows. On center 5 sts, K 1 row, P 1 row for 6 rows. Cast on 4 sts at beginning of the next 6 rows (29 sts). K 1 row, P 1 row, for 1½ inches. Dec 5 sts, K 1, P 1 for 4 rows, bind off. Sew up seams on blouse and sew buttons on left side. Push buttons thru knitted sts. Sew up skirt and panties. With embroidering needle tape yarn thru top of panties and tie. Finish skirt in same manner. S c around panties.

Olga

... *Lake Placid where Olga is called upon to do the most intricate Skating Ballet. She pirouettes and whirls on the ice like a sprite. Her tours are even more beautiful when the ruffled skirt she is wearing whirls about her. She carries a tiny muff and wears a cloche with an enormous pom-pom on top. The jacket has a bit of Angora trim and is very NEW. Even her instructor applauded the end of the scene and complimented Olga on her gorgeous four piece skating ensemble.*

Illustration 102. No. 754. *Mary's Dollies*, Volume 5, Page 12.

No. 754

Skating Outfit

1 Bone Crochet Hook, size 2.
MATERIAL—1 two-ounce ball Sport yarn, 24 yards of Angora,
4 small pearl buttons.
GAUGE—7 sts to 1 inch.

SKIRT

Ch 36 sts to measure 5½ inches. Row 1—Work 1 d c in 3rd ch from hook, *2 d c in next ch, 1 d c in next ch, repeat from *across row, ch 3, turn. Row 2—Repeat row 1. Row 3—Work 2 d c in each st, ch 3, turn. Row 4—*Work 1 d c in each of the first 3 sts, 2 d c in next st, repeat from *across row, join with a sl st, ch 3, turn. Row 5—*Work 1 d c in each of the next 6 sts, 2 d c in next st, repeat from *across row, join with a sl st, ch 3, turn. Rows—6 and 7—inc in every 8th st.

Work 1 row of s c around top of skirt (34 sts). Ch 1, turn, work another row of s c around, ch 1, turn. Work 2 more rows, increasing 4 s c in each row. Work 4 more rows even. (42 sts, 8 rows).

Ch 1, turn, work 1 s c in each of the next 9 sts, ch 1, turn. Work 8 more rows. *Ch 1, turn, work 4 s c in next 4 sts, repeat from * 4 more rows. Ch 1, turn, s c over 2 sts for slanting shoulder. Fasten thread at other end of front and work to correspond.

BACK

Skip 2 sts for underarm and work over 20 sts for back (leaving 2 sts on each side for underarm), for 11 rows. Ch 1, s c over 4 s c, ch 1, turn, work over 2 s c for slanting shoulder. Work 2 rows on other shoulder to correspond. Sew shoulder seams.

SLEEVES

Fasten thread at center of underarm and work 26 s c around armhole, join with a sl st, ch 1. Row 2—Work 3 s c in first 3 sts, 3 h d c (Y O needle, insert needle thru next st, Y O needle, draw thru, Y O needle draw thru all sts), in next 3 sts. Work 2 d c in each st to within the last 6 sts. Work 3 h d c in next 3 sts, 3 s c in last 3 sts, join with a sl st, ch 1. Row 3—Work same as row 2, but do not increase. Row 4—Work 1 row of s c in every other st, join with a sl st. Work 1 row of s c with Angora around bottom of skirt and sleeves. Work 1 row of s c around neck and right front, working 4 loops for buttonholes, fasten at left neck edge. Sew on 4 buttons.

PANTIES

Ch 36, work 1 s c in 2nd ch from hook, 1 s c in each ch to end of row. Row 2—Ch 3, turn, work 1 d c in each st, increasing 5 d c across row. Repeat row 2, 2 more times, join with a sl st, ch 3, turn. Work 3 rows of d c without increasing, join with a sl st. Sl st 1 more st. *Ch 2, turn, work 3 d c in next 3 sts, ch 2 turn, repeat from * 2 more times, break thread. Fold panties in half and sew to other side. With Angora, work 26 s c around each leg.

HAT

Ch 4, join, ch 3, work 13 d c in ring, join with a sl st, ch 3. Work 2 d c in each st, join with a sl st, ch 3. Rows 3 & 4—*Work 1 d c in each of the next 3 sts, 2 d c in next st, repeat from *for 2 rows (49 sts), join ch 1. Row 5—inc in every 6th st, Row 6—work even. Row 7—Work 1 s c in each of the next 5 sts, 5 h d c in next 5 sts, d c around row to within last 10 sts. Work 5 h d c in next 5 sts, 5 s c in last 5 sts. This is front. With Angora, work 1 row of s c around cap.

POMPOM

With a small card board, 1¼ inches in width, wrap yarn around cardboard 36 times, sew at one end, cut at other. Make 2 more in same manner, sew 3 pieces together, trim. Sew at front of cap. Lace up panties at back with a piece of yarn.

MUFF

Ch 12 sts, loosely, join, ch 1, work 1 s c in each ch, join with a sl st, ch 3. Row 2—*Work 1 d c in next st, 2 d c in next st, repeat from *around, join with a sl st, ch 3. Row 3—Work 1 d c in each st, join, ch 1. Row 4—Work 1 s c in first st, *skip 1 st, 1 s c in next st, repeat from *around, join. Ch 12, sl st in same st. Work 1 row of s c with Angora on each end.

Reprinted from *Mary's Dollies*, Volume 5, Page 13.

Mayree

. . . and so out to the race track at Santa Anita, where our heroine dons this three piece suit Bonnet, Jacket and Skirt. If you will notice the suit has a trimming of angora (or contrasting color) and the jacket has the smartest short flared sleeves, —and, if you please, buttons down the front. Bonnet ties under the chin. (Confidentially—right after the races) went to the Brown Derby, was discovered, given a movie contract and is now making her first picture.

Illustration 103. No. 755. *Mary's Dollies,* Volume 5, Page 14.

No. 755

Party Frock

1 Bone Crochet Hook, size 2

MATERIAL—1 two-ounce ball Sport yarn, 20 yards of Angora, 4 small pearl buttons.

GAUGE—7 sts to 1 inch s c.

JACKET

Back—Ch 19 sts, s c in 2nd ch from hook, s c to end of ch, ch 1, turn. Row 2—Inc 2 s c in next row. Row 3—Work even. Row 4—Inc 2 s c. Rows 5, 6, 7 & 8—Work even (22 s c). Ch 1, turn, *s c, to within last 2 sts, ch 1, turn, repeat from *once, ch 1, turn, work even until you have 18 rows from beginning. Ch 1, turn, s c over 4 sts for shoulder for 1 row. Ch 1, turn, work 2 s c for slanting shoulder, break thread. Work 1½ rows on other shoulder to correspond.

Front—Ch 11 sts, s c in 2nd ch from hook, s c to end of ch, ch 1, turn. Row 2—Inc 1 st. Row 3—Work even. Row 4—Inc 1 st. Rows 5, 6, 7, 8 & 9—Work even. Ch 1, turn, s c to within last 3 sts, ch 1, turn, work even until you have 18 rows from beginning. Ch 1, turn, s c over 4 sts for shoulder for 3 rows. Ch 1, turn, work 2 s c for slanting shoulder, break thread. Work another front exactly in same manner. Sew to back at shoulders and underarm.

Frill at sleeve—Fasten thread at center of underarm and work 26 s c around armhole. Row 2—Work 3 s c in first 3 sts, 3 h d c (Y O needle, insert needle thru next st, Y O needle, draw thru, Y O needle draw thru all sts), in next 3 sts. Work 2 d c in each st to within the last six sts. Work 3 h d c in next 3 sts, 3 s c in last 3 sts, join with a sl st, ch 1. Row 3—Work same as row 2, but do not increase, break thread. With Angora, work 1 row of s c around frill at sleeve. Work 1 row around jacket, starting at bottom of right front and ending at top of left front. Work 4 loops of ch 3, for buttonholes. Sew buttons on left side.

SKIRT

Ch 34 sts, to measure 5½ inches, work 1 s c in 2nd ch from hook, work 1 s c to end of row. Row 2—Ch 1, turn, work 1 s c in each st. Row 3—Repeat Row 2. Row 4—Ch 1, turn, *work 1 s c in next 3 sts, 2 s c in next st, repeat from *across row, thus increasing every 4th st. Row 5 & 6—Inc in every 6th st. Rows 7 & 8—Inc in every 8th st. Row 9—Inc in every 7th st. Rows 10, 11 & 12—Inc in every 12th st. Join at beg of row with a sl st, ch 1, turn. Rows 13, 14, 15, 16, 17 & 18—Inc in every 25th st, join. With Angora, s c in each st around skirt.

PANTIES

Ch 36, work 1 s c in 2nd ch from hook, 1 s c in each ch to end of row. Row 2—Ch 3, turn, work 1 d c in each st, increasing 5 d c across row. Repeat row 2, 2 more times, join with a sl st, ch 3, turn. Work 3 rows of d c without increasing, join with a sl st. Sl st 1 more st. *Ch 2, turn, work 3 d c in next 3 sts, repeat from * 2 more times, break thread. Fold panties in half and sew to other side. With Angora, work 26 s c around each leg.

BONNET

Ch 3, join, ch 1, work 7 s c in ring. Row 2—Work 2 s c in each st. Row 3—*Work 1 s c in next st, 2 s c in next st, repeat from *around row. Row 4—*Work 1 s c in each of the next 2 sts, 2 s c in next st, repeat from *around row. Now inc in every 5th st until you have 56 sts around. Work even until you have 15 rows. On 16th row dec 4 sts spaced at equal distances apart. Brim—Ch 1, turn, work 1 s c in each of the next 2 sts, 2 h d c in next 2 sts, *2 d c in next st, 1 d c in next st, repeat from *around to within 18 sts at beginning of row. Work 2 h d c in next 2 sts, 2 s c in next 2 sts, ch 1, turn. Row 2—Work 3 s c in first 3 sts, 2 h d c in next 2 sts, *2 d c in next st, 1 d c in each of the next 4 sts, repeat from *across row to within last 5 sts at beg of row below, 2 h d c in next 2 sts, 2 s c in next 2 sts. Ch 1, turn. Row 3—Repeat row 2. Row 4—Work 1 s c in each of the first 6 sts, 2 h d c in next 2 sts, *2 d c in next st, 1 d c in each of the next 6 sts, repeat from *to within last 9 sts, 2 h d c in next 2 sts, 6 s c in next 6 sts, break thread. Sew cord at beginning of brim. With Angora, work 1 row of s c over cord to end of brim. Sew cord and fasten off Angora. In 2nd row in 3rd st fasten yarn and ch 40 sts on each side of brim to tie.

THE WAVETTE

INSTRUCTIONS ON PAGE 14

Mary's Dollies

VOLUME NO. 6

Illustration 104. Cover for *Mary's Dollies*, Volume 6.

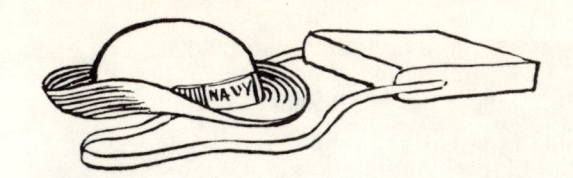

The Wavette

NEEDLES—1 *pair American Standard No. 3.*
MATERIALS—1 *two-ounce ball Navy Sport Yarn—⅛ oz. white sport yarn, 4 small brass buttons.*
GAUGE—7 *sts to 1 inch*, (*Measure garment on Doll as you make it*).

☆ JACKET

Back—Cast on 28 sts, K 3 rows, *P 1 row, K 1 row for ½ inch, K 2 tog at each end of next row, repeat from *once 24 sts. Work 1 inch even. Inc 1 st at each end and work even until piece measures 2½ inches from bottom. Bind off 3 sts at beg of next 2 rows for underarm. Work even for 1¼ inches. K 6 (put on safety pin), bind off 8 sts (tightly) for back of neck, K 6, on these 6 sts, P 1 row, K 1 row, for 7 rows. Cast on 7 sts (lapel). On right side of work, Row 1—P 7, K 6. Row 2—P 6, K 7. Row 3—P 2 tog, P 5, inc 1 st, K 5. Row 4—P 7, K 6. Row 5—P 2 tog, P 4, inc 1 st, K 6. Row 6—P 8, K 5. Row 7—P 2 tog, P 3, inc 1 st, K 7. Row 8—P 9, K 4. Row 9—P 2 tog, P 2, inc 1 st, K 8. Row 10—P 10, K 3. Row 11—P 2 tog, P 1, inc 1 st, K 9. Row 12—P 11, K 2. Row 13—P 2 tog, inc 1 st, K 10. Cast on 3 st for underarm. Continue front keeping first 2 sts on Purled rows K. Work 4 rows even, dec 1 st at seam end. Work even and make 2 increases to correspond to back. Second Revere—Pick up 6 sts from st holder, P 1 row, K 1 row for 6 rows, cast on 7 sts. On next row. K 7, P 6, then K 6, P 7, next row, K 7, P 6. K 5, inc 1 st, P 5, P 2 tog. Follow pattern back. Now K 6, inc, P 4, P 2 tog. Continue revere in this manner; on right side inc 1 st and P 2 tog at end of row, follow pattern on next row. K 2 sts border, P across. Cast on 3 sts on next row, K 12, K 2 tog, Y O (buttonhole), K 2. Continue same as Left Front, making 4 buttonholes in same manner every 6th row, bind off.

Collar—Holding wrong side of work toward you, skip 7 sts of revere, on each side, pick up 22 sts, K 2, P 18, K 2. On next row inc 1 st on 3rd st, K across and inc 1 st in 3rd st from end. Next row, K 2, P across, K last 2 sts. Inc 1 st on 3rd st, K across and inc 1 st in 3rd st from end. K 2 rows, bind off.

Sleeves—Pick up 20 center sts, P back. Pick up 3 sts at end of next 2 rows (26 sts). P 1 row, K 1 row and dec 1 st at end of every 6th row, until you have 16 sts, 4 inches. K 2 rows, bind off.

☆ SKIRT

Cast on 90 sts, K 3 rows. P 1 row, K 1 row, P 1 row. Next row, *K 8, K 2 tog, repeat from *across row. Work 5 rows even. K 7, K 2 tog across row. Now dec every 6th row, having 1 st less between every dec, until you have 45 sts, K 1 st, P 1 st for 5 rows, bind off.

☆ PANTS

Cast on 24 sts, K 1 st, P 1 st for 4 rows. K 1 row increasing 5 sts, P 1 row, K 1 row for 1½ inches. Bind off 4 sts at beg of the next 6 rows. On center 5 sts, K 1 row, P 1 row for 6 rows. Cast on 4 sts at beginning of the next 6 rows (29 sts). K 1 row, P 1 row, for 1½ inches. Dec 5 sts, K 1, P 1 for 4 rows. Bind off. Sew up skirt half way, fold panties in half and sew. With embroidering needle tape yarn thru top of panties and tie. Finish skirt in same manner. S c around panties.

☆ VESTIE

With white, cast on 3 sts, P back. K 1 row, P 1 row and inc 1 st at beg and end of every K row, until you have 15 sts. Cast on 8 sts at beg of the next 2 rows. K 1 row, P 1 row, bind off. Tie at back of neck with a piece of yarn. Draw a small piece of gros grain ribbon or Navy Yarn thru vestie tie a knot and tuck in ends under Jacket.

☆ HAT

Ch 3, join, ch 1, work 7 s c in ring. Row 2—Work 2 s c in each st. Row 3—*Work 1 s c in next st, 2 s c in next st, repeat from *around row. Row 4—*Work 1 s c in each of the next 2 sts, 2 s c in next st, repeat from *around row. Row 5—Inc in every 3rd st. Now inc in every 5th st until you have 52 sts. Work even until you have 16 rows. Next row dec 5 sts. Work 1 row even, break thread. With 2 strands of Navy, work in same direction increasing in every 3rd st for 1 row. Work 4 rows even. On next row, inc 2 sts on front spaced about 15 sts apart. Work 2 more rows even, break thread at center back. Turn up back and sides and turn down at front.

☆ BAG

Ch 14 sts, work 1 s c in 2nd ch from hook, work 1 s c across row, ch 1, turn. Work 5 more rows even. Dec 1 st at end of next 2 rows. Work 1 row even. Make other side in same manner. Ch 80, to measure 12 inches (do not stretch ch), join, ch 1, work 1 s c in each ch, do not twist ch. Sew this piece between the 2 side pieces, leaving surplus for shoulder strap. (When dressing Doll, work from feet upward, not over head).

Reprinted from *Mary's Dollies*, Volume 6, Page 14.

Judy . . . *and her mother are about to attend a party in honor of some of the representative Dolls from other nations. Just every-one will BE THERE, so Judy and her mother have decided they will look their very best in their lace Frocks fashioned with a square neck relieved with a velvet ribbon. Color—Pink.*

Illustration 106. Detail of the sleeve of the lace dress. *Mary's Dollies,* Volume 6, Page 4.

Lace Party Dress

1 *Steel Crochet Hook, size 10.*
MATERIAL—1 *ball No. 30 Mercerized Cotton or Pearl Cotton.*
GAUGE—12 *d c to 1 inch. (Measure garment on Doll as you make it)*

☆ DRESS

Starting at bottom ch 180, join with a sl st, ch 3, work 1 d c in each ch, join with a sl st. Row 2—Work 1 d c in each of the next 12 d c, *ch 3, skip 2 d c, sl st in next st, ch 3, sl st in same st (a pico made), ch 4, skip 2 d c, 1 d c in each of the next 13 d c, repeat from *around row, ending row with an open pattern, sl st in ch 3 at beg of row. Row 3—Ch 3, make a dec as follows: wrap Y O needle, insert needle in next d c, draw thru, draw thru next d c, draw thru 3 loops, draw thru 2 loops, 1 d c in each of the next 8 d c, make a dec. *Ch3, sl st in center of ch 3 of row below, ch 5, sl st in 2nd ch of next ch 4, ch 4, make a dec, d c in next 9 d c, make a dec, repeat from *ending row with an open pattern, sl st in ch 3 at beg of row. Row 4—Ch 3, work 2 d c in next 2 d c, ch 3, skip 2 d c, pico in next st, ch 4, skip 2 d c, work 3 d c in next 3 d c. *Ch 3, pico in center of ch 5, ch 4, 3 d c in next 3 d c, ch 3, skip 2 d c, pico in next st, ch 4, skip 2 d c, 3 d c in next 3 d c, repeat from *around row, join.

Row 5—Ch 3, work 2 d c in next 2 d c, *ch 3, sl st in center of ch 3 of row below, ch 5, sl st in 2nd ch of next ch 4, ch 4, 3 d c in next 3 d c, repeat from *around row, join.

Row 6—Ch 3, 2 d c in next 2 d c, ch 2, s c in center of ch 5 of row below, ch 2, work 3 d c in next 3 d c. Ch 3, pico in center of ch 5 of row below, ch 4, *3 d c in next 3 d c, ch 2, s c in center of ch 5, ch 2, 3 d c in next 3 d c. Ch 3, pico in center of ch 5, ch 4, repeat from *around row, join.

Row 7—Ch 3, work 10 d c in next 10 sts, *Ch 3, sl st in center of ch 3, ch 5, sl st in 2nd ch of ch 4, ch 4, work 11 d c, repeat from *around row, join with a sl st, ch 3. Rows 8 to 18—Follow pattern decreasing 1 d c at beg and end of every d c group on the 8th, 11th and 14th rows. Work 4 more rows even, join with a sl st. On 19th row, sl st over 3 d c, ch 3, work 2 d c in next 2 d c, follow pattern around row, ending row with 3 d c, ch 3, turn. Row 20—Follow pattern and make 1 dec in center of d c group.

Remainder of dress is made with 4 d c between open patterns. Work back and forth following pattern until you have 25 rows from beg. Work over 3 d c groups and 2 open patterns for back, for 7 rows decreasing 1 d c at armhole edge at end of 2 rows. Work 2 d c on each side of 1 open pattern at armhole side for 4 rows. On next half row for slanting shoulder, ch 3, work 1 d c in next st, ch 3, sl st in center of next ch, break thread. Fasten thread at 3 d c group at underarm and work to correspond to other side of back. Skip an open pattern for underarm and work over 5 d c groups and 4 open patterns for front for 4 rows. Work shoulder same as for back for 6 rows, work ½ row same as back. Sew shoulder seams.

Sleeves—See detailed illustration of sleeve on Page No. 15. Ch 35 sts, work 1 d c in 4th ch, d c in each ch to end of row (32 d c). Ch 3, turn, d c to end of row. Ch 3, turn, work 1 d c in each of the next 9 sts, (ch 3, skip 2 d c, pico in next st, ch 4), skip 2 d c, 3 d c in next 3 sts (ch 3, skip 2 d c, pico, ch 4), skip 2 d c, d c in each of the next 10 d c. Work 1 more row following open pattern same as for dress, increasing 2 d c in each of the 3 d c groups. Ch 1, turn, sl st over 5 d c, ch 3, follow pattern across but do not inc in first and last d c groups, working only to within last 5 d c. Row 6—Ch 2, dec 1 st, follow pattern, end row with 1 d c in last 2 d c, do not d c in the ch 3. Dec in this manner at ends and continue to inc in center group, until you have 8 rows from beginning. Work last row as follows: Ch 3, sl st in ch 5, ch 3, s c in first d c, then h d c in next st, now dec every other st to within last 2 d c, work 1 h d c, s c, ch 3 sl st in ch 5, ch 3, s c in last st. Sew up sleeves and insert into armhole, having a little fullness at top.

Reprinted from *Mary's Dollies*, Volume 6, Page 5.

May-Belle

The first person they met was May-Belle the Majorette just in from a Bond Rally, at which her dashing costume and vivacity was such an inspiration that her adoring public over-subscribed. Her costume consists of:

A white military jacket with Brass buttons and epaulettes fringed with RED. A white skirt and white panties are worn with the jacket—then to top it all off smartly there is a military hat with a huge tassel of yarn falling down the front . . . and . . . Oh, yes . . . we almost forgot . . . THE BATON . . . which May-Belle twirls as she high steps down the street. (The special boots made for May-Belle may be purchased.)

☆ ☆ ☆ ☆

Illustration 107. *Mary's Dollies*, Volume 6, Page 6.

The Majorette

1 Bone Crochet Hook, size 2 or 3.
MATERIAL—1 two ounce ball of Sport Yarn, White, 10 yards of Red Sport Yarn, 10 small brass buttons.
GAUGE—6 sts to 1 inch. (Measure garment on Doll as you make it).

☆ JACKET

Back—Ch 19 sts, s c in 2nd ch from hook, s c to end of ch, ch 1, turn. Inc 1 st at beg of the next 4 rows (22 sts). Work even until you have 11 rows. Ch 1, turn, *s c to within last 2 sts, ch 1, turn, repeat from *once. Work even until you have 21 rows from beg. Ch 1, turn, s c over 4 sts for shoulder for 1 row, ch 1, turn, work 2 s c for slanting shoulder, break thread. Work 1½ rows on other shoulder to correspond.

Left Front—Ch 14, s c in 2nd ch from hook, s c to end of ch, ch 1, turn. Row 2—Inc 1 st. Row 3—Work even. Row 4—Inc 1 st (15 sts). Work even until you have 11 rows. Ch 1, turn, s c to within last 2 sts, ch 1, turn, work even until you have 20 rows from beginning and make 2 more increases at front edge, spaced a few rows apart. Ch 1, turn, s c over 4 sts, for 3 rows, ch 1, turn, work 2 s c for slanting shoulder, break thread.

Right Front—Ch 7, work 1 s c in 2nd ch, s c to end of row, ch 1, turn, work even until you have 11 rows. Work to within 2 s c of next row and work even on 4 sts, until you have 23 rows. Ch 1, turn, work 2 s c for slanting shoulder, break thread. Sew shoulders together and sides. Work 24 s c around armhole for 2 rows.

Epaulets—Ch 6, s c 1 st in 2nd ch and s c to end of row, ch 1, turn, work even until you have 7 rows, dec 1 st at end of next 2 rows, break thread. Starting at right front work 1 s c around jacket making ch 3 loops for buttonholes and place wide end of epaulets over shoulder seams, cr to neck edge.

Fringe—Cut yarn 1 inch long, with 2 strands, tape thru each st around epaulets as shown on illustration.

☆ SKIRT

Ch 34 sts, to measure 5½ inches, work 1 s c in 2nd ch from hook, work 1 s c to end of row. Row 2—Ch 1, turn, work 1 sc in each st. Row 3 & 4—Repeat Row 2. Row 5—Ch 1, turn, *work 1 s c in next 4 sts, 2 s c in next st, repeat from *across row, thus increasing every 5th st. Rows 6 & 7—inc in every 6th st. Rows 8, 9 & 10—Inc in every 9th st. Rows 11 & 12—Inc in every 12th st. Join at beg of row with a sl st, ch 1, turn. Rows 13, 14, 15, 16, 17, 18 & 19—Inc in every 25th st, join.

☆ PANTIES

Ch 36, work 1 s c in 2nd ch from hook, 1 s c in each ch to end of row. Row 2—Ch 3, turn, work 1 d c in each st, increasing 5 d c across row. Repeat row 2, 2 more times, join with a sl st, ch 3, turn. Work 3 rows of d c without increasing, join with a sl st. Sl st 1 more st. *Ch 2, turn, work 3 d c in next 3 sts, repeat from *2 more times. Break thread. Fold panties in half and sew to other side. Work 26 s c around each leg.

☆ HAT

Ch 3, join, ch 1, work 7 s c in ring. Row 2—Work 2 s c in each st. Row 3—*Work 1 s c in next st, 2 s c in next st, repeat from *around row. Row 4—*Work 1 s c in each of the next 2 sts, 2 s c in next st, repeat from *around row. Row 5—*Work 1 s c in each of the next 3 sts, 2 s c in next st, repeat from *around row. Now inc in every 5th st, until you have 46 sts. On next row do not inc and pick up back thread only for 1 row. Work 6 rows even. *Do not break thread but with another strand of yarn, work an extra row half way around hat, increasing 2 sts, break thread, continue with first strand of yarn, work 1 row around, repeat from *4 times, do not have increases come over those of previous row. The extra rows are back of hat. With 2 strands of yarn, work 1 more row of s c around. Chin Strap—Ch 41, s c in 6th ch from hook, s c to end of row, ch 5, sl st in ch at beg of row. Sew 2 buttons at each side of hat when hat is on, fasten loops over buttons. With double stands of yarn, ch 54 sts, sew on crown as shown on illustration. Make a small tassel and sew on top of hat. Sew on buttons and embroider as shown on illustration.

☆ BATON

Ch 3, join, s c in the first single loop nearest the strand of yarn, s c in next 2 loops. Now continue crocheting around and around on 4 sts (the back loop of your previous s c), until piece measures 3 inches. Ch 8 sts for over dolls hand, sl st a few sts below beg of ch.

Reprinted from *Mary's Dollies*, Volume 6, Page 7.

Nadine

. . . who has recently returned from Bataan where she was kept very busy. Now she is instructing a Red Cross Class how to roll bandages and right after the party is giving a lesson in First Aid to some other Dolls. Her costume consists of:

A White dress and Navy Blue cape. Nadine also carries her emergency kit right with her for she is always on the alert.

☆ ☆ ☆ ☆

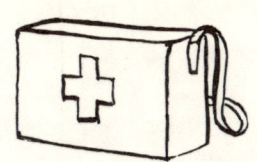

Red Cross Nurse

NEEDLES—1 *pair American Standard No. 3.*
MATERIALS—1 *ounce, Sport Yarn, Navy*—1 *ounce White, 4 yards Red, 5 small pearl buttons.*
GAUGE—7 *sts to 1 inch. (Measure garment on Doll as you make it).*

☆ DRESS

Back—Cast on 50 sts, K 3 rows. P 1 row, K 1 row for 7 rows. Next K row, K 2 tog, K 10, K 2 tog, K 5, K 2 tog, K 8, K 2 tog, K 5, K 2 tog, K 10, K 2 tog. Work 3 rows even. Make 3 more decreased rows, every 4th row (26 sts), having decreases come directly above those of previous row. P 1 row, K 1 row, for 3 rows. Next row, Dec 2 sts. Now K 1, P 1, ribbing for 4 rows. Work even until piece measures 4 inches from beginning. Bind off 3 sts at beg of the next 2 rows. Work even for 1¼ inches (12 rows). Bind off 2 sts at beg of the next 4 rows, bind off remaining 10 sts for back of neck. Right Front—Cast on 26 sts, K 3 rows. Next row, P across, K last 3 sts (border). K back. P 1 row, K 1 row for 7 rows, always keeping last 3 sts K on purled rows for border. Make decreases as follows: K 9, K 2 tog, K 5, K 2 tog, K 6, K 2 tog. P back to within last 3 sts, work buttonhole: Y 0, K 2 tog, K 1 st. K 1 row, P 1 row. Make decreases in same manner, 3 more times (every 4th row) having decreases come directly above those of previous rows, (14 sts). Work 4 more buttonholes every 11th and 12th rows or about 1 inch apart. When piece measures same as for back to ribbing, inc 1 st at seam end and K 1, P 1 for 4 rows. Work even to underarm. Bind off 2 sts at underarm, work even for 12 rows. Bind off 4 sts at neck edge, K 2 tog at beg of every row at neck edge, until you have 7 sts. Bind off 2 sts at beg of the next 2 rows at shoulder and continue to K 2 tog at beg and end at neck edge. Work left front to correspond. Sew shoulder seams. Sew up side seams and sleeves.

Collar—Skip 2 sts, on wrong side, pick up 31 sts around neck to within 2 sts on other side, K 2, P back, K last 2 sts. Next row, *K 2, inc 1 st, repeat from *across row. K 1 row, P 1 row, always knitting first and last 2 sts on purled rows for border, for 4 rows, K 3 rows, bind off loosely.

Sleeves—Pick up 14 center sts, P back, Pick up 2 sts, K 1 row, P 1 row picking up 2 sts, at end of every row, until all sts are picked up (26 sts), P back, K 1 row, P 1 row. On next row, dec 7 sts spaced at equal distances apart, K 3 rows, bind off.

☆ PANTIES

Cast on 24 sts, K 1, P 1 for 4 rows, K 1 row increasing 5 sts, P 1 row, K 1 row for 1½ inches. Bind off 4 sts at beg of the next 6 rows. On center 5 sts, K 1 row, P 1 row for 6 rows. Cast on 4 sts at beginning of the next 6 rows (29 sts). K 1 row, P 1 row for 1½ inches. Dec 5 sts, K 1, P 1 for 4 rows, bind off. Sew up panties. With embroidering needle tape yarn thru top of panties and tie. S c around pantie legs.

☆ CAPE

Cast on 28 sts, K 2 rows. Row 3—K 5, *inc 1st, K 1 st, repeat from *across row to within last 5 sts, K 5 sts. K 2 rows. Next row, K 3, P across, K last 3 sts. Repeat row 3. P 1 row, K 1 row, keeping first 3 sts K on purled rows for 3 rows, on next row, repeat row 3. Work 3 rows even in same manner. Repeat row 3. Now K 1 row, P 1 row for 3½ inches, from start, always knitting first and last 3 sts on purled rows, and inc every 6th row each end on 4th st. K 6 rows (3 ribs), bind off on wrong side. Make a ch st cord to tie cape.

☆ KIT

Ch 14 sts, work 1 s c in 2nd ch from hook, work 1 s c across row, ch 1, turn. Work 5 more rows even. Dec 1 st at end of next 2 rows. Work 1 row even. Make other side in same manner. Ch 50, join, ch 1, s c in each ch, do not twist ch. Sew this piece between the 2 side pieces. Embroider Red Cross as shown on illustration.

☆ CAP

Cast on 48 sts, K 8 rows (4 ribs). Bind off 16 sts at beg of the next 2 rows. *K 2, P across to within last 2 sts, K 2. K across increasing 4 sts, repeat from *2 times, but do not inc. K 3 rows, bind off.

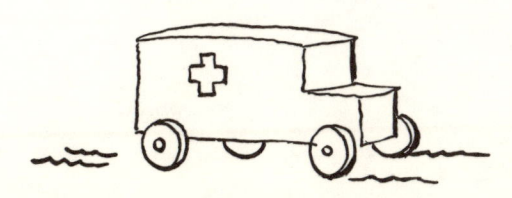

Reprinted from *Mary's Dollies*, Volume 6, Page 9.

Sonja

Sonja is going to show her American Cousins just what the practical garb is for skiing in ICELAND . . . and do the rest of the girls love it. They all feel that they will look well in the Ski-Green ski suit with its protecting hood which will have a concealing effect against the glistening snow and Fir trees of Iceland.

Sonja wears a two piece suit of Ski-Green with a hood edged in Angora. The front is trimmed with a bit of Icelandic Angora Fur in white. Don't forget to note the Ski and Ski Pole she carries. (These may be purchased for a nominal sum.)

✩ ✩ ✩ ✩

Illustration 109. *Mary's Dollies*, Volume 6, Page 10.

Skiing Costume

NEEDLES—1 *set No. 3, Double Pointed Needles, American Standard.*
MATERIAL—1 *two ounce ball Sport Yarn, Ski-Green, 12 yards Angora, White, 4 small pearl buttons.*
GAUGE—7½ *sts to 1 inch. (Measure garment on Doll as you make it).*

☆ JACKET

Cast on 26 sts for back, K 3 rows and P 1 row, K 1 row for 1 inch from start. Dec 1 st on each side, work 1 inch even, inc 1 st on each side, work 2 rows even. Bind off 3 sts at beg of the next 2 rows, work even for 1¼ inches, 12 rows. K 6, put on safety pin, bind off 8, K 6. P 1 row, K 1 row, for 5 rows, cast on 6 sts at neck edge. K 1 row, P 1 row, for 1 inch, cast on 3 sts at underarm, work same as back. Pick up 6 sts on other side, P 1 row, K 1 row, for 6 rows, work to correspond to other side.

Sleeves—Pick up 20 center sts, P back. Pick up 3 sts at end of next 2 rows, 26 sts. P 1 row, K 1 row, for 2 inches. Now dec 1 st at each end and dec 1 st at each end every 4th row, until you have 18 sts, 4 inches, K 2 rows, bind off. With angora, work 1 row around right front and neck, working 4, ch 2 loops for button holes on right front. Sew up underarms and sleeves.

☆ HOOD

Cast on 38 sts, *K 1 row, P 1 row for 3 rows, next row dec 1 st at beg and end of the next row, repeat from *2 times. Work even until piece measures 2 inches. Now K 2 tog at beg and end of every K row, until 12 sts remain, bind off. Cast on 32 sts, work 4 rows even, K 2 tog at beg and end of every K row, until 12 sts remain, bind off. Sew front and back tog having the 12 bound off sts meet. With Angora, start at bottom of cap, with wrong side toward you, pick up an inch on each side and across front (54 sts), K back. P 1 row, K 1 row for 5 rows, bind off loosely. Make a chain with angora 17 inches long. Sew bound off sts to first row on right side of hood and insert the cord when sewing. Sew hood to jacket about 3 sts from fronts.

☆ SKI PANTS

Cast on 40 sts, 12 sts on 1st needle, 12 sts on 2nd needle, 16 sts on 3rd needle, K 2, P 2 for 1 inch. Inc 8 sts, about every 5th st, 48 sts, K plain for 1¾ inches. Put 24 sts on st holder, cast on 8 sts for crotch; on these 32 sts, K 5½ inches. Cuff—K 2 sts tog until you have 16 sts, K 2, P 2 for 1 inch. Put 24 sts on 3 needles, pick up 8 sts on crotch, work to correspond to other leg.

Reprinted from *Mary's Dollies*, Volume 6, Page 11.

Lucretta

Lucretta is the star of a skating show, and hails from Russia. Today she is wearing her most beautiful costume (she had to hurry from the theatre) because the high light of the party is to be one of her dazzling skating routines ... And she's plenty dazzling herself, in her outfit of:

A long sleeved skating costume Fur trimmed in Angora with a headress ... typically "Russe." A pair of knit panties accompanies the costume. Note her Fur Muff. (The skating shoes have been made for her and may be purchased.)

P. S. We forgot to mention that the purpose of the party was to raise funds for the Red Cross. May-Belle auctioned off her costume and now the fund is enriched by $1,000.00. Don't worry! May-Belle's mother had another dress along for her. Now they're all going to the STAGE DOOR CANTEEN to entertain the BOYS.

✩ ✩ ✩ ✩

Skating Costume

1 Bone Crochet Hook, size 2.
MATERIAL—1 two ounce ball Sport Yarn, Turquoise, 20 yards of White Angora, 5 small pearl buttons.
GAUGE—7 sts to 1 inch. (Measure garment on Doll as you make it).

☆ DRESS

Starting at waist line, ch 37 sts to measure 5½ inches, work 1 s c in 2nd ch from hook, work 1 s c in each ch to end of row. Work 5 more rows in same manner. Row 7—*Work 1 s c in each of the first 3 sts, 2 s c in next st, repeat from *across row, do not inc in first and last 3 sts thru-out skirt. Now inc in every 8th st, until you have 10 rows from beginning. Work 2 rows even. Now inc in every 8th st until you have 20 rows from beginning, break thread. Work 1 row of s c around top of skirt (36 sts). Ch 1, turn, work another row of s c around, ch 1, turn. Work 2 more rows, increasing 4 s c in each row. Work 4 more rows even (44 sts, 8 rows). Ch 1, turn, work 1 s c in each of the next 9 sts, ch 1, turn. Work 8 more rows. *Ch 1, turn, work 4 s c in next 4 sts, repeat from *4 more rows. Ch 1, turn, s c over 2 sts for slanting shoulder. Fasten thread, at other end of front and work to correspond.

Back—Skip 2 sts for underarm and work over 20 sts for back (leaving 2 sts on each side for underarm), for 11 rows. Ch 1, s c over 4 s c, ch 1, turn, work over 2 s c for slanting shoulder. Work 2 rows on other shoulder to correspond. Sew shoulder seams.

Sleeves—Ch 14, s c in 2nd ch, work 1 s c to end of ch. Ch 1, turn, work 3 more rows even. *Inc 1 st at beg of the next 2 rows. Work 2 rows even, repeat from *until you have 22 rows (23 sts). On next row work to within 3 s c, ch 1, turn, work to within 3 s c of next row. Dec. 1 st at end of the next 4 rows. Sew up sleeve, insert into armhole, allowing a little fullness at top of sleeve. Fasten thread at bottom on right side and s c around fronts and neck making a ch 3 loop for buttonholes on right side, increasing 2 sts at top of fronts. With Angora starting at back, work 2 rows s c around bottom joining fronts. Tie at neck; Ch 25 sts, now work 1 s c with same thread around neck, decreasing about 5 sts, ch 25 sts at end of neck. Work 1 s c over chs and around neck, decreasing 5 more sts. S c around sleeve with Angora.

☆ PANTIES

Ch 36, work 1 s c in 2nd ch from hook, 1 s c in each ch to end of row. Row 2—Ch 3, turn, work 1 d c in each st, increasing 5 d c across row. Repeat row 2, 2 more times, join with a sl st, ch 3, turn. Work 3 rows of d c without increasing, join with a sl st. Sl st 1 more st. *Ch 2, turn, work 3 d c in next 3 sts, ch 2 turn, repeat from *2 more times, break thread. Fold panties in half and sew to other side. Work 26 s c around each leg.

☆ MUFF

Ch 14 sts, loosely, join, ch 1, work 1 s c in each ch, join with a sl st, ch 3. Row 2—*Work 1 d c in next st, 2 d c in next st, repeat from *around, join with a sl st, ch 3. Row 3—Work 1 d c in each st, join, ch 1. Row 4—Work 1 s c in first st, *skip 1 st, 1 s c in next st, repeat from *around, join. Ch 12, sl st in same st. Work 1 row of s c with Angora on each end.

☆ HAT

Ch 20, s c in 2nd ch, work 1 s c in each ch to end of row (19 s c), ch 1. *Work 3 rows even. Now dec 1 st at end of the next 2 rows, repeat from *until you have 24 rows, 11 sts, break thread. Skip 2 rows at wide end of piece, attach yarn and s c around wide end, to 2nd row on other side of piece, break thread. *Skip 3 rows from beginning of first short row and work in same manner as first row, working 3 rows longer at other side, break thread. Repeat from * (working each row 3 sts longer on each side), until you have 8 short rows. Do not break thread and work completely around piece until you have 13 rows from beginning at wide end. Work 1 row of s c around with Angora skipping about 5 sts.

MARY'S DOLLIES

"ZORINA"

INSTRUCTIONS ON PAGE 14

Illustration 111. Cover for *Mary's Dollies*, Volume 9.

VOLUME No. 9

Zorina ★ ★ ★

"MISS VICTORY" DRESSED AS A CHARMING ALLY
(illustrated on the front cover)

☆ NEEDLES
1 Bone Crochet Hook, size 2.

☆ MATERIAL
1 two-ounce ball Sport or Crepe Yarn. 12 yards of Angora. 4 small pearl buttons. 1 ball Angora for Robe.

☆ GAUGE
7 sts to 1 inch. (Measure garment on doll as you make it).

☆ COAT

Ch 88, to measure 12½ inches. S c in 2nd ch from hook, s c to end of ch. *Ch 1, turn, work 2 more rows of s c. On next row dec in every 8th st (do not dec in last 4 sts), repeat from *until you have 22 rows, 38 sts. Work 2 rows even. Inc 4 sts on next row, about every 8th st. Work 3 rows even. At beg of 29th row, inc 1 st in first s c and s c in next 13 s c. Ch 1, turn, inc 1 st every 3rd row at front edge until you have 37 rows from bottom. Work over 5 sts for shoulder for 3 rows. Ch 1, turn, work 2 s c for slanting shoulder, break thread. Skip 2 s c and work over 18 sts for back, ch 1, turn, work even until you have 12 rows from beg. Work over 5 s c for shoulder. Ch 1, turn, work over 2 s c for slanting shoulder. Work other shoulder to correspond. Starting at other front work over 5 s c leaving 2 s c for underarm, for 12 rows, work over 2 s c for slanting shoulder. Sew shoulder seams.

Sleeves—Ch 14, s c in 2nd ch, work 1 s c to end of ch. Ch 1, turn, work 3 more rows even. *Inc 1 st at beg of the next 2 rows. Work 2 rows even, repeat from *until you have 22 rows (23 sts). On next row work to within 3 s c, ch 1, turn, work to within 3 s c of next row. Dec. 1 st at end of the next 4 rows. Sew up sleeve, insert into armhole, allowing a little fullness at top of sleeve. Fasten thread at bottom on right side and s c around fronts and neck, increasing 2 sts at top of fronts. With Angora starting at bottom on right side, work 1 row of s c, making a ch 3 loop for buttonholes, continuing around neck skipping about 3 sts. Finish on left side about 7 sts from left shoulder. Ch 1, turn, work 1 more row around neck and right front, break thread.

☆ PANTIES

Ch 36, work 1 s c in 2nd ch from hook, 1 s c in each ch to end of row. Row 2—Ch 3, turn, work 1 d c in each st, increasing 5 d c across row. Repeat row 2, 2 more times, join with a sl st, ch 3, turn. Work 3 rows of d c without increasing, join with a sl st. Sl st 1 more st. *Ch 2, turn, work 3 d c in next 3 sts, ch 2 turn, repeat from *2 more times, break thread. Fold panties in half and sew to other side. Work 26 s c around each leg.

☆ HAT

Ch 3, join, ch 1, work 7 s c in ring. Row 2—Work 2 s c in each st. Row 3—*Work 1 s c in next st, 2 s c in next st, repeat from *around row. Row 4—*Work 1 s c in each of the next 2 sts, 2 s c in next st, repeat from *around row. Row 5—*Work 1 s c in each of the next 3 sts, 2 s c in next st, repeat from *around row. Now inc in every 5th st, until you have 50 sts. On next row do not inc and pick up back thread only for 1 row. Work 6 rows even. *Do not break thread but with another strand of yarn, work an extra row half way around hat, increasing 2 sts, break thread, continue with first strand of yarn, work 1 row around, repeat from *4 times, do not have increases come over those of previous row. The extra rows are back of hat. Work 2 more rows of s c around.

With Angora work 1 row of s c around bottom of Hat. Holding crown toward you work 1 row of s c on edge of crown.

☆ MUFF

Ch 14 sts, loosely, join, ch 1, work 1 s c in each ch, join with a sl st, ch 3. Row 2—*Work 1 d c in next st, 2 d c in next st, repeat from *around, join with a sl st, ch 3. Row 3—Work 1 d c in each st, join, ch 1. Row 4—Work 1 s c in first st, *skip 1 st, 1 s c in next st, repeat from *around, join. Ch 12, sl st in same st. Work 1 row of s c with Angora on each end.

☆ ANGORA ROBE

Cast on 36 sts, K 5 rows, *K 3, P across to within last 3 sts, K 3. K next row, repeat from *until piece measures 8 inches from beginning. K 5 rows, bind off.

Reprinted from *Mary's Dollies*, Volume 9, Page 14.

MARY'S DOLLIES

• volume number 9

Copyrighted 1944 by Mary Hoyer

Published by Juvenile Styles Publishing Company
1008 PENN STREET, READING, PA.

LITTLE "MISS VICTORY" *and her little Mommy*

☆ NEEDLES
1 *Steel Crochet hook, size 9*

☆ MATERIAL
1 *small pearl button.* ½ yd., ¼ in., velvet. 1 ball, 400 yds. *mercerized cotton or crepe.*

(*Measure garment on Doll as you make it.*)

Starting at waist line, ch 58 sts, to measure 7½ inches. Work 1 d c in 4th ch from hook, *ch 1, skip 1 ch, d c in next ch, repeat from *across until you have 29 d c including ch 3 at beg of row. Work 1 more d c in last ch, ch 3, turn. Row 2—D c in next d c, *ch 2, s c in next d c, ch 4, sl st in 3rd ch (pico), ch 2, s c in next d c, ch 2, d c in next d c, repeat from *across row, ending row, 2 d c, ch 3, turn. Row 3—D c in next d c, *ch 2, s c in 2nd ch (next to pico), ch 5, sl st in 3rd ch, from hook ch 3 s c in first ch from pico, ch 2, d c in next d c, repeat from *across, ending row, 2 d c, ch 3, turn. Row 4—D c in next d c, *ch 2, s c in center of ch 3, ch 5, sl st in 3rd ch, ch 3, s c in first ch from pico, ch 2, 2 d c in next d c, repeat from *across, ending row, 2 d c, ch 3, turn. Row 5—Repeat row 4, join with a sl st, ch 3. Row 6—D c in next d c, *ch 2, s c in 2nd ch (next to pico), ch 5, sl st in 3rd ch, ch 3, s c in center of next ch 3, ch 2, 2 d c in next d c, repeat from *across row, increasing 1 d c in each d c group, ending row, 2 d c, ch 3. Row 7—Repeat row 6, but do not inc. Row 8—Inc in each d c group. Row 9—Work even. Rows 10, 11 and 12, work in same manner increasing 1 d c in each d c group in each row, join, ch 7.

Scallop—*Work 2 tr cr in every d c with ch 2 between each tr cr, ch 2, s c in center of pico, ch 2, repeat from *around row, join, break thread. Top of Dress—Fasten thread at opening and repeat row 2 of skirt, ch 3, turn.

Back—Follow pattern working 1 d c, a pico pattern, 2 d c in next d c, ch 3, turn. Continue to work a pico pattern same as skirt with 2 d c on each side, until you have 5 short rows, ch 3, turn. D c in next d c, ch 2, sl st in pico, ch 3, turn. Work 1 d c in sl st, ch 2, work 2 d c, break thread. Fasten thread at other side of back and work to correspond. Front—Skip 2 pico patterns and fasten thread in next d c, ch 3, work 1 d c in same st, follow pattern across front, to within 2 pico patterns, ending row with 2 d c. Work 3 more rows, ch 3 turn. D c in next d c, ch 2, 2 d c in next 2 ch sts, ch 3 turn. Work 2 more rows for shoulder, break thread. Fasten thread at other side of front and work to correspond. Sew shoulders. Frill at sleeve—Fasten thread at underarm in first pico from back, ch 2, skip first short row at back, work 2 s c in 2nd row, work 2 s c in each row around sleeve, to within first row of front, ch 2, s c in pico, ch 2, d c in d c, ch 2, join with a sl st at beg of row, sl st to s c.

Frill—Ch 5, work 2 tr cr, in every ch, with ch 2 between tr cr to end of s c. Sl st in 4th ch at beg of row to d c at underarm, break thread. Draw ribbon or velvet thru beading, sew on button at top of dress.

☆ DUTCH CAP

Starting at center, ch 3, join with a sl st to form ring. First rnd. Ch 3 (to count as d c), 2 d c in ring, ch 3, *3 d c in ring, ch 3, repeat from *2 more times. Join with a sl st to 3rd st of starting ch. Second rnd. Sl st in each st to first ch loop, ch 3, 2 d c in loop, ch 3, 3 d c in same loop, ch 3 *(3 d c, ch 3, 3 d c) in next loop, ch 3, repeat from *2 more times. Join as before. Third rnd. Sl st in each st to first ch loop, ch 3, 2 d c in loop, ch 3, 3 d c in same loop, ch 3, 3 d c in next loop, ch 3, *(3 d c, ch 3, 3 d c) in next loop, ch 3, 3 d c in next loop, ch 3, repeat from *2 more times. Join as before. Fourth rnd. Sl st in each st to first ch loop, ch 3, 2 d c in loop, ch 3, 3 d c in same loop, ch 3, 1 d c in next loop, 3 d c over next 3 d c, 1 d c in next loop, ch 3, *(3 d c, ch 3, 3 d c) in next loop, ch 3, 1 d c in next loop, 3 d c over next 3 d c, 1 d c in next loop, ch 3, repeat from *2 more times, join. Continue in this manner, increasing 2 sts at d c groups in each rnd until there are 5 sts in each group, join, break thread. Join two blocks with 1 row of s c across one side. Join third block to side of block one and one side of block two. Join fourth block to opposite sides of blocks two and one. Keep s c loose enough to prevent drawing. Work 2 rows of s c completely around hat. S c 1 more row, decreasing 3 sts (spaced a few sts apart) at back and front of cap. Scallop—*ch 5, sl st in 3rd ch from hook, ch 3, skip 3 sts, s c in each of the next 3 sts, repeat from *around.

Reprinted from *Mary's Dollies*, Volume 9, Page 2.

Terry

... LITTLE "MISS VICTORY" *and her little Mommy*

*When it comes to party-going, there's
nothing in the fashion world as sheer and
as smart as LACE. So, our little dollie and
her little Mommy are socially prominent
in their lace party dresses.*

"MISS VICTORY" IS

Queen of the Courts

☆ Needles
1 pair American Standard No. 2

☆ Material
1 oz. crepe. ⅛ oz. crepe for trim. 4 small pearl buttons.

☆ Gauge
7 sts to 1 inch. (Measure garment on doll as you make it)

☆ DRESS

Cast on 44 sts, K 3 rows. P 1 row, K 1 row for 7 rows. Next K row, K 2 tog, K 12, K 2 tog, K 12, K 2 tog, K 12, K 2 tog. Work 3 rows even. Work 4 more decreased rows, every 4th row (24 sts), having decreases come directly above those of previous row. Work even until piece measures 4 inches from beginning. Bind off 3 sts at beg of the next 2 rows (18 sts). Work even for 1¼ inches (12 rows). K 4, bind off 10 sts for neck, K 4. On these 4 sts, P 1 row, K 1 row for 11 rows, cast on 7 sts at neck edge, keeping 2 last sts k on purled rows (border) at front edge for 9 rows. Cast on 3 sts at underarm. Work even until piece measures 2 inches from underarm. On K side, K 6, inc 1 st, K 6, inc in end st. Work 3 rows even. Inc in same manner, have increases come directly below previous increases, 4 more times, 24 sts. Work even until piece measures same as for back from underarm, K 3 rows, border, bind off.

Frill at sleeve—Holding right side toward you, skip 3 sts at underarm, pick up 18 sts, to within 3 sts at other end, P back, pick up 3 sts. K 6, inc in every st to within 3 sts, K 3 sts, Pick up 3 sts. P back. Bind off 4 sts at beg of the next 4 rows, bind off remaining 20 sts. Work other side in same manner.

Finishing—Sew up sides and bottom of frill. With contrasting shade, starting at bottom on right side at front, s c on fronts working ch 3 loops for buttonholes. S c around neck skipping 4 sts and inc 2 sts at corners of neck. Work 2 rows of s c around each frill. Sew on buttons.

☆ PANTIES

Cast on 20 sts, K 1, P 1 for 4 rows, K 1 row increasing 5 sts P 1 row, K 1 row for 1½ inches. Bind off 3 sts at beg of the next 6 rows. On center 7 sts, K 1 row, P 1 row for 6 rows. Cast on 3 sts at beginning of the next 6 rows (25 sts), K 1 row, P 1 row for 1½ inches. Dec 5 sts, K 1, P 1 for 4 rows, bind off. Sew up panties. With embroidering needle tape yarn thru top of panties and tie. S c around pantie legs.

☆ HAT

Ch 3, join, ch 1, work 7 s c in ring. Row 2—Work 2 s c in each st. Row 3—*Work 1 s c in next st, 2 s c in next st, repeat from *around row. Row 4—*Work 1 s c in each of the next 2 sts, 2 s c in next st, repeat from *around row. Row 5—Inc in every 3rd st. Now inc in every 5th st until you have 56 sts. Work even until you have 15 rows. From end of last row, count 18 sts, place pin, with 2 strands of yarn, inc 1 s c in every other st, to pin, break thread.* Turn, skip 2 sts, fasten thread in 3rd st, s c in every st across row, to within 2 sts of other end, break thread, repeat from *until you have 5 rows from beg. With 3 strands of yarn, work 1 row completely around visor working over ends and sl st in every st around back of hat. With contrasting shade, ch 42 ch sts tie on first row of visor in center.

Sunny

"MISS VICTORY" IS

Queen of the Courts

*Across the net, this doll-of-the-hour is
a sports headliner. Her "serves" are fast
as lightning ... her fore-arm strokes and
back-hands are rhythmic ... and her
tantalizing costume is a come-on for the
broad-shouldered men in the gallery!*

Illustration 113. *Mary's Dollies,* Volume 9, Page 5.

"MISS VICTORY" IS A

Modern Cinderella

... She won't be home by Twelve!

☆ NEEDLES
1 *pair American Standard No. 2.*
1 *Steel Crochet Hook size 4.*

☆ MATERIAL
2 small brass buttons. 1 ounce of Tinsel Crepe.

☆ GAUGE
7 sts to 1 inch. (Measure garment on doll as you make it).

☆ EVENING JACKET

Blouse—Cast on 20 sts, K 1, P 1 for 5 rows. K 1 row, increasing 1 st at beg and end. P 1 row, K 1 row, until piece measures 1½ inches from start. Bind off 2 sts on each side for underarm. Work even for 1 inch. K 5 sts (put on safety pin) bind off 8 sts for back of neck, K 5. On these 5 sts, P 1 row, K 1 row always keeping last 2 sts K on Purled rows for border at front for 3 rows, now inc 1 st at border edge (on 3rd st) every K row, until you have 11 sts. Cast on 2 sts for underarm, continue to inc at front edge until you have 16 sts. Work even same as for back to ribbing, K 1, P 1 ribbing, for 5 rows, bind off. Work other side to correspond.

Sleeves—On right side pick up 6 center sts, P back, pick up 2 sts, turn, K 3, inc in each of the next 4 sts, K 1, pick up 2 sts, P back. Pick up 5 sts at end of each row (24 sts). *K 2 tog at beg and end of next K row, work 3 rows even, repeat from *until you have 18 sts. Work even until piece measures 3 inches. K 1, P 1 tightly for 4 rows, bind off. Work other sleeve to correspond. Sew back to fronts, sew up sleeves. Sew on buttons, push thru sts of fronts, crossing fronts.

☆ FASCINATOR

Work ch sts loosely, for 16 inches. Row 1—Make L.K. (Lovers Knot) in every 5th ch across row as follows: *Draw up a loop about ½", work 1 s c thru back strand of elongated loop just made (1 loop made). Repeat from *once (2 loops made)—s c in 5th ch. Row 2—*To turn, make 1 loop, s c in center of first knot of row below. Make 1 loop, s c in center of 2nd knot of row below, thus decreasing 2 L.K. Now continue to make L.K. same as Row 1 and s c into each knot of row below and continue to last knot of row below. Repeat from *5 more times. Continue L.K. in same manner, decreasing 1 L.K. at beg of every row until 1 L.K. remains. Make this decreasing loop a little smaller on each end—it will fit more becomingly around the hair line. Do not break thread.

To start Frill—Draw up a loop about ¾ inches instead of ½ inch and work 2 large L.K. in each loop around Fascinator.

Flower—Ch 6, join, ch 5, work 34 tr cr in center of ring with ch 2 between each tr cr, join. Row 2—Ch 2, work 2 d c between each tr cr, join. Sew on point of fascinator.

Janie

"MISS VICTORY" IS A

Modern Cinderella

Yes, our girl-around-town finds it more fun, and more patriotic, to keep herself in circulation. She's a morale-builder at every dance . . . and she has a distinctive gown for each, as a change of scenery!

Instructions for Janie's Evening Gown as shown in Illustration 114, page 85.

Skirt—Sew 4 pieces No. 1 tog, leaving opening for vent at back, hem vent. Now sew 4 net pieces tog and gather to top of skirt. Sew band to skirt having seams on inside, turn band, sew on wrong side. Hem bottom and cut net to same length.

Panties—Cut 2 pieces No. 3, sew back seams tog, then front seams. Sew crotch. Hem bottom of each leg. Turn down hem at top of panties.

Instructions for Kathleen's Evening Gown as shown in Illustration 115, page 89.

Skirt—Sew 4 pieces No. 1 tog, leaving opening for vent at back. Now sew 4 net pieces tog and gather to top of skirt. Sew No. 4 piece to top of skirt, having seams on inside (cut to bottom line). Baste hem around top of piece. Cut net 1 inch wide, 15 inches long, fold in half, gather and baste on wrong side. Stitch on right side. Cut No. 5 piece fold in half, sew, turn, sew on dress to fit doll. Hem bottom and cut net to same length. Panties same as style on page 7.

Panties same as Janie's.

Patterns and instructions for "MISS VICTORY'S" Evening Gowns

TOP
4

CUT 2 PIECES
5
STRAPS

VENT

FOLD FOR NET ONLY

1

CUT 4 PIECES

Panties same as Janie's.

Reprinted from *Mary's Dollies*, Volume 9, Page 10.

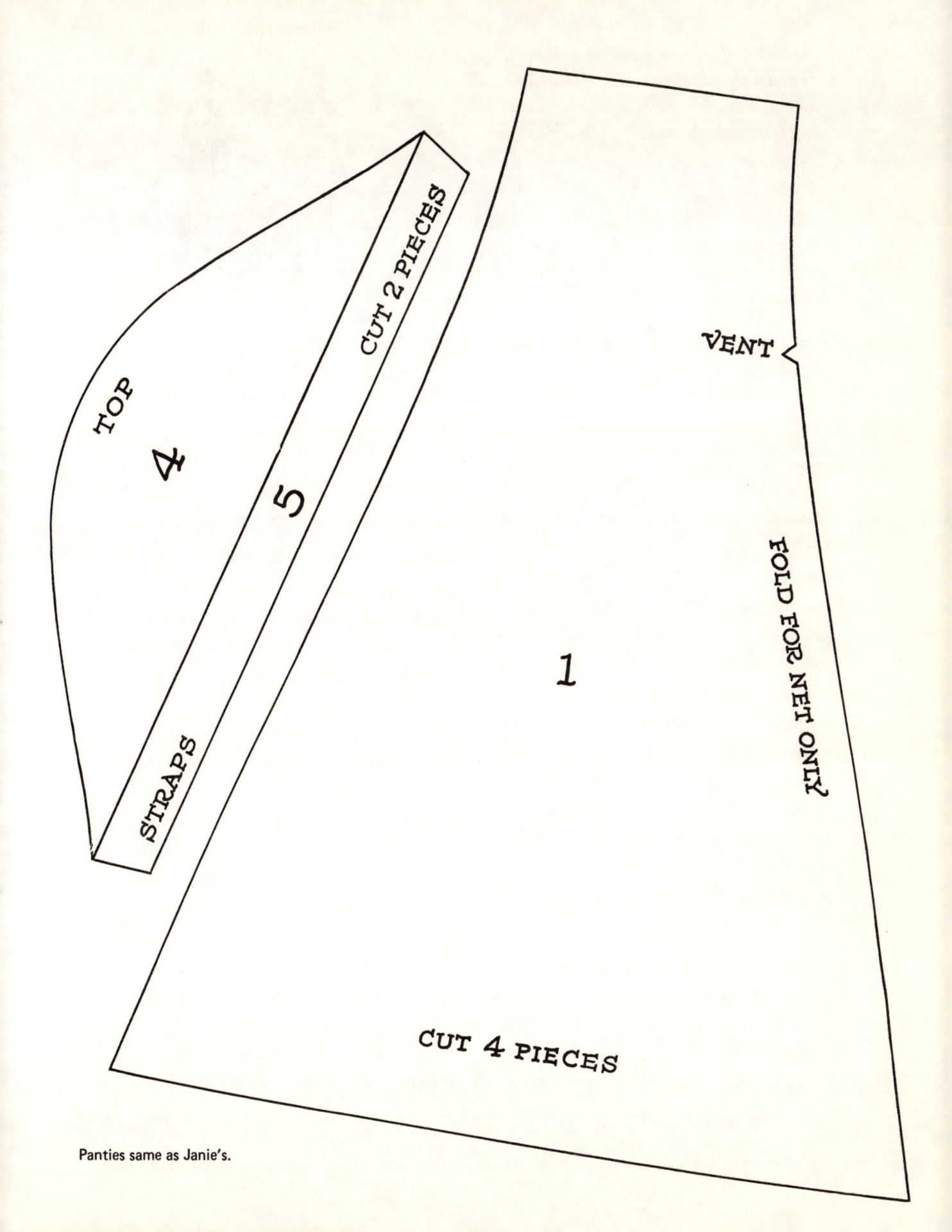

Another Dance... Another Date... Another Gown FOR "MISS VICTORY"

☆ **Needles**
1 pair American Standard No. 5.

☆ **Material**
1 ball of 100% Angora for Jacket. 1 ball of 100% Angora for Snood.

☆ **Gauge**
5 sts to 1 inch. (Measure garment on doll as you make it).

☆ **ANGORA JACKET AND SNOOD**

Jacket—Cast on 24 sts, K 3 rows. P 1 row, K 1 row for 1 inch, dec 1 st at beg and end of next row. Work even until piece measures 3 inches from start, bind off 2 sts on each side for underarm. Work even for 1 inch. K 6 sts (put on safety pin) bind off 6 sts for back of neck. K 6, on these 6 sts, work 5 rows for shoulder (always keeping first 2 sts K on purled rows at neck edge for border). On next K row, K 1, inc 1, K 4. Continue to inc in this manner on every K row, until you have 9 sts. Now P 1 row, K 1 row. Now cast on 2 sts for underarm. Work even for 1 inch, inc 1 st at seam end. Work even until piece measures same as for back, K 3 rows, bind off. Work other side to correspond.

Sleeves—On right side, pick up 6 center sts, P back, pick up 2 sts, turn, K 3, inc 1 st in each of the next 4 sts, K 1, pick up 2 sts, P back. Pick up 6 sts at end of each row (26 sts). *Dec 1 st at beg and end of next K row. Work 3 rows even, repeat from *until you have 16 sts, K 2 rows, bind off. Sew up sleeves and back to fronts.

☆ **ANGORA SNOOD**

Ch 3, join, work 7 s c in ring. Work 2 s c in each st until you have 24 sts. Now inc in every 4th st until you have 42 sts. Work even until you have 12 rows from beginning. Work Lovers Knot (L.K.) in every other st for 10 L.K. as follows: *Draw up a loop about ½ inch, work 1 s c thru back strand of elongated loop just made (1 loop made), repeat from *once (2 loops made), skip 1 s c, s c in next st. Row 2—*To turn, make 1 loop, s c in center of first knot of row below, thus decreasing 1 L.K. Now continue to make L.K. same as row 1 and s c into each Knot of row below and continue to last knot of row below. Repeat from *2 more times, break thread. With crown toward you, start at first s c of last row, work L.K. in every st across front of cap. Ch 2, s c in each L.K. around back of snood, this will tighten snood to fit under hair line.

Kathleen

Another Dance... Another Date... Another Gown
for "MISS VICTORY"

Pretty snooty... in her snood and formal weskett jacket. Miss Victory launches a heart-winning movement which is bound to succeed. She has all the charm that Cinderella had, but she'll get results without losing a slipper!

Illustration 115. *Mary's Dollies,* Volume 9, Page 11.

"MISS VICTORY" SENDS:—

V mail to her V male

☆ **Needles**
1 Steel Crochet Hook size 4.

☆ **Material**
1 ounce ball crepe. ⅛ ounce contrasting shade of crepe. 2 small pearl buttons.

☆ **Gauge**
7 sts to 1 inch. (Measure garment on doll as you make it).

☆ **SKIRT**

With main shade, ch 42 sts to measure 5½ inches. Row 1—Work 1 s c in 2nd ch from hook, s c in each ch to end of ch, ch 3, turn. Row 2—*Work 2 d c in every st across row, ch 3, turn. Row 3—*Work 1 d c in each of the next 2 d c, 2 d c in next st, repeat from *to end of row, thus increasing every 3rd st, ch 3, turn. Row 4—Inc in every 10th st, join with a sl st, ch 3, turn. Rows 5 & 6—repeat Row 4. *With contrasting shade, work 1 row of s c increasing every 10th st, drop thread, continue with first shade and work 1 row of s c even, repeat from *once more. At top of skirt, *work 1 s c row of contrasting shade, 1 row with main shade, repeat from *once. Work ch 3 loops for buttonholes on each end of band.

☆ **PANTIES**

Ch 39, work 1 s c in 2nd ch from hook, 1 s c in each ch to end of row. Row 2—Ch 3, turn, work 1 d c in each st, increasing 5 d c across row. Repeat row 2, 2 more times, join with a sl st, ch 3, turn. Work 3 rows of d c without increasing, join with a sl st. Ch 2, turn, work 3 d c in next 3 sts, ch 2 turn, work 3 d c in next 3 sts, break thread. Fold panties in half and sew to other side. With contrasting shade, work 23 s c around each leg.

Starting at top of panties, work 1 s c in each ch to end of row, ch 3, turn. Rows 2 and 3 and 4—Work d c, increasing 5 sts in each row, 53 d c, including the ch 3 at beg of row, ch 3, turn. Work 1 d c in each of the next 8 d c, ch 3, turn. Work 2 more rows, ch 3, turn. Work 1 d c in each of the next 3 d c, ch 3, turn, work 1 more row, break thread. Fasten thread at end of other side, work 2nd half of back to correspond. Skip 5 sts at underarm, fasten thread, ch 3, work 1 d c in each st to within 5 d c at other underarm, ch 3 turn. Work 1 more row of d c, ch 3, turn. Work 1 d c in each of the next 3 d c, ch 3, turn. Work 2 more rows, break thread. Work other shoulder to correspond, sew shoulders. With contrasting shade, work 1 row of s c around neck, decreasing 3 s c across front, break thread. With main color, starting at bottom of opening, work s c around opening and neck. Work 1 more row on one side of opening, working ch 3 loops for buttonholes, having buttonholes at waist line and top of dress.

☆ **SLEEVES**

Fasten thread at center of underarm and work 27 s c around armhole, join with a sl st, ch 1. Row 2—Work 3 s c in first 3 sts, 3 h d c (Y O needle, insert needle thru next st, Y O needle, draw thru, Y O needle draw thru all sts), in next 3 sts. Work 2 d c in each st to within the last 6 sts. Work 3 h d c in next 3 sts, 3 s c in last 3 sts, join with a sl st, ch 1. Row 3—Work same as row 2, but do not increase. Row 4—Work 1 row of s c in every other st, join with a sl st. With contrasting color, work 1 row of s c, break thread. With main shade work 1 more row of s c.

☆ **HAT**

Back of hat, ch 35, to measure 5 inches. Work 1 s c in 2nd ch from hook, s c to end of row, ch 1, turn. Next row, inc 9 s c, about every 4th st across row, ch 1, turn. Work even until you have 14 rows, break thread. With 2 strands of contrasting shade, starting at beg of ch, fasten thread, *ch 1, skip 1 space, s c into next st, repeat from *across side of hat. Ch 1, s c in corner, ch 1, s c in same st, repeat between *s across front of hat, work 2nd corner in same manner, work other side in same manner, do not break thread. With 2 strands of main color, starting at end of last row, work 1 row same as first row, increasing 1 st in each corner. Work 2 more rows in same manner, do not break thread.

Band at back of hat—Ch 1, turn, work 3 s c in next 3 sts (at back of hat, not bottom). Work 8 more rows, break thread, sew to other side closing at back.

Susanna

"MISS VICTORY" SENDS:—

V mail to her V male

... "She wrote a letter to her Lover,
in the Box she'll drop it." A letter
that will keep up his Morale "Over there"
while she wears a jaunty Knit Dress to
help keep up her morale "Over Here".

Illustration 116. *Mary's Dollies,* Volume 9, Page 13.

MARY'S DOLLIES

PATSY

INSTRUCTIONS ON PAGE 14

20¢

VOLUME NO. 10

Illustration 117. Cover for *Mary's Dollies*, Volume 10.

PATSY • *Illustrated on the Front Cover*

COAT HAT AND BAG

NEEDLES—1 *Bone Crochet Hook, size 2.*
MATERIAL—1 *two-ounce ball Sport Yarn, 12 yards of Angora. 4 small Pearl Buttons.*
GAUGE—7 *sts to 1 inch. (Measure garment on Doll as you make it).*

☆ COAT

Ch 87 to measure 12½ inches. S c in 2nd ch from hook, s c to end of ch. *Ch 1, turn, work 2 more rows of s c. On next row, *s c in first 7 s c, skip next st, repeat from * (thus decreasing every 8th st across row), ch 1 turn. Work 3 rows even. Dec every 8th st, every 4th row, until you have 44 sts. Work even until you have 28 rows from beg, ch 1, turn. At beg of 29th row, s c in first 9 sts, ch 1, turn. Work 8 more rows. *Ch 1, turn, work 1 s c in each of the next 4 sts, repeat from * for 4 more rows, ch 1, turn. S c over 2 sts for slanting shoulder. Fasten thread at other front and work to correspond.

Back—Skip 2 sts for underarm and work over 20 sts for back (leaving 2 sts on each side for underarm), for 11 rows. Ch 1, s c over 4 s c, ch 1, turn, work over 2 s c for slanting shoulder. Work 2 rows on other shoulder to correspond. Sew shoulder seams.

Sleeves—With angora, ch 16 sts, s c in 2nd ch, s c to end of row, ch 1, turn. Work 1 more row, break thread. Change to yarn and inc 1 st at beg and end of row (17 s c). *Work 2 more rows even. Inc 1 st at beg of the next 2 rows, repeat from * until you have 19 rows (25 sts) from beg of yarn. On next row work to within 3 s c, ch 1, turn, work to within 3 s c of next row. Dec 1 st at end of the next 4 rows. Sew sleeve seams, insert into armhole, allowing a little fullness at top of sleeve. With angora, fasten yarn at bottom on right side and s c around fronts and neck, increasing 2 sts at top of fronts, ch 1, turn, s c 1 more row in same manner dec 3 sts around neck and make a ch 3 loop for 3 buttonholes on right side, break thread.

☆ PANTIES

Ch 36, work 1 s c in 2nd ch from hook, 1 s c in each ch to end of row. Row 2—Ch 3, turn, work 1 d c in each st, increasing 5 d c across row. Repeat row 2, 2 more times, join with a sl st, ch 3, turn. Work 3 rows of d c without increasing, join with a sl st. Sl st 1 more st. *ch 2, turn, work 3 d c in next 3 sts, ch 2 turn, repeat from * 2 more times, break thread. Fold panties in half and sew to other side. Work 26 s c around each leg.

☆ HAT

Ch 3, join, ch 1, work 7 s c in ring. Row 2—Work 2 s c in each st. Row 3—*Work 1 s c in next st, 2 s c in next st, repeat from * around row. Row 4—*Work 1 s c in each of the next 2 sts, 2 s c in next st, repeat from * around row. Row 5—*Work 1 s c in each of the next 3 sts, 2 s c in next st, repeat from * around row. Now inc in every 5th st, until you have 54 sts. On next row do not inc and pick up back thread only for 1 row. Work 6 rows even. Do not break thread. Add another strand of yarn, working with 2 strands, inc 1 st every 3rd st around row for 1 row. Work 3 more rows without increasing, break thread.

Hat Band—Ch 24 inches, work 1 s c in 2nd ch from hook, s c in each ch. Block Hat and band, tie band around hat as shown on illustration.

☆ BAG

Ch 14 sts, work 1 s c in 2nd ch from hook, work 1 s c across row, ch 1, turn. Work 5 more rows even. Dec 1 st at end of next 2 rows. Work 1 row even, break thread. Work other side in same manner, do not break thread and work flat by decreasing 1 st at end of every row until you have 2 s c. Ch 3 for buttonhole and fasten off. Ch 11 inches, join, do not twist ch, work 1 s c in each ch. Sew this piece between the 2 side pieces, leaving surplus for shoulder strap. Sew buttons on coat and one on bag.

Reprinted from *Mary's Dollies*, Volume 10, Page 14.

QUEEN OF THE JUNGLES

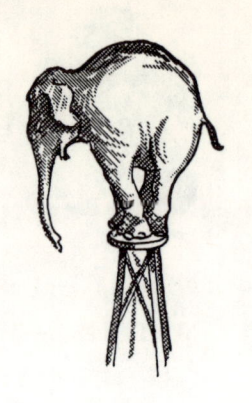

NEEDLES—1 *pair American Standard No. 2 and No. 7.*

MATERIAL—2 *ounces Crepe, 1 pack sequins, small beads, 3 small buttons or snap fasteners, 1 bead needle.*

GAUGE—8 *sts to 1 inch. (Measure garment on doll as you make it).*

☆ DRESS

With No. 2 Needles, starting at front (hip Length), cast on 30 sts, *P 1 row, K 1 row for 3 rows. On next row, dec 4 sts, (dec 1 st on each end, and K 3rd and 4th sts tog from ends). Repeat from * once, 22 sts. *Work even for 3 rows and inc 4 sts directly above decreases, repeat from * once, 30 sts. Work 2 rows even. Bind off 2 sts at beg of the next 2 rows for underarm. Inc for drop shoulder as follows: *On K rows, inc 1 st on 2nd st at beg of row and 3rd st from end of row and keep first and last 3 sts K on purled rows for border, repeat from * until you have 36 sts. On next K row, K 9 sts, put on safety pin, bind off 18 sts. Work last 9 sts even for 1 inch continuing border at armhole. Cast on 9 sts at neck edge and keep last 3 sts K on purled row for border. Now dec inside of border on K rows at armhole edge until you have 13 sts. On next row, cast on 2 sts at armhole edge and continue to dec and inc on seam end same as front continuing border at center back. Pick up 9 sts at armhole edge and work to correspond to other side.

Neck Band—On right side, pick up 48 sts around neck, *K 8 sts, K 2 tog, repeat from * across row. K 3 more rows even, bind off loosely. Sew side seams.

☆ SKIRT

With No. 2 needles, on right side, pick up 54 sts, P back. On next row, inc in every 3rd st. *Change to No. 7 needles, P 1 row, K 1 row for 5 rows. Change to No. 2 needles, inc in every 4th st, P 1 row, K 1 row even, repeat from * 5 more times, ending with 5 K rows. Bind off loosely. Sew sequins on as illustrated. Insert bead needle thru material from wrong side to right thru sequins and small bead. Now insert needle thru sequins again and fasten on wrong side. Fasten back with three snaps.

☆ CAP

With No. 2 needles, cast on 8 sts, P back. Row 2—Inc in each st (16 sts), P back. Row 4—*Inc 1 st, K 1 st, repeat from * across row (24 sts), P back. Row 6—*Inc 1 st, K 2 sts, repeat from * across row, P back. Continue in this manner having 1 more st between each inc, until you have 7 sts between increases (72 sts). K 1 row, P 1 row without increasing for 4 rows. Now dec in same manner as you increased. *K 2 sts tog, K 7, repeat from * across row, P back. Dec in this manner, having 1 st less between each dec for 2 more K rows. (56 sts). K 5 rows even and bind off loosely.

☆ PANTIES

Cast on 20 sts, K 1, P 1 for 4 rows, K 1 row increasing 5 sts P 1 row, K 1 row for 1½ inches. Bind off 3 sts at beg of the next 6 rows. On center 7 sts, K 1 row, P 1 row for 6 rows. Cast on 3 sts at beg of the next 6 rows (25 sts), K 1 row, P 1 row for 1½ inches. Dec 5 sts, K 1, P 1 for 4 rows, bind off. Sew up panties. With embroidering needle tape yarn thru top of panties and tie. S c around pantie legs.

Reprinted from *Mary's Dollies*, Volume 10, Page 5.

Illustration 118. *Mary's Dollies,* Volume 10, Page 4.

Corine

BATHING ENSEMBLE

NEEDLES—1 *Bone crochet hook, size 2.*
MATERIAL—*1 oz. ball, sport yarn, 1 small button.*
GAUGE—*7 sts to 1 inch.* (*Measure garment on doll as you make it*).

☆ BRA

Starting at back, ch 4, s c in 2nd ch, s c in each of the next 2 s c. Ch 1, turn, work 3 s c in each row, until you have 10 rows from beg. *Now inc 1 st at beg of row, 3 s c to end of row. Ch 1, work 4 s c across row. Inc 1 st at beg of every row on this end, until you have 7 s c across row. On next row, dec 1 st at same end as you increased until you have 3 s c across row, repeat from * once and finish to correspond to beg of bra. S c across bottom, ch 3 loop over end for buttonhole (skip 2 s c, s c in next st). S c over top of bra, ch 1, turn. Work 1 s c in each of the next 8 s c, *ch 1, d c in next st, ch 1, d c in same st, repeat from * to within 8 s c from other end, work 8 s c, break thread.

Straps—Skip 3 s c from end, fasten thread, and work 1 s c in each of the next 2 s c. Ch 1, turn, work in s c for 23 rows, sew to base of ruffle at front. Work other strap to correspond. Ch 45 sts, tape thru center of Bra, from top to bottom and tie.

☆ PANTIES

Front, ch 15, work 1 s c in 2nd ch from hook, s c to end of ch, ch 1, turn. Row 2—Work 1 s c in each st. Row 3—and all uneven rows, inc 1 st at beg and end of rows, until you have 8 rows from beg. Work 4 rows even, break thread. Skip 7 sts from end of last row, s c over 7 center s c. Now dec 1 st on end of every row until you have 3 sts, break thread.

Back—Ch 17, work exactly as for front, working back piece 2 sts wider. S c over 9 center sts and dec to 3 s c. Sew crotch tog. Work 1 row s c around each leg.

Ties—Ch 85 sts to measure 12 inches. Lace sides tog and tie as shown on illustration.

☆ CAPE

Ch 34 sts to measure 5 inches. Work 1 s c in 2nd ch, s c to end of ch. Row 2—Inc 1 st in every 5th st across row. Row 3—Work even. Repeat rows 2 and 3 once. Work 7 more rows, decreasing 1 st at end of each row. S c over end of cape and ch 30 sts for tie, break thread. Work other side to correspond.

Frill—Attach yarn at tie and ch 3, *work 1 d c in next st, ch 1, d c in same st, ch 1, repeat from * across sides and bottom of cape.

Paula

Illustration 119. *Mary's Dollies,* Volume 10, Page 6.

RIDING HABIT

NEEDLES—1 *set No. 1 and No. 2 Double Pointed Needles, American Standard, Steel Crochet, size 3.*

MATERIAL—1 *oz. dark shade of crepe, 1 oz. light shade crepe, 3 small pearl buttons.*

GAUGE—8 *sts to 1 inch.* (*Measure garment on doll as you make it.*)

☆ VEST

With No. 2 Needles and light shade, starting at back, cast on 22 sts, *P 1 row, K 1 row for ¾ inch, inc 1 st each side, repeat from * once. Work even until piece measures 1¾ inches. Bind off 2 sts on each side for underarm. Work 1¼ inches even. K 6 sts (put on safety pin) bind off 10 sts for back of neck, K 6 sts. On these 6 sts, P 1 row K 1 row for 7 rows. Now inc 1 st at beg of every row at neck edge until you have 12 sts. On next row at underarm cast on 2 sts. Work even for 1 inch, dec 1 st at seam end, work even until piece measures same as back. Bind off 6 sts at seam end and K 2 sts tog at beg and end of K rows until you have 2 sts, bind off. Work other side to correspond.

Sleeves—With No. 2 needles, dark shade, pick up 22 center sts, P back. Pick up 3 sts at end of next 2 rows (28 sts). P 1 row, K 1 row and dec 1 st at beg and end of every 6th row, until you have 18 sts, 3½ inches. Change to No. 1 needles, K 1, P 1 for 4 rows, bind off loosely.

Finishing—Sew back to fronts; and sleeves tog. Starting at back, with light shade, work 1 row of s c around vest increasing 2 sts at points and work ch 3 loops for button holes on right side. Sew on buttons.

☆ JODHPURS

With No. 1 needles, dark shade, cast on 44 sts, loosely, 22 sts on first needle, 12 sts on second needle, 10 sts on 3rd needle, K 1 st, P 1 st for ½ inch. Change to No. 2 needles and K 2 rows even. With first needle, inc 1 st, K 20, inc 1 st; with 2nd needle, inc 1 st, K 11, with 3rd needle, K 9, inc 1 st. Work 1 rnd even. Continue increasing (1 st beg and end of first needle, at beg of 2nd needle and end of 3rd needle), every other rnd, 5 more times. Work 4 rnds even. Now dec every other rnd same as you increased, 5 times (48 sts). Work 4 rnds even K 12 sts from first needle, place next 24 sts on st holder, cast on 8 sts for crotch, K remaining 12 sts; on these 32 sts, *K1½ inches even. Dec. 4 sts, spaced equal distances apart. Repeat from * 2 more times. Work even until piece measures 5 inches from crotch. Change to No. 1 needles, K 1, P 1 for 4 rnds, bind off loosely. Put 24 sts on 3 needles, pick up 8 sts on crotch, work to correspond to other leg. Fasten thread on side of cuff and ch 12 sts, fasten on opposite side (to hold pants in place when putting on boots.

☆ HAT

With 2 strands of crepe, light shade, ch 3, join, ch 1, work 7 s c in ring. Row 2—*Work 2 s c in each st, repeat from * around row. Row 3—*Work 1 s c in each of the next 2 sts, 2 s c in next st, repeat from * around row. Row 4—Inc in every 4th st. Now inc in every 5th st until you have 50 sts. Work even until you have 12 rows. From end of last row, count 18 sts, place pink, work 2 s c in each st to pin, break thread. *Turn, skip 2 sts, fasten thread in 3rd st, s c in every st across row to within 2 sts of other end, break thread, repeat from * until you have 5 rows from beg. With 3 strands of crepe work 1 row completely around visor working over ends and sl st in every st around back of hat. With contrasting shade, ch 42 ch sts, tie on first row of visor in center.

Reprinted from *Mary's Dollies*, Volume 10, Page 9.

Billie

Illustration 120. *Mary's Dollies*, Volume 10, Page 8.

BARE BACK RIDER

NEEDLES—1 *Bone Crochet Hook, size* 2.
MATERIALS—1 *two-ounce ball sport yarn,* 14 *yards of Angora,* 3 *small pearl buttons.*
GAUGE—7 *sts to* 1 *inch.*

Starting at top of costume, ch 42 sts to measure 7 inches. Work 1 s c in 2nd ch from hook, s c to end of row. Row 2—Work 1 s c in each st across row. Row 3—Dec 4 sts (spaced at equal distances apart). Rows 4 and 5—Work even. Row 6—Dec 4 sts. Work even for 4 rows. Row 11—Inc 4 sts. Rows 12 and 13—work even. Row 14—Inc 4 sts. Rows 15 and 16—work even, ch 3, turn.

☆ SKIRT

Work in back thread only for first row. Work 1 d c in each of the first 2 sts, *ch 1, d c in same st. Work 1 d c in each of the next 2 sts. Repeat from * across row, join with a sl st, ch 3. Row 2—Work 1 d c in each of the first 2 d c, *(d c, ch 1, d c) over ch 1 of previous row. Work 1 d c in each of the next 3 d c, repeat from * around row, join with a sl st and ch 3. Work 3 more rows in same manner having increases come directly above those of previous increases with 2 more d c between increases.

Second part of Skirt—Fasten yarn at center back of skirt and work on front thread for first row, working second part of skirt in same manner as first part, for 4 rows. Work 1 row s c on back of dress, working 3, ch 3 loops for buttonholes on one side.

Straps—Skip 5 sts from end at top of dress, fasten thread and s c in next 3 s c sts ch 1, turn. Work 3 s c for straps for 21 rows. Fit on doll and sew to front. Work other side to correspond. Fasten yarn at back of dress and s c around top of dress and over straps. Ch 3, turn, work 1 d c in first s c, *ch 1, d c in same st, ch 1, d c in next st, ch 1, d c in next st, repeat from * across row.

☆ FLOWERS

With yarn, ch 3, join, with a sl st, ch 1, work 8 s c in ring, join. Ch 1, pick up back thread only, work 2 s c in each st with ch 1, between each s c, join. With angora *ch 1, sl st, repeat from * in each st around row. With angora, work 1 s c in each st on front thread in ring, with ch 1 between each st. Work 2nd flower in same manner.

☆ PANTIES

Ch 36, work 1 s c in 2nd ch from hook, 1 s c in each ch to end of row. Row 2—Ch 3, turn, work 1 d c in each st, increasing 5 d c across row. Repeat row 2, 2 more times, join with a sl st, ch 3, turn. Work 3 rows of d c without increasing, join with a sl st. Sl st 1 more st. *Ch 2, turn, work 3 d c in next 3 sts, ch 2 turn, repeat from * 2 more times, break thread. Fold panties in half and sew to other side. Work 26 s c around each leg.

Reprinted from *Mary's Dollies*, Volume 10, Page 11.

Jackie

Illustration 121. *Mary's Dollies*, Volume 10, Page 10.

MARY'S DOLLIES

Illustration 122. Cover for *Mary's Dollies*, Volume 11.

VOLUME NO. 11

20¢

Illustration 123. *Mary's Dollies,* Volume 11, Page 4.

Anita

103

Skiing Costume

NEEDLES—1 set of *No. 1 and No. 3* double pointed needles, American Standard.

MATERIAL—1⅞ oz. Sport Yarn, 14 yds. of Angora, 4 small pearl buttons.

GAUGE—7½ sts to 1 inch.

(*Measure garment on Doll as you make it.*)

☆ JACKET

With No. 1 needles, cast on 22 sts, K 1, P 1, ribbing for 5 rows. Change to No. 3 needles, K 1 row, increasing 4 sts at equal distances apart. P 1 row, K 1 row, until piece measures 1¾ inches from start. Bind off 2 sts on each side for underarm. Work even for 1 inch. K 5 sts (put on safety pin) bind off 12 sts for back of neck, K 5. On these 5 sts, work 2 rows for shoulder. Change to angora and work 3 more rows. Cast on 5 sts for front. K 1 row, P 1 row, for 1¼ inches. At armhole edge, cast on 2 sts, work even for 1½ inches. With yarn, K 1 row, change to No. 1 needles, casting on 4 sts at front edge. K 1, P 1, for 4 rows, keeping 4 sts at front edge, K in garter st, bind off. Pick up 4 sts at border edge and K in garter st for band at front for 2½ inches, place on st holder. Work other side to correspond working buttonhole as follows: K 2, Y O, K 2 tog, working buttonhole in 3rd row of band and 3rd row in neck band, and 2 more at equal distances apart. Sew bands to angora fronts stretching border slightly.

Neck Bands—With No. 1 needles and yarn, pick up 32 sts, including front bands, K 1, P 1 for 5 rows, bind off, K 1, P 1.

Sleeves—Pick up 3 center sts, P back, pick up 1 st, turn, K 1, inc 1 st in each of the next 3 sts, pick up 1 st at end of each row (24 sts). Now K 1 row, P 1 row for ½ inch, dec 1 st on each side. Work 1 inch even, dec 1 st on each side. Work even until sleeve measures 3 inches from underarm (20 sts) Change to No. 1 needle. K 1, P 1 for 5 rows, bind off.

☆ PANTS

Cast on 40 sts, 12 sts on 1st needle, 12 sts on 2nd needle, 16 sts on 3rd needle, join. K 1, P 1, for 1 inch. Inc 8 sts, about every 5th st, 48 sts. K plain for 1¾ inches. Put 24 sts on st holder, cast on 8 sts for crotch; join, on these 32 sts, K 6 inches.

Cuff—K 2 sts tog until you have 16 sts, change to No. 1 needles. K 1, P 1 for 1 inch. Put 24 sts on 3 needles, pick up 8 sts on crotch, work to correspond to other leg.

☆ TASSEL CAP

With No. 3 needles, cast on 16 sts, K 1 row, P 1 row for 5 rows. Next K row, * inc 1 st, K 3, repeat from * across row. Work 5 rows even. *Inc, K 4, repeat from * across row. Repeat these last 2 rows having 1 st more between each inc until you have 56 sts, working angora stripes as follows: first stripe, with angora, K 1 row 1½ inches from start. Work 2 more stripes 1¼ inches apart, 2nd stripe 2 rows, 3rd stripe 3 rows. Work even until cap measures 7 inches from start. Change to No. 1 needles, K 1, P 1 ribbing for 1 inch, bind off K 1, P 1. Sew tog. Draw the 16 sts tog at beginning of cap.

☆ TASSEL

Wrap 10 strands of yarn around a 4 inch cardboard, cut at one end and with 2 strands of yarn tape thru other end, sew to top of cap. Take a piece of yarn and wrap around tassel ½ inch below top. Sew to top of cap.

Dolores

Skating Costume

NEEDLES—1 *bone crochet hook, size 2.*

MATERIALS—1 *two ounce ball Sport Yarn, 20 yards of angora, 3 small buttons.*

GAUGE—7 *sts to 1 inch.*

(*Measure garment on Doll as you make it.*)

☆ DRESS

Starting at waist line, ch 37 sts to measure 5½ inches, work 1 s c in 2nd ch from hook, work 1 s c in each ch to end of row, ch 1, turn. Work 3 more rows in same manner. Row—5—*Work 1 s c in each of the first 3 sts, 2 s c in next st, repeat from *across row, do not inc in first and last 3 sts thru-out skirt. Now inc in every 7th st, until you have 10 rows from beginning. Work 2 rows even, join ch 1, turn. Now inc in every 8th st until you have 18 rows from beginning, break thread. Work 1 row of s c around top of skirt (36 sts). Ch 1, turn, work another row of s c around, ch 1, turn. Work 2 more rows, increasing 4 s c in each row. Work 4 more rows even (44 sts, 8 rows). Ch 1, turn, work 1 s c in each of the next 9 sts, ch 1, turn. Work 10 more rows, ch 1, turn, work 5 s c in next 5 sts, ch 1, turn, s c over 2 sts for slanting shoulder. Fasten thread at other end of back and work to correspond.

Front—Skip 2 sts for underarm and s c across front (leaving 2 sts on each side for underarm), for 11 rows. Ch 1, s c over 5 s c, ch 1, turn, work over 2 s c for slanting shoulder. Work 2 rows on other shoulder to correspond. Sew shoulder seams.

Sleeves—Ch 14, s c in 2nd ch, work 1 s c to end of ch. Ch 1, turn, work 3 more rows even. *Inc. 1 st at beg of the next 2 rows. Work 2 rows even, repeat from *until you have 22 rows (23 sts). On next row work to within 3 s c, ch 1, turn, work to within 3 s c of next row. Dec. 1 st at end of the next 4 rows. Sew up sleeves, insert into armhole, allowing a little fulness at top of sleeve.

Finishing—Fasten thread on left side of waist line and s c around backs and neck, making 3 ch 3 loops for buttonholes on right side, increasing 2 sts at top of backs. With Angora starting at back, work 1 row of s c around bottom. Work 1 row of s c around neck, skipping 3 sts. Embroider as shown on illustration (take white sewing thread, make your outline, then embroider with angora).

☆ PANTIES

Ch 36, work 1 s c in 2nd ch from hook, 1 s c in each ch to end of row. Row 2—Ch 3 turn, work 1 d c in each st, increasing 5 d c across row. Repeat row 2, 2 more times, join with a sl st, ch 3, turn. Work 3 rows of d c without increasing, join with a sl st. Sl st 1 more st. *Ch 2, turn, work 3 d c in next 3 sts, ch 2, turn, repeat from *2 more times, break thread. Fold panties in half and sew to other side. Work 26 s c around each leg.

☆ CAP

Ch 3, join, ch 1, work 7 s c in ring. Row 2—Work 2 s c in each st. Row 3—*Work 1 s c in next st, 2 s c in next st, repeat from *around row. Row 4—*Work 1 s c in each of the next 2 sts, 2 s c in next st, repeat from *around row. Now inc in every 5th st until you have 56 sts around. Work even until you have 15 rows. On 16th row dec 4 sts spaced at equal distances apart. Ch 1, turn, s c to within 14 s c at beg of row, ch 1, turn. Work 3 more rows around front of cap decreasing 1 st at end of each row, ch 1, turn. Work 1 more row, decreasing 3 sts, evenly distributed. Ch 27 sts for chin strap. Work 1 s c in 4th ch from hook, s c to end of ch, sl st, fasten off. Work 1 row, with angora around front and back of cap, decreasing 2 sts at back of cap.

☆ MITTS

Ch 20, loosely, join, work 19 s c rnd ch. Row 2—Work 1 row even. Row 3—Dec 5 sts evenly distributed. Row 4—Work even. Row 5—Inc 3 sts. Row 6—Inc 2 sts. Row 7—Ch 2, skip 3 sts for thumb. Work 2 rows even, working 2 s c over ch 2 sts. Now dec 3 s c every row, until you have 3 s c left, sew tog.

Thumb—Fasten thread and work 1 s c in each st around thumb hole for 2 rows. Dec 2 sts in next row, draw tog and sew. Work 1 row, with angora, of s c around top of mitts.

Illustration 125. *Mary's Dollies,* Volume 11, Page 10.

Lucille

Roller Skating Outfit

NEEDLES—1 *pair American Standard Nos. 1 and 3.*

MATERIAL—*1 oz. Fingering, light shade; 1 oz. Fingering, dark shade; 4 small buttons.*

GAUGE—*7½ sts to 1 inch, on Jumper.*

(*Measure garment on Doll as you make it.*)

☆ JUMPER

With No. 3 needles, and M C, starting at bottom, cast on 150 sts, K 2 rows. K 61 (P 1, K 2, P 1), K 20 (P 1, K 2, P 1), K 61. Next row P 61 (K 1, P 2, K 1), K 20 (K 1, P 2, K 1), P 61. Work 2 more rows of pattern. Next row dec and work cable as follows: *K 8, K 2 tog, repeat from * to within 3 sts of first purled st, K 2 tog, K 1, P 1 (cable, K the back of 2nd st, leave on needle, K in front of first st, take 2 sts off tog), P 1, K 1, K 2 tog. Now K to within 3 sts of next purled st, K 2 tog, K 1, P 1 work 2nd cable in same manner, P 1, K 1, K 2 tog, dec in same manner to end of row. Work 3 rows even following pattern. On next row twist cable and dec as follows: K 7, K 2 tog, decreasing and twisting for cable in same manner as first dec, having 1 st less between each dec (following center dec) until you have 80 sts, P back. On next row, K 2 tog to first cable, follow pattern, dec 3 sts on front panel, follow 2nd cable, K 2 tog to end of row. Change to No. 1 needles, K 1, P 1 ribbing following cable for 4 rows. Bind off 15 sts, place next 6 sts on st holder, bind off 5 sts, place next 6 sts on st holder, bind off remaining sts. Work 6 inches for shoulder straps, bind off and work ch 3 loop for buttonholes.

☆ PANTIES

With No. 1 needles, and C C cast on 22 sts, loosely, K 1, P 1 row for 4 rows. Change to No. 3 needles, K 1 row increasing 3 sts, P 1 row, K 1 row for 1½ inches. Bind off 3 sts at beg of the next 6 rows. On center 7 sts, K 1 row, P 1 row for 6 rows. Cast on 3 sts at beginning of the next 6 rows (25 sts), K 1 row, P 1 row for 1½ inches. Dec 3 sts, change to No. 1 needles, K 1, P 1 for 4 rows, bind off. Sew panties. S c around pantie legs.

☆ BLOUSE

With No. 1 needles, and C C pick up 22 sts from pants, P back. Next K row inc 4 sts, P back. Change to No. 3 needles, *K 1, Y O, repeat from * across row ending K 1. With No. 1 needles, P back dropping the Y O sts. Repeat these last 2 rows until blouse measures 1½ inches. Bind off 4 sts at beg of the next 2 rows (18 sts left): bind off Y O sts with K sts. Work 3 rows even. Bind off center 10 sts, place first 4 sts on st holder. On last 4 sts work even for 1½ inches for shoulder, cast on 4 sts at neck edge. Work even until piece measures same as front to underarm. Cast on 3 sts for underarm. Work even until piece measures same as for front, bind off. Work other side to correspond.

Sleeve—Holding right side toward you, with No. 1 needles, pick up 30 sts, P back. Follow pattern knitting 2 sts tog each side every 4th row, until you have 18 sts. Change to No. 1 needles, K 1 st, P 1 st (decreasing 2 sts on first row) for 5 rows, bind off. Work other sleeve to correspond.

☆ FINISHING

Sew sleeves and sides, sew blouse to back of panties. Work 1 row of s c around backs and neck working a ch 3 loop for buttonhole at top of blouse. Sew 1 button on blouse and 3 on back of skirt.

☆ HAT

With No. 3 needle and 2 strands of yarn, M C, cast on 8 sts, P back. Next row inc in each st, P back. Inc in first st, K 2, inc, place marker, inc, K 2, inc, place marker, inc, K 2, inc, place marker, inc, K 2, inc. P back. Next row, inc on each side of marker and at beg and end of every K row in same manner having 2 sts more between each marker (thus increasing 8 sts every K row) until you have 96 sts. P back on right side (to make ridge for turning). Now K 2 tog on each side of marker and at beg and end of row until you have 48 sts. With No. 1 needles K 1, P 1 for 4 rows, bind off K 1, P 1. Sew tog.

Reprinted from *Mary's Dollies*, Volume 11, Page 11.

MARY'S DOLLIES

"THE WESTERNER"
INSTRUCTIONS ON PAGE 13

VOLUME No. 12

20¢

Illustration 126. Cover for *Mary's Dollies*, Volume 12.

The Westerner

(illustrated on front cover)

NEEDLES—1 *pair No. 2 American Standard. 1 each Steel Crochet Hooks, size 1 and 3.*

MATERIALS—*1½ ounces light weight Yarn and ½ ounce contrasting shade. 5 small buttons. 1 Westerner belt with buckle.*

GAUGE—*8 sts to 1 inch (measure garment on doll as you make it).*

☆ PANTS

With dark shade, starting at bottom, cast on 22 sts. K 3 rows. P 1 row, K 1 row for ½ inch. *Inc 1 st at beg and end of next row. Work ¾ inch even, repeat from *until piece measures 5½ inches, 36 sts. *On next K row, bind off 2 sts (place marker) this will be front edge, at end of row, K 2 tog. Work 3 rows even, repeat from *2 more times 27 sts. Work even until piece measures 2 inches measuring from first 2 bound off sts. On next K row dec 2 sts. On next purled row, P 20 sts, turn, slip first st, K to back edge, P 15, K back, P 10, K back, P 5, K back. Now K 2 rows, P 1 row, K 1 row for 5 rows. K 2 rows, bind off. Work other leg to correspond. On wrong side sew fronts tog, then backs. Sew leg seams.

☆ BLOUSE

With light shade, starting at back, cast on 26 sts, K 3 rows. *P 1 row, K 1 row for ½ inch. Inc 1 st each side, repeat from *once. Work even until back measures 1¾ inches from start. Bind off 3 sts at beg of the next 2 rows, 24 sts. Work even for 1 inch. K 6 sts (put on safety pin) bind off 12 sts loosely for back of neck, K 6. On these 6 sts, P 1 row, K 1 row for 7 rows. Cast on 7 sts at neck edge. K 1 row, P 1 row for 1¼ inches, always keeping first 3 sts K for border. At armhole edge, cast on 3 sts, work even for 1¾ inches. K 3 rows, bind off. Work other side to correspond.

Collar—Skip 2 sts, on wrong side, pick up 31 sts around neck to within 2 sts on other end. K 2, P back, K last 2 sts. Next row, *K 2, inc 1 st, K to within last 4 sts, inc, K 3. Repeat these two rows until you have 9 rows, K 3 rows border, bind off loosely.

Sleeves—Pick up 5 center sts, P back, Pick up 1 st, turn, K 2, inc in each of the next 3 sts, K 1, pick up 1 st at end of each row (26 sts). Now K 1 row, P 1 row for 1 inch dec 1 st on each side. Work even until sleeve measures 3¼ inches from underarm. On next K row dec 7 sts, K 4 rows, bind off. Sew sleeve seams. Sew on buttons as illustrated, push buttons thru knitted sts.

Bolero—Right side—Cast on 9 sts, P back. Cast on 3 sts—this is front edge, K 1 row P 1 row and cast on 3 sts at front edge 1 more time, K back and on next row at underarm, bind off 4 sts. On next row at front edge inc 1 st. Dec 1 st at armhole edge once. Now K 1 row, P 1 row for 6 rows. Now K 2 tog at front edge every K row, 5 times. On next row at armhole bind off 3 sts at beg of the next 2 rows.

Left side, Work to correspond.

Back—Cast on 28 sts, K 1 row P 1 row, 4 rows. Bind off 4 sts at beg of the next 2 rows, 20 sts left. Work even for 1 inch. K 6 (put on safety pin) bind off 8 sts loosely, K 6. Bind off 3 sts at beg of the next 2 rows at shoulder edge. Work other side to correspond. S c around armhole and bolero.

☆ HAT

With No. 3 Cr hook, ch 3, join, ch 1, work 7 s c in ring. Row 2—Work 2 s c in each st. Row 3—*Work 1 s c in each of the next 2, 2 s c in next st, repeat from *around row. Now inc in every 6th st until you have 30 sts. Now inc in every 10th st until you have 50 sts. Inc in every 15th st until you have 60 sts. Work even until you have 24 rows from beg. On next row dec 4 sts, break thread. With No. 1 cr hook and 2 strands of yarn, with wrong side of crown toward you, work 1 row of s c increasing in every 3rd st around row. Work 3 rnds even. On next rnd inc in every 7th st. Work 3 more rnds even. With contrasting shade, over cast around bolero and hat as follows: Starting at back of bolero over cast as shown on illustration completely around, break thread, with contrasting color work back in opposite direction.

110

Reprinted from *Mary's Dollies*, Volume 12, Page 13.

Peggy

Peggy's beautiful traveling outfit is not complete without her Dolly Suitcase.

Illustration 127. *Mary's Dollies,* Volume 12, Page 4.

Travel Costume

COAT, HAT and BAG

NEEDLES—1 *Steel Crochet Hook, size 3.*
MATERIAL—1 *two-ounce ball Sport Yarn. 8 yards of Angora. 4 small pearl buttons.*
GAUGE—*7 sts to 1 inch. (measure garment on doll as you make it.)*

☆ COAT

Ch 90 sts to measure 14½ inches. S c in 2nd ch from hook, s c to end of ch. *Ch 1, turn, work 2 more rows of s c. On next row, *s c in first 7 s c, skip next st, repeat from * (thus decreasing every 8th st across row), ch 1, turn. Work 3 rows even. Dec every 8th st, every 4th row (do not dec in last 4 sts), until you have 50 sts, meantime on 22nd row, work buttonhole as follows: work across row to within last 3 sts, ch 1, skip 1 s c, s c in last 2 sts. Work 2 more buttonholes, 7 rows apart. Work even until you have 27 rows from beg, 50 sts, ch 1, turn. At beg of 28th row, s c in first 13 sts, ch 1, turn. Work 8 more rows. *Ch 1, turn, work 1 s c in each of the next 8 sts, ch 1, turn. Dec 2 sts at end of row at neck edge, repeat from * once, ch 1, turn. S c over 2 sts for slanting shoulder. Fasten thread at other front and work to correspond.

Back—Skip 2 sts for underarm and work over 20 sts for back (leaving 2 sts on each side for underarm), for 11 rows. Ch 1, s c over 5 s c, ch 1, turn, work over 3 s c for slanting shoulder. Work 2 rows on other shoulder to correspond. Sew shoulder seams. Sleeves—Ch 14, s c in 2nd ch, work 1 s c to end of ch. Ch 1, turn, work 3 more rows even. *Inc 1 st at beg of the next 2 rows. Work 2 rows even, repeat from *until you have 22 rows (23 sts). On next row work to within 3 s c, ch 1, turn, work to within 3 s c of next row. Dec 1 st at end of the next 4 rows. Sew up sleeve, insert into armhole, allowing a little fullness at top of sleeve.

Collar—Skip 3 s c at front, fasten yarn and work 32 s c around neck to within 3 s c at beg of right front. *Ch 3, turn, work 1 row of d c in each st increasing 1 st at beg and end of row. Ch 1, turn, work 1 row of s c, increasing 1 st at beg and end of every row, repeat from *1 more time. With Angora, starting on right side, work 1 row of s c completely around collar increasing 2 sts in each corner. Sew on buttons.

☆ HAT

Ch 58 sts, to measure 9 inches, join, being careful not to twist sts, work 1 s c in each ch around row. Work 3 more rows of s c, place marker. Now work 1 s c in each of the next 6 sts, 3 h d c in next 3 sts, 2 d c in each st until you have 32 d c. Work 3 h d c, 12 s c. Ch 1, turn. Work 6 s c in first 6 s c, 3 h d c in next 3 sts. Work *5 d c in next 5 d c, 2 d c in next st, repeat from *across row to within 6 s c (of marker) at beg of row, end row with 3 h d c, 6 s c. Ch 1, turn, work 3 s c in next 3 sts, 3 h d c in next 3 sts. Now work 1 d c in each st increasing in every 4th st to within 9 sts at beg of row, ending row with 3 h d c, 3 s c, ch 1, turn. Work 6 s c in next 6 sts, 3 h d c in next 3 sts, d c across row (do not inc) to within 9 sts at beg of row below, ending row, 3 h d c, 3 s c, break thread. With Angora, work 1 row of s c completely around brim.

☆ BAG

Ch 14 sts, work 1 s c in 2nd ch from hook, work 1 s c across row, ch 1, turn. Work 5 more rows even. Dec 1 st at end of next 2 rows. Work 1 row even, break thread. Work other side in same manner, do not break thread and work flap by decreasing 1 st at end of every row until you have 2 s c. Ch 3 for buttonhole and fasten off. Ch 6½ inches, join, do not twist ch, work 1 s c in each ch. Sew this piece between the 2 side pieces, leaving surplus for strap. Sew button on bag.

☆ PANTIES

Ch 36, work 1 s c in 2nd ch from hook, 1 s c in each ch to end of row. Row 2—Ch 3, turn, work 1 d c in each st, increasing 5 d c across row. Repeat row 2, 2 more times, join with a sl st, ch 3, turn. Work 3 rows of d c without increasing, join with a sl st. Sl st 1 more st. *Ch 2, turn, work 3 d c in next 3 sts, ch 2, turn, repeat from *2 more times, break thread. Fold panties in half and sew to other side. Work 26 s c around each leg.

Reprinted from *Mary's Dollies*, Volume 12, Page 5.

Greta

This authentic reproduction of Wooden Shoes as worn by the children of Holland, fit Greta to a tee.

Illustration 128. *Mary's Dollies,* Volume 12, Page 6.

A Dutch Treat

MATERIALS—⅞ ounce sport yarn ⅛ ounce contrasting shade, 3 small pearl buttons.

NEEDLES—1 steel crochet hook, size 3.

GAUGE—7 sts to 1 inch.

☆ S K I R T

Ch 36 sts to measure 5½ inches. Row 1—Work 1 d c in 3rd ch from hook, *2 d c in next ch, 1 d c in next ch, repeat from *across row, ch 3, turn. Rows 2 and 3—Repeat row 1. Rows 4 and 5. *Work 1 d c in each of the first 3 sts, 2 d c in next st, repeat from *across row, join with a sl st, ch 3, turn. Row 6—Inc in every 6th st, join with a sl st, break thread.

Work 1 row of s c around top of skirt (34 sts), ch 1, turn, work 4 more rows even, sl st in last st and ch 3 for buttonhole, sl st in 3rd row at end. Sew button on opposite side. Skip 11 s c from end of row and s c across row to within 11 s c from other end, ch 1, turn. S c on these center 12 sts, for 12 rows. Ch 1, turn, work over 2 s c, ch 1, turn. Work 2 s c for strap until piece measures 3½ inches, ch 3 for loop, skip 1 st, sl st in next st, fasten off. Work other strap to correspond, do not break thread but s c on center edges of straps and around front at neck edge.

☆ J A C K E T

With contrasting shade, Ch 33 sts, work 1 s c in 2nd ch from hook, s c to end of row, ch 1, turn. Work 3 more rows even.* On next row inc 4 sts at equal distances apart. Work 1 row even, repeat from *once, 8 rows, 40 sts. Ch 1, turn, work over 7 s c for front. Work armhole edge even and dec 1 st at front edge until 4 st remain. Work even on 4 sts until you have 20 rows from beg. Ch 1, turn, work over 2 sts for slanting shoulder. Work other front to correspond.

Back—Skip 2 sts for underarm, s c to within 2 sts on other side, ch 1, turn. Work even until you have 20 rows from beg. Sew shoulder seams tog. Starting at right side on left front fasten thread and work 1 row of s c to other side of front. Ch 3, turn, skip 1 s c, *work 1 s c in each of the next 3 sts, Ch 3, repeat from *2 more times. S c around neck, work loops on opposite side to correspond.

Lacer—With double strands, ch 76, break thread. Lace as shown on illustration.

Sleeves—Fasten thread at center of underarm and with contrasting color work 27 s c around armhole, join with a sl st, ch 1. Row 2, with main color work 3 s c in first 3 sts, 3 h d c (Y O needle, insert needle thru next st, Y O needle, draw thru, Y O needle draw thru all sts), in next 3 sts. Work 2 d c in each st to within the last 6 sts. Work 3 h d c in next 3 sts, 3 s c in last 3 sts, join with a sl st, ch 1. Row 3—Work same as row 2, but do not increase. Row 4—Work 1 row of s c in every other st, join with a sl st. Work 1 row even.

☆ P A N T I E S

Ch 36, work 1 s c in 2nd ch from hook, 1 s c in each ch to end of row. Row 2—Ch 3 turn, work 1 d c in each st, increasing 5 d c across row. Repeat row 2, 2 more times, join with a sl st, ch 3, turn, Work 3 rows of d c without increasing, join with a sl st. Sl st 1 more st. *Ch 2, turn, work 3 d c in next 3 sts, ch 2 turn, repeat from *2 more times, break thread. Fold panties in half and sew to other side. Work 26 s c around each leg.

☆ C A P

Starting at center, ch 3, join with a sl st to form ring. First rnd, Ch 3 (to count as d c), 2 d c in ring, ch 3, *3 d c in ring. Ch 3, repeat from *2 more times. Join with a sl st to 3rd st of starting ch. Second rnd. Sl st in each st to first ch loop, ch 3, 2 d c in loop, ch 3, 3 d c in same loop, ch 3 * (3 d c, ch 3, 3 d c) in next loop, ch 3, repeat from *2 more times. Join as before. Third rnd. Sl st in each st to first ch loop, ch 3, 2 d c in loop, ch 3, 3 d c in same loop, ch 3, 3 d c in next loop, ch 3, *(3 d c, ch 3, 3 d c) in next loop, ch 3, 3 d c in next loop, ch 3, repeat from *2 more times. Join as before. Make 3 more blocks. Join two blocks with 1 row of s c across one side. Join third block to side of block one and one side of block two. Join fourth block to opposite sides of blocks two and one. Keep s c loose enough to prevent drawing. Work 1 row of s c completely around cap. S c 1 more row decreasing 3 sts (spaced a few sts apart) at back and front of cap, working scallop on corners as follows. On center d c group (about 8 s c from center point) ch 3, skip 2 s c, d c in next st, ch 3, sl st in first st (peco), d c in same st, ch 3, skip 2 s c, s c in next st, ch 3, skip 2 d c in center (at point) peco and d c in same st, continue same as beg of scallops. Work other corner in same manner.

Finishing—Sew 2 more buttons on back of skirt (about ½ inch from center button).

Jo-Ann

This sea-worthy rubber bathing cap as worn by Jo-Ann, comes complete with snap and fastener. Fits her perfectly.

Illustration 129. *Mary's Dollies,* Volume 12, Page 10.

Swimming Suit

NEEDLES—1 pr. American Standard No. 2.

MATERIAL—½ oz. Fingering Yarn.

GAUGE—9 sts to 1 inch.

PATTERN—P 2, K 1. Next row, P 1, K 2.

Starting at top, cast on 21 sts, K 2 rows. K 2 (border), *P 2, K 1 repeat from *across row, ending row, K 2. Next row, K 1, inc 1 st, follow pattern to within last 2 sts, inc 1 st, K 1. Continue to inc in every other row keeping first and last 2 sts K for border, until you have 39 sts. Cast on 7 sts for back, K 9 sts, follow pattern across row, cast on 7 sts. On next row, *K 9 follow pattern across row to within 9 sts, K 9, repeat from *once. Discontinue borders and work in pattern for 3¼ inches, measuring straight from center of front. Work over 13 sts, bind off 5 sts, follow pattern for 17 sts, bind off 5 sts, work to end of row (place 1 back and front on st holder). Work over 13 sts in pattern. Now bind off 2 sts at beg of every row at side only, until 3 sts remain, bind off. Pick up sts on front, and K 2 tog at beg of every row until 5 sts remain, bind off. Work other back to correspond. Pick up 28 sts around legs, K 4 rows, bind off on wrong side. Sew bottom and back tog. Fasten thread on each side of front and work 40 chs.

MARY'S DOLLIES

VOLUME No. 13

Illustration 130. Cover for *Mary's Dollies*, Volume 13.

20¢

Mary Hoyer Twins
(illustrated on front cover)

NEEDLES—1 pair American Standard No. 1 and No. 3
MATERIAL—1 oz. Fingering M C; 1/8 oz. C C, 7 small buttons.
GAUGE—8 sts to 1 inch.
(Measure garment on Doll as you make it.)

BOBBY

☆ CARDIGAN

Left Front—With No. 1 needles and M C, starting at bottom, cast on 16 sts. K 1, P 1, ribbing, for 5 rows, always keeping first and last 3 sts K on purled rows for border on front. Change to No. 3 needles. Row 1—With M C K 6, drop M C and with C C K 1 (always being careful to pick up new color from underneath the dropped one). With M C K 9. Row 2—K 3, P 5, C C P 3, M C P 5. Row 3—K 4, C C K 5, M C K 7. Row 4—K 3, P 5, C C P 3, M C P 5. Row 5—K 6, C C K 1, M C K 9. Row 6—K 3, P 6, C C P 1, M C P 6. Next row, K 5, C C K 3, M C K 8. Continue in pattern until piece measures 2 inches from start. Bind off 2 sts at beg of next row at underarm. Continue pattern for 1 inch. Bind off 5 sts on front at beg of next row and K 2 tog at beg of next row at neck edge, 2 times. Complete 6th diamond and work even until armhole measures 2 inches. Place on stitch holder.

Right Front—Work ribbing to correspond to left front and start pattern as follows: with No. 3 needles, P 6, C C P 1, M C P 6, K 3 border. Continue pattern to correspond to left front. Now with right sides toward you, cast on 8 sts for neck, join right front and K 1 row, P 1 row for 1 inch. Cast on 2 sts at end of next 2 rows at underarm (26 sts). K 1 row, P 1 row, for 1½ inches. Change to No. 1 needles and dec 3 sts, K 1, P 1, ribbing for 5 rows, bind off.

Sleeves—With No. 3 needle, pick up 22 center sts, P back. Pick up 3 sts at end of next 2 rows (28 sts). P 1 row, K 1 row and dec 1 st at beg and end of every 6th row until you have 20 sts. Work even until sleeve measures 3¼ inches. Change to No. 1 needles, K 1, P 1 for 4 rows, bind off loosely. Sew sleeves and side seams tog.

Neck Band—With right side toward you, and No. 1 needles, pick up 34 sts, K 1, P 1 ribbing for 5 rows, bind off loosely in K 1, P 1.

☆ PANTS

With No. 1 needles, cast on 22 sts, K 1, P 1 for 5 rows. Change to No. 3 needles, K 1 row, increasing 4 sts. P 1 row, K 1 row for 1¾ inches. Bind off 4 sts at beg of the next 4 rows. Bind off 2 sts at beg of next 2 rows. On center 6 sts, K 1 row, P 1 row for 6 rows. Cast on 2 sts at beg of next 2 rows and cast on 4 sts at beg of next 4 rows. (26 sts). K 1 row, P 1 row for 1 1/3 inches. Dec. 4 sts, change to No. 1 needles, K 1, P 1 for 5 rows, bind off loosely. With No. 1 needles, pick up 32 sts around legs, K 1, P 1 ribbing for 5 rows, bind off loosely. Sew side seams.

☆ BEANIE

With No. 3 needles, cast on 8 sts, P back. Row 2—Inc in each st (16 sts), P back. Row 4—*Inc 1 st, K 1 st, repeat from *across row (24 sts), P back. Row 6—*Inc 1 st, K 2 sts, repeat from *across row, P back. Continue in this manner having 1 more st between each inc, until you have 7 sts between increases (72 sts). K 1 row, P 1 row without increasing for 4 rows. Now dec in same manner as you increased. *K 2 sts tog, K 7, repeat from *across row, P back. Dec in this manner having 1 st less between each dec for 1 more K row. (56 sts). Change to No. 1 needles, K 1, P 1 ribbing for 4 rows, bind off loosely.

☆ SLIP-OVER

Front—With No. 1 needles and C C starting at bottom, cast on 22 sts, K 1, P 1, ribbing for 4 rows. Change to No. 3 needles, K 1 row, P 1 row until piece measures 1¾ inches from beg. Bind off 2 sts at beg of next 2 rows for underarm. Work even for ¾ inch. On next row, K 5, bind off 8 sts loosely, K 5. Work 1 inch on these 5 sts, cast on 7 sts at neck edge keeping 2 sts K on purled rows for border at back. K 1 row, P 1 row, for 1 inch and cast on 2 sts at underarm. Continue in pattern to correspond to front in length. Continue from other shoulder to correspond.

Sleeve Bands—With No. 1 needles, pick up center 20 sts, K 1, P 1, pick up 2 sts at end of next 2 rows. K 1, P 1, for 3 more rows, bind off loosely in K 1, P 1. Sew side seams. Sew on 3 buttons at back and push thru K sts.

Neck Band—With No. 1 needles, pick up 38 sts, K 1, P 1, for 4 rows, bind off K 1, P 1 loosely.

BETTY

☆ CARDIGAN—Same as for Boy.
☆ SLIP-OVER—Same as for Boy.
☆ BEANIE—Same as for boy.
☆ PANTIES—Same as for boy, but instead of picking up bands for legs, s c around pantie legs. Tape yarn thru top of panties and tie.
☆ SKIRT

Cast on 143 sts, K 3 rows. P 1 row, K 1 row, P 1 row. Next row, *K 9, K 2 tog, repeat from *to end of row. Work 3 rows even. K 8, K 2 tog across row. Continue to dec every 4th row having 1 st less between every dec, until you have 52 sts. Work 5 rows even. Change to No. 1 needles, dec 4 sts across row and K 1, P 1 ribbing for 4 rows, bind off loosely. With double strand of yarn tape thru center of ribbing and tie at back. Sew skirt ½ way from bottom.

Reprinted from *Mary's Dollies*, Volume 13, Page 13.

Nancy AND Dick

Illustration 131. *Mary's Dollies*, Volume 13, Page 4.

DUDE RANCH

The Cow Boy and Girl

NEEDLES—1 pair No. 1 and No. 3 American Standard.

MATERIAL—1 ounce Fingering Yarn, 1/8 ounce C C, 3 small buttons, 1 two-gun holster.

GAUGE—7½ sts to 1 inch.

(Measure garment on Doll as you make it.)

DICK

☆ PANTS

With M C, starting at bottom, cast on 22 sts. K 3 rows, P 1 row, K 1 row for ½ inch. *Inc 1 st at beg and end of next row. Work ¾ inch even, repeat from *until piece measures 5½ inches, 36 sts. *On next K row, bind off 2 sts (place marker) this will be front edge, at end of row, K 2 tog. Work 3 rows even, repeat from *2 more times 27 sts. Work even until piece measures 2 inches measuring from first 2 bound off sts. On next K row dec 2 sts. On next purled row, P 20 sts, turn, slip first st, K to back edge, P 15, K back, P 10, K back, P 5, K back. Now K 2 rows, P 1 row, K 1 row for 5 rows. K 2 rows, bind off. Work other leg to correspond. On wrong side sew fronts tog, then backs. Sew leg seams.

☆ JACKET

With M C, starting at back, with No. 1 needles; cast on 24 sts, K 1, P 1 ribbing for 4 rows. Change to No. 3 needles, K 1 row, P 1 row increasing 3 sts at equal distances apart. P 1 row, K 1 row, until piece measures 2 inches from start. Now bind off 2 sts on each side for underarm. On next row K 11, with C C K 1, drop C C, with M C K 11 (always being careful to pick up new color from underneath the dropped one). Next row, M C P 10, C C P 3, M C P 10. Continue in this manner having 2 more sts in C C in each row until you have 7 sts in C C; at end of row, break thread on M C and continue to K 1 row, P 1 row with C C to complete yoke. When piece measures 2 inches from underarm, K 6, place on st holder, bind off 11 sts loosely for back of neck, K 6. On these 6 sts, P 1 row K 1 row for 7 rows. Cast on 7 sts at neck edge. K 1 row, P 1 row for 1 inch, always keeping first 3 sts K for border on front. On next row at neck edge, K 9, M C K 4, next row M C P 5, C C P 5, K 3. Continue in this manner working 1 more st in M C on each row to form yoke, until all sts are in M C (continue to keep 3 border sts in C C). Now cast on 2 sts at underarm and work length same as for back following pattern for ribbing at bottom. Work right side to correspond.

Sleeves—M C, pick up 21 center sts, P back and pick up 3 sts at end of next 2 rows (27 sts). K 1 row, P 1 row and dec 1 st at beg and end of every 6th row until you have 19 sts, P back, on next row with M C K 9, C C K 1, M C K 9. Next row, P 8, C C P 3, M C P 8. Continue center C C until you have 7 sts, break M C. With C C, K 1 row. Next row, with No. 1 needles, K 1, P 1 ribbing for 3 rows, bind off loosely.

Collar—Skip 2 sts, on wrong side of work, pick up 28 sts around neck to within 2 sts on other end. K 2, P across row, K 2. Next row, inc in first st, K to within last 2 sts, inc 1 st, K 1. Repeat these 2 rows until you have 7 rows. K 2 rows for border, bind off loosely on wrong side.

Finishing—Sew sleeve and side seam. Sew on buttons, push buttons thru knitted sts. Embroider hat and jacket as shown on illustration.

NANCY

☆ JACKET—Same as for Boy.

☆ SKIRT

Cast on 90 sts, K 3 rows. P 1 row, K 1 row for 5 rows. Next row, *K 8, K 2 tog, repeat from *across row. Work 5 rows even. K 7, K 2 tog across row. Now dec every 6th row, having 1 st less between every dec, until you have 45 sts. Work 3 rows even after last dec. P 1 row on K side. Now P 1 row, K 1 row for 6 rows, K 2 rows, bind off loosely. Sew skirt ½ way from bottom. Tie at back.

☆ PANTS

Same as for Betty's on Page 14.

Hans AND Tina

Illustration 132. *Mary's Dollies,* Volume 13, Page 6.

"The Pond's Sweethearts"
Hans and Tina

NEEDLES—1 *set Nos. 1 and 3 double pointed needles, American Standard.*
MATERIAL—*2 oz. Sport Yarn, 1/8 ounce C C, 8 buttons.*
GAUGE—*7½ sts to 1 inch.*
(Measure garment on Doll as you make it.)

DUTCH BOY

☆ JACKET

With No. 1 needles, cast on 24 sts, K 1, P 1, ribbing for 5 rows. Change to No. 3 needles, K 1 row, increasing 4 sts at equal distances apart. P 1 row, K 1 row, until piece measures 1¾ inches from start. Bind off 2 sts on each side for underarm. Work even for 1 inch. On next purled row, P 5, K 14, P 5. K next row. P 5, K 2 bind off 10, K 2, P 5. On these 7 sts, K 1 row, P 1 row, keeping first 2 sts K on Purled rows for border at front. When piece measures 2 inches from bound off sts at neck, cast on 2 sts for underarm, work even to correspond to back. Work other front to correspond.

Sleeves—Pick up center 20 sts, P back, pick up 3 sts at end of next 2 rows, 26 sts. Work 1 inch even. Now dec. 1 st each side and continue to dec. 1 st each side every inch until you have 3 inches, 20 sts. Change to No. 1 needles, K 1, P 1 for 4 rows, bind off.

☆ JACKET BIB

With No. 3 needles and C C cast on 12 sts, K 2 rows. K 1 row, P 1 row for ¾ inch, keeping first and last 2 sts K on purled rows for border on sides. Inc 1 st in 3rd st from beg and 4th st from end, on K rows, 3 times, ¾ inches apart. (18 sts) K 2 rows, border, bind off on wrong side. Sew buttons on Jacket (4 on each side) and make buttonholes by pushing buttons thru on 2nd st on borders.

☆ PANTS

With No. 1 needles, cast on 40 sts, 12 sts on first needle, 12 sts on 2nd needle, 16 sts on 3rd needle, join, K 1, P 1, for 1 inch. Change to No. 3 needles, *inc in first 2 sts, K 1, repeat from *around row (68 sts). K plain for 2½ inches. Put 34 sts on st holder, cast on 8 sts for crotch; join, on these 42 sts, K 5 inches.

Cuff—K 2 sts tog until you have 16 sts, change to No. 1 needles, K 1, P 1 for 1 inch, bind off loosely. Put 34 sts on 3 needles, pick up 8 sts on crotch, work to correspond to other leg.

☆ HAT

With No. 3 needles, cast on 8 sts, P back. Row 2—Inc in each st (16 sts), P back. Row 4—*Inc 1 st, K 1 st, repeat from *across row (24 sts), P back. Row 6—*Inc 1 st, K 2 sts, repeat from *across row, P back. Continue in this manner having 1 more st between each inc until you have 9 sts between increases (88 sts). P 1 row, K 1 row without increasing for 5 rows. Dec in same manner as you increased; *K 2 tog, K 9, repeat from *across row, P back. Dec in this manner having 1 st less between each dec for 3 more K rows (56 sts). Change to No. 1 needles, K 10 rows (5 ribs), garter st. Bind off loosely 20 sts, K 16 sts, (visor of cap), turn, change to No. 3 needles, P back on these 16 sts. K 2 tog, at beg of row, K 3, inc 1 st, K 4, inc 1 st, K 3, K 2 tog, P back. K 2 tog at beg and end of next 2 K rows. On next P side, K 1 row (to turn visor). K 1 row, P 1 row. Now inc 1 st at beg and end of K rows until this side measures same as front side of visor (about ¾ inch). Bind off loosely. Bind off remaining 20 sts. Sew sides of visor and bottom. Sew cap tog on wrong side.

☆ SCARF

With No. 3 needles, cast on 8 sts, work in garter st for 2 inches. Dec 2 center sts, continue in garter st, for 6 inches. Inc 2 sts, continue for 2 more inches, bind off loosely. Work fringe on each end 1 inch long.

DUTCH GIRL

☆ JACKET—Same as for Boy.

☆ SKIRT

With M C and No. 3 needles, cast on 140 sts, K 3 rows for border. P 1 row, K 1 row for 7 rows and dec as follows: K 8, K 2 tog for 1 row. Work 3 rows even. **Stripe: With C C * K 1, Y O, 2 times, repeat from *across row. With M C, P back, dropping the Y O sts. K 1 row, P 1 row and make another dec: K 7, K 2 tog. K 1 row, P 1 row until you have 9 rows from C C. Repeat from first stripe ** 2 more times having 1 st less between each decreased row; and 7 rows between C C instead of 9. Work 1 inch even after last dec: K 4, K 2 tog for 1 row. Work even until piece measures 5½ inches. *K 2 tog, K 1, repeat from *across row. Change to No. 1 needles, K 1, P 1 ribbing for 5 rows, bind off loosely. With 2 strands of yarn, tape thru center of beading and tie at back. Sew skirt tog, 5 inches from bottom.

☆ CAP

Back, starting at bottom, with No. 3 needles, cast on 10 sts, K in garter st for 7 rows (4 ribs). *Inc 1 st at beg and end of next row. K 6 rows even, repeat from *until you have 18 sts. Work even until you have 33 rows (17 ribs) from beg. Dec 1 st at beg and end of every row until you have 10 sts, bind off.

Starting at bottom of front piece, cast on 14 sts (K in garter st), inc 1 st at beg of every row on front edge, until you have 21 sts. Work

3 rows even. Now dec on front edge until you have 16 sts. Work even until you have 32 ribs from beg. Inc to 21 sts on front edge. Work 3 rows even and dec to 14 sts, bind off. Sew back piece of cap to straight piece of front of cap. Over-cast with contrasting shade around back of piece just sewed, work back thru same st, over-casting in opposite direction. Work 1 row of S C around front of cap working 2 s c at points. Overcast front of cap in same manner. Embroider flower in points.

☆ TIES

Ch 32, fold point of cap back about ¼ inch S C over back of cap, work other side to correspond.

☆ SCARF—Same as for Boy.

☆ PANTIES

With No. 1 needles, Cast on 22 sts, K 1, P 1 for 5 rows. Change to No. 3 needles, K 1 row, increasing 4 sts. P 1 row, K 1 row, for 1¾ inches. Bind off 4 sts at beg of the next 4 rows. Bind off 2 sts at beg of next 2 rows. On center 6 sts, K 1 row, P 1 row for 6 rows. Cast on 2 sts at beg of next 2 rows and cast on 4 sts at beg of next 4 rows. (26 sts). K 1 row, P 1 row for 1¾ inches. Dec 4 sts, change to No. 1 needles, K 1, P 1 for 5 rows, bind off loosely. Sew panties. S C around pantie legs.

Reprinted from *Mary's Dollies*, Volume 13, Page 7.

Carol

Suit and Hat
CAROL

NEEDLES—1 *Steel Crochet Hook, size 3.*

MATERIAL—1 *two ounce ball sport Yarn, 24 yards Astrican Wool or Angora. 4 small buttons.*

GAUGE—7 *sts to 1 inch.*

(Measure garment on Doll as you make it.)

☆ JACKET

Ch 41 sts to measure 6 inches. S c in 2nd ch from hook, s c to end of row, ch 1, turn. Work 3 more rows of s c. On next row, inc 6 sts (about every 6th st across row), 46 sts. Work even until you have 9 rows from beg. Ch 1, turn, work 1 s c in each of the next 10 s c, ch 1, turn, work over these 10 sts, until you have 18 rows from beg. Ch 1, turn, work over 6 s c, ch 1, turn, work 4 more rows, decreasing 1 st at neck edge at end of next 2 rows. Ch 1, turn, work over 2 s c for slanting shoulder, break thread. Fasten thread at other end of front and work to correspond.

Back—Skip 3 s c at underarm and s c to within 3 s c of other front. Work even across back until you have 19 rows from beg, ch 1, turn, work over 6 s c, ch 1, turn, work over 2 s c for shoulder. Work other shoulder for 2 rows to correspond. Sew shoulder seams. Holding right side toward you, start yarn at bottom of front on right side, work s c up front making 4 buttonholes as follows: ch 3, skip a small space, s c in next st, work about 5 s c between buttonholes. Work 2 s c to turn corners around neck. S c down left front. Continue for first row of peblum on bottom, increasing in every 3rd st across row, Ch 1, turn, work 1 row even, do not s c in last st at end of row, thru out peblum. Row 3—Inc every 4th st. Row 4—Work even. Row 5—Inc every 5th st, break thread.

Collar—On right side, skip 2 s c and work around neck (to within 2 s c from other front), increasing every 4th st across row and do not work in last st at end of row thru out collar. Work 4 rows even. Now inc in every 5th st, break thread.

Sleeves—Ch 15, s c in 2nd ch, work 1 s c to end of ch, ch 1, turn. Work 3 more rows even. *Inc 1 st at beg of the next 2 rows. Work 2 rows even, repeat from *until you have 20 rows (22 sts). On next row work to within 3 s c, ch 1, turn, work to within 3 s c of next row. Dec 1 st at end of next 4 rows. Sew sleeve, insert into armhole, allowing a little fullness at top of sleeve.

☆ SKIRT

Ch 42 sts, to measure 6 inches, work 1 s c in 2nd ch from hook, work 1 s c to end of row. Ch 1, turn. Work 3 rows even. Row 5. *Inc in every 5th st across row. Work 1 row even, repeat from * until you have 12 rows from beg, join at beg of row with a sl st, ch 1, turn. *Next row inc in every 10th st. Work 2 rows even repeat from * until you have 20 rows from beg.

☆ MUFF

Ch 14 sts, loosely, join, ch 1, work 1 s c in each ch, join with a sl st, ch 3. Row 2—*Work 1 d c in next st, 2 d c in next st, repeat from *around. Join with a sl st, ch 3. Row 3—Work 1 d c in each st, join, ch 1. Row 4—Work 1 s c in first st. *Skip 1 st, 1 s c in next st, repeat from *around, join, break thread. Work 2 rows of s c with yarn on each end. Ch 14, sl st in same st.

☆ BONNET

Ch 3, join, ch 1, work 7 s c in ring. Row 2—Work 2 s c in each st. Row 3—*Work 1 s c in next st, 2 s c in next st, repeat from *around row. Row 4—*Work 1 s c in each of the next 2 sts. 2 s c in next st, repeat from *around row. Now inc in every 5th st until you have 58 sts around. Work even until you have 16 rows. On 17th row dec 4 sts spaced at equal distances apart. Ch 1, turn, work to within 15 sts at beg of row. *Ch 1, turn, work to within 1 st at beg of row below, repeat from *once, ch 1, turn.

Brim—*Inc in every other st to within 2 sts at beg of row, ch 1, turn, repeat from *once. Now work in same manner to within 3 sts at end of rows, increasing about 2 sts in each row, until you have 9 rows from beg of first increased row of brim. S c over end and sl st across back and s c over other end at beg of 9th row.

Finishing—Work 1 row of trimming around collar and peblum. Work 1 row around brim of bonnet. With 2 strands of yarn, tape thru 2nd row on top of skirt and tie at back. Tie panties at back. Sew on buttons.

☆ PANTIES

Ch 36, work 1 s c in 2nd ch from hook, 1 s c in each ch to end of row. Row 2—Ch 3, turn, work 1 d c in each st, increasing 4 d c across row. Repeat row 2, 2 more times, join with a sl st, ch 3, turn. Work 3 rows of d c without increasing. Join with a sl st. Sl st 1 more st. *Ch 3, turn, work 4 d c in next 4 sts, repeat from * 2 more times, break thread. Fold panties in half and sew to other side. With trimming work 27 s c around each leg.

Reprinted from *Mary's Dollies*, Volume 13, Page 11.

MARY'S DOLLIES

LOUISE
INSTRUCTIONS ON PAGE 13

ANIMATED NURSERY TALES

VOLUME No. 14   Illustration 134. Cover for *Mary's Dollies*, Volume 14.   20¢

Travel in the Best Circles

— LOUISE —

(*illustrated on front cover*)

NEEDLES—1 *steel crochet hook size 4.*

MATERIAL—1 *one-ounce skein fingering yarn. 12 yards trimming. 2 small buttons.*

GAUGE—7 *sts to 1 inch.*

☆ DRESS

Starting at top, ch 52 sts to measure 7½ inches. Work 1 s c in 2nd ch from hook, s c in each ch across row, ch 3, turn. Row 2—Work 1 d c in each of the next 8 sts. Frill at sleeve—*Ch 1, d c in next st, ch 1, d c in same st, repeat from *8 more times, ch 1. Work 2 d c in each st across front to within 18 s c, repeat between stars for (frill at sleeve) ch 1, work 1 d c in last 9 sts, back, ch 1, turn. Row 3—Work 1 s c in each of the next 8 sts, ch 4. Skip frill at sleeve, s c across front to ch 1 at beg of 2nd frill at sleeve, ch 4, skip frill, s c in last 9 s c across back, ch 3, turn. Row 4—Work 1 d c in each st across row, ch 1, turn. Row 5—Work 1 s c in each st across row, ch 3 turn. Row 6—Repeat row 4, ch 1, turn. Row 7—S c in first 9 sts *skip 1 s c, work 1 s c in each of the next 2 s c, repeat from *across row to within 9 s c. Work 1 s c in last 9 s c, ch 1, turn. Rows 8-9-10-11-12 work even in s c, ch 3, turn. Row 13—*Work 1 d c in each of the next 3 sts, 2 d c in next st, repeat from *across row, thus increasing in every 4th st across row, ch 1, turn. Work 1 s c in each st across row. Repeat last 2 rows until you have 3 d c rows from waist line, join with a sl st, ch 1, turn continue in pattern, joining each row and turning. When skirt has 5 d c rows from waist line, inc in every 6th st (7 d c rows). Finish with a s c row.

Finishing—Fasten thread at left side of back and make a ch 3 loop for buttonhole and a loop at top. Sew on buttons. With trimming fasten at underarm, s c to ch 1, frill at sleeve *ch 1, sl st between s c, repeat from *around frill, s c and fasten off at underarm. Work 1 row of s c in each st around neck, dec across front if necessary to fit neck line.

Cord—Ch 30 inches, sl st in each ch. Tie around waist as shown on illustration.

☆ PANTIES

Ch 38, work 1 s c in 2nd ch from hook, 1 s c in each ch to end of row. Row 2—Ch 3, turn, work 1 d c in each st, increasing 4 d c across row. Repeat row 2, 2 more times, join with a sl st, ch 3, turn. Work 3 rows of d c without increasing, join with a sl st. Sl st 1 more st. *Ch 3, turn, work 3 d c in next 3 sts, ch 2, turn, repeat from *2 more times, break thread. Fold panties in half and sew to other side. Work 28 s c around each leg.

☆ HAT

Tie ribbon around hat and tie bow in back. Sew flowers on front.

Connie

Illustration 135. *Mary's Dollies,* Volume 14, Page 4.

127

Short and Sweet

— CONNIE —

NEEDLES—1 *pair No. 1 and No. 3, American standard.*

MATERIAL—*2 oz. Sport Yarn, 3 small pearl buttons*

GAUGE—*7½ sts to 1 inch. (Measure garment on doll as you make it).*

☆ COAT

With No. 3 needles, cast on 20 sts. Row 1—K 2 front (inc in next st, place marker, inc in next st, seam) K 1 sleeve, inc, place marker, inc, K 6 back, inc, place marker, inc, K 1 sleeve, inc, place marker, inc, K 2 front. Row 2—P back. Row 3—Inc 1 st, K 1 front, inc before and after each marker across row and inc in last st. Row 4—P back. Row 5—Cast on 2 sts at end of next 2 rows and continue to inc before and after each marker. Row 6—P back, keeping first and last 3 sts K at beg and end on purled rows for border down fronts. Row 7—Follow pattern, inc before and after each marker. Repeat last 2 rows until you have 106 sts. K across front for 16 sts, place on st holder, K 24 sts, sleeve, now place remaining sts on st holder. On these 24 sts for sleeve, *P 1 row, K 1 row for ¾ inch, dec 1 st at beg and end of row, repeat from * 2 more times. When sleeve measures 3 inches. K 1 row on the P side, to turn for cuff. Now P 1 row, K 1 row, inc 1 st at each end of K row. Work 2 more rows without increasing. K 2 rows, bind off on wrong side. Place sts of other sleeve on needle and work to correspond. K across back (increasing 5 sts on back) K right front following pattern, P back and continue left front. Work 4 rows even. Now inc 2 sts at each underarm (thus increasing 4 sts across row). Inc in this manner 3 more times, 6 rows apart. When coat measures 3½ inches, K 4 rows for border, bind off on wrong side loosely.

Collar—Skip 2 sts, on wrong side of work, with No. 1 needle, pick up 28 sts around neck to within 2 sts on other end. K 2, P across, K 2. Next row, with No. 3 Needles, K 2, inc, K to within last 4 sts, inc. K 3. Repeat these 2 rows until you have 11 rows. K 2 rows for border, bind off loosely on wrong side.

Finishing—Sew sleeve and cuff, turn back. Sew on buttons, push thru knitted sts.

☆ BERET

With No. 3 needles, cast on 8 sts, P back. Row 2—Inc in each st (16 sts), P back. Row 4—*Inc 1 st, K 1 st, repeat from *across row (24 sts), P back. Row 6—*Inc 1 st, K 2 sts, repeat from *across row, P back. Continue in this manner having 1 more st between each inc until you have 9 sts between increases (88 sts). P 1 row, K 1 row without increasing for 10 rows. Dec in same manner as you increased; *K 2 tog, K 9, repeat from *across row, P back. Dec in this manner having 1 st less between each dec for 3 more K rows (56 sts). Change to No. 1 needles, K 1, P 1 for 5 rows, bind off loosely.

☆ PANTIES

With No. 1 needles, cast on 24 sts, loosely K 1, P 1 row for 4 rows. Change to No. 3 needles, K 1 row increasing 2 sts, P 1 row, K 1 row for 1½ inches. Bind off 3 sts at beg of the next 6 rows. On center 8 sts, K 1 row, P 1 row for 6 rows. Cast on 3 sts at beginning of the next 6 rows (26 sts), K 1 row, P 1 row for 1½ inches. Dec 2 sts, change to No. 1 needles, K 1, P 1 for 4 rows, bind off. Sew panties. S.C. around pantie legs.

Nan and Jack

Illustration 136. *Mary's Dollies*, Volume 14, Page 6.

The Ship's In
— NAN —

NEEDLES—1 *steel crochet hook, size 3.*

MATERIALS—1 *two ounce ball Sport Yarn, small amount of White for Trim, 3 small buttons.*

GAUGE—7 *sts to 1 inch.* (*Measure garment on doll as you make it*).

☆ COAT

Starting at waist line, ch 44 sts to measure 6 inches, work 1 d c in 4th ch from hook, work 2 d c in next st, thus increasing in every other st across row, ch 3 turn. Row 2—Inc in every 4th st across row, ch 3, turn. Work 5 more rows increasing every 6th st in each row, but do not increase in first and last 6 sts, break thread (7 rows). Starting at waist line, skip 1 st and s c across row, skipping 3 sts across back about 3 sts apart to within 1 st at end of row, ch 1, turn. Work 3 rows even. On next row, inc 4 sts spaced at equal distances apart. Work 3 rows even. On next row inc 4 more sts, ch 1, turn. Work 1 more row even (10 rows from beg). Ch 1, turn, work 1 s c in each of the next 10 sts, ch 1, turn, dec 1 st at end of every row at front edge until you have 6 sts. Work even until you have 12 rows from underarm, ch 1, turn. Work 3 s c (for slanting shoulder), break thread. Fasten thread at other end and work to correspond.

Back—Skip 2 sts for underarm and s c across back to within 2 sts at other front, ch 1, turn. Work even for 12 more rows, ch 1, turn, work 6 s c in next 6 sts, ch 1, turn, s c over 3 sts, break thread. Fasten thread at other end of back and work slanting shoulder to correspond.

Sleeves—Ch 14 loosely, s c in 2nd ch, work 1 s c to end of ch. Ch 1, turn, work 3 more rows even. *Inc 1 st at beg of the next 2 rows. Work 2 rows even, repeat from *until you have 22 rows (23 sts). On next row work to within 3 s c, ch 1, turn, work to within 3 s c of next row. Dec 1 st at end of the next 4 rows. Sew sleeves, insert into armhole, allowing a little fullness at top of sleeve.

Collar—Ch 16, work 1 s c in 2nd ch from hook, s c in each st across ch, ch 1, turn. Work 5 rows even. Work over 4 s c for 6 rows. Dec 1 st on inside of collar and work over 3 s c for 4 rows. Dec 1 st at inside and work over 2 s c for 4 rows. Dec to 1 st. Now work other side of collar to correspond. On outside of collar work 1 row of s c around increasing 2 s c at corners. With white work 1 row of s c in same manner. Sew on coat.

☆ PANTIES

Ch 36, work 1 s c in 2nd ch from hook, 1 s c in each ch to end of row. Row 2—Ch 3, turn, work 1 d c in each st, increasing 4 d c across row. Repeat row 2, 2 more times, join with a sl st, ch 3, turn. Work 3 rows of d c without increasing, join with a sl st. Sl st 1 more st. *Ch 3, turn. Work 3 d c in next 3 sts, ch 2, turn, repeat from *2 more times, break thread. Fold panties in half and sew to other side. Work 26 s c around each leg.

☆ HAT

Ch 3, join, ch 1, work 7 s c in ring. Row 2—Work 2 s c in each st. Row 3—*Work 1 s c in next st, 2 s c in next st, repeat from *around row. Now inc in every 5th st until you have 56 sts rnd. Now inc in every 10th st until you have 90 sts rnd, break thread. Starting band, ch 4, work 1 s c in each ch (3 s c), ch 1, turn. Work in this manner for 60 rows from beg, sew tog, s c in each st along one side, join with a sl st. Now work around increasing in every 4th st. Work 2 rows even. Row 5, Inc in every 10 st for 1 rnd. Now inc in every 15th st until you have 90 s c around, break thread. With white, ch 4, work 3 s c, same as band for 110 rows.

Finishing—Sew white strip to top of crown and sew bottom piece of hat to other side of strip. Work 1 row of s c up right side of front, starting at bottom of skirt, working ch 3 loops for 3 buttonholes as shown on illustration, (at equal distances apart) to collar. S c on other side of coat. Sew on buttons.

Reprinted from *Mary's Dollies*, Volume 14, Page 7.

The Ship's In
— JACK —

NEEDLES—1 *set No. 3 double pointed, American Standard.*

MATERIAL—*2 oz. Sport Yarn, 3 yards White Yarn.*

GAUGE—*7½ sts to 1 inch.* (*Measure garment on doll as you make it*).

☆ JACKET

With No. 3 needles, cast on 26 sts, K 3 rows border. *P 1 row, K 1 row (always keeping first and last 2 sts, K on purled rows for border at sides for ½ inch. K 3rd and 4th sts tog at beg and end of next row, repeat from *1 more time. Work even until piece measures 1½ inches from bottom. Inc in 3rd st from ends and K 4 center sts on purled row, K back. On next row, K 12 keeping first and last 2 sts K on purled rows (put remaining 12 sts on st holder). When piece measures 2½ inches from bottom, bind off 2 sts at beg of the next 2 rows. On center of Jacket K 2 tog at beg of every row at neck edge until 7 sts remain. Work even until armhole measures 1¾ inches from 2 bound off sts. Work from st holder to correspond to other side. Cast on 8 sts for back of neck and K 1 row, P 1 row for 1½ inches. Cast on 2 sts at underarms and work same as front on side seams.

Collar—Cast on 18 sts, K 1 row, P 1 row, 1¼ inches, K 5, bind off 8, K 5. Work 1 inch even. K 2 tog at neck edge every other row until 1 st remains. Work other side to correspond. Work 1 row of s c around collar in white.

Sleeves—Pick up 20 center sts, P back. Pick up 2 sts at end of next 2 rows, 24 sts. P 1 row, K 1 row for ½ inch. Now dec 1 st at each end, and dec 1 st at each end every 4th row, until you have 18 sts. When piece measures 3½ inches, change to No. 1 needles, K 3 rows, bind off loosely on wrong side.

Finishing—Ch about 65 sts for lacer at neck. Ch 36 sts for lacers at side openings. Sew on collar. Sew underarms, starting 1½ inches from bottom, continue sewing sleeves. When dressing Doll put blouse on first, starting at feet. Put both arms in sleeves from back. Tape lacers thru after sweater is blocked and on doll.

☆ PANTS

Cast on 40 sts, 12 sts on first needles, 12 sts on 2nd needle 16 sts on 3rd needle, join, K 1 P 1, for 5 rows. Inc 6 sts, about every 5th st, 46 sts. K plain for 2 inches. Put 23 sts on st holder, cast on 6 sts for crotch; join, on these 29 sts, K 3 inches (inc 3 sts, 1 inch apart), on inside of leg. When leg measures 5¾ inches, K 4 rows, bind off on wrong side. Put 23 sts on 3 needles, pick up 6 sts on crotch, work to correspond to other leg.

☆ HAT

Ch 3, join, ch 1, work 7 s c in ring. Row 2—Work 2 s c in each st. Row 3—*Work 1 s c in next st, 2 s c in next st, repeat from *around row. Row 4—*Work 1 s c in each of the next 2 sts, 2 s c in next st, repeat from *around row. Now inc in every 5th st until you have 56 sts around. Work even until you have 16 rows. On 17th row dec 4 sts spaced at equal distances apart. Cr this row a little tighter. Sl st last st, ch 1, turn.

Brim—Work 1 s c in next 3 sts, 2 s c in next st, thus increasing every 4th st around row. Work 6 more rows increasing only 2 sts in each round. Now sl st in each st on last row, loosely. Break thread.

Janette

Illustration 137. *Mary's Dollies*, Volume 14, Page 10.

.... in the Spotlight
— JANETTE —

NEEDLES—1 *pr. American Standard Nos. 1 and 3*

MATERIAL—1 *two ounce ball Sport Yarn, 4 small buttons.*

GAUGE—7 *sts to 1 inch. (Measure garment on doll as you make it)*.

☆ SKIRT

With No. 1 needles, cast on 48 sts, K 1, P 1, for 5 rows. Change to No. 3 needles, *P 1, K 3, repeat from *across row, inc in 2nd st from end, ending row, P 1. Next row, K 1, P 3 across row ending, K 1. These 2 last rows are pattern. Follow pattern and on 4th row, *inc 1 st in center of each panel. Work 3 rows even. Inc 1 st in center of each panel every 4th row and on end sts every 6th row, until skirt measures 3½ inches. K 4 rows for border. Bind off on wrong side.

☆ TURTLE NECK SWEATER

With No. 1 needles, cast on 25 sts, K 3 rows, border. Change to No. 3 needles, *P 1 row, K 1 row, P 1 row, on next K row, dec 1 st at beg and end, repeat from *once. Work even until piece measures 1½ inches from bottom. Inc 1 st on each end and work 3 rows even. Make another inc, 25 sts. When piece measures 2¼ inches from bottom, bind off 2 sts at beg of the next 2 rows for underarm. On next purled row, K the center st and K 2 more sts on purled rows thereafter (1 on each side), until you have 15 sts in yoke. K 7, put on safety pin, bind off 7 loosely, K 7. P 1 row, K 1 row on these last 7 sts for 7 rows, cast on 6 sts at neck edge, P 1 row, K 1 row always keeping last 2 sts K on purled rows for border at back for 1 inch, cast on 2 sts at underarm, work same as front, on side seams. Pick up 7 sts on other side, P 1 row, K 1 row, for 8 rows, work to correspond to other side.

Sleeves—Pick up 22 center sts, P back. Pick up 2 sts at end of next 2 rows, 26 sts. P 1 row, K 1 row for ½ inch, now dec 1 st at each end, and dec 1 st at each end every 4th row, until you have 18 sts. When sleeve measures 3½ inches, change to No. 1 needles, K 1, P 1 for 5 rows, bind off loosely.

Collar—With No. 1 needle, on right side, Pick up 38 sts, K 1, P 1 ribbing, for 10 rows, bind off loosely.

Finishing—Sew underarms and sleeves. Sew on 4 buttons. Buttons are pushed thru knitted sts to close. Sweater can be worn to open on back or front. Sew skirt half way at back. With double strand of yarn tape thru back of skirt and tie.

☆ PANTIES

With No. 1 needles, cast on 24 sts, loosely, K 1, P 1 row for 4 rows. Change to No. 3 needles, K 1 row increasing 2 sts, P 1 row, K 1 row for 1½ inches. Bind off 3 sts at beg of the next 6 rows. On center 8 sts, K 1 row, P 1 row for 6 rows. Cast on 3 sts at beginning of the next 6 rows (26 sts), K 1 row, P 1 row for 1½ inches. Dec 2 sts, change to No. 1 needles, K 1, P 1 for 4 rows, bind off. Sew panties. S.C. around pantie legs.

☆ CAP

With No. 3 needles, cast on 50 sts, K 1, P 1, ribbing always keeping first and last 2 sts K at beg and end of every row, for 3 inches, bind off. Fold in half, sew bound off sts tog for back of cap.

Ties—Ch 35 sts on each side of cap.

Pompon—Wrap yarn around a cardboard about 1 inch deep, cut one side, sew other end, sew to top of cap.

Reprinted from *Mary's Dollies*, Volume 14, Page 11.

Mary's Dollies

"DOLLY MADISON"

20¢

VOLUME No. 15

Illustration 138. Cover for *Mary's Dollies*, Volume 15.

Illustration 139. *Mary's Dollies,* Volume 15, Page 4.

Reneé

Reneé...
☆ Crocheted Sun Dress and Cape

☆ **Needles**
1 Steel Crochet hook, size 5.

☆ **Materials**
Two ounces Crepe, 5 small pearl buttons.

☆ **Gauge**
7 sts to 1 inch. (Measure garment on doll as you make it).

☆ **DRESS**

Starting at waist line, ch 42 sts to measure 5½ inches, work 1 s c in 2nd ch from hook, work 1 s c in each ch to end of row, ch 3, turn. Row 2—*Work 1 d c in next 4 d c, 2 d c in next st (thus increasing every 5th st), repeat from *across row, ch 1, turn. Row 3—Work 1 s c in each st across row, ch 3, turn. Row 4—Inc in every 6th d c across row. Repeat rows 3 and 4 until you have 5 d c rows from beginning. Work 1 s c row, join with a sl st, ch 5, turn.

Pattern—Skip 1 s c, work 2 d c in next s c, ch 1, 2 d c in same st. *Skip 1 s c, work 1 d c in next st. Skip 1 s c, work 2 d c in next st, ch 1, work 2 d c in same st, repeat from *around row, ending row with shell pattern, sl st in 4th ch at beg of row, ch 5, turn. Row 2—*Work 2 d c in center of shell of row below, ch 1, work 2 d c in same place, ch 1, work 1 d c in d c of row below. Ch 1, repeat from *around row, ending with a shell pattern, ch 1, sl st in 4th ch at beg of row, ch 6, turn. Row 3—Work same as Row 2, having 2 ch sts before and after shell pattern, instead of 1 ch, ending row, ch 2, sl st in 4th ch at beg of row, ch 2, turn. Row 4—*Work 6 d c in center of shell, ch 2, sl st in d c, ch 2, repeat from *across row, ending ch 2, sl st in ch at beg of row, fasten off.

Top of Dress—At back, skip 1 st, fasten thread in 2nd st, ch 3, work 1 d c in each st to within last st. Ch 1, turn, work 1 s c in each st to end of row, ch 3, turn. Row 3—D c in each st across row, increasing 4 d c spaced at equal distances apart, ch 1, turn. Row 4—Work 1 s c in each st across row. Repeat rows 3 and 4 twice (4 d c rows, ending with a s c row), ch 1, turn.

Back—Work over 9 s c, ch 1, turn for strap, work over 3 s c, ch 1, turn. Continue on these 3 sts until you have 22 rows, or 2¼ inches, break thread, leaving 4 inch end to sew. Start other end of back and work to correspond. Skip 10 s c on each side at underarm and sew to front of dress. Holding right side of dress toward you, fasten thread at waist line (at center back) and work 3 ch 3 loops for buttonholes. Continue working s c over straps and front of dress and continue to s c on other side of back. Sew on buttons to correspond to buttonhole loops.

☆ **CAPE**

Ch 34 (to measure 5 inches). Work 1 s c in each ch, ch 1, turn. Row 2—Work 1 s c in next 3 sts, 2 s c in next st, repeat from *across row (do not inc in last 3 sts thruout yoke), ch 1, turn. Row 3—Work even. Row 4—Work same as Row 2. Row 5—Work even. Row 6—Inc every 10th st. Work 4 rows even, ch 5 turn.

Pattern—Row 1—Skip 1 s c, work 2 d c in next st, ch 1, 2 d c in same st. *Skip 1 st, work 1 d c in next st, skip 1 s c work 2 d c in next st, ch 1, work 2 d c in same st, repeat from *across row, ending row 1 d c in last st, ch 5, turn. Row 2—*Work 2 d c in center of shell of row 1, ch 1, work 2 d c in same place, ch 1, work 1 d c in d c of row below, ch 1, repeat from *across row, ending row, ch 2, d c in 3rd ch at beg of row, ch 6, turn. Row 3—Work same as row 2 having 2 chs before and after d c instead of 1 ch, ch 2, turn. Row 4—*Work 6 d c in center of shell, ch 2, sl st in d c, ch 2, repeat from *across row, ending ch 2, sl st in 3rd ch. Sl st over end of pattern to yoke. Ch 3 for buttonhole loops. S c to end of yoke, ch 3, sl st for 2nd buttonhole, fasten off.

☆ **PANTIES**

Ch 40, work 1 s c in 2nd ch from hook, 1 s c in each ch to end of row. Row 2—Ch 3 turn, work 1 d c in each st, increasing 5 d c across row. Repeat row 2, 2 more times, join with a sl st, ch 3, turn. Work 3 rows of d c without increasing, join with a sl st. Sl st 2 more sts. *Ch 3, turn, work 5 d c in next 5 sts, ch 3, turn, repeat from *2 more times, break thread. Fold panties in half and sew to other side. Work 30 s c around each leg. Tape double string thru panties and tie.

Isabelle

Illustration 140. *Mary's Dollies,* Volume 15, Page 6.

Isabelle...
☆ Knitted Skating Costume

☆ **NEEDLES**
No. 0 and No. 2. No. 2 double pointed needles for Hat.

☆ **MATERIALS**
1 Oz. Fingering Yarn, 20 Yards of Angora. 2 small Pearl Buttons.

☆ **GAUGE**
8 sts to 1 inch. (Measure garment on doll as you make it).

☆ **DRESS**

With Angora and No. 2 needles, cast on 160 sts, loosely, K 2 rows. With yarn, K 1 row, P 1 row, for 1 inch. On next K row, dec as follows: *K 1, K 2 tog, repeat from *across row, ending K 1 (107 sts). Work 1 inch even, *K 1, K 2 tog, repeat from *across row, ending K 2 (72 sts). Work 3 rows even. K 2 tog across row, 36 sts. With No. 0 needles, K 5 rows. With No. 2 needles, K 1 row, P 1 row. K 8, inc in next 2 sts, K 15, inc 2 sts, K remaining sts. Work 3 rows even. Inc 4 more sts having increases come directly above previous increases. K 9, bind off 3 sts, K 20, bind off next 3 sts, K to end of row.

Back—Dec 1 st at beg of every row at back edge (at 3 bound off sts), until you have 6 sts. Work even until armhole measures 1¼ inches. Bind off 3 sts at beg of the next 2 rows at armhole edge.

Front—Work over 10 sts, at front edge dec 1 st at beg of every row, 3 times. Now continue to dec at neck edge and inc at armhole edge, 5 times. Bind off 3 sts at beg of armhole edge 2 times and at neck edge once more. Work other front to correspond. Continue back to correspond to first back.

Finishing—Sew shoulder seams. Sew vent tog for 1½ inches from bottom. With yarn, starting at waist line on back, work 1 row of S C completely around backs and neck, making ch 3 loops for buttonholes, 2 times. Work 1 row around sleeves. With Angora, work 1 row around neck only and sleeves.

☆ **CAP**

With Angora and set of No. 2 needles, cast on 54 sts, 18 sts on each needle. With 4th needle, join and K 1 round. P 1 row with angora. Break thread. With yarn, K 1 round increasing 6 sts. On next round K 2 tog, 2 times. K 26, K 2 tog, 2 times. K to end of round. K 1 row even. Dec in same manner every other round, having decreases come directly over those of previous row, until 26 sts remain. Weave tog or bind off, and sew.

☆ **PANTIES**

With No. 2 needles, cast on 24 sts loosely, K 1 st, P 1 st, for 4 rows. Now K 1 row, increasing 6 sts. P 1 row, K 1 row for 1½ inches. Bind off 3 sts at beg of the next 6 rows. On center 12 sts, K 1 row, P 1 row for 6 rows. Cast on 3 sts at beg of the next 6 rows (30 sts.). K 1 row, P 1 row for 1½ inches. Dec 6 sts, K 1, P 1 for 4 rows, bind off. Sew side seams. S c around pantie legs.

IV. Original Styles by Mary Hoyer

Patterns from the kits designed for the Mary Hoyer Doll

Mary Hoyer not only designed knit and crochet patterns for her doll, she also created original patterns which were offered as kits. These became a very popular and successful part of the mail order business. Also, the McCall Pattern Company printed two patterns: McCall Printed Pattern 1564 in 14in (35.6cm) size only and McCall's Printed Pattern 1891 in sizes 14in (35.6cm) and 18in (45.7cm). Both were designed by Mary Hoyer. These McCall patterns are out of print and no longer for sale.

This chapter contains a selection of the original kit patterns created by Mary Hoyer as well as the McCall Pattern Company patterns which she designed.

To get the *Most* out of this book

you'll need THIS DOLL

only $3.95

(Gown and Veil Not Included)

The MARY HOYER DOLL

as advertised in

McCall's Needlework Magazine

Every Costume in This Book Was Designed for The Mary Hoyer Doll

The costumes in all Mary Hoyer Dolly Books will fit her perfectly. They were especially created to fit the original Mary Hoyer Doll.

As durable as it is beautiful, this lovely doll is 14 inches tall. The hair is hand-combed and hand-curled. Your choice of blonde, medium or dark brown.

Mail $3.95 check or money order
Plus 50¢ Postage (East of the Rockies)
Plus 75¢ Postage (West of the Rockies)
to . . . . .

Of Special Interest to those of you who already have a Mary Hoyer Doll---

Kit including all necessary materials and complete directions to make Bridal Gown as illustrated available to those who already have a Mary Hoyer Doll at only $1.50.

MARY HOYER DOLL MFG. CO., 1008 Penn St., Reading, Pa.

Illustration 141. *Mary's Dollies,* Volume 10, Page 12.

BRIDE DRESS and VEIL

Material: Taffeta -- 1/2yd (0.46m)
Net -- 3/4yd (0.69m)
Ruffle on bottom of skirt: 3yds (2.74m) long, 1-3/4in (4.5cm) wide
Ruffle on neck: 14in (35.6cm) long, 1in (2.5cm) wide
Bows on veil: 1/2yd (0.46m) long, 1-1/4in (3.2cm) wide

Be sure to measure the garment on the doll as you sew.

BODICE: Lay net lining on right side of front, sew neck edges together, turn. Sew ruffle on neck edge. Topstitch bottom of front. Backs: Lay net on right side of back, sew

The Bridesmaid DOLL

This beautiful, exclusive doll is the most outstanding doll value on the market today. There isn't a child whose little heart won't miss a beat when she gets her first glimpse of the Bridesmaid Doll . . . and you'll love her too!

Her gown is net over satin, with pointed bodice, sweetheart neckline. Bouffant skirt is edged with a net ruffle. Hat of satin and matching net. Dollie's purse may be purchased for a nominal sum.

Sturdily constructed of a hard durable composition, the Mary Hoyer Bridesmaid Doll has movable head, arms and legs. She has attractive movable eyes with eye-lashes and real hair that has been hand-curled. Your choice of blonde, medium, dark brown and red.

The Mary Hoyer Doll with *Bridesmaid* Gown $6.45
(*including Hat and Panties*)

PLUS 20c POSTAGE (EAST OF THE ROCKIES) 30c POSTAGE (WEST OF THE ROCKIES)

The *Bridesmaid* Gown $3.50
(*including Hat and Panties*)

The costumes in all Mary Hoyer Dolly Books will fit the doll perfectly.

Mail Check or Money Order to

JUVENILE STYLES PUBLISHING COMPANY
1013 Penn Street, Reading, Pennsylvania

Illustration 143A. *Mary's Dollies,* Volume 11, Page 8.

RIGHT: Illustration 143B. Bridesmaid Dress and Hat. *Mary's Dollies,* Volume 11, Page 9. See instructions and pattern on pages 141-143.

Illustration 142. Bride Dress and Veil. See instructions and pattern on pages 140-144.

KIT *to make ensemble* $1.75

If you already have a Mary Hoyer Doll, may we suggest that you purchase a Kit, which includes all necessary materials to make the ensemble she is wearing—already cut to fit.

Dollie's Purse may be purchased for a nominal sum. See price list.

Add 10c for postage

backs and net together, turn. With right sides facing, sew shoulder seams.

SLEEVES: Make two small darts at notches on sleeve. Hem bottom of sleeves. Insert sleeves into armholes, having fullness at top of sleeves. Sew side seams and sleeves together.

SKIRT: Taffeta: Hem bottom of skirt. Hem vent at back to notch. Hem vent at back on net skirt. Gather net for ruffle, sew ruffle on bottom of net skirt. Lay net skirt on taffeta skirt and sew together at top. With right sides facing, sew skirts to bodice (be sure to have centers meeting at point). Sew backs of skirts together separately, on wrong side.

VEIL: Make two bows of net about 1-1/2in (3.8cm) from end of veil as shown in Illustration 142. Sew two snaps on back of dress.

BRIDESMAID DRESS and HAT

Material: Taffeta - - 1/2yd (0.46m)
           Net - - 3/4yd (0.69m)
Net trimming for Hat: 1-1/4yds (1.14m) long, 1-3/4in (2.0cm) wide

DRESS: See Bride Dress for chart and instructions.
HAT: Cut two separate lengths of net 20in (50.8cm) long and 1-3/4in (4.5cm) wide. Fold in half and sew ends together on each strip separately, turn. Now fold each strip in half lengthwise and place one on top of the other, sew raw edges together. Place net on right side of taffeta,

vent back

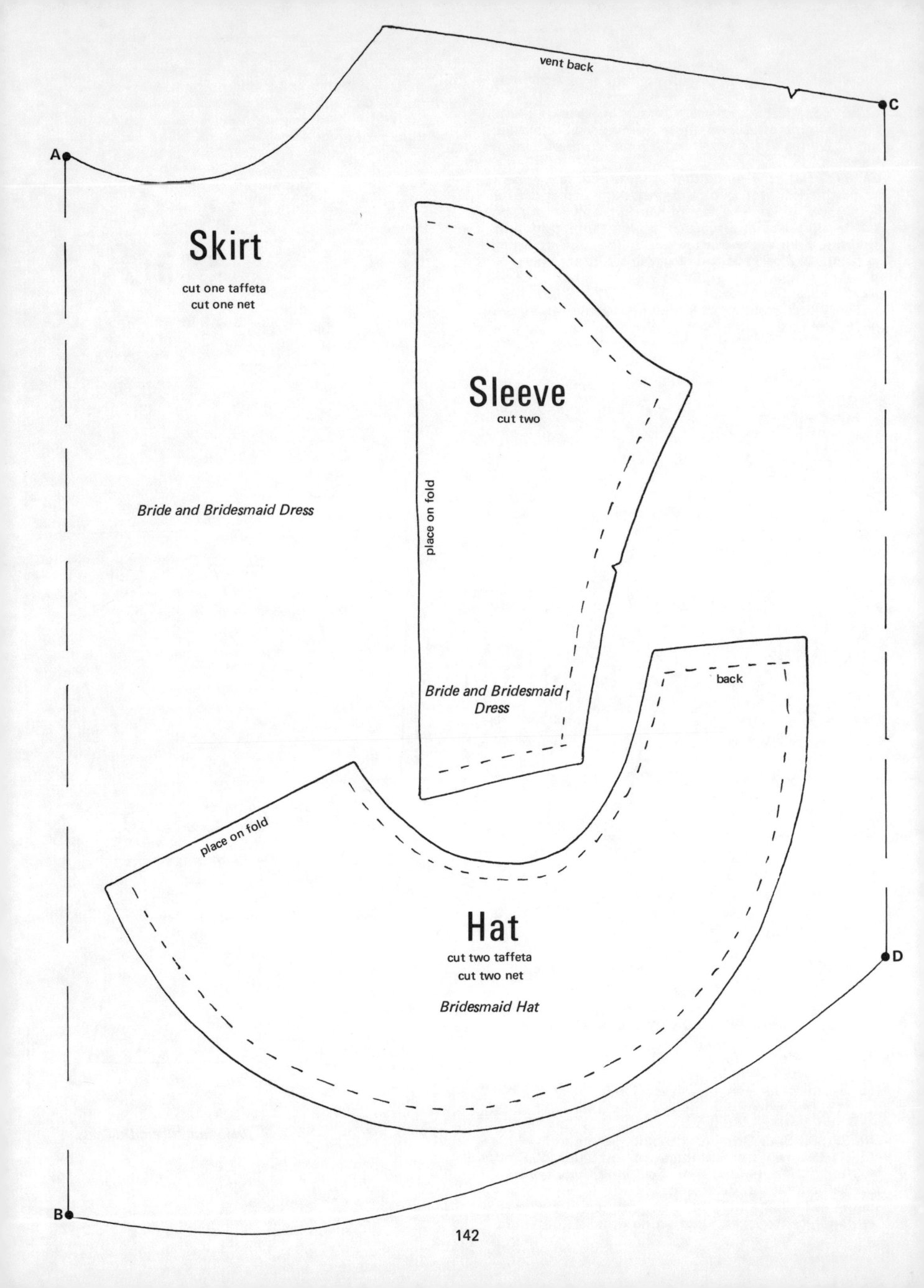

Skirt

cut one taffeta
cut one net

Bride and Bridesmaid Dress

Sleeve

cut two

place on fold

Bride and Bridesmaid Dress

place on fold

back

Hat

cut two taffeta
cut two net

Bridesmaid Hat

sew around outer edge of hat. Place net strips on right side of hat (net side is the right side) 1/4in (0.65cm) from end of hat, sew around outer edge of hat. Now sew net to taffeta on other piece of hat. Place right sides of hat pieces together (net bands are on the inside of pieces), baste first then sew, turn on right side. Separate the two net pieces as shown in Illustration 143B. Place hat on doll before sewing binding on inside of hat. Fold one piece of net in half and sew raw edges on inside of hat, turn to other side and topstitch. Sew backs together to fit doll, topstitch ends.

Skirt
cut one taffeta
cut one net

Veil
cut one net

Bride and Bridesmaid Dress

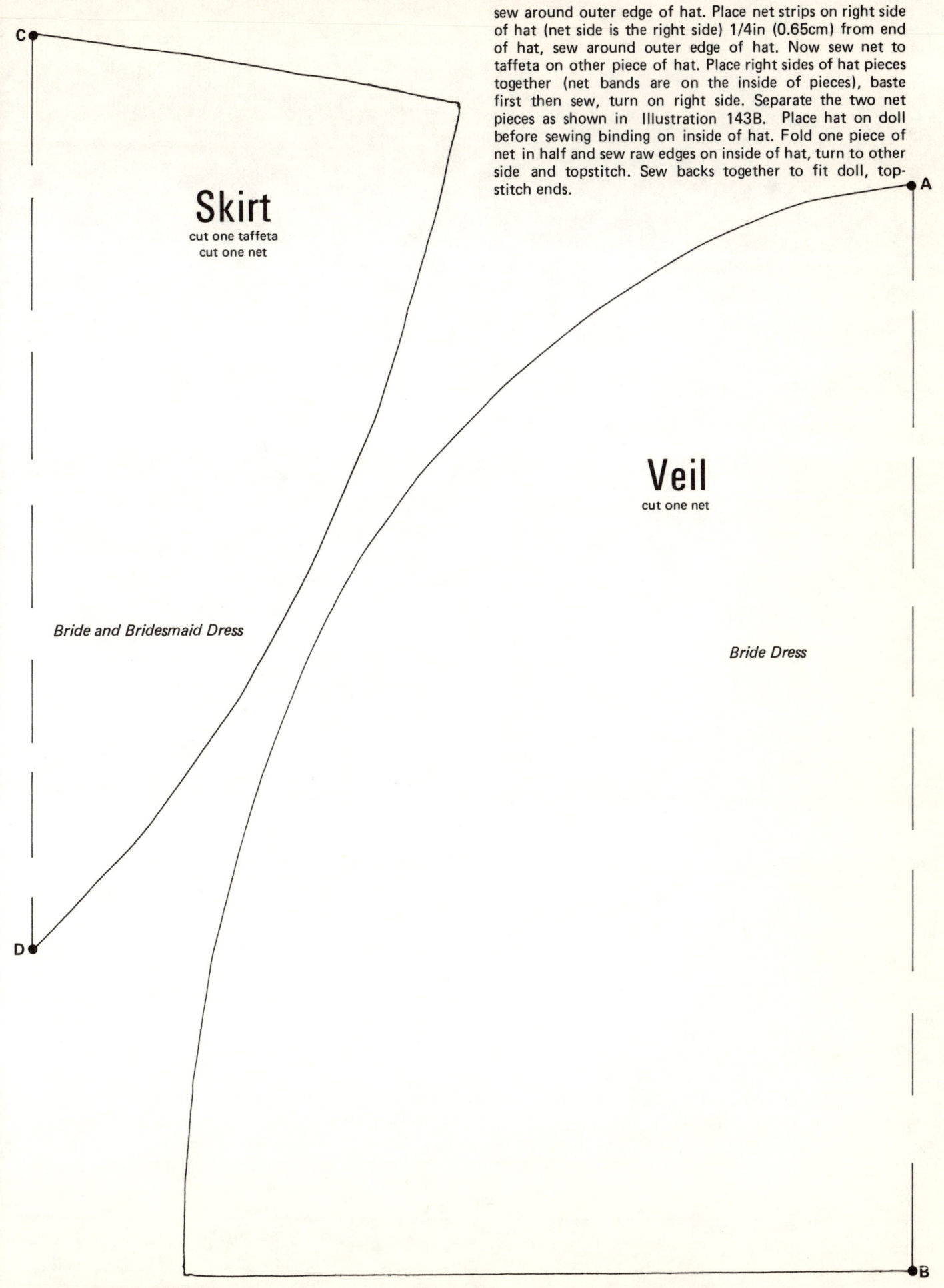

Bride Dress

Veil
cut one net

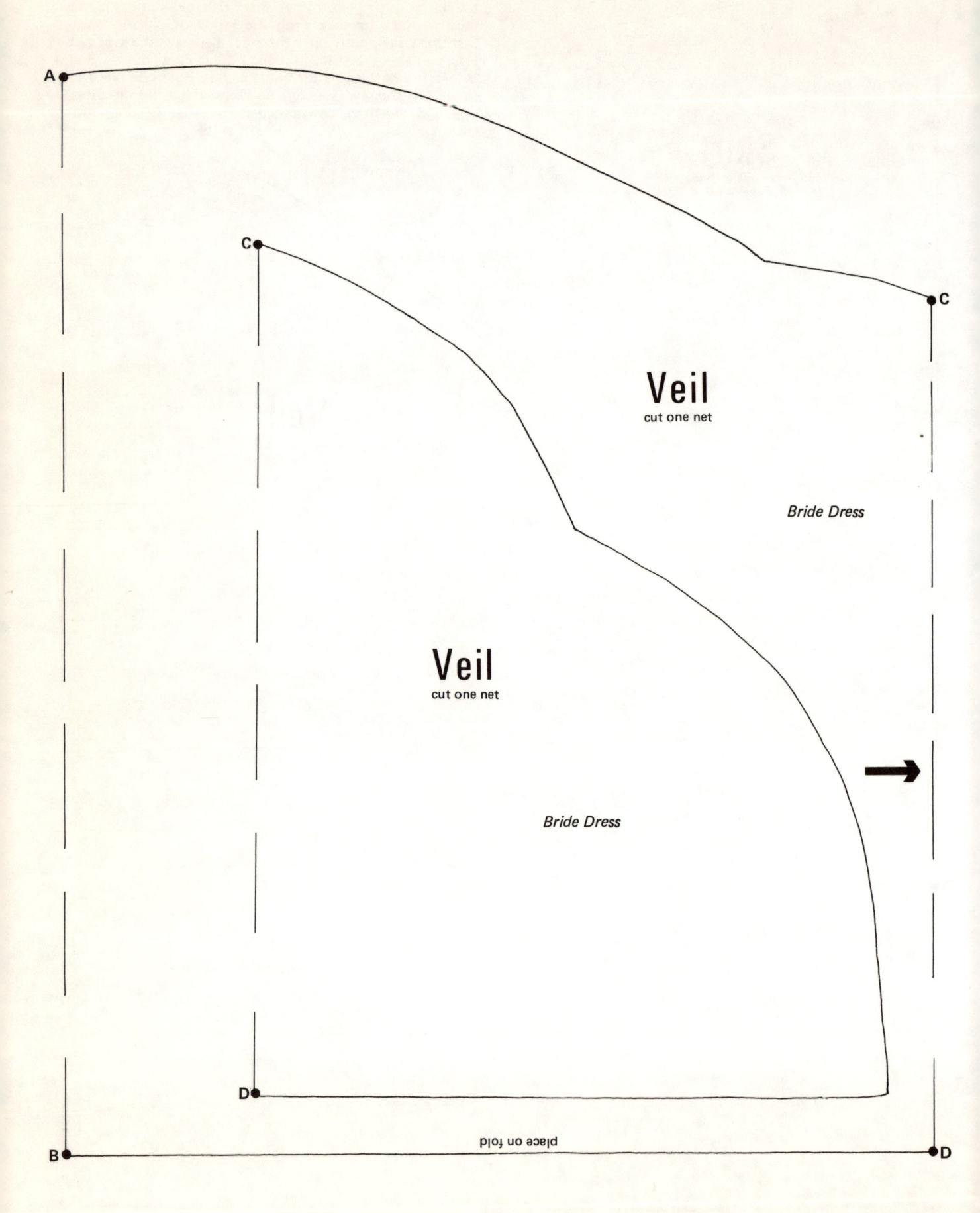

Bride Dress

Veil
cut one net

Bride Dress

place on fold

BALLERINA

Material: Taffeta - - 1/4yd (0.23m)
          Net - - 1/4yd (0.23m)
Net Skirt: 6-1/4in (15.9cm) long, 1-1/4yds (1.14m) wide
Be sure to measure the garment on the doll as you sew.
BODICE: Backs - With right sides facing, sew lining and taffeta together, starting at back and neck edge. Sew armhole edges.
         Front - Sew net to taffeta around neck edge and armholes. Turn all pieces to right side. With right sides facing, sew shoulder seams and side seams.
SKIRT: Cut ends of net skirt to slope at back same as taffeta skirt. Hem bottom of taffeta skirt and vent. Hem vent of net skirt. Mark center of taffeta skirt and center top of net skirt and gather net to taffeta starting at center of skirts. Now gather both skirts to measure same as for bodice. Sew skirts to bodice with right sides facing (be sure to have points of bodice and skirts meet) and sew. Turn and topstitch, turning raw edges toward bodice. Sew back of taffeta skirt together. Sew back of net skirt together. Sew two snaps on bodice and sew on ribbon bow as shown in Illustration 145. When sewing on ribbon, make a few gathers at point.
PANTIES: Turn back and hem panty legs. Hem vent at back. Sew seams on sides of panties. Hem top of panties and sew on snaps.

Introducing

The *Ballerina*

Here is a sturdily constructed 14-inch doll that will bring endless hours of joy to that little lady in your home. The Mary Hoyer Ballerina has movable head, arms and legs, as well as movable eyes and real hair that has been hand-curled! Four lovely shades; blonde, medium, dark brown and red.

Her lovely costume is net over bridal satin, with pointed bodice and full skirt, studded with gleaming sequins. V-neckline has satin ribbon bow with full streamers.

The Mary Hoyer Doll
with *Ballet Costume* . . . $5.25
(including ballet slippers and panties)
Plus 20c Postage (East of Rockies) 30c Postage (West of Rockies)

The *Ballet Costume* . . . $1.95

The costumes in all Mary Hoyer Dolly Books will fit the doll perfectly.

Mail Check or Money Order to
JUVENILE STYLES PUBLISHING COMPANY
1008 PENN STREET IN READING, PENNSYLVANIA

Illustration 144. *Mary's Dollies,* Volume 12, Page 8.

KIT *to make Ballet Costume*

If you already have a Mary Hoyer Doll, may we suggest that you purchase a Kit, which includes all necessary materials to make Ballet Costume she is wearing—already cut to fit. Ballet Slippers may be purchased for 25c.

$1.25
Add 10c for postage

Illustration 145. Ballerina. *Mary's Dollies,* Volume 12, Page 9. See instructions and pattern on pages 145-147.

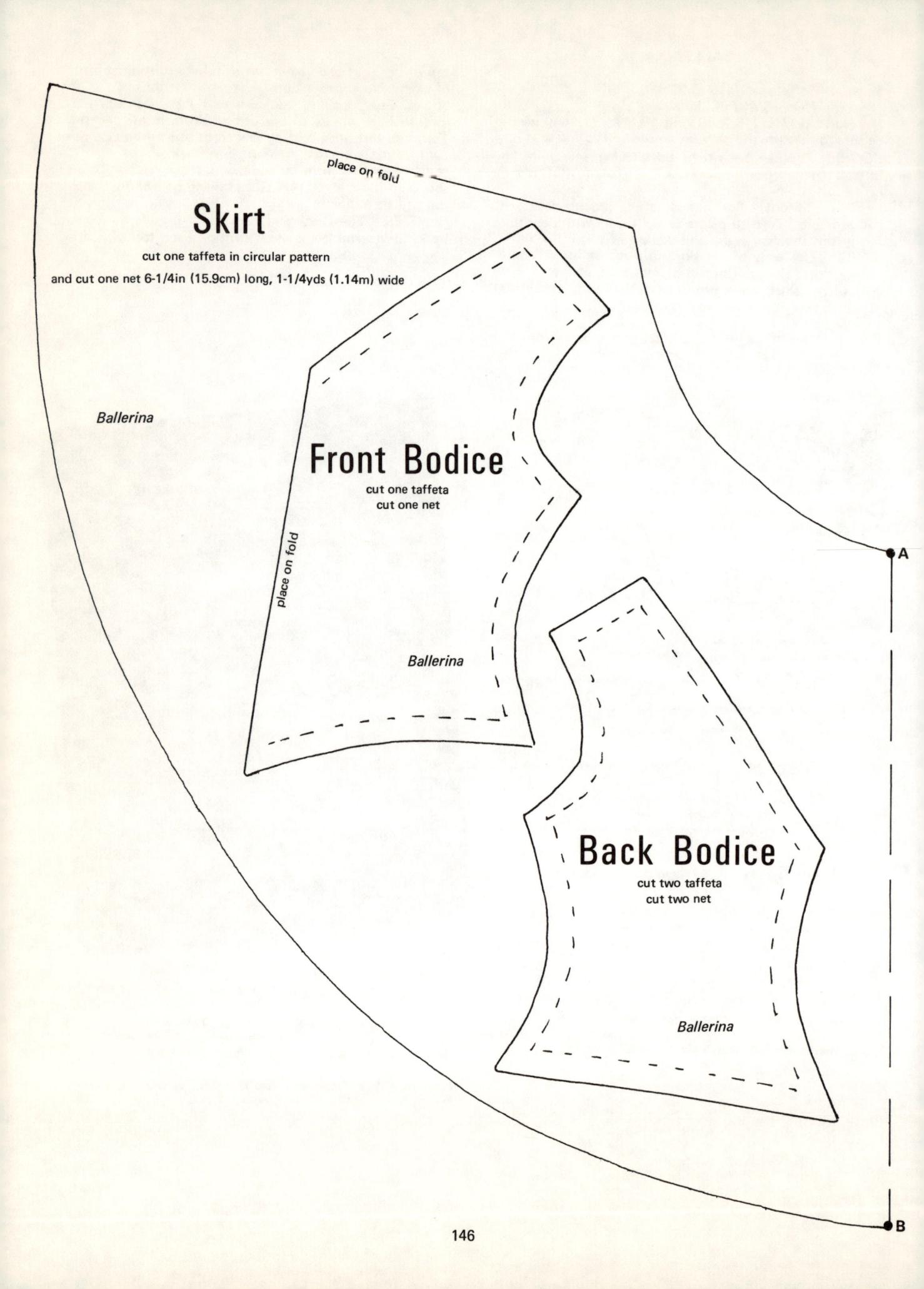

Skirt

cut one taffeta in circular pattern
and cut one net 6-1/4in (15.9cm) long, 1-1/4yds (1.14m) wide

Ballerina

place on fold

Front Bodice

cut one taffeta
cut one net

Ballerina

Back Bodice

cut two taffeta
cut two net

Ballerina

• A

• B

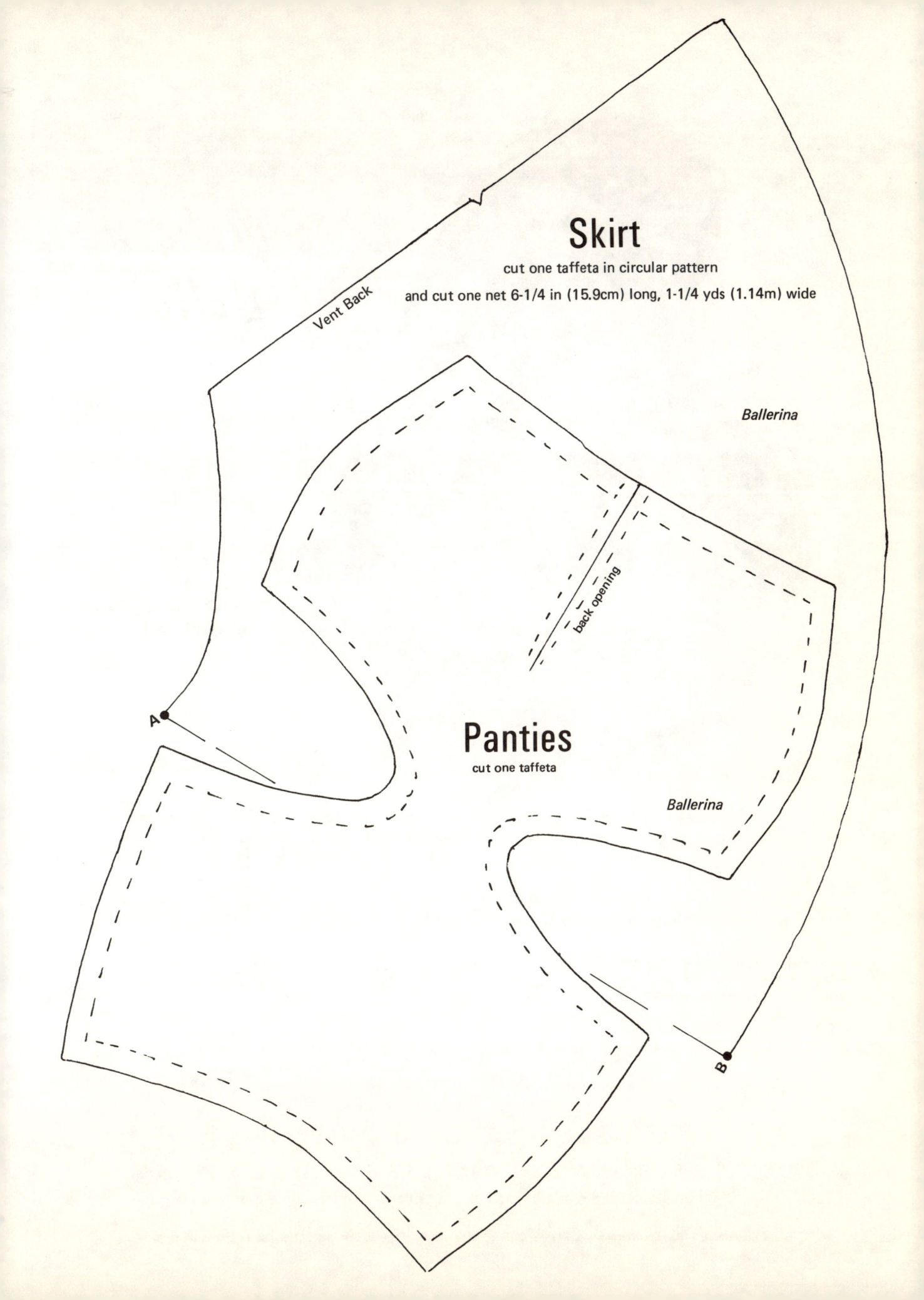

Skirt
cut one taffeta in circular pattern
and cut one net 6-1/4 in (15.9cm) long, 1-1/4 yds (1.14m) wide

Vent Back

Ballerina

back opening

Panties
cut one taffeta

Ballerina

A

B

Southern Belle

AN OUTSTANDING ACHIEVEMENT

A dainty and prim little miss, clothed in a superb creation devised by the masterful hand of Mary Hoyer. This lovely ensemble seems to live and breathe the romantic magic of the Old South.

To see this masterpiece is a treat and to own it a must. It will excite endless appreciation in little girls from three years of age to eighty.

Doll Dress Kit, cut and fitted ready to sew; including parasol frame and material, also matching shoes $2.95

Complete parasol that opens and closes $1.25

Doll Costume ready for doll to wear, with completed parasol and matching shoes $4.50

Add 15c postage on above items if ordered separately.

Doll undressed, with shoes to match costume, and Real Hair Wig $3.50

Doll undressed, with shoes to match costume, and DuPont Nylon Wig $4.95

Add 20c postage; 30c west of Chicago.

Mail Check or Money Order to

JUVENILE STYLES PUBLISHING COMPANY
1013 PENN STREET IN READING, PENNSYLVANIA

Illustration 146. Southern Belle. *Mary's Dollies,* Volume 14, Page 9. See instructions and pattern on page 149.

SOUTHERN BELLE

Material: Dress and Parasol: Dotted Swiss - - 1yd (0.91m)
Lining: Organdy or sheer material: 1/4yd (0.23m)
Eyelet insertion: 1yd (0.91m) long, 1-1/2in (3.8cm) wide
Narrow trimming: 3/4yd (0.69m) long, 3/8in (0.9cm) wide
Skirt: 5-1/4in (13.4cm) long, 1yd (0.91m) wide
Skirt ruffle: 2yds (1.83m) long, 2-3/4in (7.1cm) wide
Skirt lining: 7-1/2in (19.1cm) long, 1yd (0.91m) wide
Ribbon: 1-3/4yd (1.60m) long, 1/4in (0.65cm) wide
Parasol ruffle: 3yds (2.74m) long, 3-1/2in (8.9cm) wide
Parasol top ruffle: 18in (45.7cm) long, 2-1/2in (6.4cm) wide
Parasol: Eight pieces of satin

Be sure to measure the garment on the doll as you sew.

BODICE: Place front of lining under bodice, sew two darts on wrong side. Gather narrow trimming on bodice as shown in Illustration 148. Backs: With lining and backs (right sides facing), sew back seams, turn. With right sides facing, sew shoulder seams.

SLEEVES: Sew two small darts at notches. Hem bottom of sleeves, and sew on narrow trim. Insert sleeves into armholes, having fullness at top of sleeve. Sew narrow trim to neck edge. Sew sleeve seams and bodice together.

SKIRT: Sew two pieces of narrow ruffle together having right sides facing. Hem bottom and gather top of ruffle to measure 1yd (0.91m). On wide piece of skirt, turn under 1/4in (0.65cm) and sew eyelet insertion on right side. Now sew ruffle 1/4in (0.65cm) under eyelet edge as shown in Illustration 148. Hem vents at back.

SKIRT LINING: Hem bottom, hem vents at back. Place wrong side of skirt on top of right side of lining and gather to fit waistband. Sew skirts to bodice, with right sides facing, turn and topstitch. Hem backs of skirts together, separately on wrong sides.

FINISHING: Insert ribbon through eyelet and sew small bow on yoke. Sew snaps on bodice.

PARASOL: See Dolly Madison pattern and instructions on page 159 for making parasol.

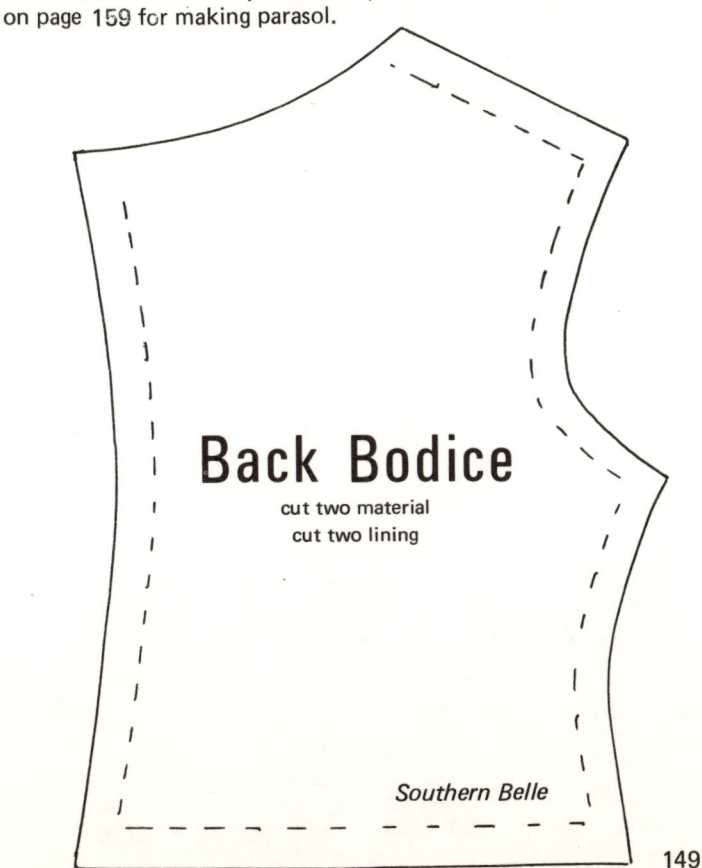

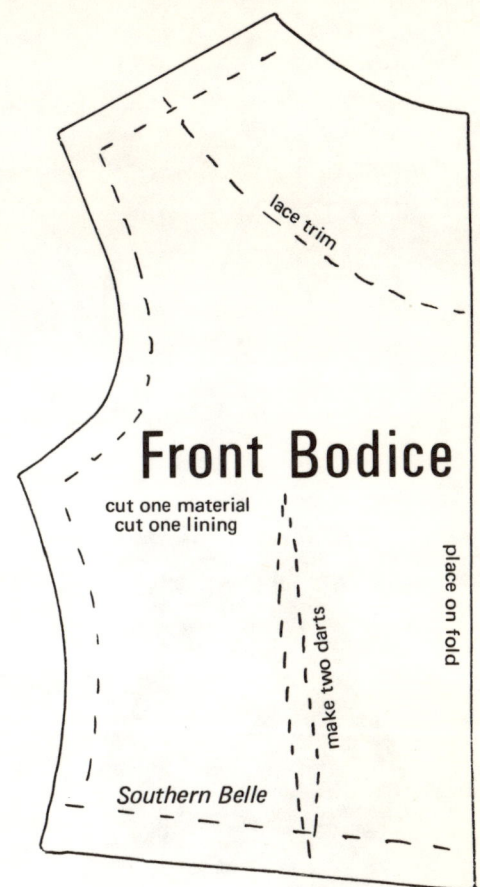

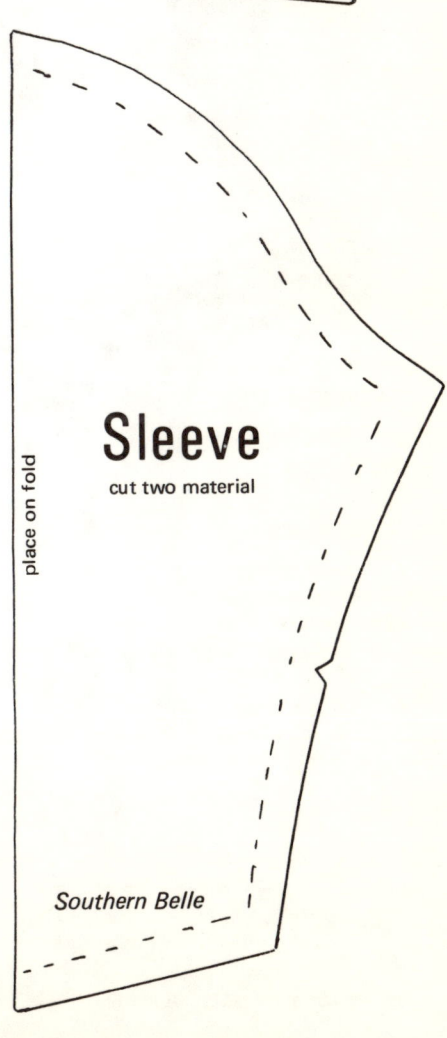

VOLUME 15

Mary's Dollies

by MARY HOYER

THE MARY HOYER DOLL
has a Special Message for Little Mothers and Fathers

Boys and girls, mothers and grandmothers, too; I'd like to tell you about the many services and new ideas my creator, Mary Hoyer, has to offer you.

You know, once in a while I have an accident—a broken arm or leg . . . well, there's no reason for too much worry for all parts of me are replaceable—arms, legs, body, head and wig! Just return me for repairs and I'll be sent back to you as good as new. (Cost of repairs is listed in our price list).

Then too, several attractive hair-do's are now available—curls, upsweep, long flowing beautifully waved Alice wigs, and all of these may be washed, combed and waved. They are made especially for me!

And . . . here's a new idea in Sewing Kits by Mary Hoyer, that are carefully cut to fit me. The Kit includes a special Child's Pattern, so simple that any child can sew it together, and so economical that everyone can afford to buy it.

What's more—a complete Accessory Line is available, made just for me . . . ice skates, roller skates, skis, tennis rackets, hand bags, etc. . . . even many shoe styles in colors for every costume.

Why not write today for free price lists!

ALICE BLUE PINAFORE
$2.95
for the Completed Costume

KIT-ready to sew, with illustration and instructions.
$1.50
Both include matching shoes.

Mary Hoyer Doll Mfg. Co.
1013 PENN STREET IN READING, PENNSYLVANIA

Illustration 147. Alice Blue Dress and Pinafore. *Mary's Dollies,* Volume 15, Page 3. See instructions and pattern on page 151.

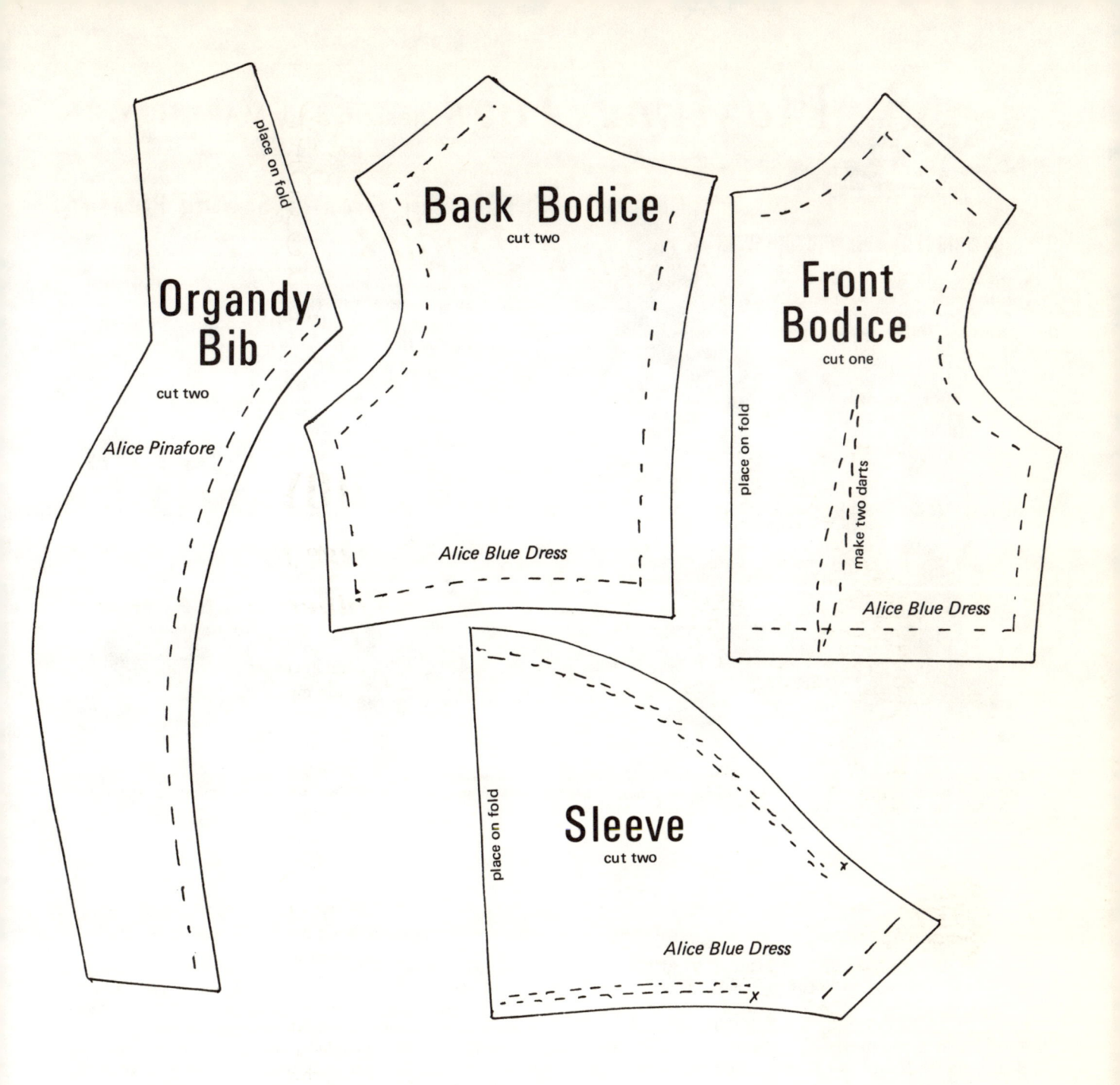

ALICE BLUE DRESS and PINAFORE

Materials: Pinafore: Organdy - - 1/4yd (0.23m)
Dress: Material without nap - - 1/4yd (0.23m)
Skirt: 4-1/2in (11.5cm) long, 30in (76.2cm) wide
Neck Band: 6in (15.2cm) long, 3/4in (2.0cm) wide
Sleeve Bands: 3in (7.6cm) long, 1in (2.5cm) wide
Pinafore: 3-3/4in (9.6cm) long, 13in (33.0cm) wide
Tie: 24in (61.0cm) long, 1-1/2in (3.8cm) wide

Be sure to measure the garment on the doll as you sew.

BODICE: Sew two darts on front. Sew shoulder seams. Sew neck band on neck edge on right side, raw seams facing. Turn band to wrong side and topstitch on right side.
SLEEVES: Gather bottom of sleeve to measure 3in (7.6cm). Sew on bands same as for neck binding. Gather top of sleeves, insert into armholes. Turn hems on backs 1/4in (0.65cm) to fit doll. Sew sleeve seams and sides of bodice together.
SKIRT: Hem bottom of skirt. Sew vents at back. Gather top of skirt to fit bodice and sew skirt and bodice together on wrong sides, turn and topstitch. Hem back of skirt.
PINAFORE: Sew upper edges of bib together, turn. Gather lace on raw edges. Hem bottom and sides of pinafore. Gather top to measure 3in (7.6cm). Sew lace on bottom of pinafore, easing lace as you sew.
SASH: Fold and press 1/4in (0.65cm) to inside of sash on both edges. Fold sash in half lengthwise and press. Mark center of sash and center of pinafore and topstitch sash to pinafore. Baste bottom of bib to center of skirt band inside of folds. Baste ends of bib at ends of apron. Topstitch upper edge of sash, including bib.

Playtime Togs designed by MARY HOYER

TERRY CLOTH BEACH ROBE WITH SUN GLASSES

- **THE DOLL** Has the washable curled wig. $4.50.
- **COMPLETED COSTUME** Made of Terry Cloth with contrasting trimming. $1.25. Sun glasses—25c extra.
- **READY CUT KIT** Contains complete instructions and illustration. 60c.

SLACKS WITH BELT AND SHIRT

- **THE DOLL** Has a real boy haircut. $3.50.
- **COMPLETED COSTUME** Made of cotton shirt with contrasting slacks, belt included. $1.50.
- **READY CUT KIT** Contains complete instructions and illustration, ready to sew together. 85c.

For Your Greater Sewing Pleasure!

You'll get great enjoyment sewing these fashion-right Playtime Togs designed by Mary Hoyer especially for the Mary Hoyer Doll and your youngster will thrill to dressing the Mary Hoyer Doll in the clothes you have made. Kits contain all necessary materials cut and fitted ready to sew, also illustrations and sewing instructions. You may also purchase the completed costumes, exactly as illustrated on these two pages.

Accessories Available

There are many accessories available designed especially for the Mary Hoyer Doll. They're real replicas of ice skating shoes, roller skates, parasols, sun glasses, etc., in miniature—correct scale to conform with the Mary Hoyer Doll. Write for Complete Price List.

SHORTS AND HALTER

- **THE DOLL** Has a flowing washable wig. $4.95.
- **COMPLETED COSTUME** Cotton halter and shorts in matching cotton. $1.00.
- **READY CUT KIT** Contains complete instructions and illustration and materials already cut to sew. 50c.

Illustration 148. *Mary's Dollies,* Volume 15, Page 8. See instructions and pattern for Terry Cloth Beach Robe on pages 152 and 153. See instructions and pattern for Slacks and Shirt on pages 152, 154 and 155.

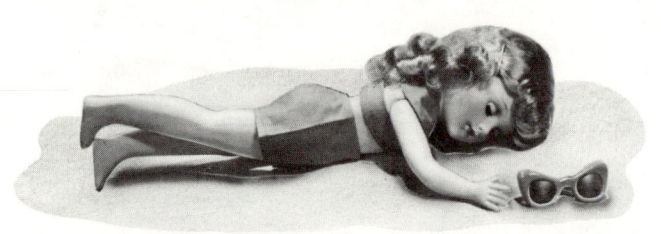

Illustration 149. *Mary's Dollies,* Volume 15, Page 9. See instructions and pattern for Shorts and Halter on page 152, 153 and 155.

TERRY CLOTH BEACH ROBE - - SLACKS - - SHIRT - - SHORTS - - HALTER

Material: Poplin or Cotton - - 1/2yd (0.46m)
Terry Cloth Beach Robe: Terry Cloth - - 1/4yd (0.23m)
Bias Tape for Halter and Terry Cloth Beach Robe - - 4yds (3.66m)

Be sure to measure the garment on the doll as you sew.

TERRY CLOTH BEACH ROBE: With right sides facing, sew shoulder seams. Open and lay right side of binding on right side of sleeve opening, turn 1/4in (0.65cm) hem on inside of binding and stitch binding. Turn binding on other side and topstitch. Sew side seams and underarm. Starting at back, sew on binding completely around robe same as for sleeves.
BELT: Fold both ends of binding towards center, stitch together open ends. Fit robe on doll and stitch center of belt at back.
SLACKS: Sew fronts together with right sides facing, from top to crotch. Hem vents at back to notch. Turn top of slacks down 1/4in (0.65cm) and hem. Hem bottom of legs. Sew backs together from bottom of vents to crotch. With right sides facing, sew legs together. Turn and press seams and crease in fronts. Sew on snap at back.
SHIRT: With right sides together, sew shoulder seams. Sew two small darts in sleeve. Insert sleeves into armhole, easing top of sleeve. Hem bottom of sleeves. Sew underarm and sleeve seams. Stitch ends of collar on wrong side, turn. Now baste collar on right side of shirt, having notch of collar and back meet. Fold facing at notch, lay facing (on top of collar) and machine stitch across top of shirt having notches meet. Stitch facing at bottom of shirt, on both sides. Turn on right side and hem remaining bottom of shirt. Sew on snap at front and two small buttons if desired.
SHORTS: Sew same as for slacks only turn hems (on top of shorts and bottom of shorts) under twice.
HALTER: With right sides facing, sew two pieces at notch. Sew two other pieces together at notch. Press seams open. With right sides together, sew ends and inside of halter, turn. Open and lay right side of binding on edge of halter, allow 1/4in (0.65cm) hem at each end of binding to turn under. Stitch binding to outside of halter.

Front
cut two

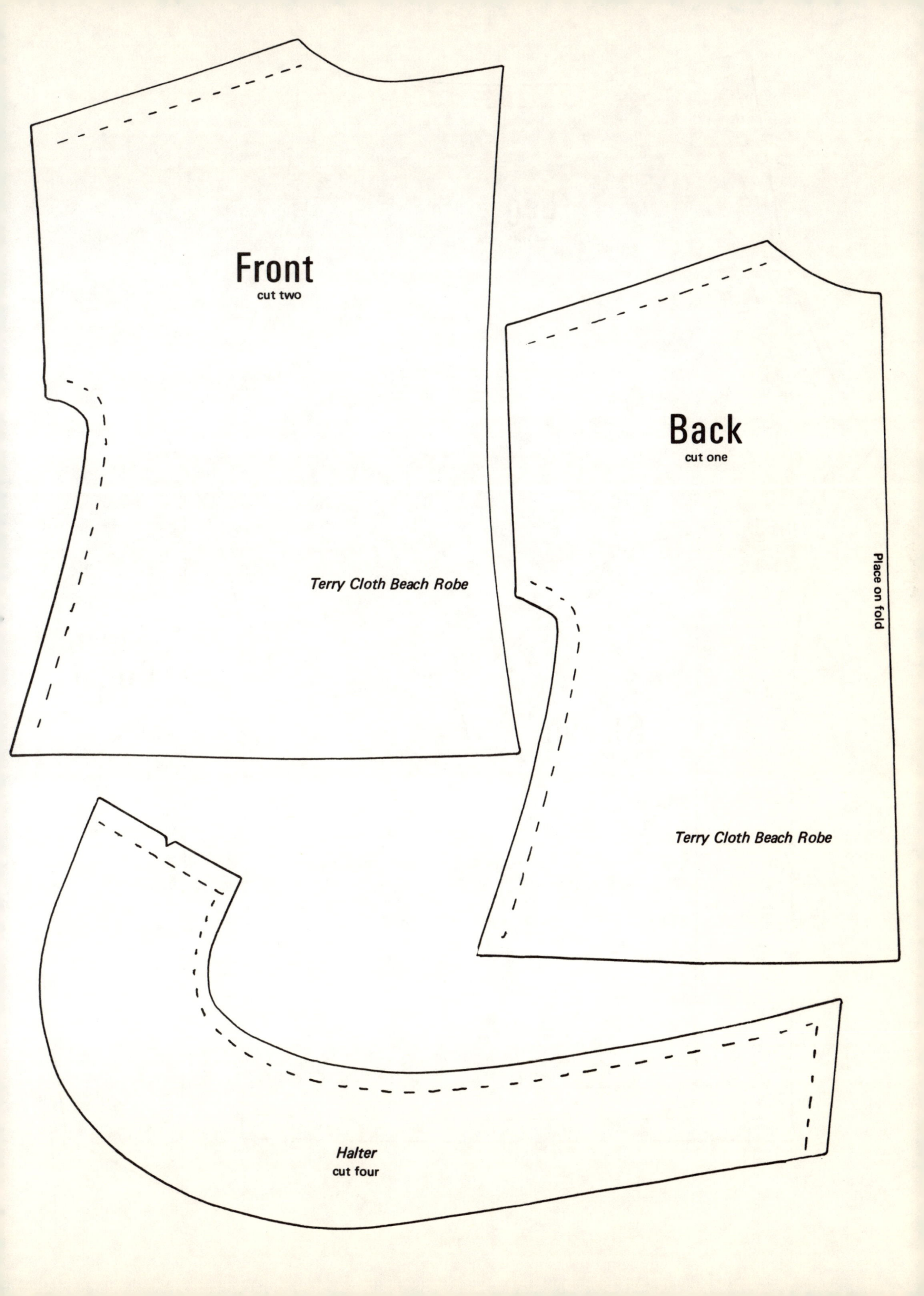

Terry Cloth Beach Robe

Back
cut one

Place on fold

Terry Cloth Beach Robe

Halter
cut four

Leg
cut two

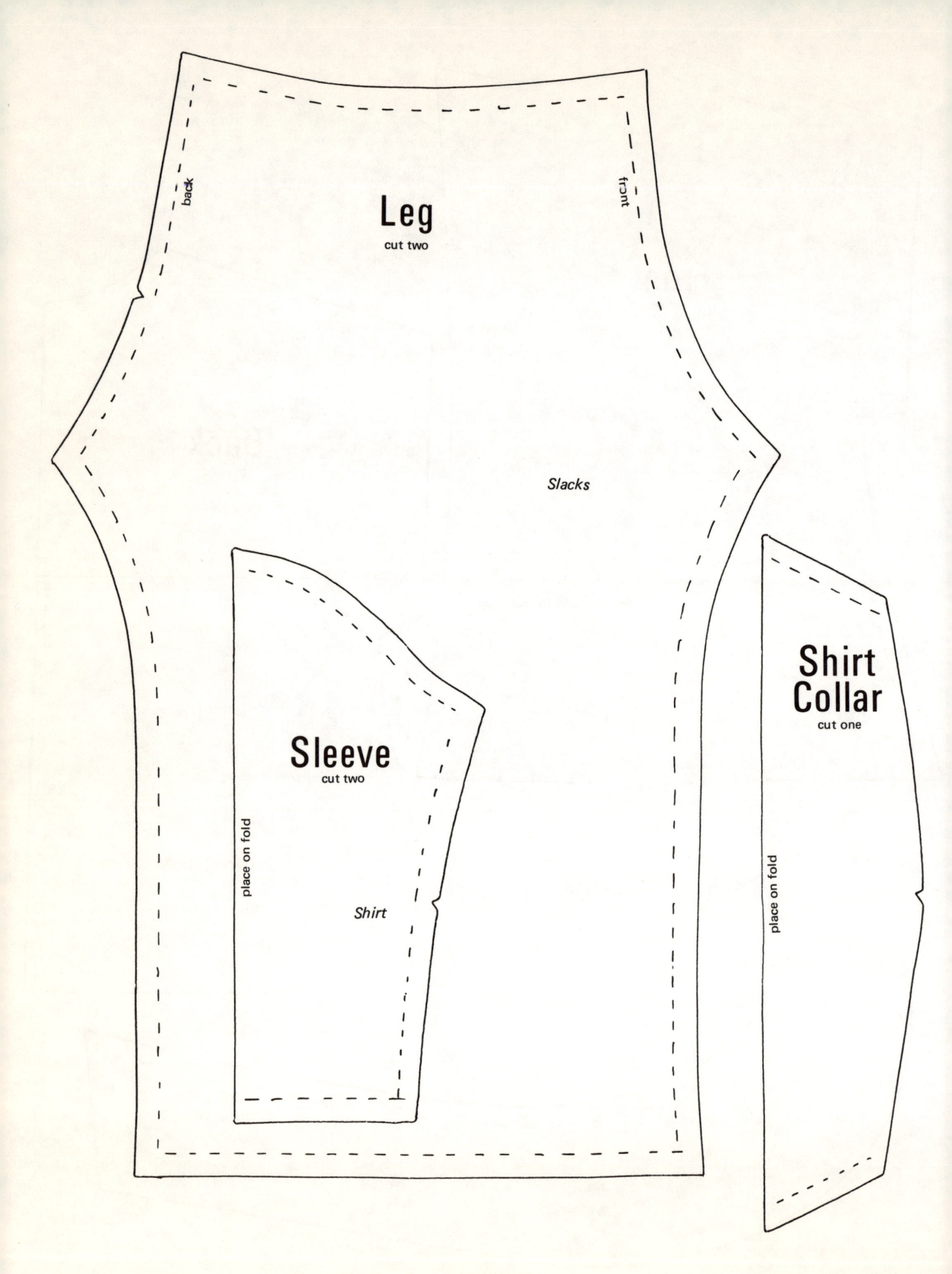

back

front

Slacks

Sleeve
cut two

place on fold

Shirt

Shirt Collar
cut one

place on fold

Front
cut two

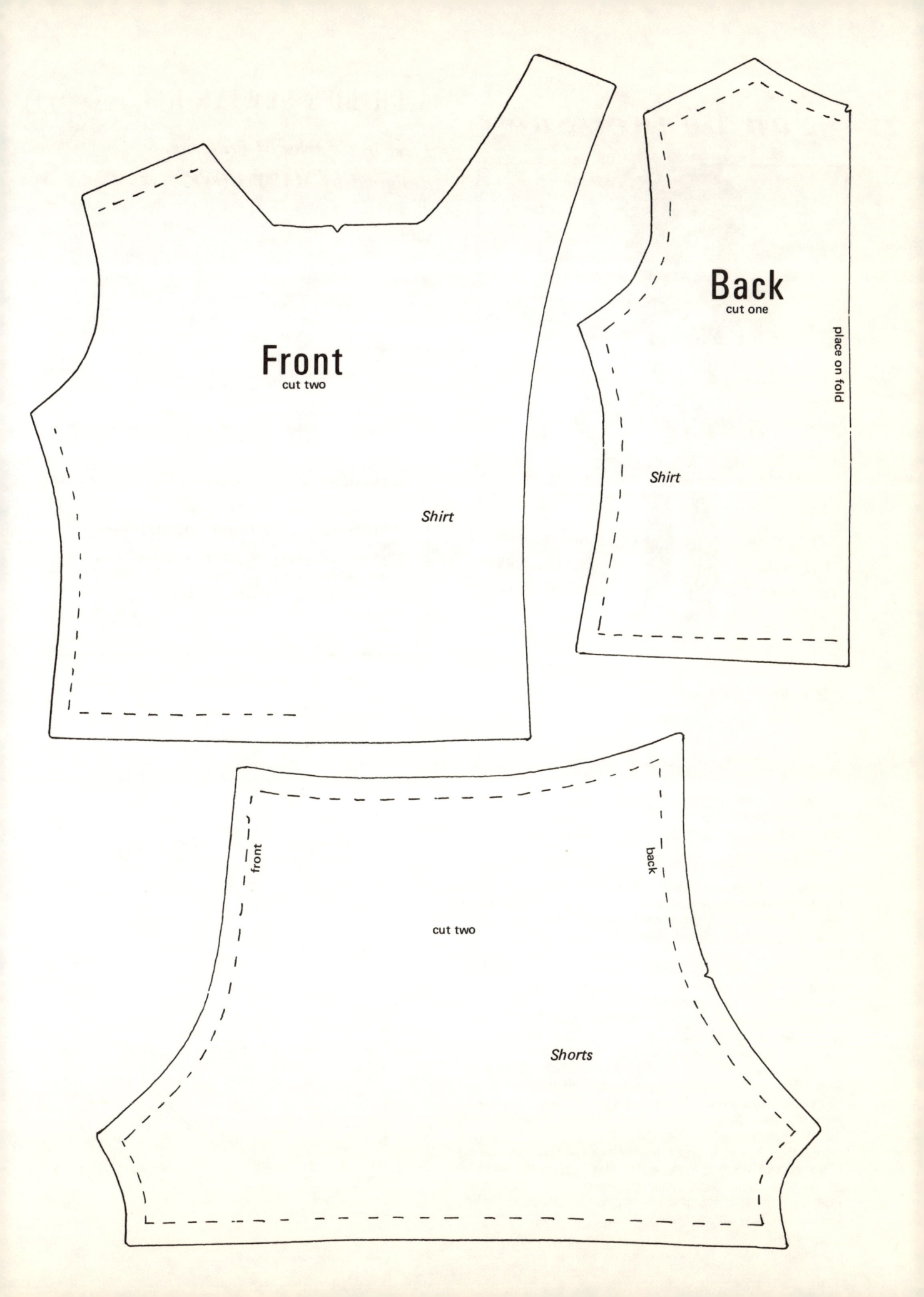

Shirt

Back
cut one

place on fold

Shirt

front

back

cut two

Shorts

Sun Bonnet Sue

YOUR CHILD CAN MAKE THIS OUTFIT

KIT INCLUDES ILLUSTRATIONS AND INSTRUCTIONS

Illustration 150. *Mary's Dollies,* Volume 15, Page 10.

A CHILD'S SEWING KIT

First in a Series of Patterns designed by MARY HOYER....

Children just love to use their little hands, whether to model in clay, dabble in finger paints or one hundred and one other pastime pleasures.

They're forever asking mother "What can I do now?" It's been many years since we mothers were youngsters and we too often forget that little hands must be kept busy in order to keep them out of trouble. Yes, normal children have active little bodies and minds—they want to be kept occupied.

Mary Hoyer, internationally-known designer of hand-knits for children, has a daughter, too, who is no different than your child, who has often asked the same question you mothers are confronted with—"What can I do now?"

So long as children are willing to do something, we mothers might just as well have them work on a worthwhile project . . . one that will entertain as well as educate them.

Mary Hoyer now presents the first in a series of such projects—SUN BONNET SUE (See illustration on opposite page) A CHILD'S SEWING KIT! Just think of the fun your child will get dressing her Mary Hoyer Doll in a costume which she herself has made!

Of course, the SUN BONNET SUE OUTFIT including cotton dress and bonnet trimmed with matching braid, may be purchased "Ready to Wear", for only **$1.50**

Educational .... Economical!

This educational kit, first in a series designed by Mary Hoyer, contains everything to make the SUN BONNET SUE OUTFIT, including illustrations and instructions—so simple your child can make it! Here is her first lesson in sewing—learning to do something for herself—something worthwhile. It's economical, too! **75¢**

Illustration 151. *Mary's Dollies,* Volume 15, Page 11.

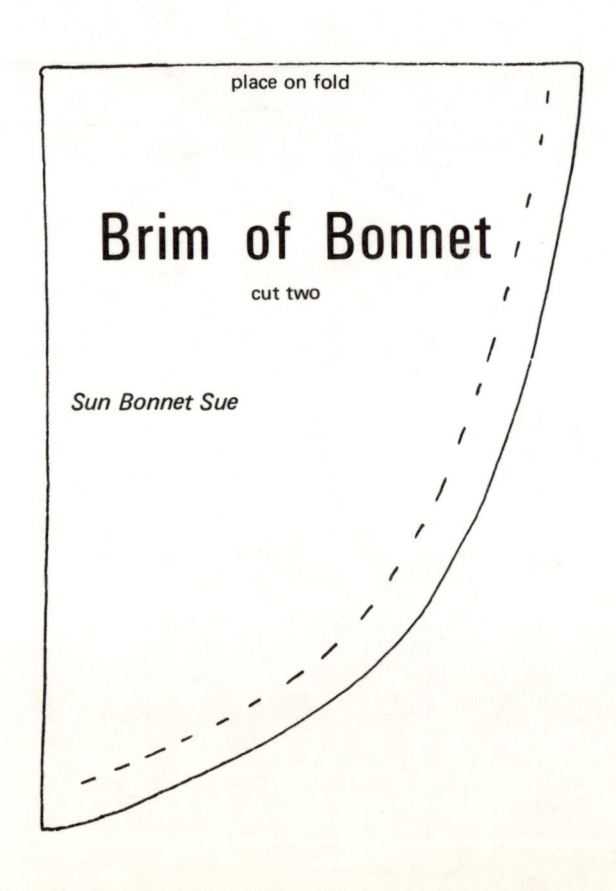

SUN BONNET SUE

Material: Poplin or Polished Cotton - - 1/4yd (0.23m)
Rickrack: 1yd (0.91m)
Skirt: 4-1/2in (11.5cm) long, 36in (91.4cm) wide

Be sure to measure the garment on the doll as you sew.

BODICE: Turn back hems on bodice at armhole edge, front and backs. Place right sides together and sew shoulder seams. Sew rickrack on armhole edges. Hem backs. Hem neck edge, sew on rickrack. Sew side seams.
SKIRT: Turn back hem 1/2in (1.3cm) and sew on rickrack. Gather skirt to fit bodice. Sew vents at back of skirt. Right sides facing, sew skirt to bodice. Hem back of skirt. Sew two small snaps on bodice.
BONNET: Back of bonnet: Place right sides together and sew 1/4in (0.65cm) seam on bottom. Turn to right side and press. Gather between x's.
BRIM: Place right sides together (curve of brim), sew and turn. Mark center back of cap on gathered edge and center of brim on raw edge side, baste together, then sew, having centers meet. Sew rickrack on inside of brim allowing 7in (17.8cm) on each side to tie.
PANTIES: Sew fronts together with right sides facing (from top to crotch). Hem vents at back. Hem top and legs of panties. Sew backs together from notch to crotch. Fold in half so center seams meet, with right sides facing, sew crotch. Sew on small snap.

place on fold

Brim of Bonnet
cut two

Sun Bonnet Sue

Illustration 152. Sun Bonnet Sue. See instructions and pattern on pages 156 and 158.

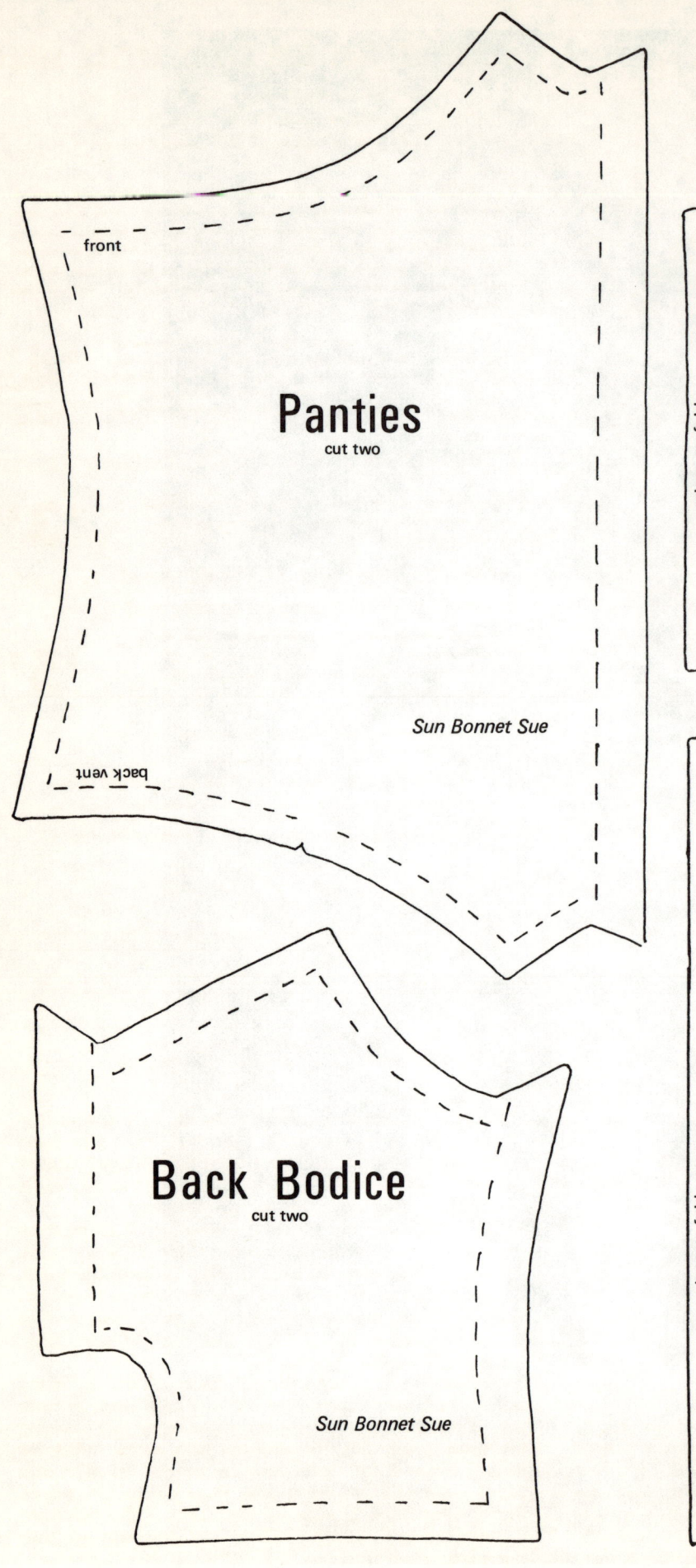

Panties
cut two

front

back vent

Sun Bonnet Sue

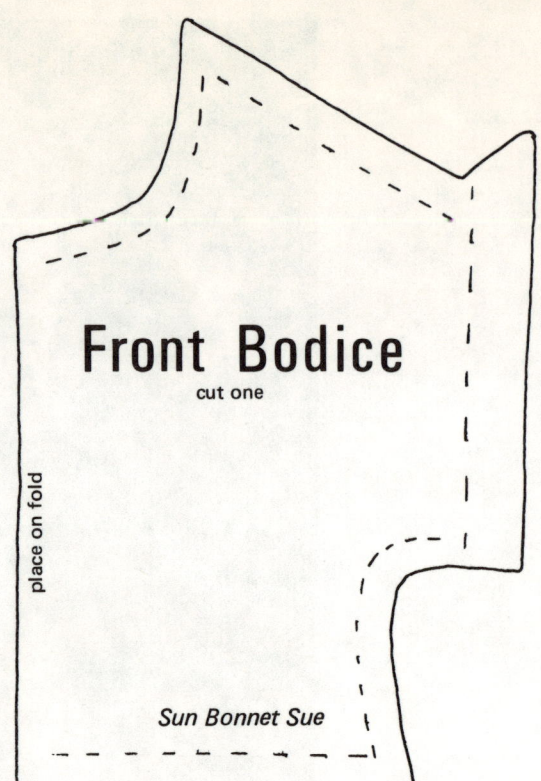

Front Bodice
cut one

place on fold

Sun Bonnet Sue

Back Bodice
cut two

Sun Bonnet Sue

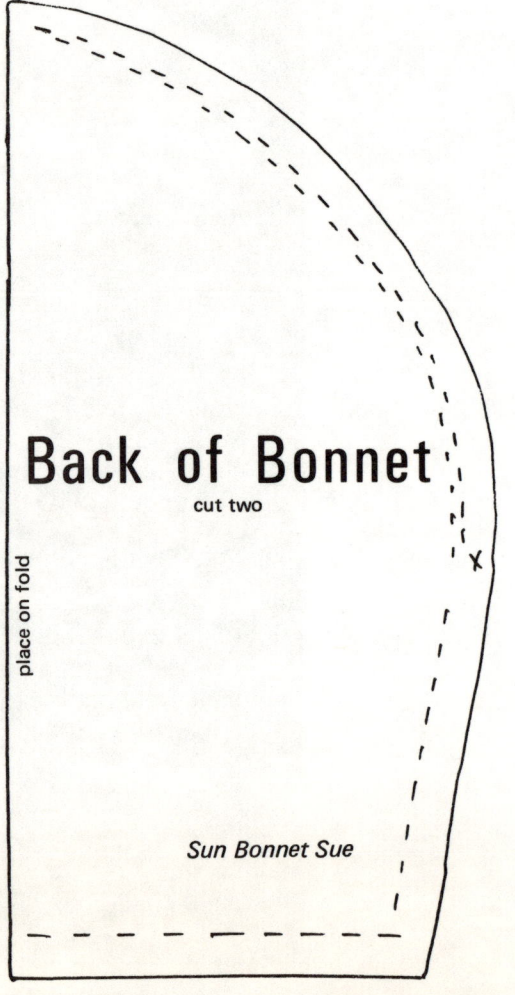

Back of Bonnet
cut two

place on fold

Sun Bonnet Sue

Dolly Madison

MOST BEAUTIFUL DOLL IN AMERICA!

Illustration 153. *Mary's Dollies,* Volume 15, Page 12.

YEARS OF *fun* FOR EVERY LITTLE GIRL!

she'll have fun shampooing and curling her lovely hair
... dressing her perfect little body ... playing with her;
you'll have fun making her many beautiful costumes!

Little girls ... big girls, too, will get a big thrill and endless hours of enjoyment dressing the Mary Hoyer Doll in the beautiful costumes you have made. You'll find her so easy to knit, crochet and sew for—she has such a perfect little body. The creation of Mary Hoyer, this lifelike 14-inch doll is made of finest durable plastic, is fully jointed and has moving eyes. Her lovely hair has been hand-curled. Shades of Wigs—blonde, medium, dark brown and auburn. Yes, there isn't a child whose little heart won't miss a beat when she gets her first glimpse of the Mary Hoyer Doll ... and is she a little beauty, you'll love her, too!

$3.50 PLUS POSTAGE with MOHAIR WIG

There's a Mary Hoyer Doll for the boys, too! Actually he's her twin brother—exact in every detail. You will find on many occasions, a boy doll is a "must" to fill your needs. He has a boy hair cut. Your choice of medium or dark brown hair. Only $3.50 plus postage. BOTH DOLLS COME UNDRESSED, but with shoes and stockings.

$4.95 PLUS POSTAGE with WASHABLE WIG can be Combed and Waved

◀ **COMPLETE KIT TO MAKE *Dolly Madison* COSTUME**

Kit contains all necessary materials (bridal satin and nylon net) cut and fitted ready to sew costume and cover parasol frame; matching slippers; also illustrations and sewing instructions.

$3.25

Dolly Madison COSTUME (ready to wear)

AS ILLUSTRATED ON OPPOSITE PAGE

Here is, without a doubt, the most beautiful, precisely made doll costume ever offered at anywhere near the price. Of bridal satin and nylon net, the DOLLY MADISON COSTUME and PARASOL comes complete with matching slippers to fit the Mary Hoyer Doll perfectly!

$5.95

(Add 25c postage—40c West of Chicago) for each Doll ordered.

Mail Check or Money Order to

MARY HOYER DOLL MANUFACTURING CO.
1013 PENN STREET IN READING, PENNSYLVANIA

Illustration 154A. *Mary's Dollies,* Volume 15, Page 13.

DOLLY MADISON

Material: Satin - - 1/4yd (0.23m)
　　　　　Dotted Flocked nylon net - - 1/4yd (0.23m)
Satin skirt: 9in (22.9cm) long, 36in (91.4cm) wide
Flocked nylon ruffle: 3yds (2.74m), 28in (71.1cm) long, 4-1/4in (11.5cm) wide
Sleeve bands: 3in (7.6cm) long, 1in (2.5cm) wide
Sleeve ruffle: 9in (22.9cm) long, 1in (2.5cm) wide
Neck ruffle: 24in (61.0cm) long, 1in (2.5cm) wide
Parasol ruffle: 3yds (2.74m) long, 3-1/2in (8.9cm) wide
Parasol top ruffle: 18in (45.7cm) long, 2-1/2in (6.4cm) wide
Parasol: Eight pieces of satin

Be sure to measure the garment on the doll as you sew.

NET YOKE: Place right sides together. Sew around backs and neck, turn. Sew two darts in bodice on front. Sew shoulder seams. Mark center of bodice yoke and center of net yoke, holding right sides together. Baste yoke to bodice; starting at center front, topstitch. Finish hems on backs. Gather frilling for yoke. Sew on yoke as shown in Illustration 154B.

SLEEVES: Gather bottom of sleeves to measure 3in (7.6cm). Sew sleeve band on right side, then turn band under and topstitch. Gather ruffle on top of band. Gather top of sleeve, having most fullness at top of sleeve, insert into armhole. Sew side seams and sleeve seams.

SKIRT: Hem bottom of skirt. Gather ruffle to measure same as skirt. Sew on skirt leaving 1/2in (1.3cm) below skirt hem. Hem vents at back 3-1/4in (8.3cm) from top. Gather top of skirt to measure same as bottom of bodice. Mark center of bodice and center of skirt. Sew skirt to bodice, then turn and topstitch. Sew back of skirt. Sew three small snaps on bodice.

PARASOL: Join eight pieces taking 1/4in (0.65cm) seams. Press seams open. Turn bottom edge back on right side, topstitch. Open parasol and measure parasol covering on frame to see if it fits properly. Now gather ruffle for parasol same as for dress. Sew on parasol on right side about 1/8in (0.31cm) from edge. Place parasol on opened frame. Sew seams to ends of ribs. Gather 18in (45.7cm) ruffle to fit top of parasol. Draw up tightly and sew over raw edges.

Illustration 154 Dolly Madison. See instructions and pattern on pages 159 and 161.

Back Bodice
cut two

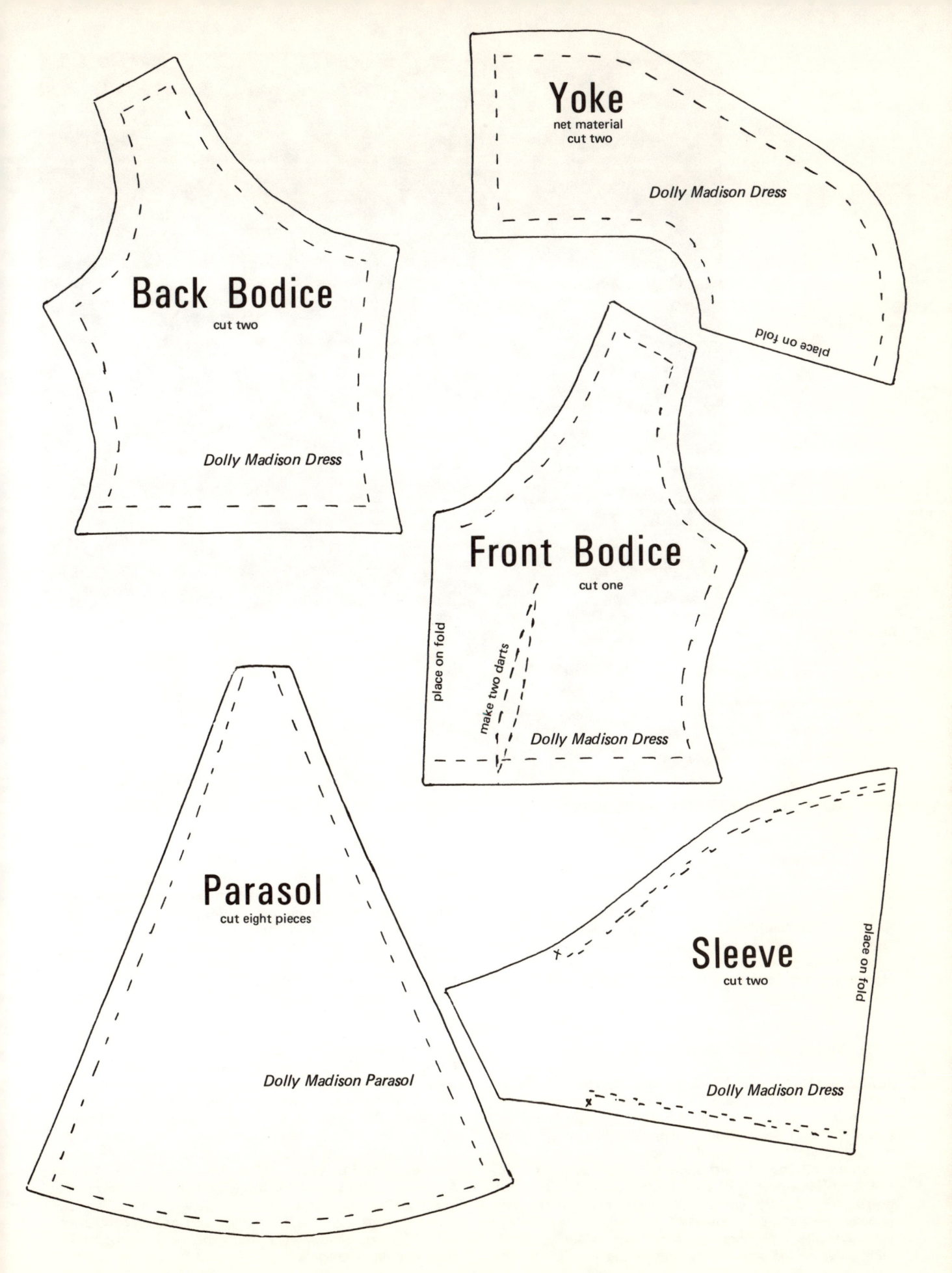

Dolly Madison Dress

Yoke
net material
cut two

Dolly Madison Dress

place on fold

Front Bodice
cut one

place on fold

make two darts

Dolly Madison Dress

Parasol
cut eight pieces

Dolly Madison Parasol

Sleeve
cut two

place on fold

Dolly Madison Dress

161

Illustration 155. Scotch Plaid Jumper and Blousette. Note the doll's plaid handbag and the matching child's handbag, both of which could be purchased separately from the Mary Hoyer Doll Mfg. Co. See instructions and pattern on pages 162-164.

SCOTCH PLAID JUMPER and BLOUSETTE

Material: Scotch Plaid - - 1/4yd (0.23m)
Organdy - - 1/4yd (0.23m)
Lace - - 3/4yd (0.69m) long, 1/4in (0.65cm) wide
Leg bands: 4-3/4in (12.2cm) long, 1in (2.5cm) wide
Skirt: 4in (10.2cm) long, 28in (71.1cm) wide
Skirt band: cut one plaid, cut one organdy - - 7-1/2in (19.1cm) long, 1-1/8in (2.8cm) wide
Hat band: cut one plaid - - 10-1/2in (26.7cm) long, 1in (2.5cm) wide

Be sure to measure the garment on the doll as you sew.

JUMPER SKIRT: Hem bottom of skirt 1/4in (0.65cm), and sew vent at back about 2in (5.1cm) from top. Mark center of skirt, make a box pleat - - folding under each pleat about 1/2in (1.3cm). Now continue folding pleats under on each side of box pleat. Pin each pleat at top of skirt and bottom. Top of skirt should measure about 7-1/2in (19.1cm). Now on top of skirt, place pleats closer together overlapping slightly 6-1/2in (16.5cm). Press skirt, then remove pins and sew top of skirt.

WAISTBAND: On organdy band turn 1/4in (0.65cm) hem on ends and sew on skirt on wrong side. With right side of plaid band, sew on right side of skirt in same manner.

JUMPER BIB: Place right side of plaid bib on organdy lining, sew together on inside and outside of bib (do not sew ends). Tape a narrow ribbon from bottom of bib on each side to ends of bib. Fasten securely at ends. Pull through to turn bib on right side; press bib. Now baste right side of bib to right side of plaid waistband and ends of bib (having lining facing you). Place ends of bib about 1/4in (0.65cm) from end of band, being sure ends are turned inside, and topstitch.

BERET: Brim: Place right side of band to right side of brim of beret and sew. Turn band under and topstitch (try on doll for size). Sew ends together to fit doll, separate ends and topstitch.

CIRCLE of BERET: Baste lining on wrong side of circle, sew around edge. Lay right sides of beret pieces together and baste, then sew. Turn to right side and press.

BLOUSETTE: Turn ends of sleeves under 1/4in (0.65cm) and sew on narrow lace. Gather sleeves to measure 3in (7.6cm). With right sides facing, starting at end of sleeves, hem sides of blousette. Gather leg openings to measure 4-1/2in (11.5cm). Sew leg bands on right side, turn under and topstitch. Sew crotch together on wrong side. Sew lace on neck edge same as for sleeves and gather to measure 6in (15.2cm). Hem vent at back and sew on small snap. Sew snap on skirt band.

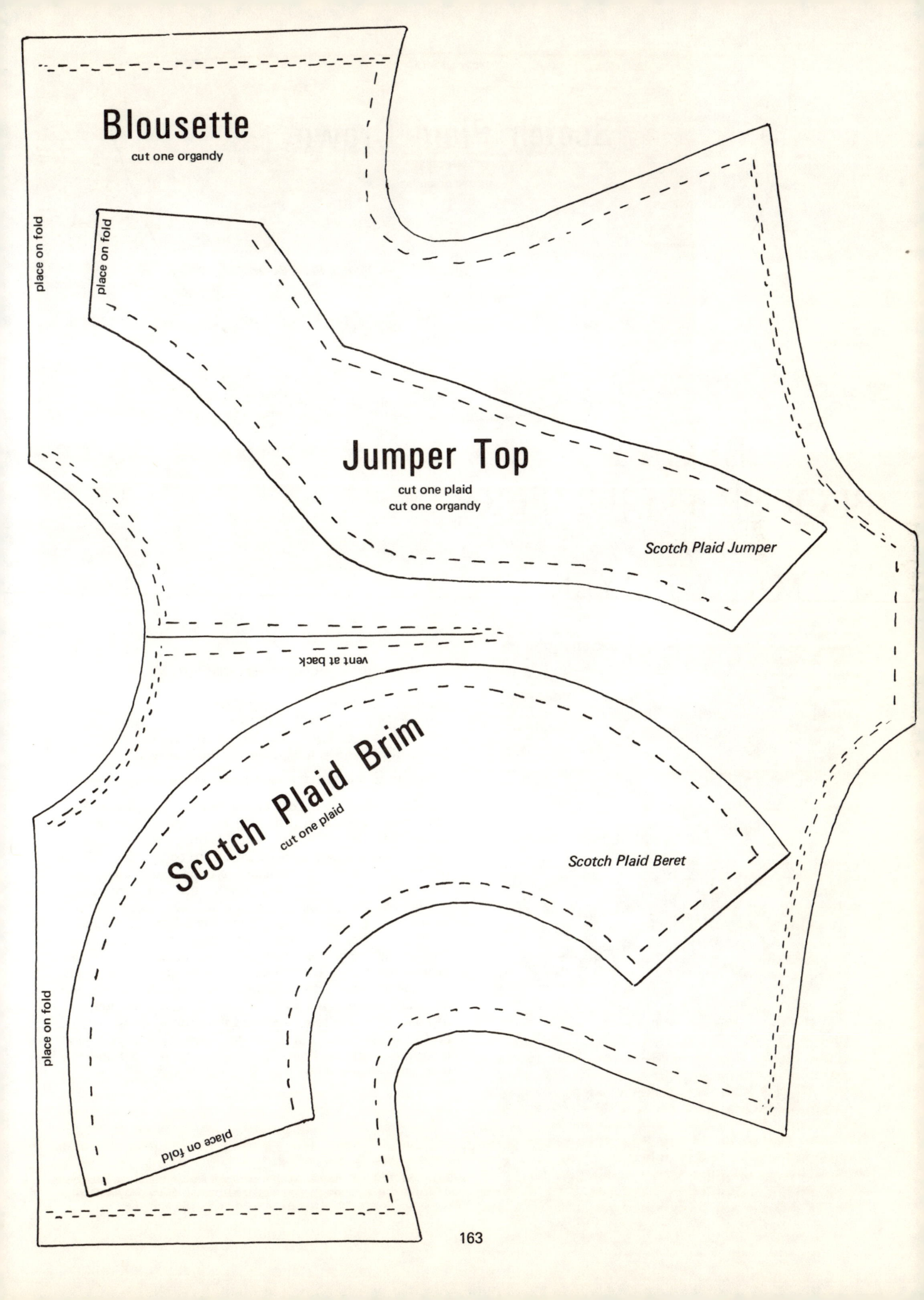

Blousette
cut one organdy

place on fold

place on fold

Jumper Top
cut one plaid
cut one organdy

Scotch Plaid Jumper

vent at back

Scotch Plaid Brim
cut one plaid

Scotch Plaid Beret

place on fold

place on fold

place on fold

Scotch Plaid Crown

cut one plaid
cut one organdy

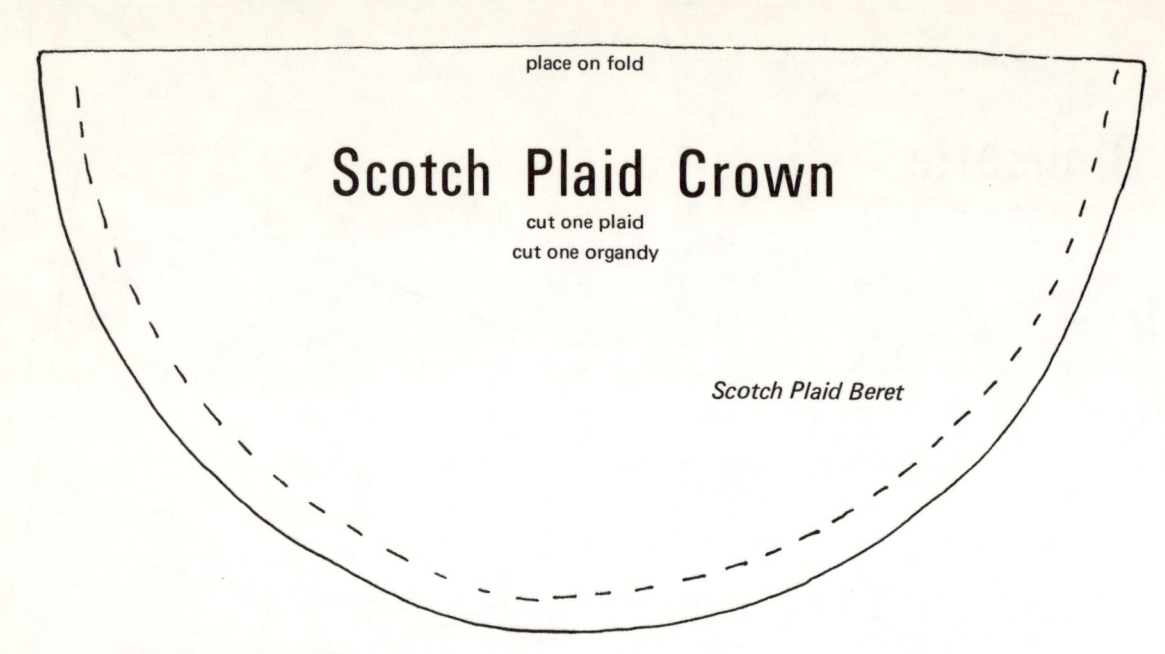

Scotch Plaid Beret

BECKY
BLOUSE and JUMPER
Designed by
MARY HOYER

BLOUSE and JUMPER

Jumper: Corduroy - - 1/4yd (0.23m)
Blouse: Organdy - - 1/4yd (0.23m)
Lace trim: 1yd (0.91m) long, 3/8in (0.9cm) wide
Skirt: 4in (10.2cm) long, 24in (61.0cm) wide

Be sure to measure the garment on the doll as you sew.

BLOUSE: With right sides facing, sew shoulder seams. Hem bottom of sleeves and gather on trim. Sew two small darts at notches. Insert sleeves into armholes, easing top of sleeves. Sew side and sleeve seams. Turn back 1/2in (1.3cm) on fronts and 1/4in (0.65cm) around neck edge, sew. Starting at left neck edge, gather lace and continue to gather lace 2in (5.1cm) from top of neck edge; continue to sew lace on edge of right front. Hem bottom of blouse.

JUMPER: Front - Place right side of front to organdy lining; sew neck and armholes only; turn. Backs - Sew backs from top to bottom and armholes same as for front, turn. With right sides together, sew shoulder seams and underarms. Now sew two small darts at back to fit doll.

SKIRT: Hem bottom of skirt; gather top to measure same as top of jumper. Sew vents to notch. Sew skirt to top of jumper and topstitch. Sew back seam of skirt and sew snap on bodice and one snap at top of blouse.

Illustration 156. Blouse and Jumper designed for the vinyl *Becky* doll. Note the steel doll stand designed by the Mary Hoyer Doll Mfg. Co. See instructions and pattern on pages 164 and 165.

Front Bodice
cut two organdy

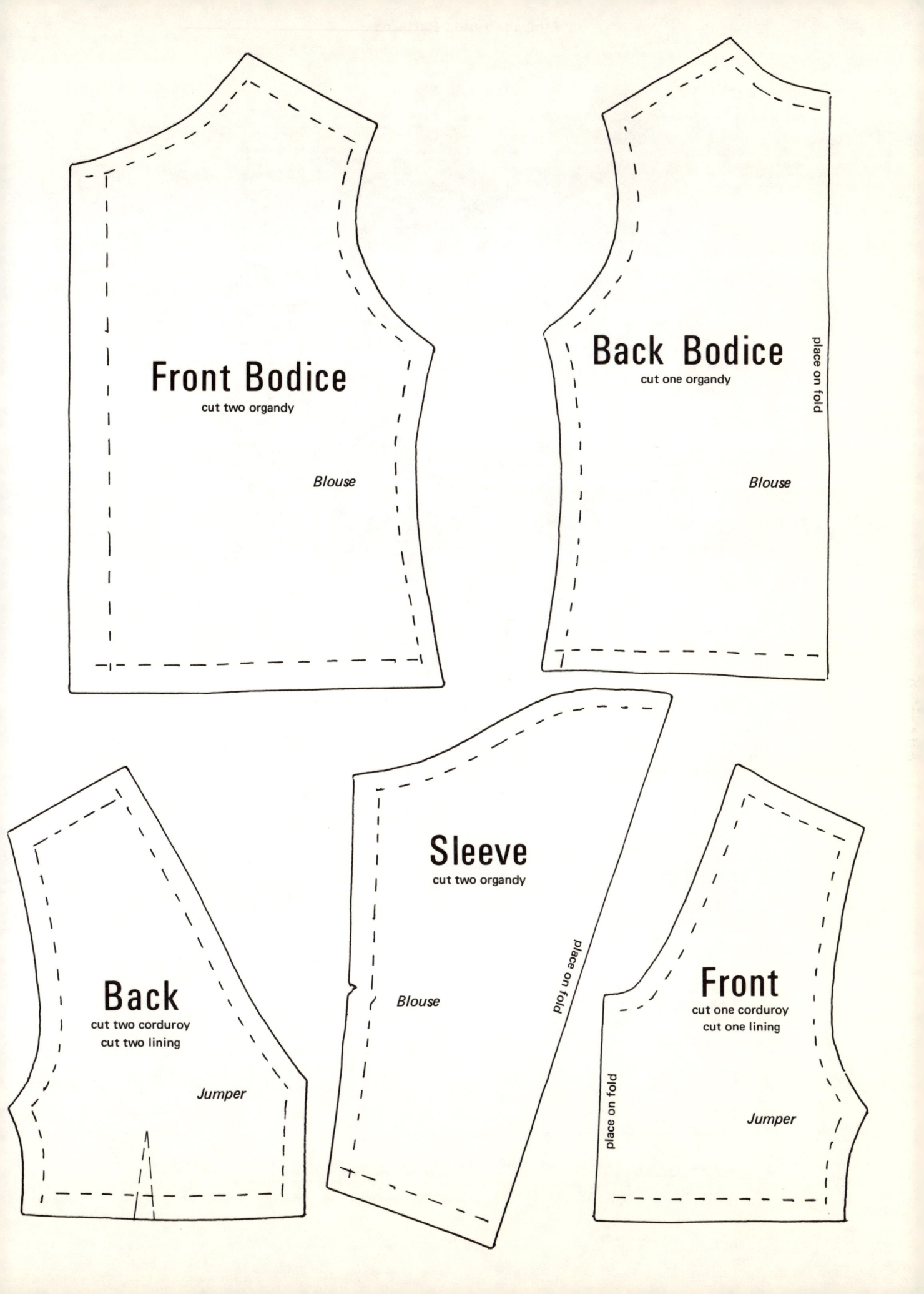

Blouse

Back Bodice
cut one organdy

place on fold

Blouse

Back
cut two corduroy
cut two lining

Jumper

Sleeve
cut two organdy

Blouse

place on fold

Front
cut one corduroy
cut one lining

place on fold

Jumper

McCall Printed Patterns

Set of Doll Clothes
Fits the "Mary Hoyer" Doll

McCALL PRINTED PATTERN 1564 ONE SIZE 35c

THE PATTERN WITH THE PRINTED CUTTING LINE
Cut through the white center of the double cutting line. Sew on broken lines.

INCLUDING: CUT AND SEW GUIDE
1. Cutting layouts for this size
2. Assembling, sewing and finishing details
3. General directions

McCALL PRINTED PATTERN No. 1564 — 1 Piece

MATERIAL REQUIRED	One Size 14"
VIEW A—Ballet Costume	
Waist, Panties & Hat Band—39" Satin or Taffeta	¼ yds.
Hat Ruffle, Skirt and Sleeves, 72" Maline	½ "
VIEW B—Evening Dress and Cap	
72" Maline	¼ "
Lining, 39" Taffeta	½ "
Trimming—Fancy Gold Edging	1⅜ "
VIEW C—Sunsuit and Bonnet	
35" Material	⅜ "
½" Wide Lace Trimming	2½ "
Brim Interfacing, 28" Crinoline	⅛ "
VIEW D—Slip and Panties	
35" or 39" Organdy	⅜ "
¼" Wide Lace Edging	1¾ "
¼" Ribbon for Bows	½ "
VIEW E—Cape	
39" Velvet	¼ "
Lining, 39" Taffeta	¼ "
Ties, Maline, One piece 3¾" x 21" or	
½" Wide Ribbon	⅝ "
VIEW F—Skating Costume—2 ounces of Sport Yarn, 20 yds. of Angora, plastic crochet hook No. 2 and 3 small pearl buttons.	
CORRESPONDING BODY MEASUREMENTS	One Size 14"
Chest	7⅜ ins.
Waist	6 "
Hip	7½ "
Headsize (With Wig)	9¾ "
Neck	4⅜ "
Circular Crotch Depth from Neck	11 "
Outer Leg Length	7⅜ "
Outer Arm Length to Wrist	4⅛ "

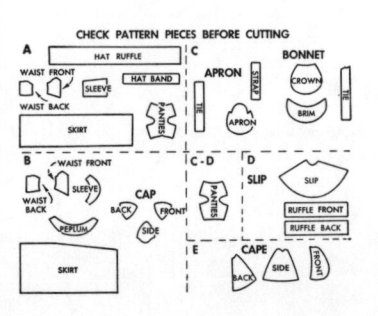

IMPORTANT All seams are indicated by broken lines, all cutting lines by continuous double lines. Cut apart each pattern piece then CUT PATTERN AND MATERIAL TOGETHER THROUGH THE WHITE CENTER OF THE DOUBLE LINE. The margin falls away as you cut through the pattern and material. Every mark is important for the construction, so before removing the pattern from the material, mark carefully with tracing wheel, tailor's chalk or thread markings.
United States Patents Nos. 1,387,723, 1,527,518, 1,982,005. Foreign Patents and Pending U. S. and Foreign Applications. Copyright 1950, by McCall Corporation. Made in U. S. A.

CROCHETED SKATING SUIT (F)

1564

CROCHETED SKATING SUIT (F)

Needles - 1 bone crochet hook, size 2.

Materials- 1 two-ounce ball sport yarn, 20 yards of Angora, 3 small pearl buttons.

Gauge - 7 sts to 1 inch. Measure garment on doll as you make it.

DRESS - Starting at waistline, ch 37 tc measure 5-1/2 inches, work 1 s c in 2nd ch from hook, work 1 s c in each ch to end of row, ch 1, turn. Work 3 more rows in same manner. Row 5 - * Work 1 s c in each of the first 3 sts, 2 s c in next st, repeat from * across row, do not inc in first and last 3 sts throughout skirt. Now inc in every 7th st in each row until you have 10 rows from beginning. Work 2 rows even, join, ch 1, turn. Now inc in every 8th st in each round until you have 18 rounds from beginning, break thread. Work 1 row of s c around top of skirt (36 sts). Ch 1, turn, work another row of s c, ch 1, turn. Work 2 more rows, increasing 4 s c in each row. Work 4 more rows even (44 sts, 8 rows), ch 1, turn, work 1 s c in each of the next 9 sts, ch 1, turn. Work 10 more rows even, ch 1, turn, work 5 s c in next 5 sts, ch 1, turn, s c over 2 sts for slanting shoulder. Fasten thread at other end of back and work other side to correspond.

Front - Skip 2 sts for underarm and s c across front (leaving 2 sts on each side for underarm) for 11 rows. Ch 1, s c over 5 s c, ch 1, turn, work over 2 s c for slanting shoulder. Work 2 rows on other shoulder to correspond. Sew shoulder seams.

Sleeves - Ch 14, s c in 2nd ch, work 1 s c to end of ch. Ch 1, turn, work 3 more rows even. *Inc 1 st at beg of next 2 rows. Work 2 rows even, repeat from * until you have 22 rows (23 sts). On next row work to within 3 s c, ch 1, turn, work to within 3 s c of next row. Dec 1 st at end of next 4 rows. Sew up sleeves, insert into armhole, allowing a little fulness at top of sleeve.

Finishing - Fasten thread on left side of waistline and s c around backs and neck, making 3 ch 3 loops for buttonholes on right side, increasing 2 sts at top of backs. With Angora, starting at back, work 1 row of s c around bottom of skirt. Work 1 row of s c around neck, skipping 3 sts. Embroider as shown on illustration (take white sewing thread, make your outline, then embroider with Angora) in outline and lazy daisy stitches, detail 1.

PANTIES - Ch 36, work 1 s c in 2nd ch from hook, 1 s c in each ch to end of row. Row 2 - Ch 3, turn, work 1 d c in each st, increasing 5 d c across row. Repeat row 2, 2 more times, join with a sl st, ch 3, turn. Work 2 rounds of d c without increasing, join each rnd with a sl st, ch 3. Sl st 1 more st. *Ch 2, turn, work 1 d c in each of next 3 sts, ch 2, turn, repeat from *2 more times, break thread. Fold panties in half and sew crotch to other side. Work 26 s c around each leg.

CAP - Ch 3, join, ch 1, work 7 s c in ring. Row 2 - Work 2 s c in each st. Row 3 - * Work 1 s c in next st, 2 s c in next st, repeat from * around row. Row 4 - * Work 1 s c in each of the next 2 sts, 2 s c in next st, repeat from * around row. Now inc in every 5th st until you have 56 sts around. Work even until you have 15 rows. On 16th row dec 4 sts spaced at equal distances apart. Ch 1, turn, s c to within 14 s c at beginning of row, ch 1, turn. Work 3 more rows around front of cap dec 1 st at end of each row, ch 1, turn. Work 1 more row, decreasing 3 sts, evenly distributed. Ch 27 sts for each chin tie. Work 1 s c in 4th ch from hook, s c to end of ch, sl st, fasten off. Work 1 row, with Angora, around front and back of cap, decreasing 2 sts at back of cap.

MITTS - Ch 20, loosely, join, work 19 s c in ring. Row 2 - Work 1 row even in s c. Row 3 - Dec 5 sts evenly distributed. Row 4 - Work even. Row 5 - Inc 3 sts. Row 6 - Inc 2 sts. Row 7 - Ch 2, skip 3 sts for thumb. Work 2 rows even, working 2 s c over the ch - 2. Now dec 3 s c every row until you have 3 s c left, sew together.

Thumb - Fasten thread and work 1 s c in each st around thumb hole for 2 rows. Dec 2 sts in next row, draw together and sew. Work 1 row, of s c with angora around top of mitts.

ACTUAL SIZE

McCALL CUT AND SEW GUIDE
1564

I. Cutting layouts for all sizes.
II. Assembling, sewing and finishing details.

I. Diagrammes de coupe pour toutes les tailles.
II. Détails de l'assemblage, couture et finissage.

I. Divisiones para el courte de todos los tamanos.
II. Confeccion, costura y detalles para el acabado.

HOW TO CUT
Cut pattern and material through the white center of the double line.

Do not cut off the margin before cutting material. The margin falls away as you cut through pattern and material.

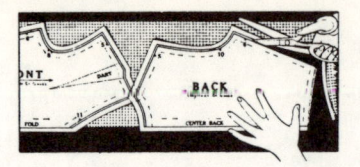

CUTTING WITH PINKING SHEARS
Pinking shears may be used for cutting out the garment. This is suitable for most materials, such as silks, cottons, woolens, rayons, velvets, etc.

Pinking automatically finishes the seam edges, thus saving time.

Avoid pinking on loosely woven materials that ravel easily.

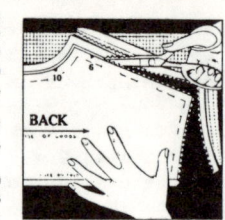

TAILOR'S TACKS
Make tailor's tacks before removing pattern, after garment is cut.

A—With double thread, baste through pattern and material, forming loops; then clip each loop to remove pattern.

B—Raise upper layer of material slightly and clip through center of thread.

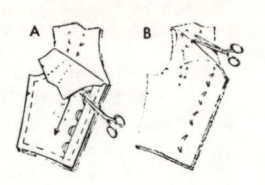

For plain material, as cottons, linens, etc., a tracing wheel may be used.

I. CUTTING LAYOUTS FOR ALL SIZES

The diagrams below show how to lay the pattern pieces on the material.
Pin the pattern pieces on material and cut pattern and material together through the white center of the double line. The margin falls away as you cut through pattern and material. See diagram above on "How to Cut."
IMPORTANT—The pattern pieces, shaded in the diagrams, are to be laid face down.

FOR NAP MATERIALS—For materials that have a raised nap, such as velveteen, etc., pattern pieces should be laid all in one direction with nap running upward.
For materials with a flat nap, such as pan velvet, broadcloth, etc., pattern should be laid in one direction with the nap running downward.
FOR ONE-WAY DESIGN MATERIALS, lay pattern pieces all in one direction.

VIEW A
1564
BALLET COSTUME
39" MATERIAL

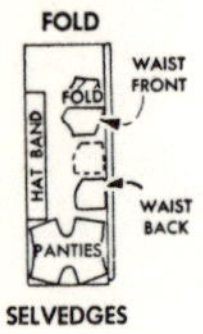

72" MATERIAL

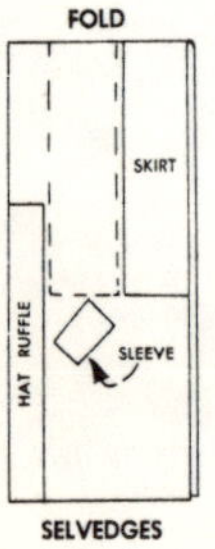

VIEW B
EVENING DRESS AND CAP
72" MATERIAL

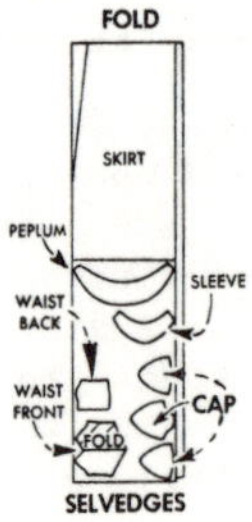

LINING
39" MATERIAL

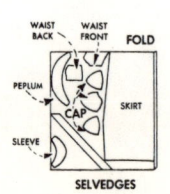

VIEW C
SUNSUIT AND BONNET
35" MATERIAL

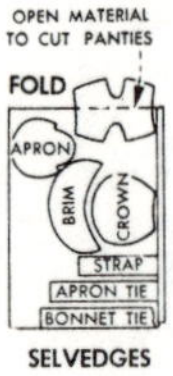

VIEW D
SLIP AND PANTIES
35 or 39" MATERIAL

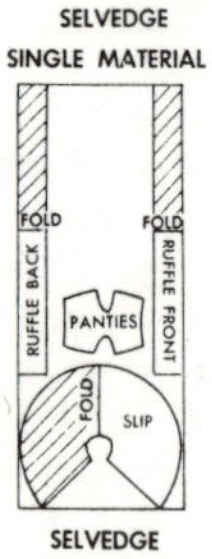

VIEW E
CAPE
39" MATERIAL

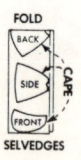

168

II. ASSEMBLING, SEWING AND FINISHING DETAILS

Join the seams by matching the corresponding notches. **The notches in the pattern are numbered in the order in which the seams should be joined.**

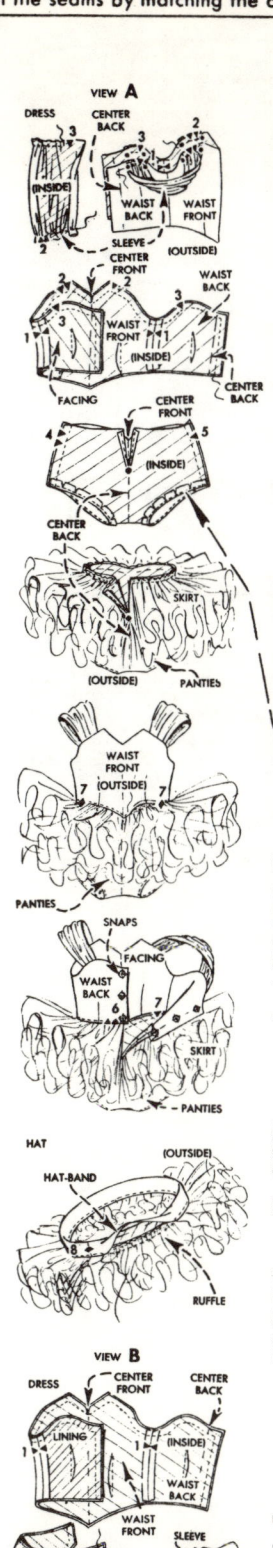

1564

NOTE: 1/4" seams allowed on all edges unless otherwise specified on the pattern.

For VIEW F (Wool Crocheting Skating Outfit) see instructions on Sheet 2.

VIEW A

DRESS

DARTS -- Make darts in waist front and backs, stitching together along dotted lines on wrong side of material. Press darts toward centers.

SEAMS - Notches 1 -- Join front to backs at sides. Press seams open.

SLEEVES -- Turn under on lines indicated, then gather notched edges along seam lines.

2. Baste sleeve to waist
3. between circles (right sides together).

WAIST FACING -- Make darts and join seams in waist. Stitch facing to waist along upper and back edges, joining in sleeves. Clip seam at curves and corners. Turn waist right side out, press. Baste lower edges.

PANTIES -- Turn under seam allowance on un-notched leg edges, clipping along curve. Edge-stitch.

Slash down center back to circle. Turn under seam allowance indicated on pattern, edge-stitch.

4. Join side seams.
5. .

SKIRT -- Place 2 sections of skirt together, matching centers and raw edges. Fold on line indicated, press. Gather through all thicknesses along line indicated and 1/8" outside.

Baste ruffle to upper edge of panties, edges even, matching centers and adjusting gathers.

JOINING WAIST TO SKIRT & PANTIES
6. Turn under and baste
7. lower edges of waist, clipping along curves. Top-stitch over gathered edge of skirt, matching centers and joining in panties.

FINISHING--Separate layers of skirt to make them stand out, paste on star sequin trimming. Sew snaps to back opening edges.

HAT -- Prepare ruffle in same manner as skirt.

8. Join center back seam in hat band, press seam open.

Join one edge of hat band to ruffle, having ends of ruffle at center back. Turn in seam allowance on free edge, top-stitch over seam on outside.

Separate layers of ruffle, trim with sequins as for skirt.

VIEW B

DRESS

WAIST - Notches 1 -- Make darts and join side seams as for VIEW A. Repeat for lining.

Stitch lining to waist along upper and back edges (right sides together). Clip seam at curves and corners. Turn right side out, press. Baste lower edges.

SLEEVES--Line sleeve (right sides together) leaving free between circles. Turn and press. Gather free edge to 2-1/2", fasten threads.

Lap ends of sleeve about 1/4" under top of waist between circles, stitch to position.

VIEW B (CONTINUED)

PEPLUM--Line peplum (right sides together) leaving notched edge free. Turn and press. Sew braid to finished edge. Gather notched edge along seam line.

Turn under and baste seam allowance at lower edge of waist. Baste over gathered edge of peplum, with ends at centers front and back, matching notches 3 and 4.

SKIRT AND LINING -- Turn under lower edge of skirt lining 1/4" and edge-stitch. Baste skirt over lining along upper and back edges.

2. Join center back seam in skirt and lining (right sides together) leaving free above circle for opening. Turn under seam allowance on opening edges and edge-stitch.

Gather upper edge along seam line.

3. Lap and baste waist over
4. skirt, matching seam lines and centers front and back. Top-stitch over seam.

FINISHING--Sew braid along top of waist and gathered edge of sleeve. Fasten back opening with snaps.

CAP

Baste cap sections over corresponding lining sections (right sides up).

SEAMS--Join cap sides to front
5. and back. Trim seams
6. to 1/8".
For facing, cut a bias strip 1" x 12". Fold lengthwise through center, press. Stitch to lower edge of hat along seam line (right sides together) raw edges even, joining ends at center back. Trim seam. Clip along curves.

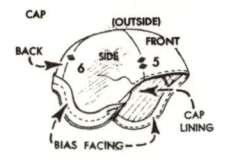

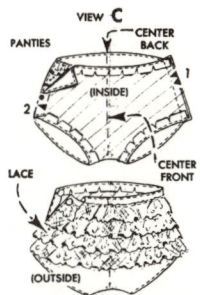

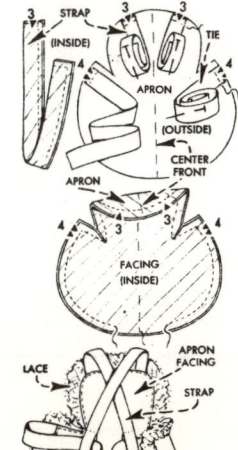

Turn bias facing to inside, edge-stitch hat. Trim with sequins.

VIEW C

PANTIES

Turn under and baste seam allowance on un-notched upper and leg edges, clipping along curves. Edge-stitch.

LACE TRIMMING--Cut 4 pieces 1/2" wide lace, each 6-3/4" long. Gather lace by drawing thread in straight edge and stitch each row to position indicated on pattern, starting with lowest row.

SEAMS- Notches 1 and 2 --- Join side seams (right sides together), leaving left side free above circle for opening. Turn under seam allowance on opening edges, edge-stitch. Lap front over back 1/4", snap at waistline.

APRON

STRAPS AND TIES--Fold lengthwise (right sides together) and stitch, leaving notched ends open. Turn and press.

Baste straps to position on apron, matching notches 3, seams toward center. Baste ties to position, seams upward, matching notches 4.

APRON FACING -- Stitch to
3. outer edges of apron
4. (right sides together) joining in ends of straps and ties, being careful to keep finished edges free of stitching. Leave a 2" opening at inner edge for turning. Clip seam at curves and corners.

Turn apron right side out, slip-stitch opening. Cut lace twice measurement of outer edges. Gather as for panties and stitch to outer edges (right sides up) joining ends at an inner corner.

Turn under ends of straps on lines indicated, hem to position, forming loops. Cross straps in back, slip ties through loops and tie bow at center back.

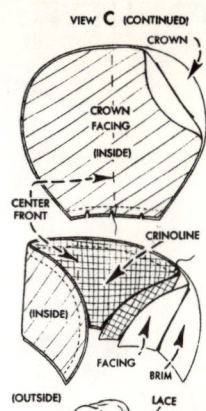

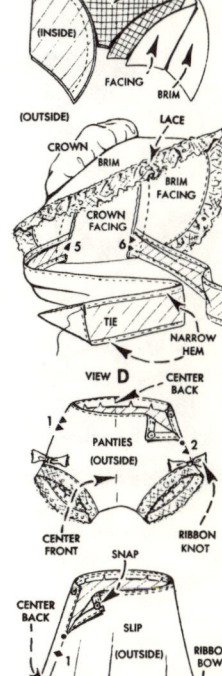

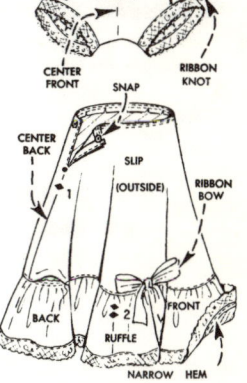

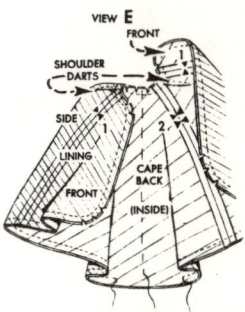

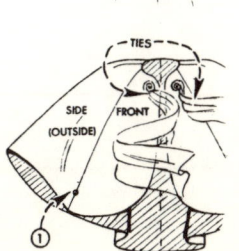

VIEW C (CONTINUED)

BONNET

CROWN -- Face crown (right sides together) and stitch lower back edge between circles. Clip seam along curve. Turn crown right side out, baste raw edges together then gather on seam line.

BRIM -- Face brim (right sides together) having 1 thickness crinoline interfacing on top and leaving notched edge free. Turn brim right side out, press.

5. Join brim to crown (right
6. sides together) matching centers and adjusting gathers.

Stitch gathered lace (twice full) to outer edge of brim as an apron, turning under raw ends of lace.

TIES -- Narrowly hem long edges. Turn in seam allowance on straight end, fold on line indicated and slip-stitch to long edge.

Form pleat at opposite end as indicated and sew to position on underside of brim.

VIEW D

PANTIES

PANTIES -- Turn under and baste seam allowance on un-notched upper and leg edges, clipping along curves. Stitch 1/4" lace flat to leg edges.

SEAMS -- Notches 1 and 2 -- See instructions under VIEW C.

TRIMMING-- Cut 1/4" ribbon 2" long. Tie in knot and tack to side seams above lace.

SLIP

CENTER BACK SEAM- Notches 1- Join seam, leaving free above circle for opening. Turn under seam allowance on edges of opening and edge-stitch.

Turn under seam allowance at upper edge, clipping along curves and stitch twice.

RUFFLE -- Join seams in ruf-
2. fle and press open. Finish lower edge with narrow machine-stitched hem. Stitch 1/4" lace flat to hemmed edge, joining ends at a seam.

Gather along seam line at raw edge of ruffle. Turn under seam allowance on lower edge of slip, stitch over gathered edge of ruffle, matching centers and adjusting gathers evenly.

FINISHING -- Cut 1/4" ribbon 12" long. Tie bow and tack to position at right front. Sew snap at back opening.

VIEW E

CAPE

Make shoulder dart seam at top of cape side, stitching together along dotted lines on wrong side. Trim seam to 1/8".

SEAMS - Notches 1 and 2 -- Join cape side to cape front and cape back. Steam seams open.

LINING--Make same as cape. Stitch lining to cape (right sides together) leaving a 3" opening across lower edge of back for turning. Clip seam along curves.

Turn cape right side out, slipstitch opening.

TIES -- Cut net or maline 3-3/4" wide and 10-1/2" long for each tie (or ribbon may be used). Roll up 1" at end tightly to form knot and sew to position. Repeat for other tie. Tie ends in a bow.

NOTE: If jacket effect is desired, tack together at corresponding circles (1).

169

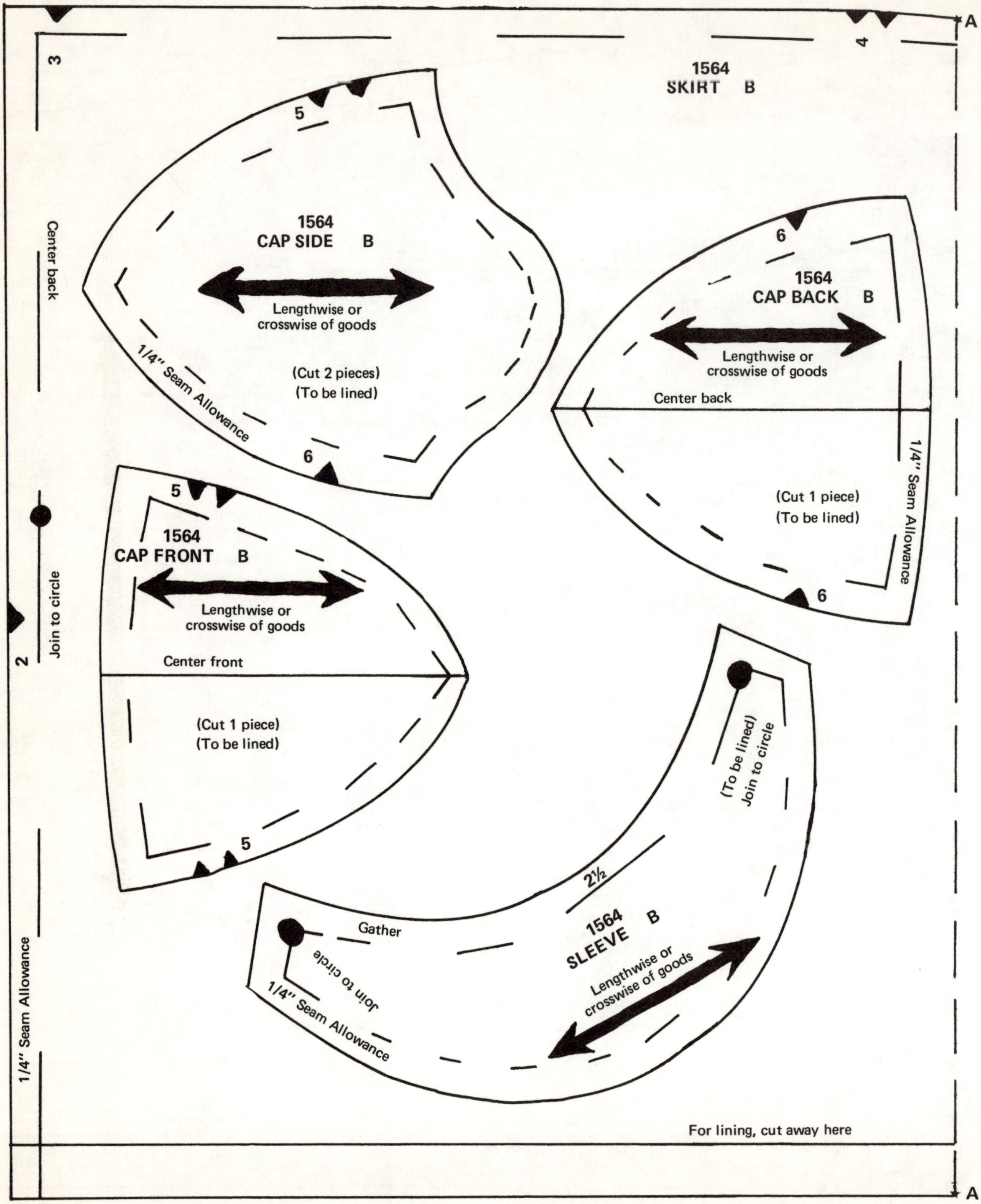

1564
SKIRT B
3
4
A
Center back
Join to circle
2
1/4" Seam Allowance
1564
CAP SIDE B
Lengthwise or crosswise of goods
(Cut 2 pieces)
(To be lined)
1/4" Seam Allowance
5
6
1564
CAP BACK B
Lengthwise or crosswise of goods
Center back
(Cut 1 piece)
(To be lined)
1/4" Seam Allowance
6
1564
CAP FRONT B
Lengthwise or crosswise of goods
Center front
(Cut 1 piece)
(To be lined)
5
1564
SLEEVE B
Lengthwise or crosswise of goods
Gather
2½
(To be lined)
Join to circle
Join to circle
1/4" Seam Allowance
For lining, cut away here
A

1/4" Seam Allowance
Gather this edge

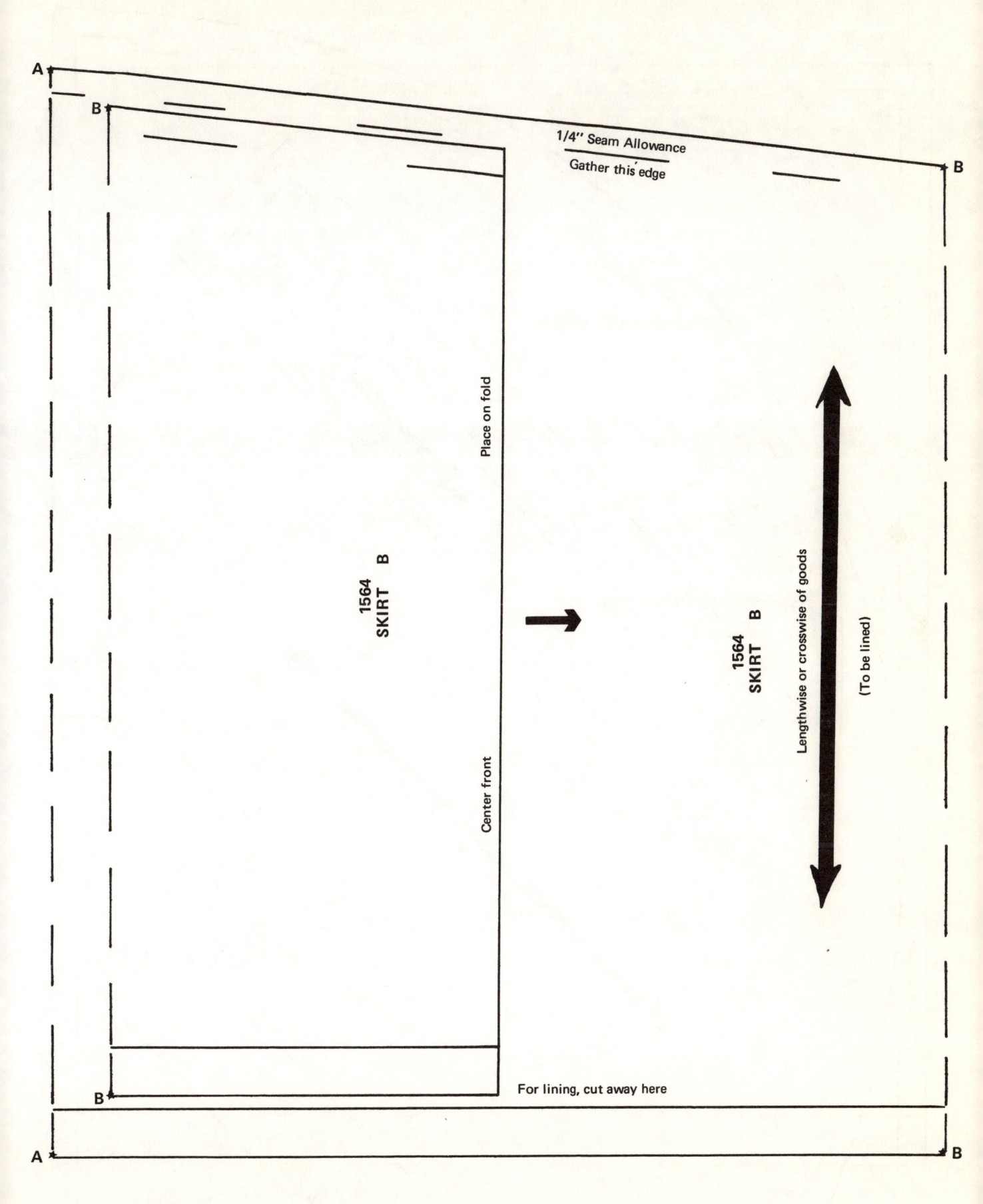

Place on fold

1564
SKIRT B

Center front

1564
SKIRT B

Lengthwise or crosswise of goods

(To be lined)

For lining, cut away here

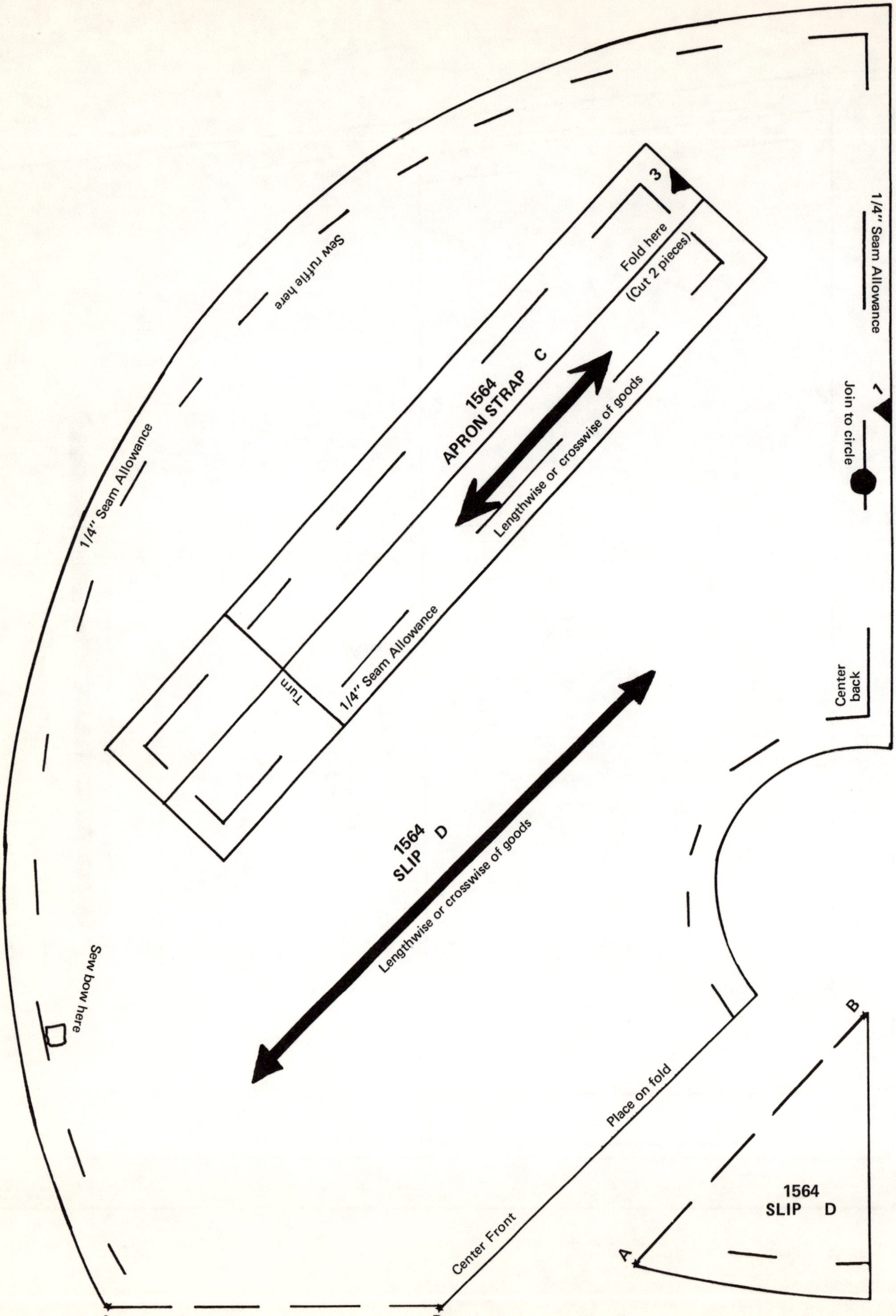
1564
APRON STRAP C
Fold here
(Cut 2 pieces)
Lengthwise or crosswise of goods
1/4" Seam Allowance
Turn
3
Sew ruffle here
1/4" Seam Allowance
1/4" Seam Allowance
Join to circle
1
Center back
1564
SLIP D
Lengthwise or crosswise of goods
Sew bow here
Place on fold
Center Front
A
B
1564
SLIP D
A
B

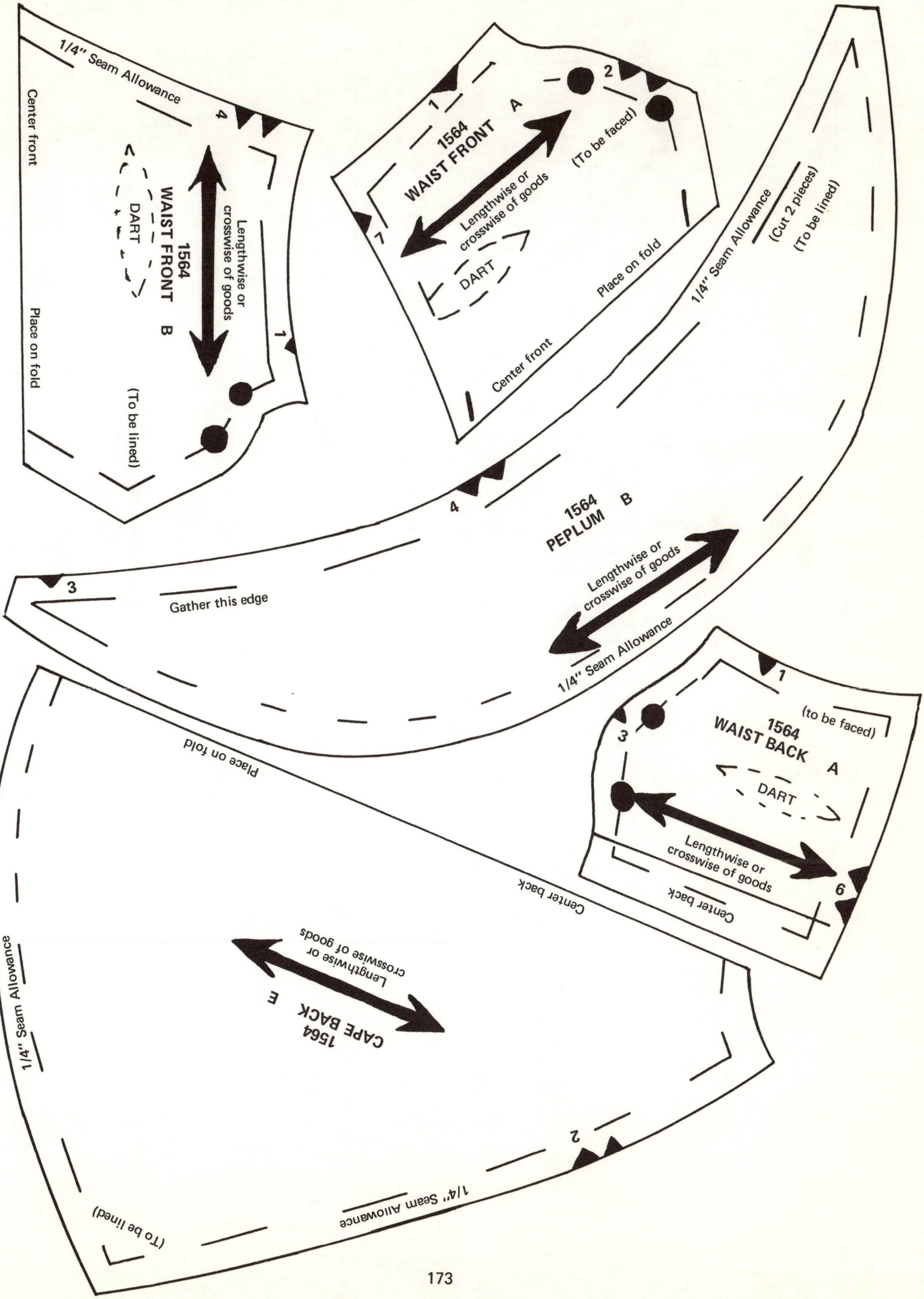
1564
WAIST FRONT B
Lengthwise or crosswise of goods
1/4" Seam Allowance
Center front
Place on fold
DART
(To be lined)
1564
WAIST FRONT A
Lengthwise or crosswise of goods
(To be faced)
DART
Place on fold
Center front
1564
PEPLUM B
Lengthwise or crosswise of goods
1/4" Seam Allowance
(Cut 2 pieces)
(To be lined)
Gather this edge
1564
WAIST BACK A
(to be faced)
DART
Lengthwise or crosswise of goods
Center back
1564
CAPE BACK E
Lengthwise or crosswise of goods
Place on fold
Center back
1/4" Seam Allowance
(To be lined)

174

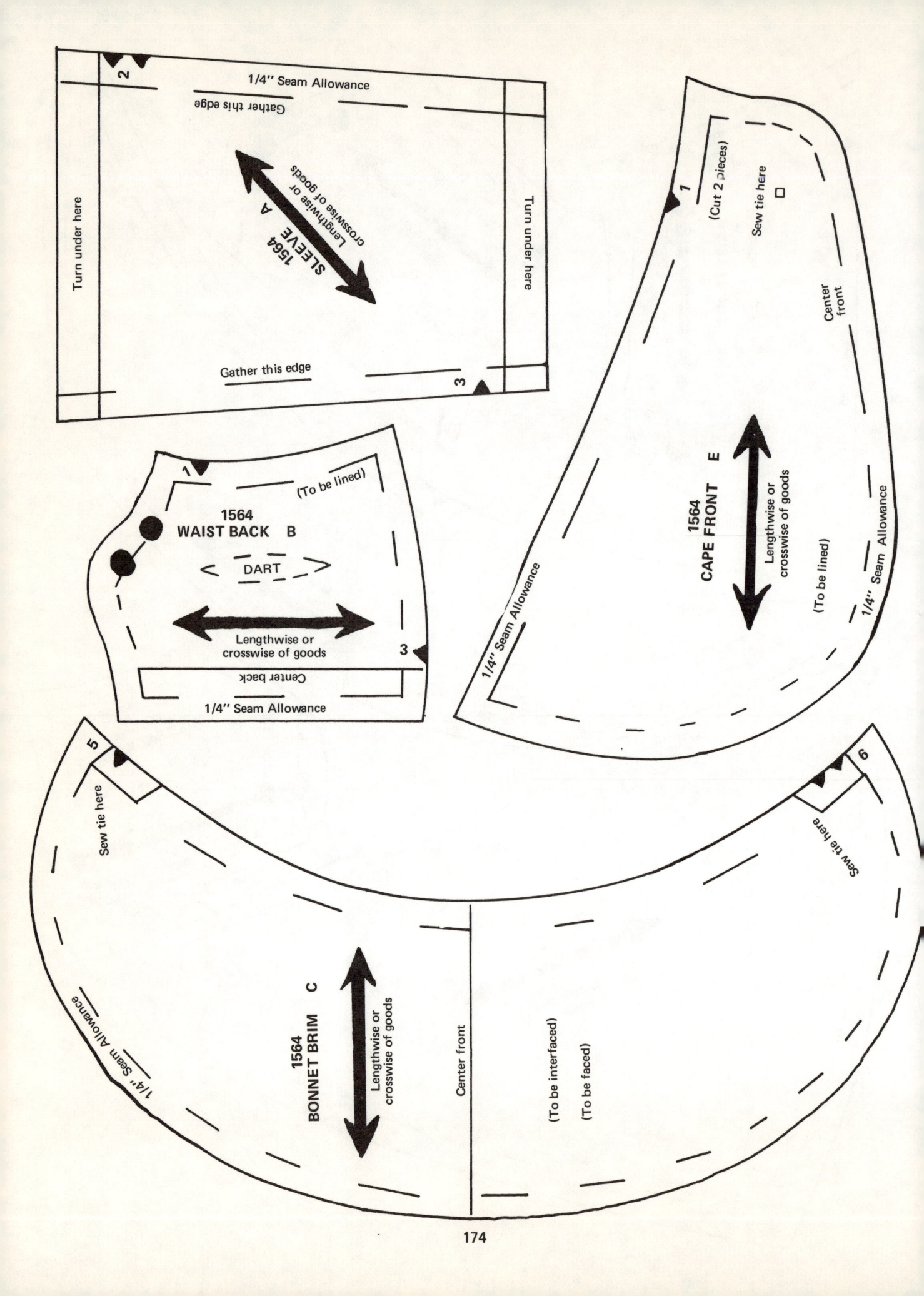

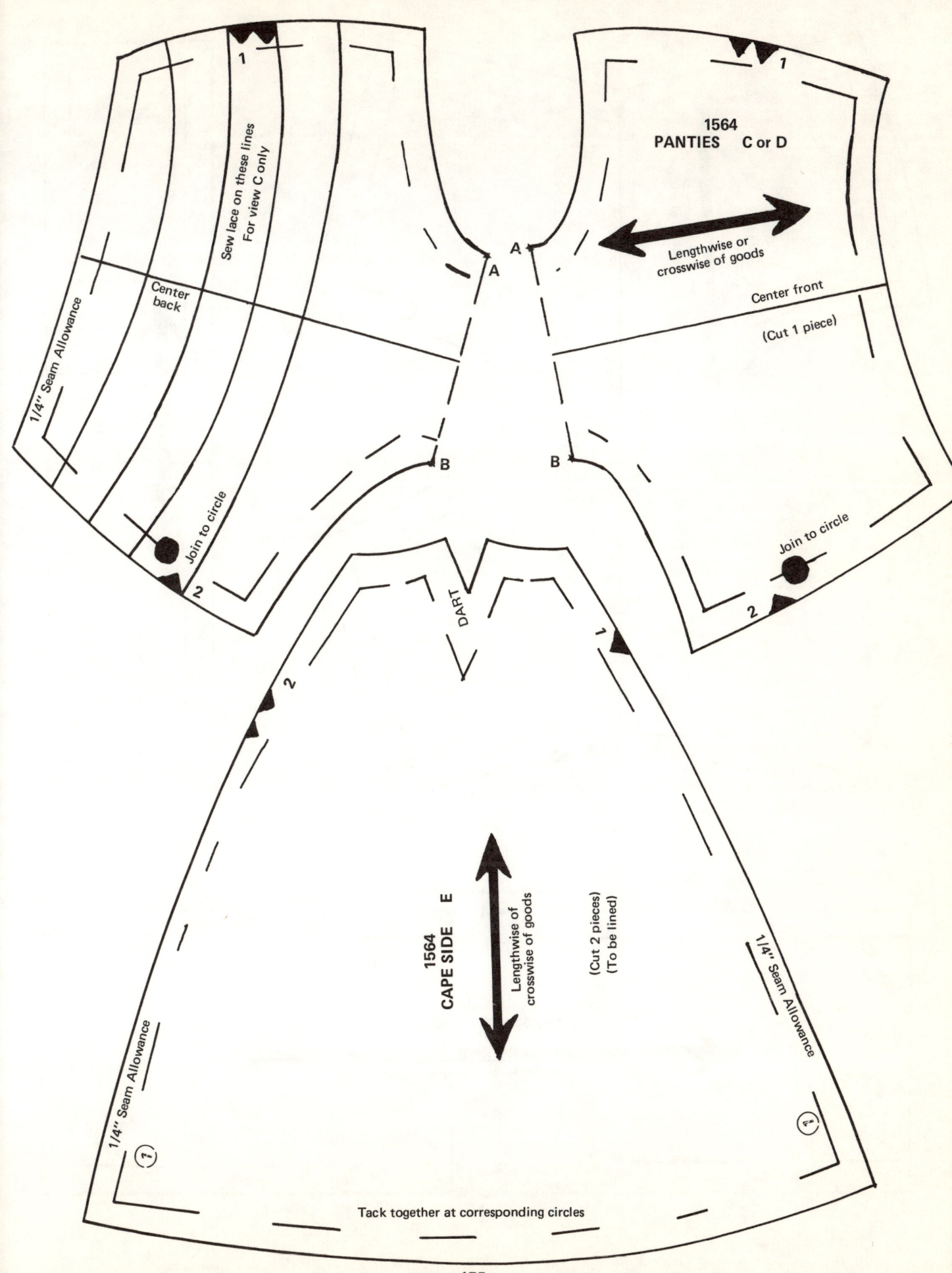

175

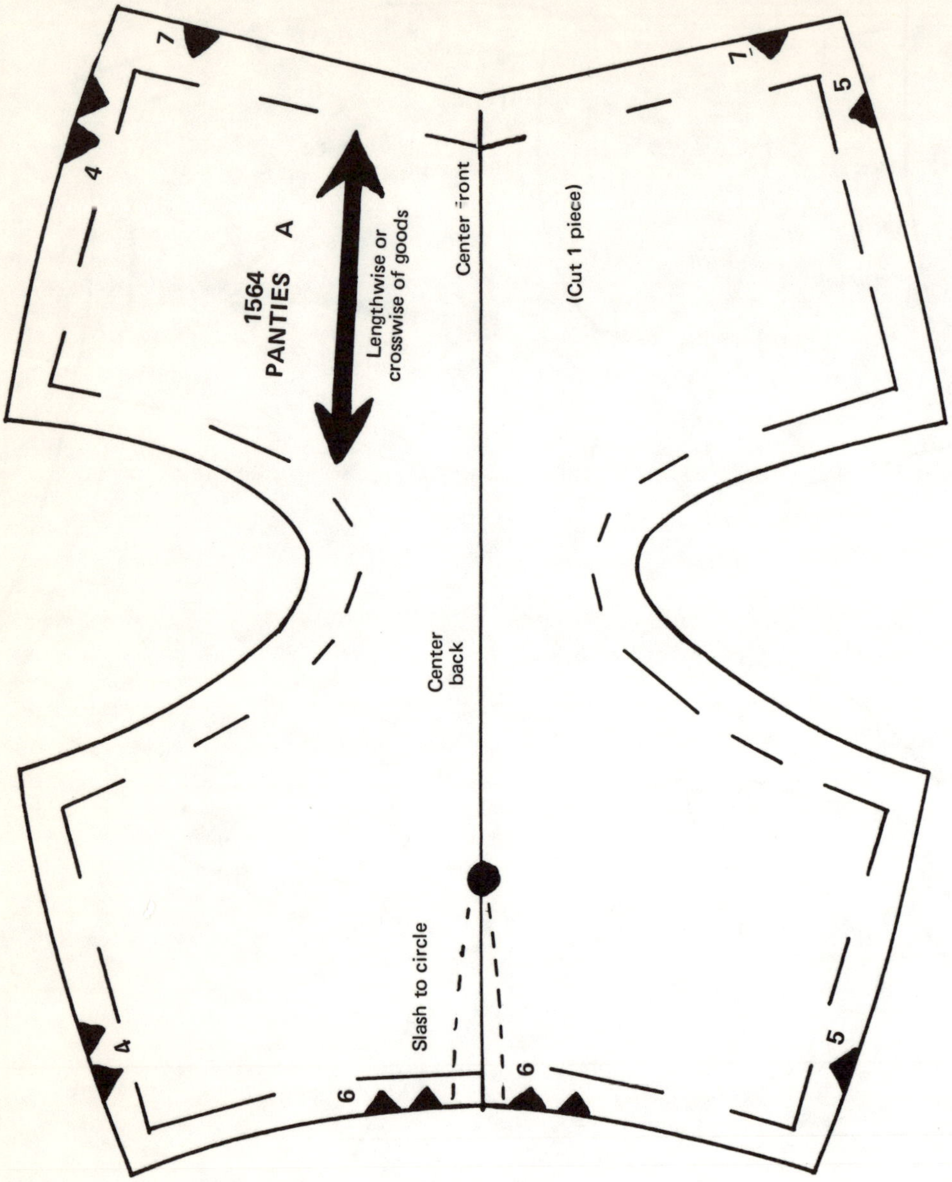
1564
PANTIES A
Lengthwise or crosswise of goods
Center front
(Cut 1 piece)
Center back
Slash to circle
4
5
6
7

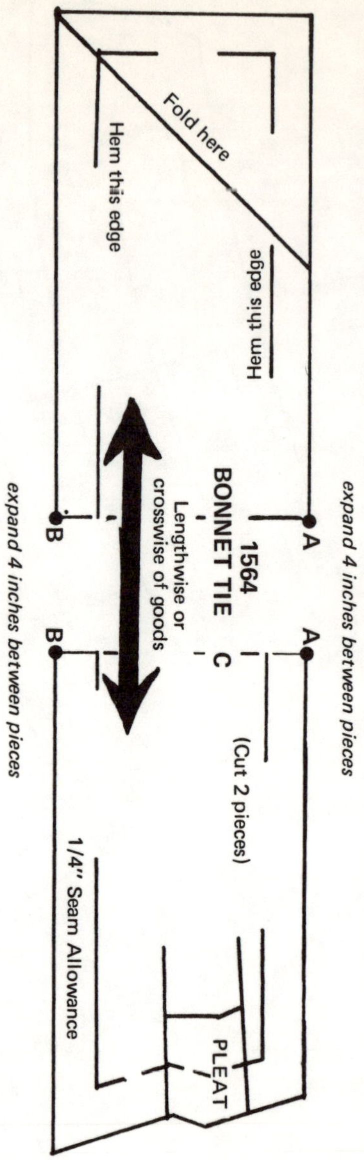
expand 4 inches between pieces
Fold here
Hem this edge
Hem this edge
1564
BONNET TIE C
Lengthwise or crosswise of goods
(Cut 2 pieces)
1/4" Seam Allowance
PLEAT
A
B
expand 4 inches between pieces

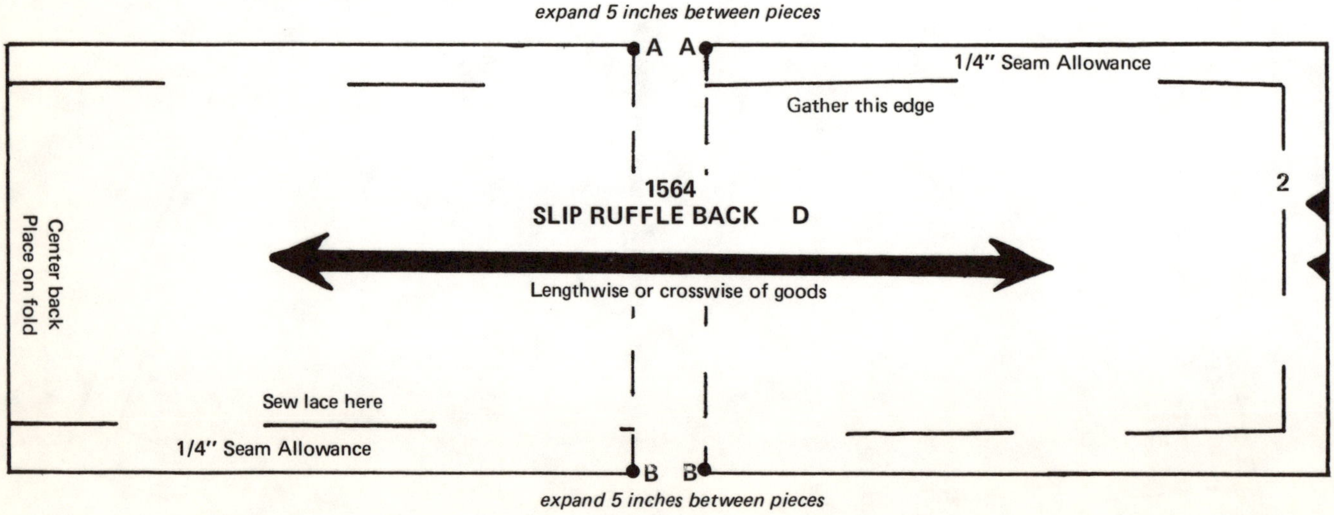
expand 5 inches between pieces
A A
1/4" Seam Allowance
Gather this edge
1564
SLIP RUFFLE BACK D
Lengthwise or crosswise of goods
Center back
Place on fold
Sew lace here
1/4" Seam Allowance
2
B B
expand 5 inches between pieces

1564 SKIRT A

Lengthwise or crosswise of goods

Center back

Gather along this line

Fold here

(Cut 2 pieces)

Center front

Place on fold

expand 11 inches between pieces

1564 APRON TIE C

Lengthwise or crosswise of goods

1/4" Seam Allowance

Fold here

(Cut 2 pieces)

expand 6 inches between pieces

1564 HAT BAND A

Lengthwise or crosswise of goods

1/4" Seam Allowance

Center back

Fold here

(Cut 1 piece)

expand 5 inches between pieces

177

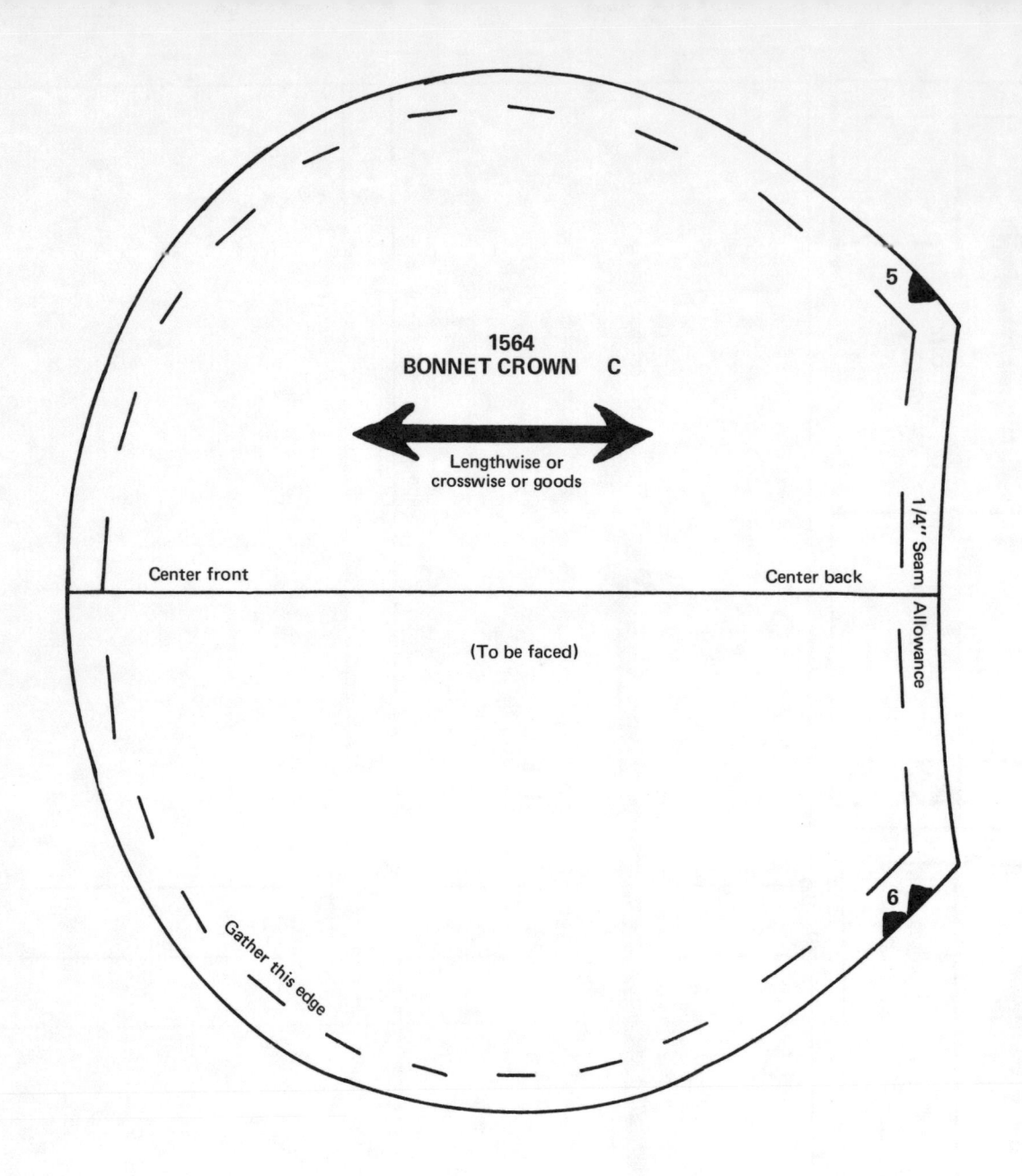

1564
BONNET CROWN   C

↔ Lengthwise or crosswise or goods

Center front   Center back

1/4" Seam Allowance

(To be faced)

Gather this edge

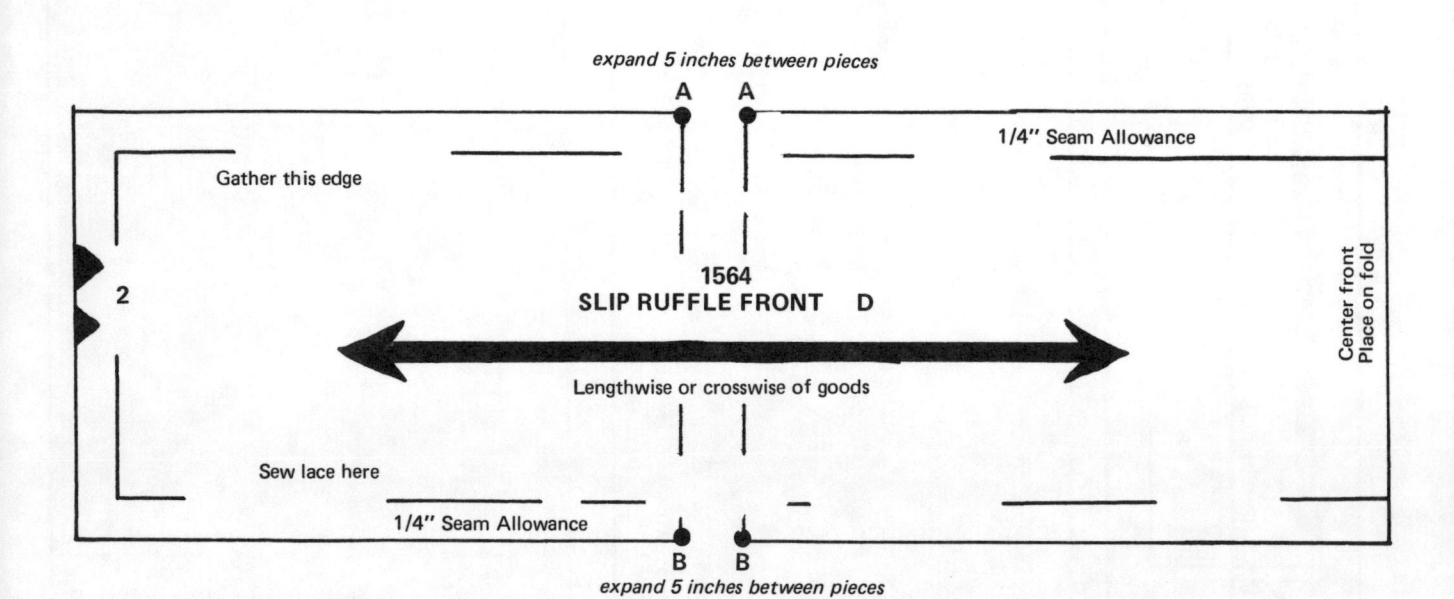

5

6

---

expand 5 inches between pieces

A   A

1/4" Seam Allowance

Gather this edge

2

1564
SLIP RUFFLE FRONT   D

↔ Lengthwise or crosswise of goods

Center front
Place on fold

Sew lace here

1/4" Seam Allowance

B   B

expand 5 inches between pieces

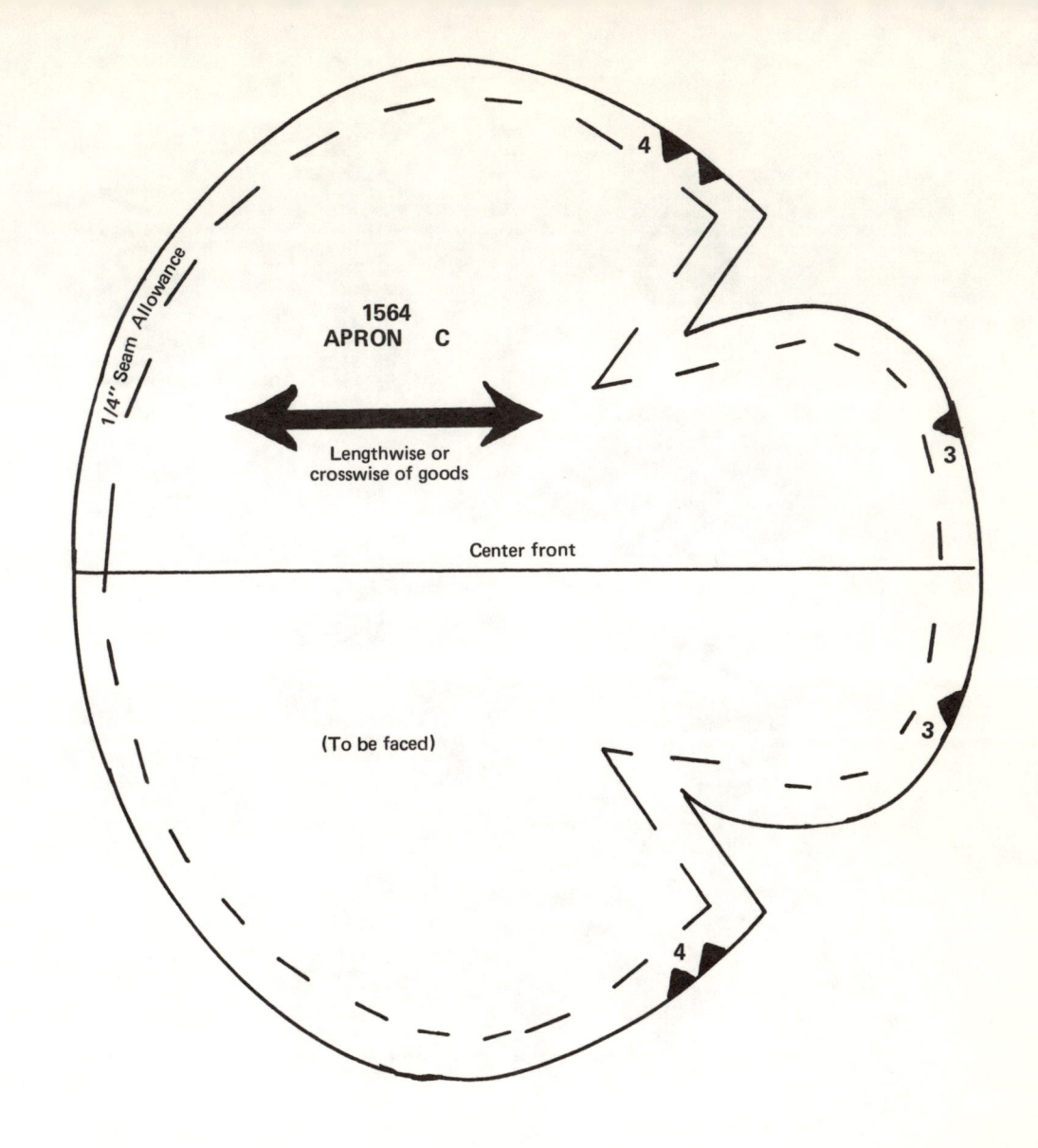

1564 APRON C

1/4" Seam Allowance

Lengthwise or crosswise of goods

Center front

(To be faced)

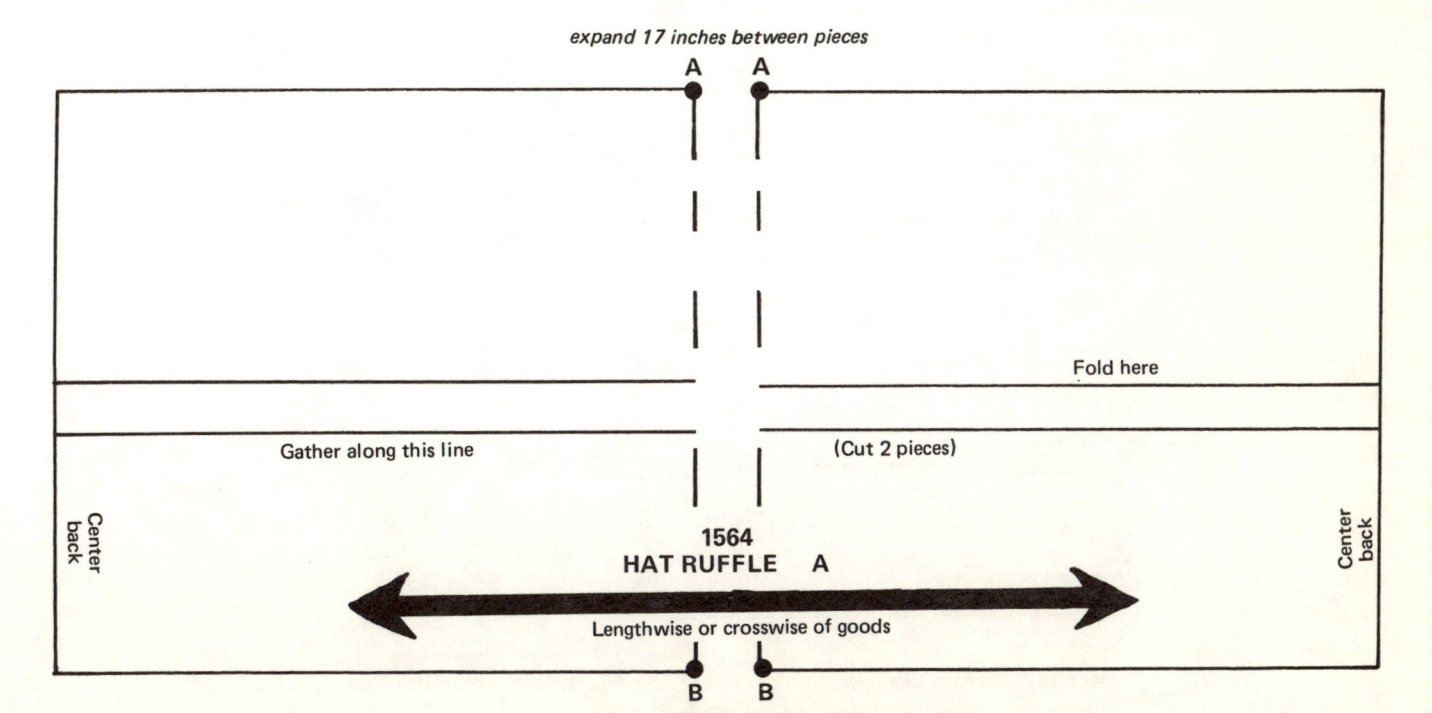

expand 17 inches between pieces

A   A

Fold here

Gather along this line   (Cut 2 pieces)

Center back

Center back

1564 HAT RUFFLE A

Lengthwise or crosswise of goods

B   B

expand 17 inches between pieces

E
F
D
A
C
G
B
McCall's
PRINTED PATTERN
1891
SIZE 18
35c
Set of Doll Clothes
Fits the
"Mary Hoyer" Doll

This pattern includes Cut and Sew Guide with instructions for cutting, sewing, and finishing.

McCALL'S PRINTED PATTERN No. 1891 — 2 Pieces

Trademark Reg. U. S. Pat. Off. Marca Registrada

FABRIC REQUIRED Sizes	14″	18″	
VIEW A—Dress			
Bodice—One Piece of Fabric 9″ x 19½″ or 35″ Fabric Without Nap*	⅛	¼	yds.
Contrast Skirt, Binding, etc., 35″ Fabric Without Nap*	¼	¼	"
VIEW B—Dress and Parasol Cover			
35″ or 39″ Fabric Without Nap*	⅝	¾	"
Overbodice, Overskirt, etc.			
54″ Nylon Tulle or Net	⅝	¾	"
3½″ Wide Pleated Nylon Tulle Ruffling	4	4¾	"
One 36-yd. Spool Metallic Sewing Thread. For Parasol Frame See Note Below.			
VIEW C or D—Peignoir with Nightgown			
35″ Fabric Without Nap*	¾	1	"
39″ " " "	⅝	⅞	"
Baby Ribbon for Bow and Ties	⅞	⅞	"
½″ Wide Lace Edging for Nightgown	2¼	2⅝	"
VIEW E or F—Lingerie			
Long Petticoat and Panties—35″ or 39″ Fabric	½	½	"
To Trim Long Petticoat—2″ Wide Ruffling	1¼	1⅜	"
" " " " ½″ Wide Horsehair Braid	1¼	1⅜	"
Short Petticoat and Panties—35″ or 39″ Fabric	⅜	⅜	"
To Trim Short Petticoat—1¼″ Wide Embroidered Ruffling	⅞	1⅛	"
To Trim Panties—½″ Wide Lace or ⅝″ Wide Ruffling	⅜	⅜	"

VIEW G—Cape, Headband & Muff—2 Balls Angora (10 grams), No. 6 Knitting Needles.

NOTE: A Parasol frame that opens mechanically may be purchased from Doll Mfg. Co.

*WITHOUT NAP means fabric with either way design, or without nap or pile.

CORRESPONDING BODY MEASUREMENTS Sizes	14″	18″	
Chest	7⅜	8⅞	ins.
Waist	6	7⅛	"
Hip	7½	9	"
Neck	4⅜	5⅛	"
Circular Crotch Depth from Neck	11	14	"
Outer Leg Length	7⅜	8¼	"
Outer Arm Length to Wrist	4⅛	5⅜	"

CHECK PATTERN PIECES BEFORE CUTTING

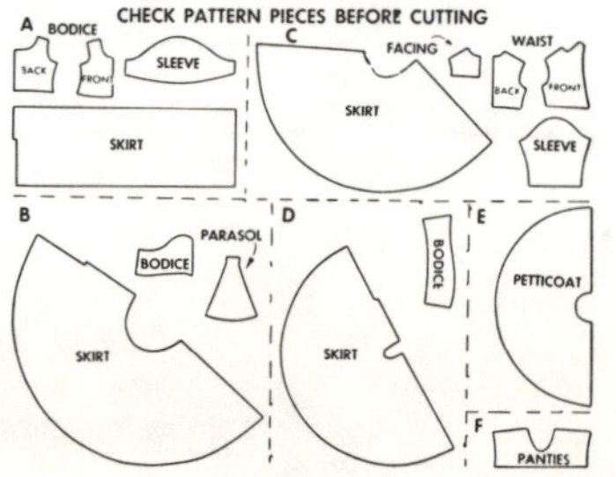
A
BODICE
BACK
FRONT
SLEEVE
SKIRT
C
FACING
WAIST
BACK
FRONT
SKIRT
SLEEVE
B
BODICE
PARASOL
SKIRT
D
BODICE
SKIRT
E
PETTICOAT
F
PANTIES

McCALL CORPORATION, PUBLISHERS, 230 PARK AVENUE, NEW YORK

United States Patents Nos. 1,387,723, 1,527,518, 1,982,005. Foreign Patents and Pending U. S. and Foreign Applications. Copyright 1954, by McCall Corporation. Made in U. S. A.

II. ASSEMBLING, SEWING AND FINISHING DETAILS

Join the seams by matching the corresponding notches. The notches in the pattern are numbered in the order in which the seams should be joined.

1891

IMPORTANT: 1/4" seams allowed on all edges unless otherwise specified on the pattern. When joining seams, be sure to take up the full seam allowance as indicated on the pattern.

PRESS SEAMS AND SECTIONS as the work progresses. **PRESS EACH SEAM OPEN** after stitching unless the directions state otherwise.

DRESS A

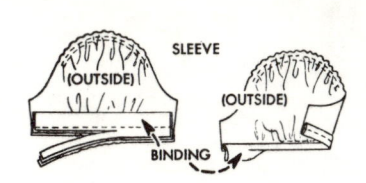

SLEEVES
Gather upper and lower edges on seam lines between crosses, also 1/8" outside. Draw up lower gathers as indicated on pattern, fasten threads.
FOR BINDING, cut straight fabric 1-1/4" wide to fit lower edge of sleeve. Fold lengthwise, then join to lower edge in 1/4" seam. Trim seam to 1/8", turn binding over edge and stitch close to seam on outside.

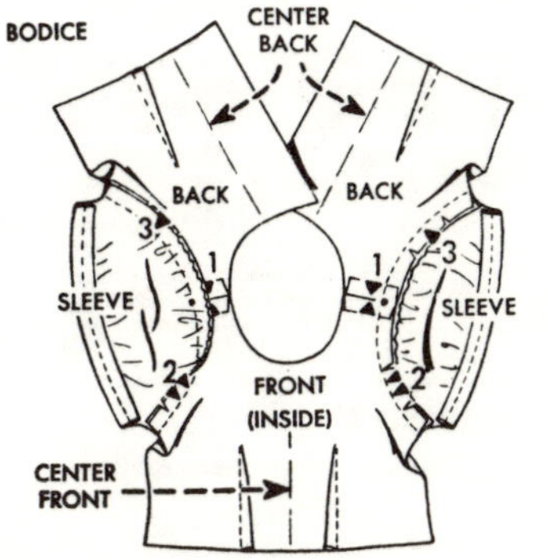

BODICE
Make darts in front and back, stitching together along dotted lines on wrong side of fabric. Press toward centers.

Notches 1. Join shoulder seams.

2,3. Join sleeves to armhole edges, shoulder seams at circles, adjusting gathers. Press seams toward sleeves.

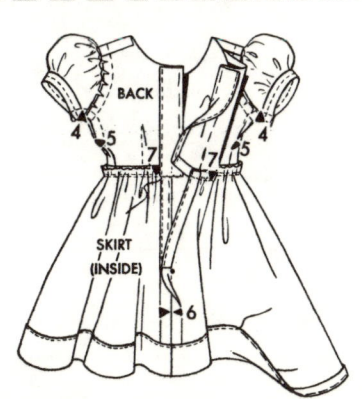

4,5. Join underarm seams in sleeve and bodice.

SKIRT
6. Join center back seam as far as circle.

Turn under 1/4" on back opening edges, stitch. Turn in RIGHT edge on center line, baste.

Turn hem on line indicated, turn in raw edge and stitch flat to skirt.

Gather upper edge along seam line and 1/8" outside.

7. Join bodice to skirt, matching centers and adjusting gathers. Press seam toward bodice.

BACK HEMS
Turn under 1/8" on back edges of bodice, stitch. Turn under on hemlines, baste. Hem lower ends to position.

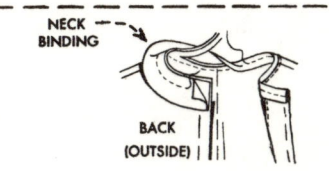

NECK BINDING
Cut straight fabric 1-1/4" wide. Fold lengthwise and baste to neck edge, turning in ends. Stitch 1/4" seam, trim to 1/8". Turn binding over edge, stitch close to seam on outside.

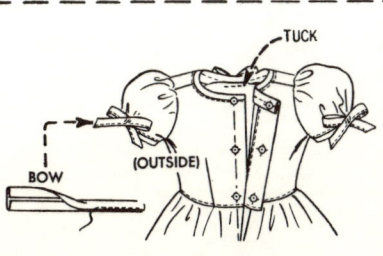

FINISHING
Make tuck in bodice front, stitching together along dotted lines.

Fasten back edges of bodice with snaps.

For 3 bows, cut straight fabric 1/2" x 12". Turn in 1/8" on long edges, then fold through center and stitch. Cut in 4" lengths. Form loops and ends for bows. Tack one at center front over tuck and one to each sleeve.

DRESS B

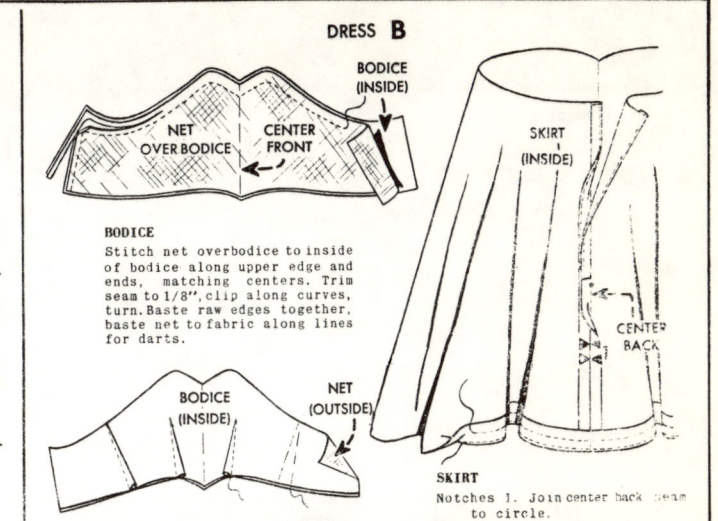

BODICE
Stitch net overbodice to inside of bodice along upper edge and ends, matching centers. Trim seam to 1/8", clip along curves, turn. Baste raw edges together, baste net to fabric along lines for darts.

Make darts, stitching together along dotted lines on inside of bodice. Press toward center front.

SKIRT
Notches 1. Join center back seam to circle.

Turn under 1/4" on back opening edges, stitch. Turn hem on line indicated, stitch close to edge and 1/4" above.

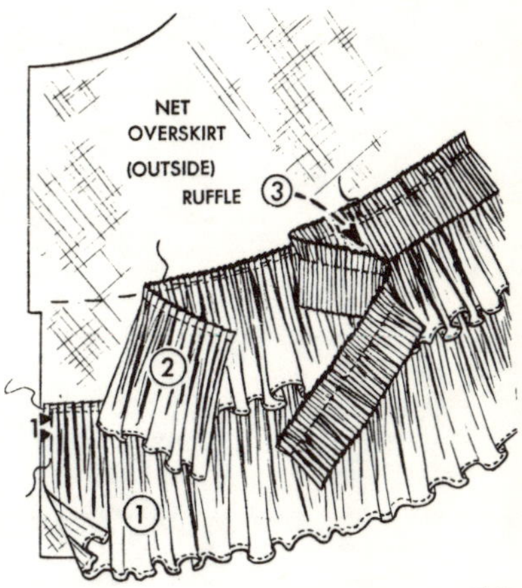

NET OVERSKIRT AND RUFFLES
RUFFLES (1) AND (4) -- Cut 3-1/2" wide ruffling 1-1/2 yds. long for 14" doll, 1-7/8 yds. long for 18" doll. Machine stitch 2-7/8" from lower edge for ruffle (1), trim away upper part 1/8" from stitching. Remove binding, then stitch through center of cut away section to be used for ruffle (4).

RUFFLES (2) AND (3) -- Cut 3-1/2" wide ruffling 1-1/4 yds. long for 14" doll, 1-5/8 yds. long for 18" doll. Machine stitch 2-3/8" from lower edge for ruffle (2), trim away upper part 1/8" from stitching. Remove binding, then stitch 1/4" from upper edge of cut away section to be used for ruffle (3).

Using metallic sewing thread in bobbin of machine, stitch 1/8" from lower edge of ruffles (1) and (2) wrong side up, opening out pleats.

Baste ruffle (1) to net overskirt with stitching along line indicated, easing in fulness. Using metallic sewing thread in bobbin, stitch to position (wrong side of overskirt up).

Baste ruffle (2) to position in same manner, then baste ruffle (3) over ruffle (2). Stitch to position as for ruffle (1).

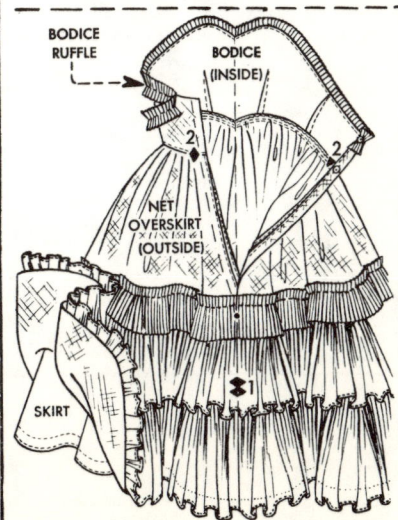

Join center back seam in overskirt and finish back opening edges as for skirt. Baste net overskirt to skirt along upper edge.

WAISTLINE SEAM
Gather upper edge of skirts along seam line and 1/8" above.

2. Join skirts to bodice, matching centers and adjusting gathers. Press seam toward bodice, top-stitch.

RUFFLE (4)
Baste stitching line of ruffle close to upper edge of bodice, then stitch to position, using metallic thread as for overskirt ruffles.

BACK CLOSING
Turn under right opening edge on center line, tack. Fasten bodice with snaps.

181

1891 (CONTINUED)

PARASOL B

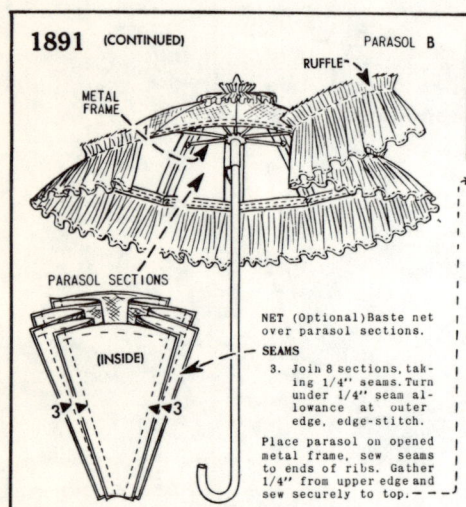

NOTE: A parasol frame that opens mechanically may be purchased from Mary Hoyer Doll Mfg. Co., 1013 Penn Street, Reading, Pa. Order parasol frame according to doll size.

Use 1-1/4 yds. 3-1/2" wide ruffling for 14" or 18" doll. Machine stitch 1-1/2" from lower edge of ruffling, then trim away upper part 1/2" from stitching. Stitch 1" from lower edge of cut away section, remove binding.

Trim lower edges of ruffles with metallic thread as for dress. Baste wider ruffle to outer edge of parasol with stitching line 1/8" from turned edge. Keeping metallic thread in bobbin, stitch to position from under side of parasol, being careful to stop machine at EACH RIB, take long stitch across metal (so that you do not break needle) then continue around entire edge in this manner.

Using 16" of narrower ruffle, gather along stitching line, draw up tightly and sew securely over raw edges at top of parasol.

SEAMS

3. Join 8 sections, taking 1/4" seams. Turn under 1/4" seam allowance at outer edge, edge-stitch.

Place parasol on opened metal frame, sew seams to ends of ribs. Gather 1/4" from upper edge and sew securely to top.

NET (Optional) Baste net over parasol sections.

PEIGNOIR C

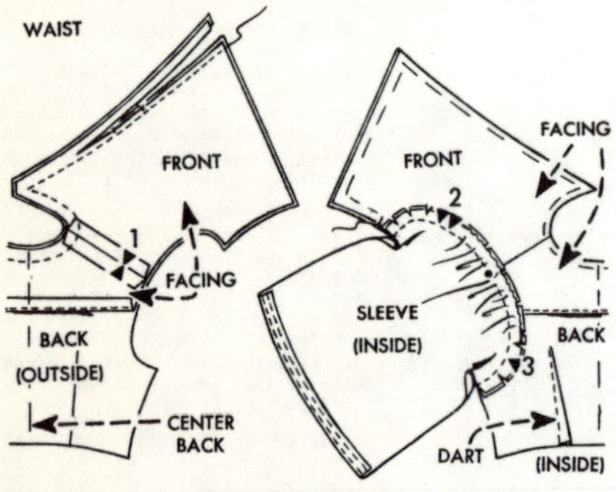

WAIST

Make waistline darts in back, stitching together along dotted lines on wrong side of fabric. Press toward center.

Notches 1. JOIN fronts to back at shoulder seams. Join front facings to facing (for back) in same manner.

Turn under seam allowance at lower back edge of facing, stitch.

Face waist (right sides together) matching shoulder seams. Stitch 1/4" seams at neck and front edges. Trim seam, clip along curves.

Turn facing to inside, baste raw edges together.

SLEEVE, ETC.

Turn under lower edge on seam line, stitch edge and 1/8" inside. Gather upper edge on seam line between crosses and 1/8" outside.

2, 3. Join sleeve to armhole edges, shoulder seam at circle, adjusting gathers. Press seam toward sleeve.

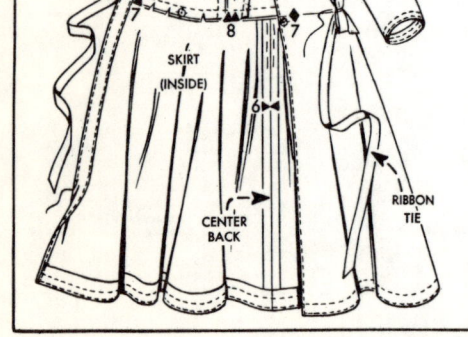

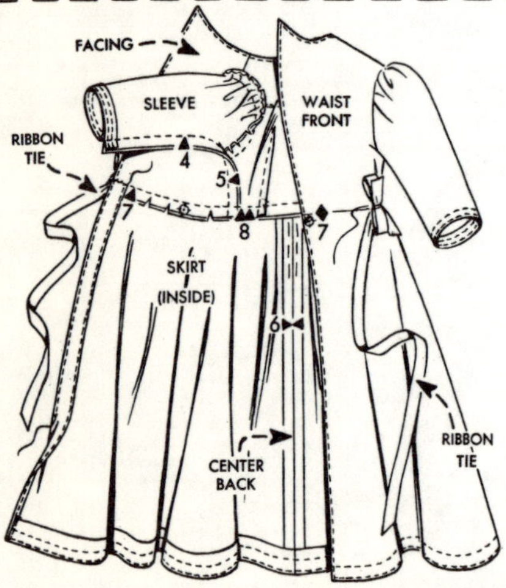

4, 5. Join entire underarm seams.

SKIRT

6. Join center back seam.

Make inverted pleat on outside as indicated on pattern, baste.

Turn hem on line indicated, stitch edge and 1/4" inside.

7, 8. Join skirt to waist, matching center backs, having front edges at hem lines on skirt. Press seam toward skirt, clipping along curves.

Turn under 1/8" on front edges of skirt, edge-stitch. Turn hems on lines indicated, stitch turned edge. Hem ends to waistline seam and lower edge.

RIBBON TIES

Cut baby ribbon 12" long for each tie. Form 1" bow at one end with 2 loops on one side and 1 loop and end on other side. Tack securely through center.

Lap right front over left, sew one bow tie to right front edge and other one to left front at waistline seam. Snap free left front edge to right front at waistline seam. Tie free ends of ribbon in a bow.

NIGHTGOWN D

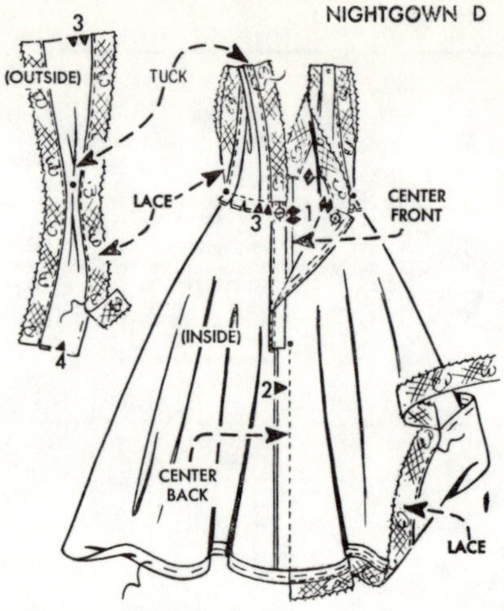

BODICE

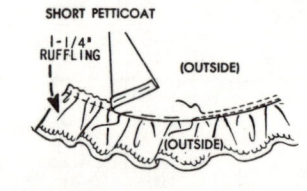

Turn under and baste 1/4" seam allowance on long edges. Stitch 1/2" wide lace 1/8" over turned edges.

Make shoulder tuck, stitching together along dotted lines on wrong side of fabric.

Press tuck open like box pleat, tack through center.

Lap lace on front edges at waistline, leaving 1/4" between front edges of bodice fabric, baste. Lap back over front at underarm, matching circles, baste.

SKIRT

Notches 1 and 2. Join center front and center back seams, leaving back free above circle. Press back seam toward right side. Turn under 1/8" on back opening edges, stitch.

3, 4. Join skirt to waist, matching centers, back edges of lace even with center lines. Press seam toward skirt, clipping along curves, top-stitch.

Turn under right back opening edge of skirt on center line, edge-stitch. Fasten opening with snap at waistline.

LOWER EDGE

Turn under 1/4" seam allowance, baste. Stitch 1/2" wide lace 1/8" over turned edge.

RIBBON BOW

Tie 6" of baby ribbon in bow. Tack to bodice front as shown on envelope.

PETTICOAT E

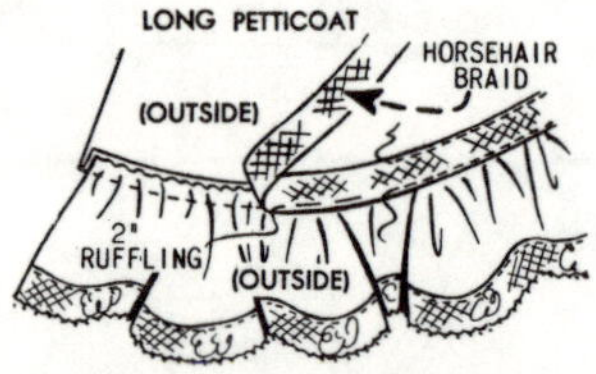

TO JOIN RUFFLING TO LOWER EDGE

If ruffling has a binding, remove it.

SHORT PETTICOAT: Turn under 1/4" at lower edge, baste. Stitch to 1-1/4" wide ruffling along gathering line.

LONG PETTICOAT: Join ruffling to lower edge (wrong sides together) having gathering line of ruffling even with 1/4" seam line. Press seam toward petticoat. Baste 1/2" wide horsehair braid on outside, with lower edge at seam line. Stitch both edges of braid.

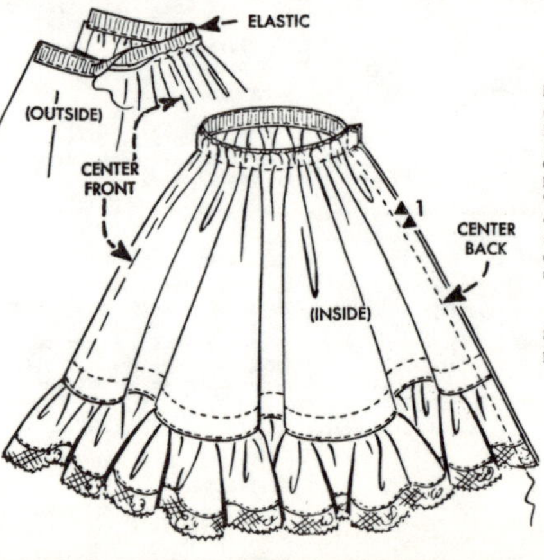

ELASTIC WAISTBAND

Cut 1/4" wide elastic 6-1/2" long for 14" doll or 7-5/8" long for 18" doll. Stitch one edge of elastic 1/8" over top of petticoat on inside, stretching elastic to fit while stitching.

Turn elastic to outside, stitch to line indicated, stretching elastic to fit fabric flat while stitching.

SEAM

Notches 1. Join center back edges, taking up 1/4" seam allowance.

182

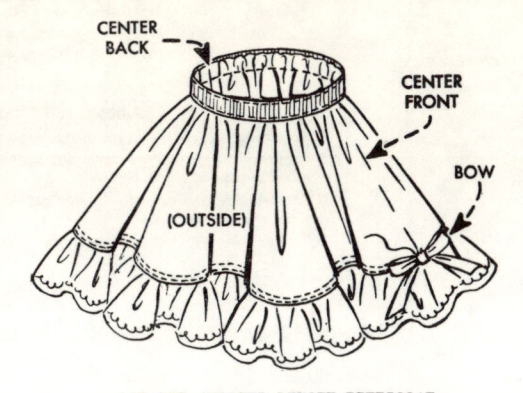

BOW FOR SHORTER LENGTH PETTICOAT
Tie 6" of baby ribbon in a bow. Tack to center front at ruffle seam.

PANTIES F

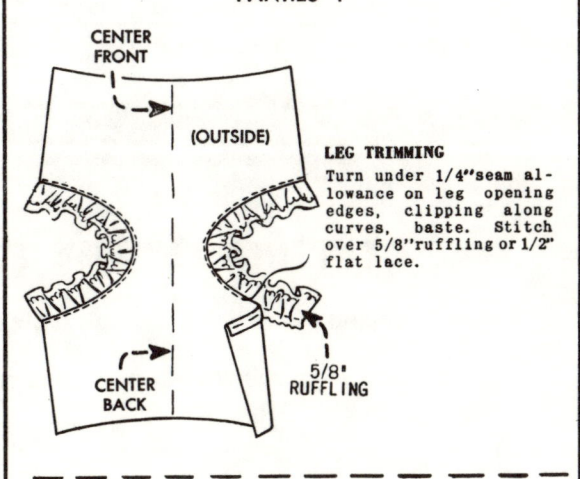

LEG TRIMMING
Turn under 1/4" seam allowance on leg opening edges, clipping along curves, baste. Stitch over 5/8" ruffling or 1/2" flat lace.

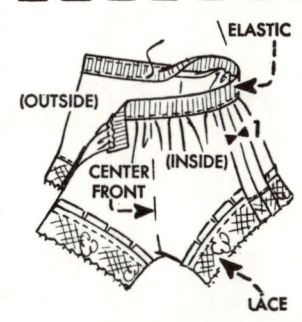

SEAM
Notches 1. Join one side seam, taking up 1/4" seam allowance.

ELASTIC WAISTBAND
Cut 1/4" wide elastic 6" long for 14" doll or 7-1/8" long for 18" doll. Join to upper edge of panties as instructed for petticoat.

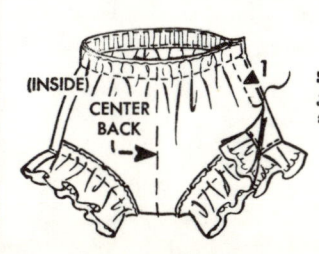

SEAM
Join other side seam in same manner as above.

BOWS (OPTIONAL)
Cut 6" of baby ribbon for each bow. Tie bows, tack at side seams above trimming.

KNITTED CAPE, HEADBAND, AND MUFF (G)

SIZES - Directions are for doll size 14". Changes for doll size 18" are in parentheses.

MATERIALS - 2 (10 gram) Balls Angora and Standard Knitting Needles No. 6. (Or, English size No. 7).

CAPE - Cast on 14 (18) sts, p back. Row 2 - Inc 1 st, k across row, inc in last st. Row 3 - P back, cast on 2 sts. Row 4 - K 2, * inc 1 st, k 1, repeat from * across row, cast on 2 sts making 28 (34) sts. Row 5 - K 3 sts for border, p across, k last 3 sts for border. Row 6 - K 2, * inc 1 st, k 1, repeat from * across row, do not inc in last 2 sts. Row 7 - K 3, p back to within last 3 sts, k 3, always keeping first and last 3 sts k on purled rows for border through out cape. Work 2 rows even. Row 10 - K 8, inc 1 st in each of the next 6 sts, k to within last 14 sts, inc in next 6 sts, k 8. Row 11 - P back. Row 12 - Repeat row 10. Row 13 - P back. Work 2 (6) rows even. Row 16 (20) - K 1, inc 1 st, k across row to within last 3 sts, inc 1 st, k 2, p back. Work 2 rows even. Now repeat last 4 rows, 2 more times. On next k row, inc in every 8th st across row. K 4 more rows in garter st for border, bind off loosely. At top of cape, make a ch 4 loop. Sew on button.

HEADBAND - Knit in garter stitch. Cast on 4 (6) sts, k 1 row even. * Now inc 1 st at beg and end of next row. K 1 row even. Repeat last 2 rows until you have 12 (14) sts. K 1 row even. Now dec 1 st at beg and end of every other row until you have 4 (6) sts, k 1 row. Repeat from * 2 more times, bind off 4 (6) sts.

MUFF - Cast on 10 (12) sts loosely, k 2 rows. Now inc in every other st across row. P 1 row, k 1 row for 8 (10) rows. Dec every other st, k 2 rows, bind off loosely. Ch 10 (12), join at beg of ch to form loop for wrist. Fold muff in half and sew.

McCALL'S CUT AND SEW GUIDE 1891

I. Cutting layouts for all sizes.
II. Assembling, sewing and finishing details.

I. Diagrammes de coupe pour toutes les tailles.
II. Details de l'assemblage, couture et finissage.

I. Divisiones para el corte de todos los tamanos.
II. Confeccion, costura y detalles para el acabado.

HOW TO CUT

Cut pattern and material through the white center of the double line.
Do not cut off the margin before cutting material.
The margin falls away as you cut through pattern and material.

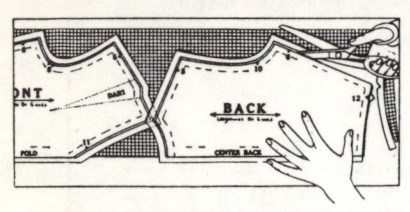

The diagrams below show how to lay the pattern pieces on the material.

Pin pattern to material, overlapping the margin to save material. Then cut pattern and material together through the white center of the double line. The margin falls away as you cut through pattern and material (see diagram above on "HOW TO CUT").

FOR NAP OR ONE-WAY DESIGN MATERIALS, lay pattern pieces all in one direction as shown in layouts marked "WITH NAP".

FOR VELVETEENS, ETC., the nap on material should run upward; for materials with a flat nap as PANNE VELVET, BROADCLOTH, ETC., nap should run downward.

IMPORTANT—The pattern pieces, shaded in the diagrams, are to be laid face down.

TAILOR'S TACKS

Make tailor's tacks before removing pattern, after garment is cut.
Mark center front and back with long basting stitches.

MARKING WITH THREAD

1 Pin through pattern and fabric along the printed lines of dart.
2 Turn section over with the fabric side up; then baste through one layer of fabric only along pinned outline
3 Remove pins from underneath; then pin through the two layers of fabric along the basting lines.
4 Turn section over and baste through the second layer only. Remove pins.

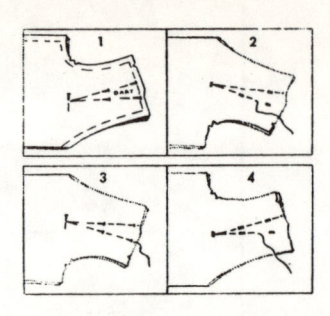

MARKING WITH TRACING WHEEL

Place fabric over carbon tracing paper. Trace lines of pattern with a tracing wheel. For double layer of fabric remove pattern; then trace other side along traced markings.

I. CUTTING LAYOUTS FOR ALL SIZES

VIEW A — DRESS

BODICE
ONE PIECE OF FABRIC
9" × 19½"
1891 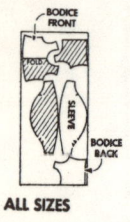
ALL SIZES

or 35" FABRIC
ALL SIZES

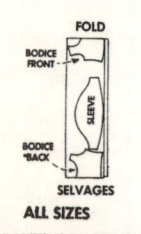

CONTRAST SKIRT ETC.
35" FABRIC
ALL SIZES

VIEW B

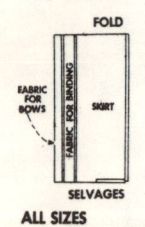

DRESS AND PARASOL COVER
35 or 39" FABRIC
ALL SIZES

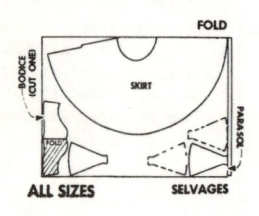

OVERBODICE, OVERSKIRT ETC.
54" TULLE OR NET
ALL SIZES

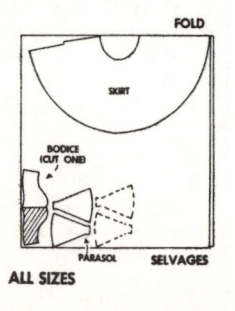

VIEW C or D

PEIGNOIR WITH NIGHTGOWN
35" FABRIC 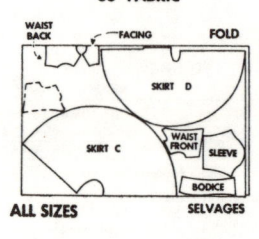
ALL SIZES

39" FABRIC
SIZE 14

SIZE 18

VIEW E or F — LINGERIE

LONG PETTICOAT AND PANTIES
35 or 39" FABRIC 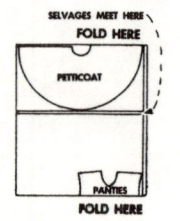
ALL SIZES

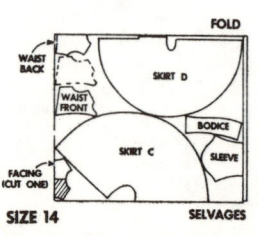

SHORT PETTICOAT AND PANTIES
35 or 39" FABRIC 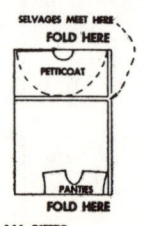
ALL SIZES

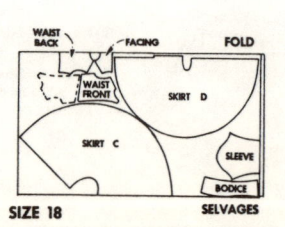

Evening Dress and Cap, View B, from McCall Printed Pattern No. 1564.

Nightgown, View D, from McCall's Printed Pattern No. 1891.

Ballet Costume, View A, from McCall Printed Pattern No. 1564.

Sunsuit and Bonnet, View C, from McCall Printed Pattern No. 1564.

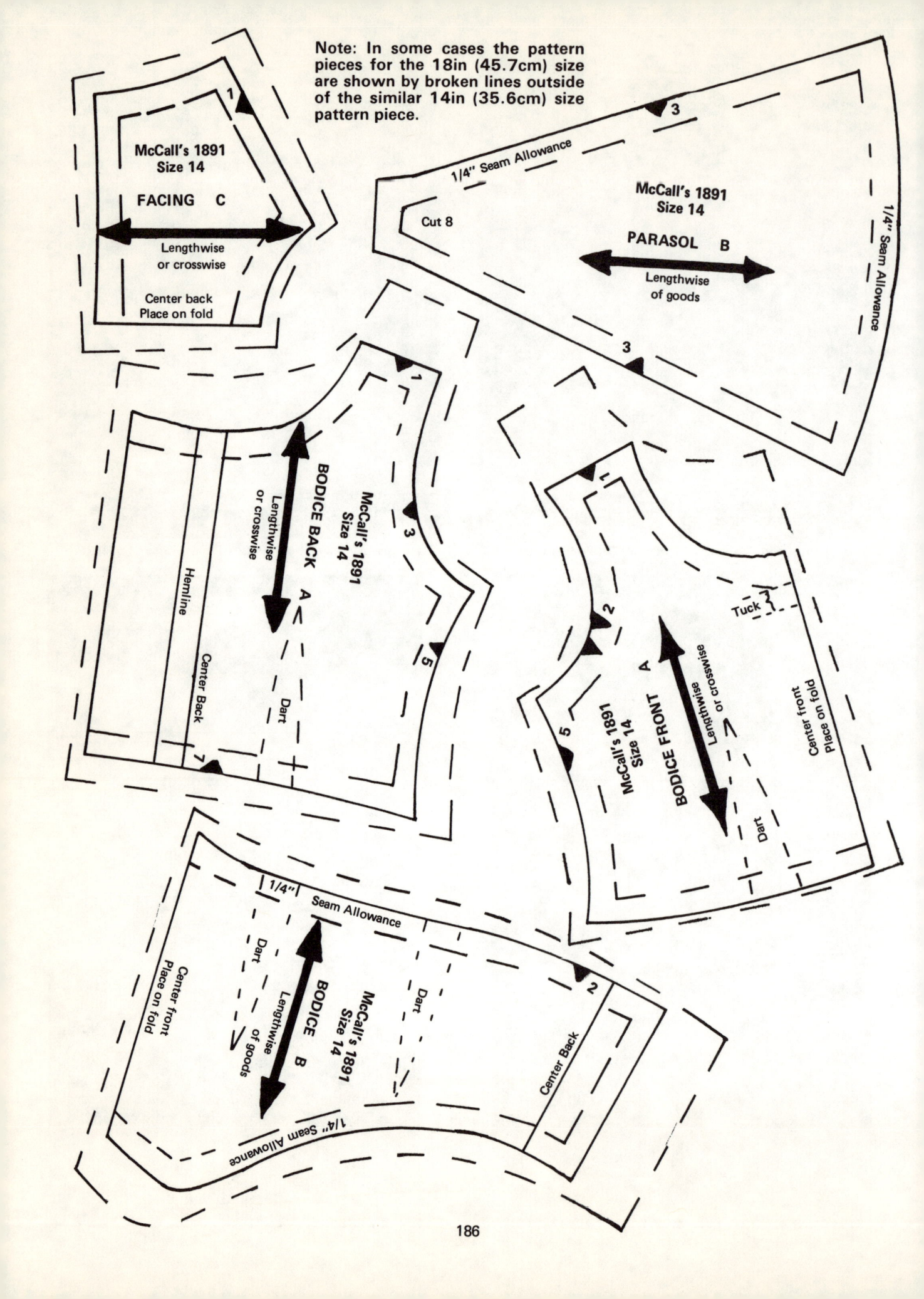

Note: In some cases the pattern pieces for the 18in (45.7cm) size are shown by broken lines outside of the similar 14in (35.6cm) size pattern piece.

187

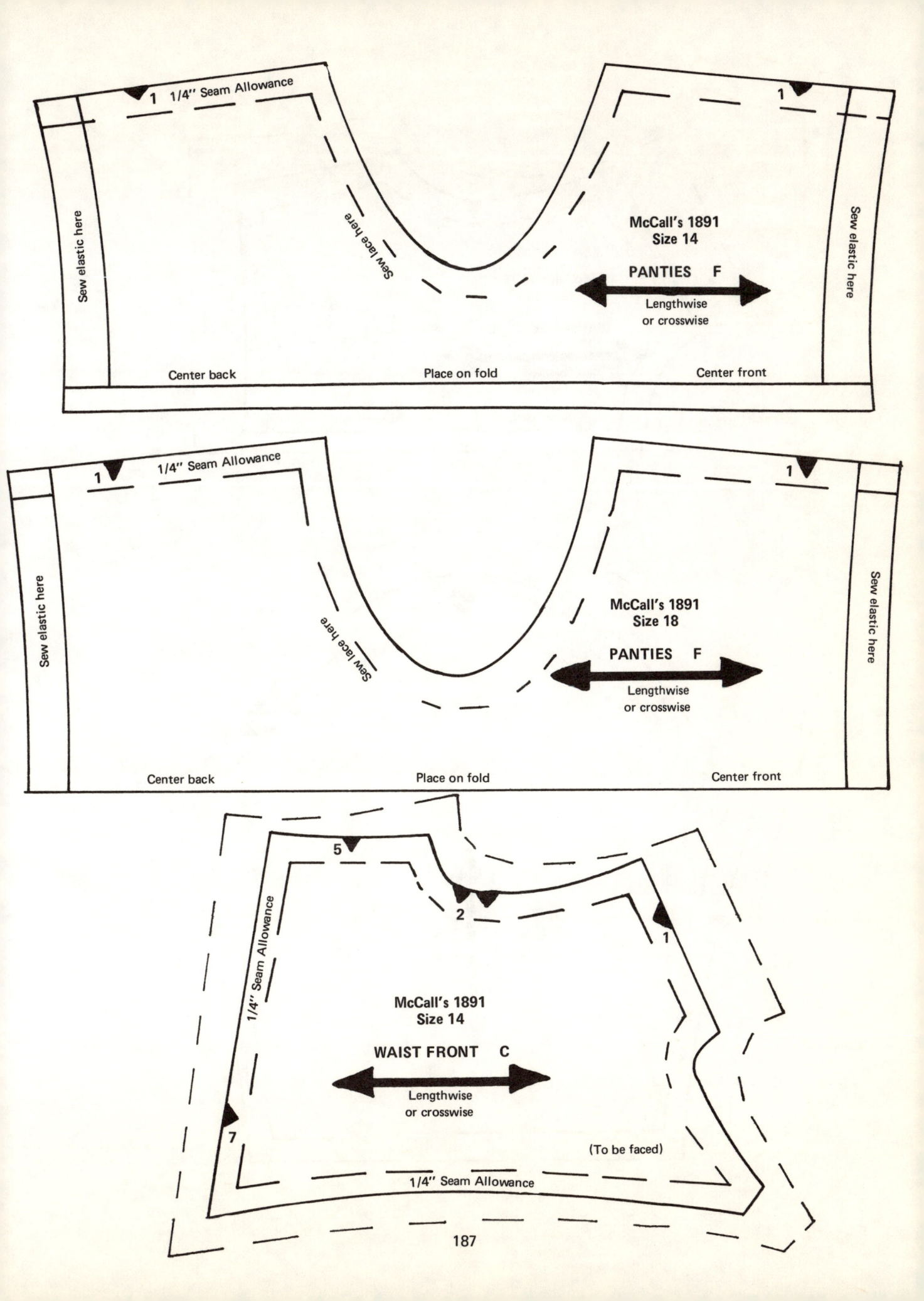

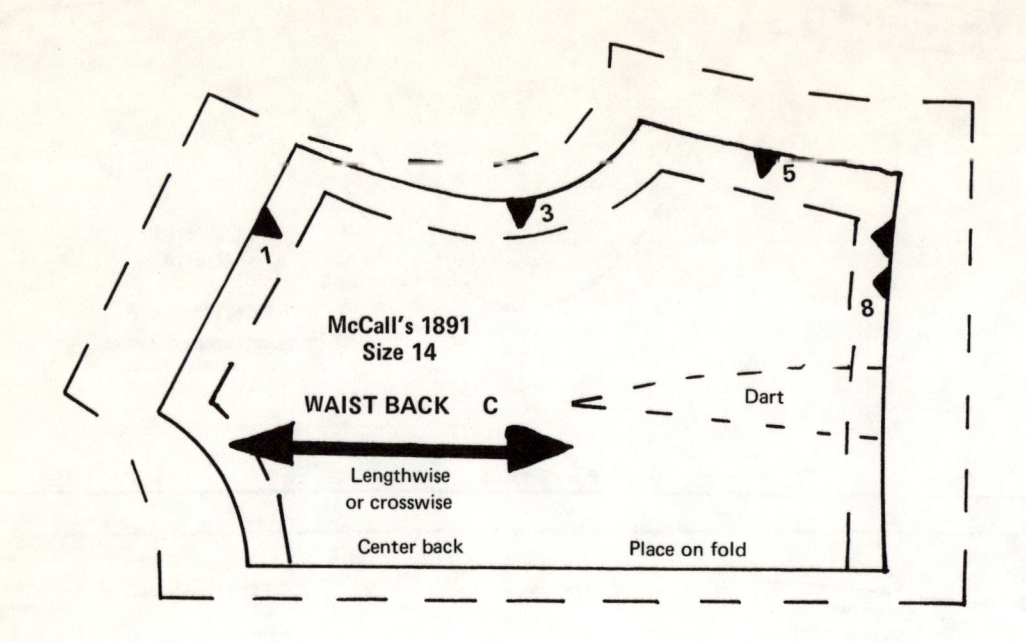

McCall's 1891 Size 14
WAIST BACK C

Lengthwise or crosswise

Center back

Place on fold

Dart

McCall's 1891 Size 14
SLEEVE C

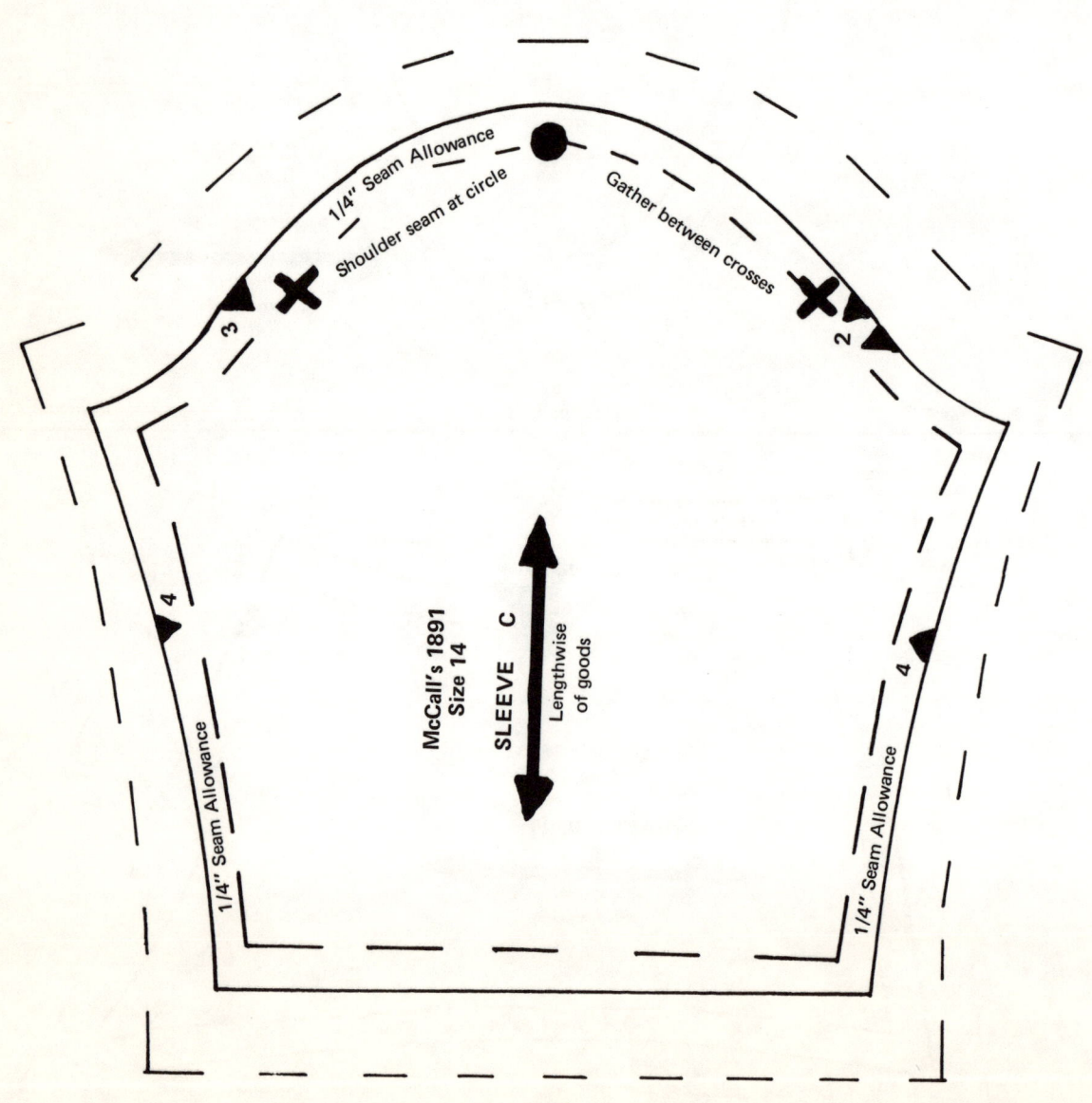

1/4" Seam Allowance

Shoulder seam at circle

Gather between crosses

Lengthwise of goods

1/4" Seam Allowance

1/4" Seam Allowance

189

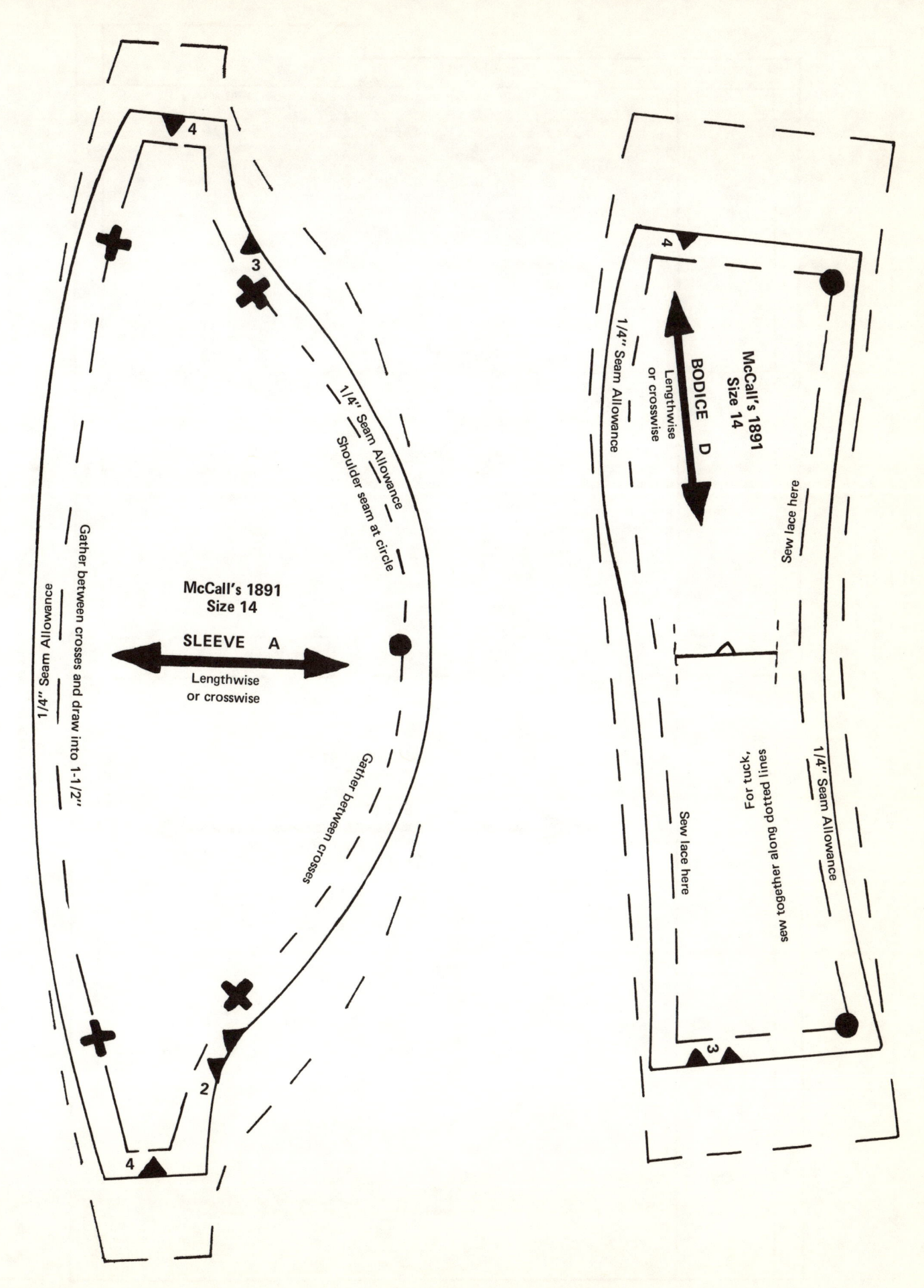

Join to circle

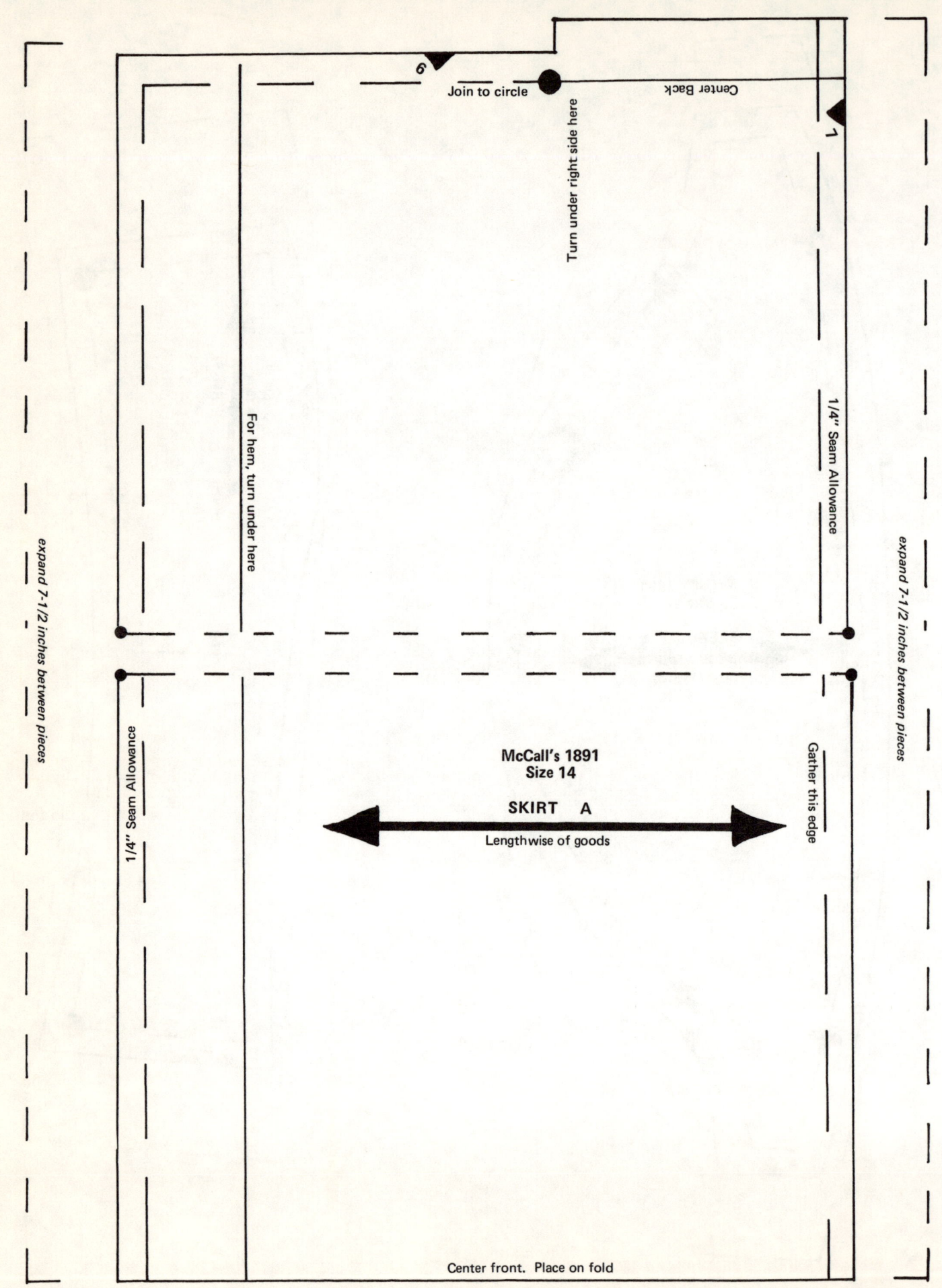

Center Back

Turn under right side here

1/4" Seam Allowance

For hem, turn under here

expand 7-1/2 inches between pieces

expand 7-1/2 inches between pieces

1/4" Seam Allowance

Gather this edge

McCall's 1891
Size 14

SKIRT   A
Lengthwise of goods

Center front. Place on fold

190

add 1/4 inch

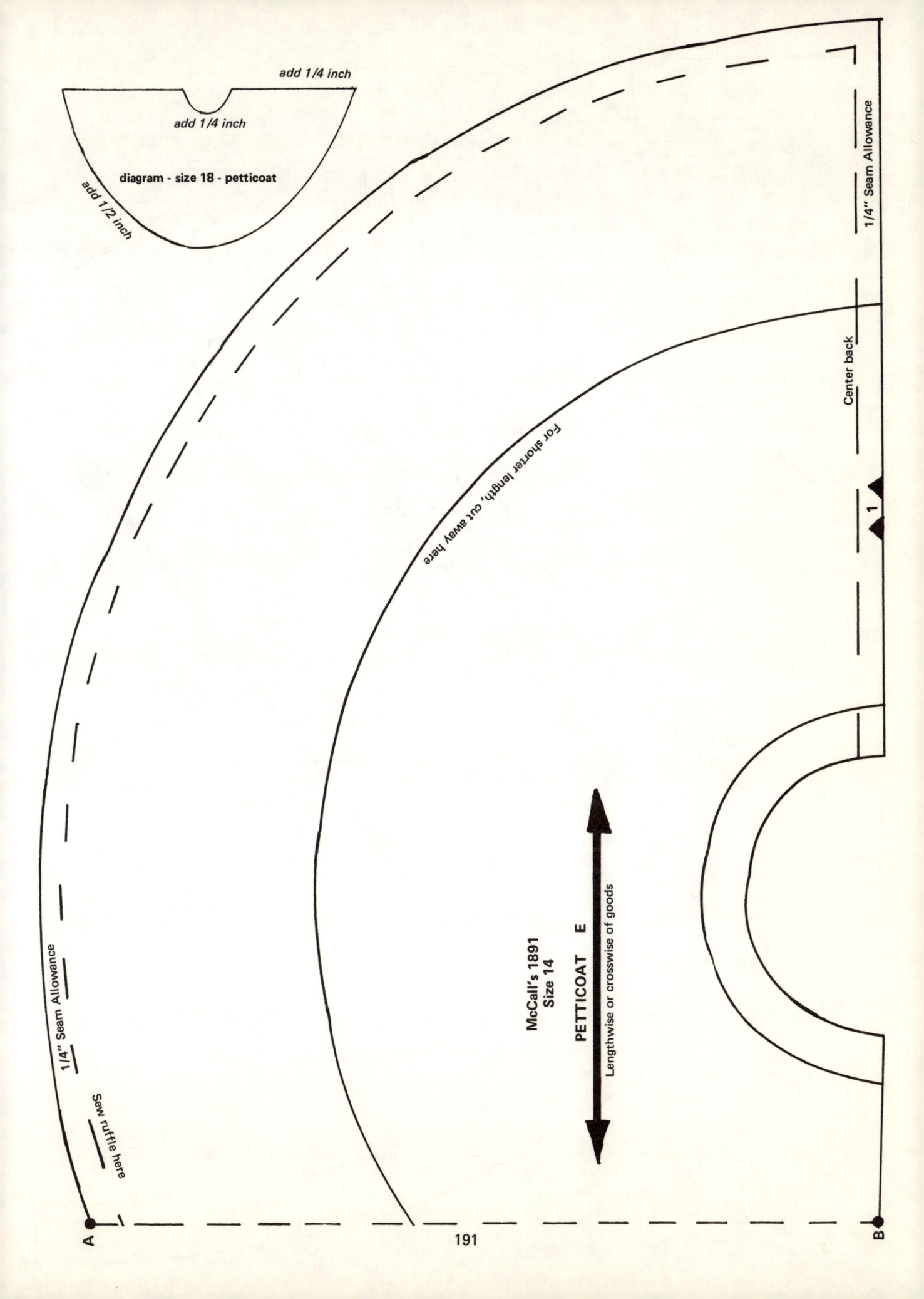

add 1/4 inch

add 1/2 inch

diagram - size 18 - petticoat

1/4" Seam Allowance

Center back

1

For shorter length, cut away here

McCall's 1891
Size 14

PETTICOAT E

Lengthwise or crosswise of goods

1/4" Seam Allowance

Sew ruffle here

A

B

191

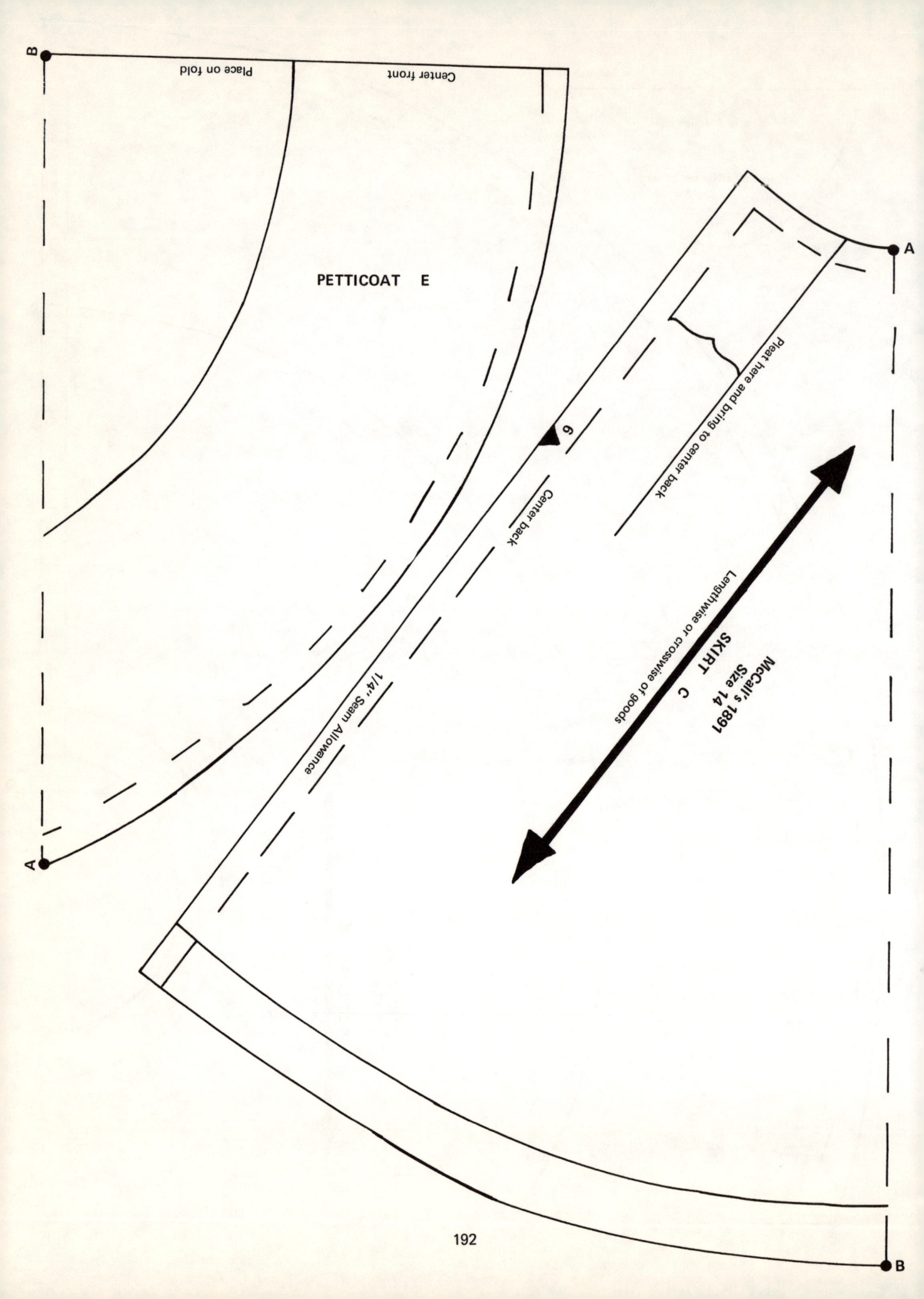

C

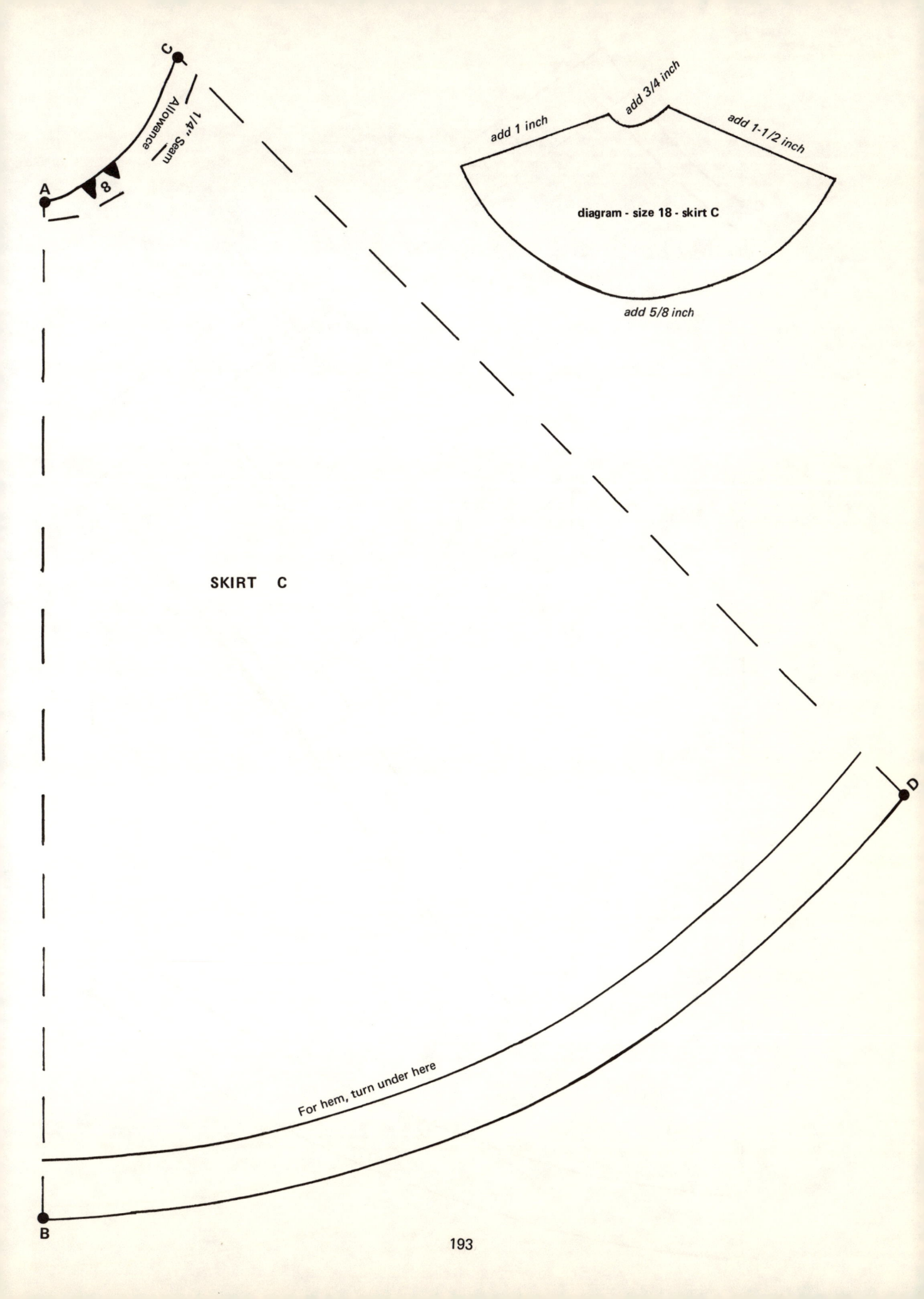

A 8 1/4" Seam Allowance

diagram - size 18 - skirt C

add 1 inch   add 3/4 inch   add 1-1/2 inch

add 5/8 inch

SKIRT C

D

For hem, turn under here

B

193

SKIRT C

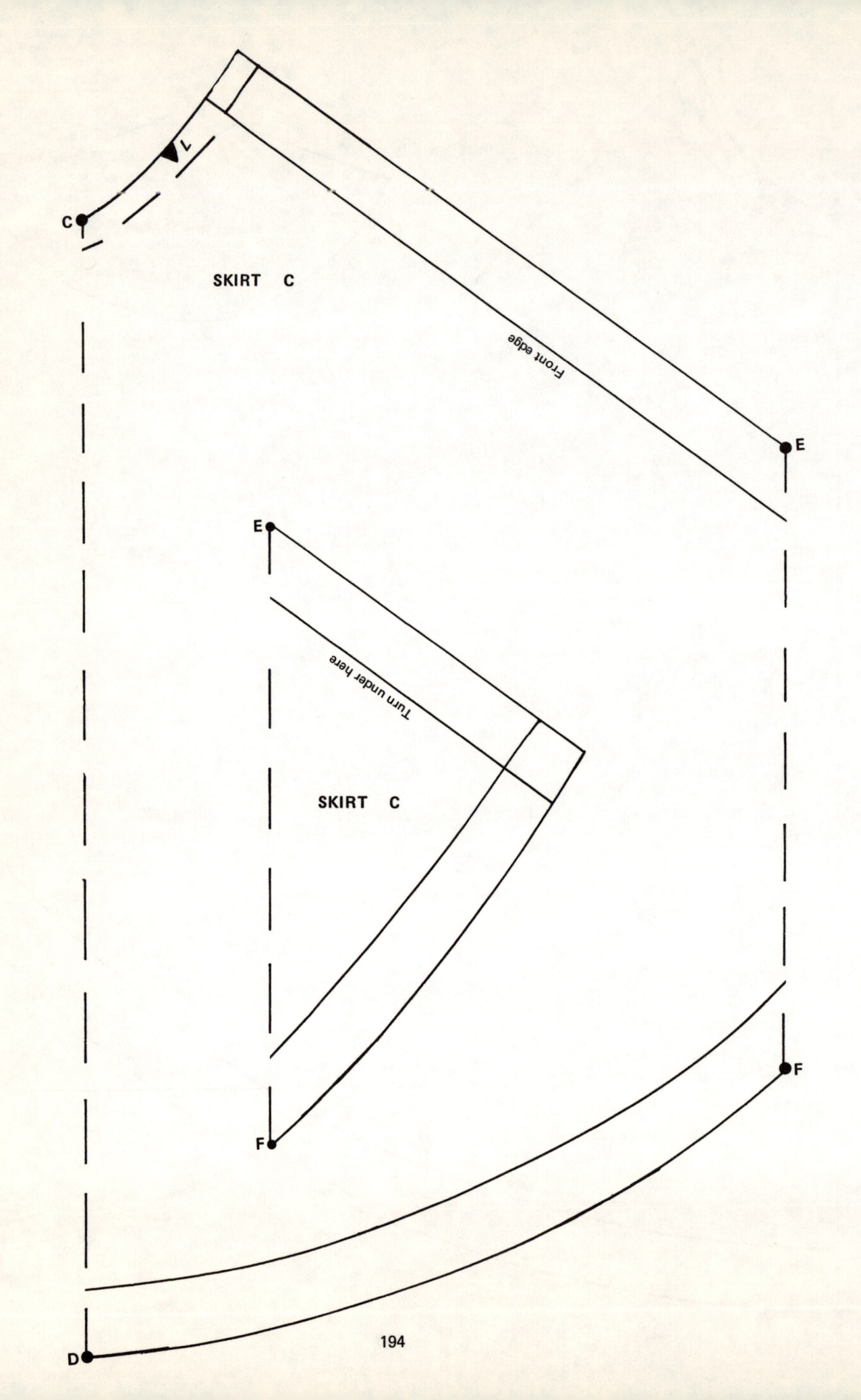

Front edge

Turn under here

SKIRT C

• A

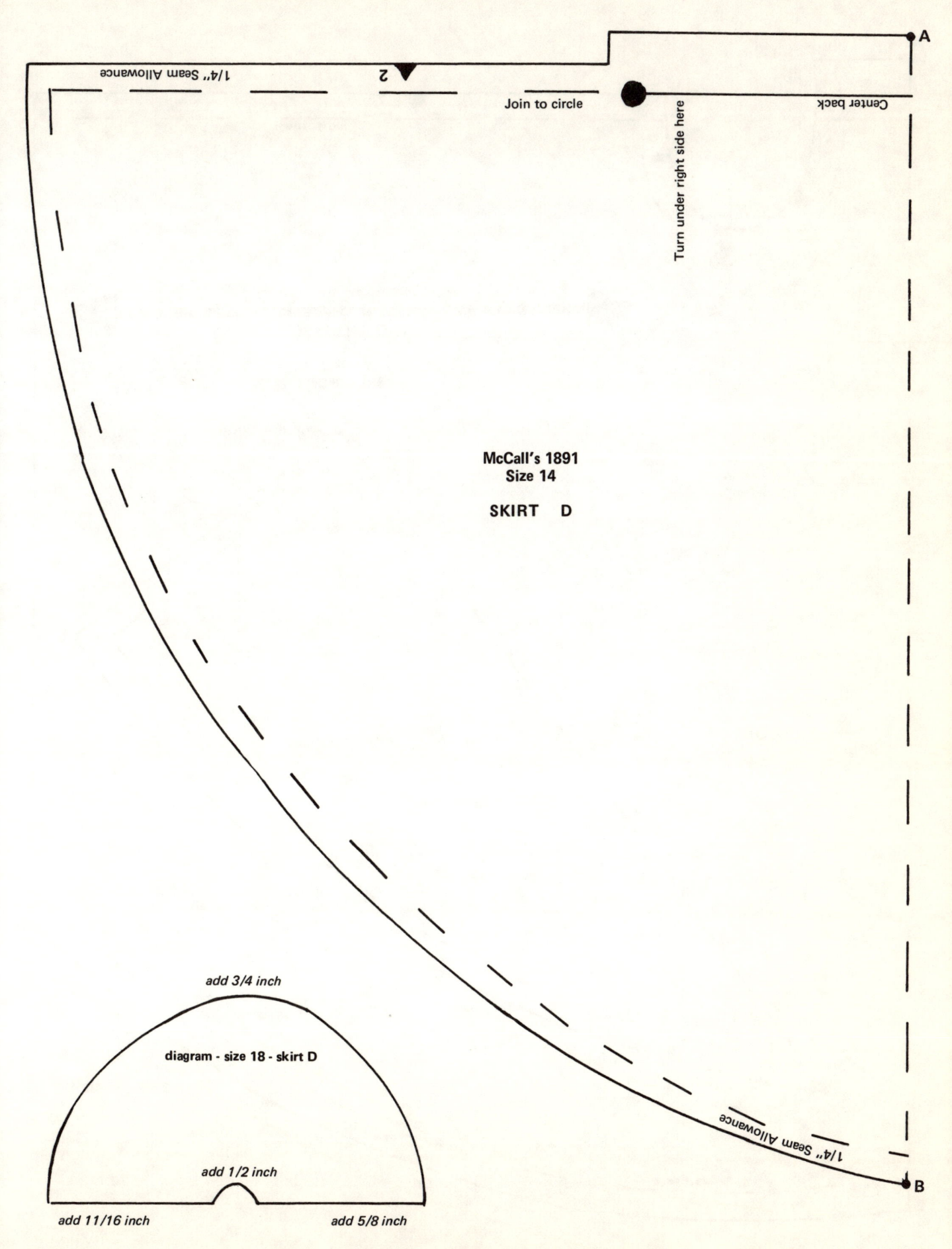

1/4" Seam Allowance

2

Join to circle

Turn under right side here

Center back

McCall's 1891
Size 14

SKIRT   D

add 3/4 inch

diagram - size 18 - skirt D

add 1/2 inch

add 11/16 inch

add 5/8 inch

1/4" Seam Allowance

• B

196

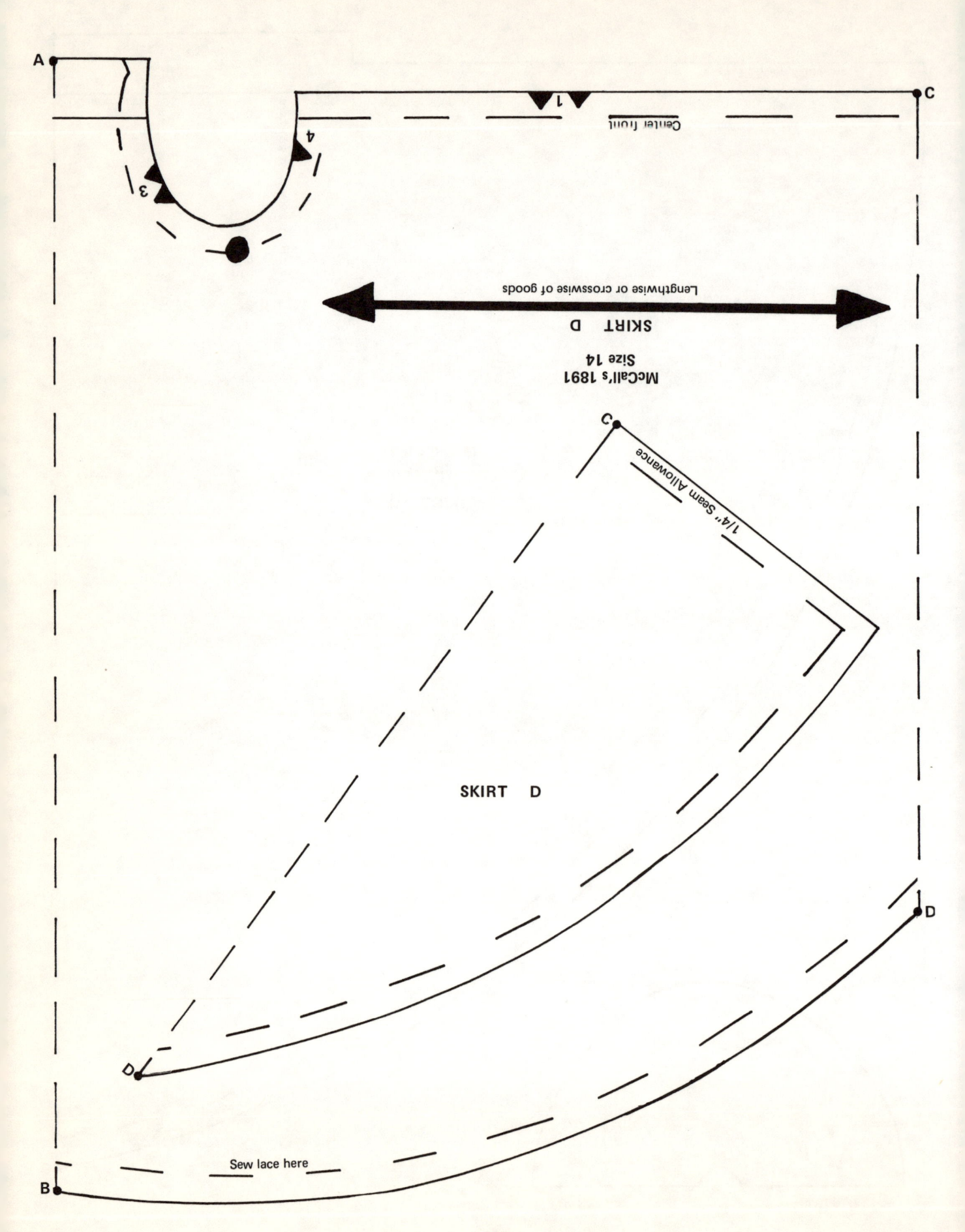

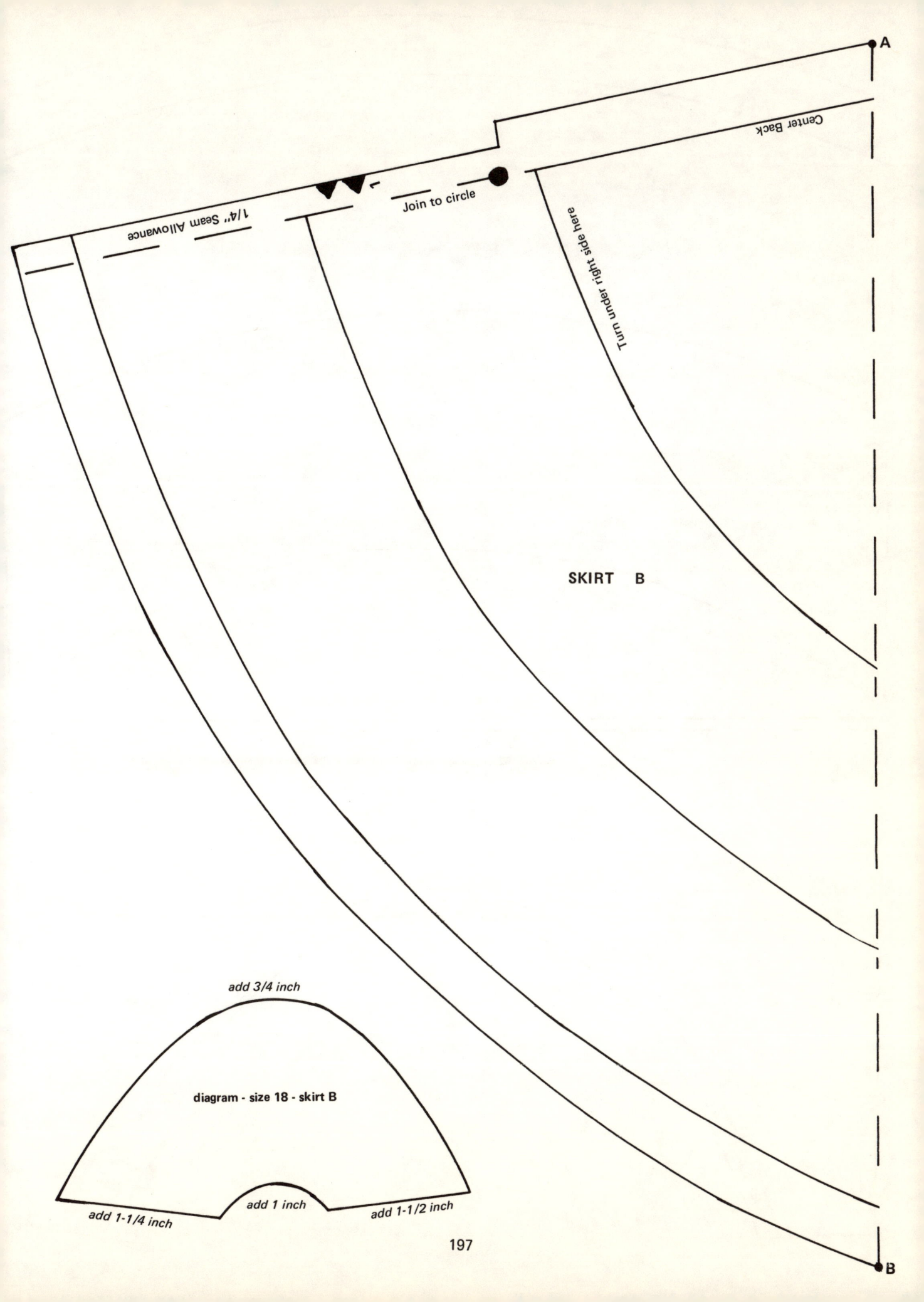

- A
- Center Back
- 1/4" Seam Allowance
- Join to circle
- Turn under right side here
- SKIRT B
- add 3/4 inch
- diagram - size 18 - skirt B
- add 1-1/4 inch
- add 1 inch
- add 1-1/2 inch
- B

For hem, turn under here

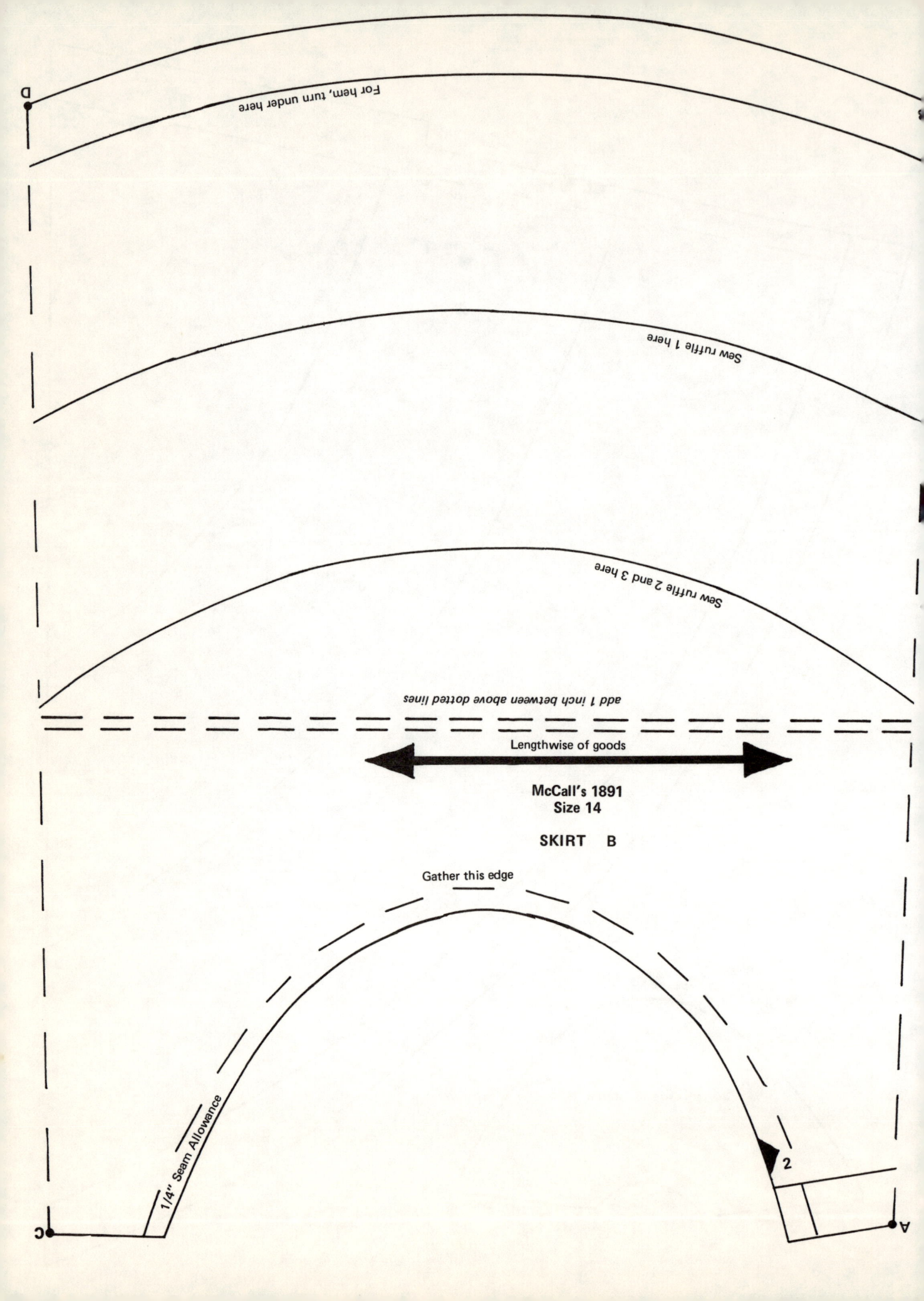

Sew ruffle 1 here

Sew ruffle 2 and 3 here

add 1 inch between above dotted lines

⟷ Lengthwise of goods

**McCall's 1891
Size 14**

SKIRT   B

Gather this edge

1/4" Seam Allowance

2

SKIRT B

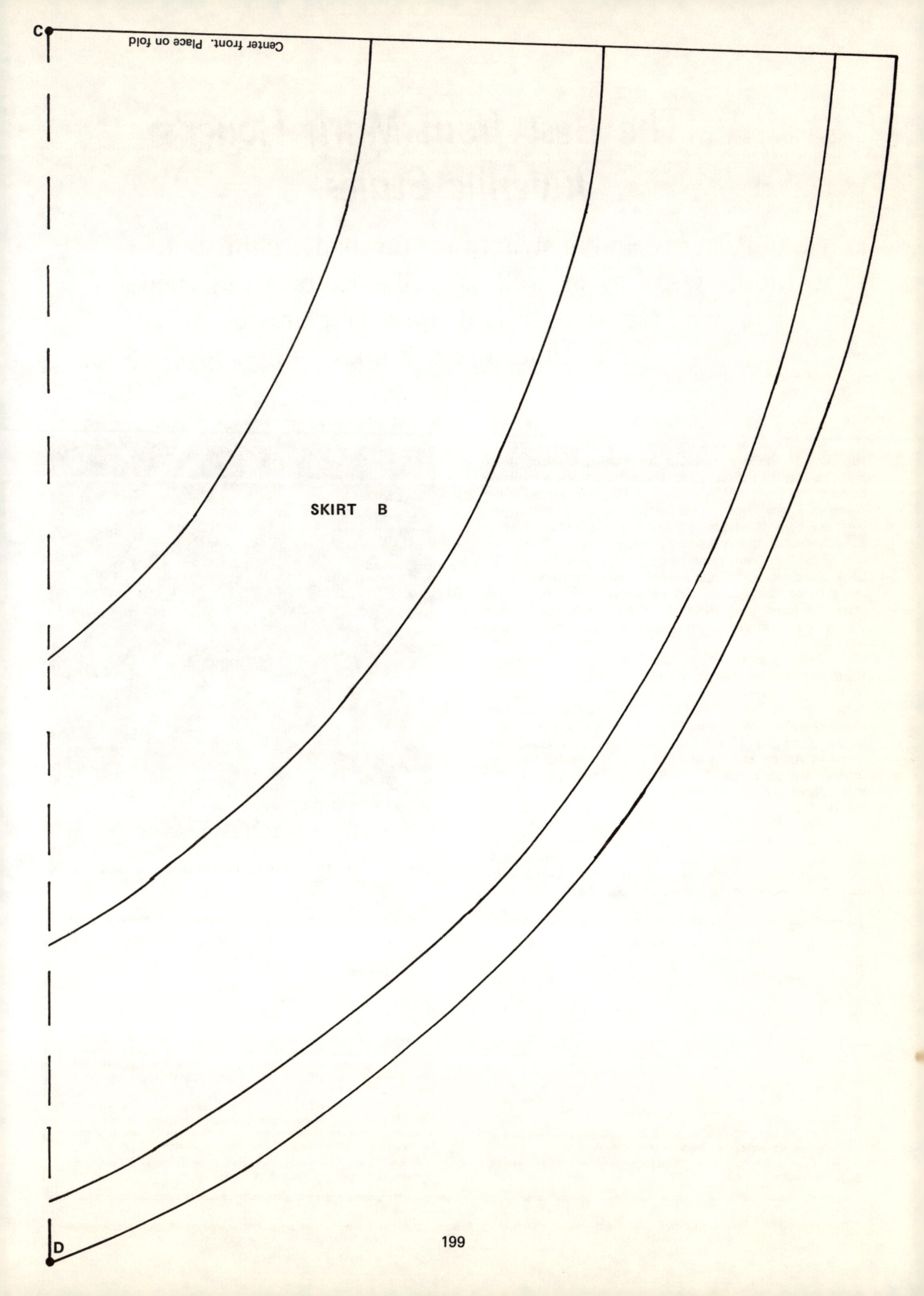

Center front. Place on fold

V. The Best from Mary Hoyer's Juvenile Styles

Patterns and instructions for baby, child and adult fashions as well as doll costumes designed by Mary Hoyer and appearing in her Juvenile Styles books.

As the chapter title indicates, this chapter contains a selection of the *best* fashions for babies, children, teenagers, adults and dolls alike. These outfits were designed through the years by Mary Hoyer and were presented in her *Juvenile Styles* books. The patterns selected and shown here are considered timeless and are as popular today as they were when they were first designed.

The first book published by Mary Hoyer was a hat book she designed for the Ber-Mel Yarn Company. Modeling the hats and accessories were her daughter, Arlene, several children from Reading and two adult models from Apeda Studio in New York where all of the photographs were taken.

Upon completion of the hat book, Mary Hoyer started to compile a book of baby and children's garments. In 1936 Mr. Hoyer formed a publishing business under the name "Juvenile Styles" and Mrs. Hoyer published her first knitting and crocheting book of children's fashions. Some of the photographs in the first *Juvenile Styles* books were taken in Apeda Studios and the remainder were taken by professional photographers in Reading. The models, for the most part, were local children who were friends of the family.

Most of the photographs in the *Juvenile Styles* books were taken out of doors. It was like an outing and fun for the children and the natural settings made pleasing backgrounds for the pictures, although it was sometimes difficult and time-consuming for the photographer.

Illustration 157. The boy and girl eating ice cream cones. *Juvenile Styles,* Volume 3, Page 15.

ABBREVIATIONS USED IN KNITTING AND CROCHET INSTRUCTIONS

The following abbreviations are used throughout the book:

K	—Knit	s c	—Single crochet
P	—Purl	d c	—Double crochet
ch	—Chain	tog	—Together
h d c	—Half double crochet	st	—Stitch
cr	—Crochet	sts	—Stitches
sl st	—Slip stitch	y o	—Yarn over
rnd	—Round	P	—Picot
beg	—Beginning	m c	—Main color
tr cr	—Triple crochet	c c	—Contrasting color

P.s.s.o.—Pass slip stitch over

*(asterisk). When this symbol appears, continue working until instructions refer you back to this symbol.

Even means that a row must be worked without increasing or decreasing.

Work means to continue with the stitch as described.

Half Double Crochet—Yarn over, draw up a loop in st, yarn over and draw through all 3 loops on hook.

Slip Stitch—Insert hook in next st, yarn over and draw through both loops on hook.

Blocking—Pin the garment, with rust proof pins, wrong side out, on a pressing board in exactly the measurements desired. Place a damp cloth over garment and with a moderately hot iron, press lightly, allowing the steam to go through. Lay on a flat surface until thoroughly dry.

Needle Gauge—When making a garment—work a swatch, using the needles called for to determine whether or not your work measures the same number of stitches to the inch as given in the scale. Change size of needles accordingly.

When Using Colors—In changing colors always K the first row on right side regardless of pattern.

Illustration 158. This chart shows all the abbreviations used in the following knit and crochet patterns. *Juvenile Styles,* Volume 8, Page 34.

Illustration 159. Cover of the book, *Crocheted hats Styled by BER-MEL*, Vol. XIII, which was designed and published by Mary Hoyer for the Ber-Mel Yarn Company in 1936.

Illustration 160. Arlene Hoyer modeling the hat named for her (Arlene, No. 860) from the book shown in Illustration 159. *Crocheted hats Styled by BER-MEL*, Vol. XIII, Page 15.

ARLENE
NO 860

Headsize 20 inches

Materials—
    1 four-ounce skein Ber-Mel Lustra-worsted
    1 ball "La Boule De Neige" French Angora
    1 Ber-Mel Non-inflammable Bone Crochet Hook, size 4

Scale — 5½ stitches = 1 inch   5½ rounds = 1 inch

CROWN—Ch 3, join in ring and work 6 s c in ring, then work 2 s c in each st until there are 24 sts around. *Work 1 s c in each of the next 4 sts, 2 s c in next st, repeat from * (thus increasing in every 5th st) until there are 50 sts around; then increase in every 15th st until there are 100 sts around. Work even until crown measures 5 inches from center to edge. *Work 1 s c in each of the next 20 sts, skip next st, repeat from * (thus decreasing every twenty-first st) or about 4 decreases to the round, until crown measures 6 inches from center to edge, or desired headsize. Break thread.

BRIM—First row: turn and work in opposite direction starting 2½ inches from end of last row. Work 1 s c in each of the next 3 sts and 2 s c in next st (thus increasing every 4th st) for one round. *Work 1 s c in each of the next 19 sts and 2 s c in next st, repeat from * (thus increasing every 20th st) for 8 rows. Work 1 row even.

ANGORA BOW—Ch 14 sts, work 1 s c in 2nd st from hook, 1 s c in each st to end of row (13 s c in row). Ch 1 and turn, skip first s c and work 1 s c in each st to end of row (12 s c in row). Continue working in this manner, skipping 1 s c in each row, after you ch 1 and turn, until you have 3 sts left. Work 4 rows even. Ch 1, turn and work 2 s c in first st, 1 s c in each st to end of row (4 sts in row). Ch 1, turn, work 2 s c in first st, 1 s c in each st, to end of row (5 sts in row). Increase in this manner until you have 13 s c across row. Tie into knot and sew on top of hat. See illustration.

Blocking instructions on page 20.

◆

DIRECTIONS FOR BLOCKING HATS

Fold a turkish towel over a bowl smaller than hat, place hat over bowl, place a damp cloth over hat, and then a dry cloth over the wet one, press lightly with a hot iron, allowing the steam to go thru the hat. By carefully following these instructions the appearance of your hat will be greatly improved.

Whenever possible give hat to an experienced hatter for draping and blocking.

Reprinted from *Crocheted hats Styled by BER-MEL*, Vol. XII, Page 14.

The photographs in Volume 3 of *Juvenile Styles* were taken in the City Park in Reading. The photograph on page 15 (see Illustration 157) was taken on a very hot day and both of the children were wearing heavy sweaters. Mary Hoyer remembers: "I tried to keep the children cool and amused with ice cream cones. An ice cream vendor happened to be present at the time and the children were on their third cones before we got the photograph. I think the little girl was amazed that her ice cream cone was melting so fast again."

In addition to designing clothes for dolls, infants, children, teen-agers and adults, Mrs. Hoyer did some designing for the Spool Cotton Company. These designs were children's dresses made with mercerized cotton. Alfred, Meyer and Weissman of Boston, Massachusetts, not only distributed her books but purchased some of her thread designs which were then used for tablecloths and other items.

Through the years Mary Hoyer published six volumes of *Juvenile Styles* and a selection of the designs contained therein are presented here.

A YOKE COAT FOR DOLLY AND HER MAMMA

CHILD'S COAT AND HAT NO. 552
Size 3-5 Years

These instructions are written in size 3; changes needed to make size 5 are found in parentheses.

1 Pr. Steel Needles, American Standard, No. 2.
1 Circular Needle, American Standard, No. 5.
1 Bone Crochet Hook, Size 4.

Scale: Garter Stitch, 5 sts to 1 inch.
Crochet Stitch, 5 sts to 1 inch (Hat).

Material: Scotch Tweed, 4 Fold, 3 Skeins; 1½ yards of Velvet, ¾ inch wide; 1 yard Hat Wire; 3 Wooden Buttons.

Coat

With No. 2 Needles, cast on 100 sts. K 2, P 2 for 3 rows. Work across row to within 9 sts of end. Bind off next 6 sts, for buttonhole, K 1, P 2. On next row, cast on 6 sts over those bound off on previous row. Continue ribbing for 1 inch. Change to No. 5 circular needle. Yoke is worked in garter st. K 10 sts, then increase every 6th st across row to within last 10 sts; K 10 sts plain (do not increase in first and last 10 sts). Increase when holding right side of work toward you. Work ½ inch even. Increase in every 6th st for 1 row, every half inch, until there are 191 sts on needle. Then increase every inch until there are 252 sts on needle. When work measures 3 inches from neck, make another buttonhole as follows: K across row to within 7 sts from edge. Bind off 4 sts, K 3 sts. On next row cast on 4 sts over those bound off on previous row. When work measures 5½ inches from neck, make another buttonhole in same manner. Continue garter st until work measures 6 inches from neck (size 5, 6½ inches), or desired length. Break thread. Put 36 sts on string (front), K next 60 sts (sleeve), put remaining sts on string, continue to P 1 row, K 1 row on sleeve for 4½ inches. K 5th and 6th st together across row (50 sts), then change to No. 2 needles and K 2, P 2 for 3½ inches or desired length. Skip 60 sts (back) and work next 60 sts (sleeve) to correspond with other sleeve. Pick up sts, joining fronts and back and K first 10 sts, then increase every 4th st to within 10 sts, (border), 160 sts on needle. Continue stockinet st for 8 inches, always working first 10 sts at each end in garter st. Increase 1 st at each underarm every inch, being careful to keep increases directly below preceding ones. Finish with 2 inches of garter st (10 inches from yoke), or desired length.

Illustration 161. "Yoke Coat and Hat No. 552. She'll look smart in this knitted outfit of Tweed Yarn that's mainly stockinet stitch with a contrasting yoke of garter stitch. Dolly is dressed like her little mamma." The doll shown was the first doll dressed by Mary Hoyer, before she had her own doll made. This unknown doll belonged to her daughter. *Juvenile Styles,* Volume 1, Page 4.

Bind off loosely on wrong side of work. Work 1 row of s c on fronts and around neck.

Hat

Crown—Ch 3, join in ring and work 7 s c in ring, then work 2 s c in each st until there are 28 sts around. * Work 1 s c in each of the next 4 sts, 2 s c in next st, repeat from * until there are 50 sts around. Then increase in every 15th st until there are 105 sts around. Work even until crown measures 5 inches from center to edge. Then skip 4 decreases to each round, but do not have decreases come over those of previous row, until crown measures 5½ inches from center to edge or desired headsize. Do not break thread.

Brim—Row 1: Place a marker when starting brim, this will be center back. Work in same direction, increasing every 5th st to within 4 sts of center back. Break thread. When starting each row, work 2 s c in 2nd st, to keep work flat. Row 2: Turn, skip

4 sts, work 1 row even in opposite direction on same side, to within 4 sts of beginning of center back. *Row* 3: Turn, skip 4 sts, work 1 row increasing in every 10th st to within 4 sts of beginning of last row. Each row will be 4 sts shorter at beginning and end. Work 6 rows in same manner increasing every 20th st. Work over wire for 1 complete round, increasing whenever necessary to cover wire.

A Yoke Coat for Dolly

Dolly's Coat and Hat No. 552

14 Inch Doll
1 Pr. Steel Needles, American Standard No. 2.
1 Circular Needle, American Standard, No. 5.
1 Bone Crochet Hook, Size 4.
Scale: 5 sts to 1 inch (Coat) 5 sts to 1 inch (Hat).
Material: Scotch Tweed, 4 Fold, 1 Skein; 3 Small Buttons.

Coat

With No. 2 needles, cast on 48 sts, K 2, P 2 for 2 rows. K 2 sts, bind off 4 sts, for buttonhole. On next row, cast on 4 sts over those bound off on previous row. Continue ribbing for 1 more row. Change to No. 5 needle, work yoke in garter st. Increase in every 4th st across row (do not increase in last 4 sts throughout yoke), 59 sts. Increase in every 4th st, every 4th row until you have 136 sts on needle. When work measures 1¼ inches from neck, work 2 sts, bind off 3 sts for buttonhole, K to end of row. Make another buttonhole 1¼ inches below, in same manner. Break thread. Put 25 sts on string (front), K next 22 sts (sleeve), put remaining sts on string, continue to P 1 row K 1 row on sleeve for 1½ inches, or desired length. Then change to No. 2 needles and K 2, P 2 for ¾ inch. Skip 42 sts (back) and work next 22 sts (sleeve) to correspond with other sleeve. Pick up sts, joining fronts and back and K first 6 sts (border), then increase every 6th st to within 6 sts. Continue stockinet st for 3 inches, always working first 6 sts at each end in garter st. Finish with 4 ribs of garter st, or desired length. Bind off loosely.

Hat

Crown—Ch 3 join in ring and work 6 s c in ring, then work 2 s c in each st until there are 24 sts around. Increase in every 5th st until there are 70 sts around. Then decrease 3 sts to each round until you have 50 sts remaining.

Brim—*Row* 1: Place a marker when starting brim, this will be center back. Work in same direction, increasing every 3rd st to within 4 sts of center back. Break thread. When starting each row, work 2 s c in 2nd st, to keep work flat. *Row* 2: Turn, skip 2 sts, work 1 row even in opposite direction on same side, to within 4 sts of beginning of center back. *Row* 3: Turn, skip 2 sts, work 1 row increasing in every 6th st to within 2 sts of beginning of last row. *Row* 4: Repeat row 3. Break thread. Starting at center back, holding brim toward you, work 1 complete row around hat.

Reprinted from *Juvenile Styles,* Volume 1, Page 5.

LACE DRESS and HAT

STYLE No. 609
Size 2-4 Years

Material: Crepelane, Cravenette or material equivalent to this weight, 6 ounces; 3 yards of Narrow Velvet; 1 Steel Crochet Hook, size 4.

DRESS

Ch 80 sts loosely (ch should measure approximately 13 inches), work 1 d c in 4th st from hook. Ch 1 st between each d c throughout yoke. This will not be mentioned again). Ch 1, work 1 d c in each ch to end of row (76 d c in row).

Row 2: Ch 3, work 1 d c between each d c to end of row.

Row 3: Ch 3, * work 1 d c between each d c for 9 d c then work 2 d c in next d c repeat from * around yoke, 82 d c in row.

Row 4: Work even.
Row 5: Increase every 20th st.
Row 6: Work even.
Row 7: Increase every 10th st.
Row 8: Work even.
Row 9: Increase every 20th st.
Row 10: Increase every 10th st.

Row 11: Increase every 3rd st (143 d c including the ch 3 at beginning of row).

Pattern—(Work pattern loosely), join yoke (center front) with sl st and ch 4, skip 2 d c and work 4 d c between 2nd and 3rd d c. Ch 1, work 1 d c between 4th and 5th d c. Ch 1, work 4 d c between 6th and 7th d c. Continue this pattern around yoke skipping 2 d c between 4 d c and 1 d c. Row ends with 4 d c in between 2nd and 3rd d c. Ch 1 and sl st in 3rd ch st of beginning of first pattern row.

Row 2: Ch 4, * work 4 d c between 4 d c of previous row. Ch 1, work 1 d c in d c of previous row. Ch 1 and repeat from * 5 times (6 patterns across front).

Left Cape at Sleeve—Work in same manner, working 6 d c in shell for 7 patterns.

Back—Work 10 patterns with 4 d c in each shell. Cape at sleeve—work same as left cape—7 patterns (6 d c in each shell).

Left Front—Work 6 patterns with 4 d c in each shell. Continue in

203

Illustration 162. Lace Dress and Hat, No. 609. *Juvenile Styles*, Volume 2, Page 17.

Reprinted from *Juvenile Styles*, Volume 2, Page 16.

this manner for 3 more rows (working 6 d c in shell for cape at sleeve). From center front, work 6 patterns and ch 12 sts (underarm), then skip next 7 patterns for cape sleeve (do not skip the d c at beginning and end of 7 patterns, these are included in body of dress). Continue around back of dress for 10 patterns and work right underarm to correspond with left. Work 6 patterns for right front. Ch 1 and sl st in ch 3 at beginning of row, ch 4 and continue pattern for 1 row and work 3 patterns at underarm. When first row of pattern at underarm is completed, work the remainder of dress with 6 d c in shell instead of 4. Work even for 9 inches or desired length. Finish last shell with 8 d c. Attach velvet ribbon as shown on illustration, or make 4 small loops and use 4 small buttons.

HAT

Band—Ch 15 sts, work 1 d c in 5th st from hook, * ch 1, skip 1 st and work 1 d c in next st, repeat from * to end of ch. (6 d c in row). Ch 5, turn, work 1 d c in first d c of row below, * ch 1 and work 1 d c in next d c, repeat from * across row (6 d c in row). Ch 5, turn work 6 d c in each row, until band measures 61 rows (this should measure loosely around head). Sew band together, this will be center back. Fasten yarn in 3rd row from center back to right side. Ch 4, and * work 1 d c in next row (or d c), ch 1, repeat from * until you have 7 d c in row, including the ch 4 st beginning of row. Ch 5, turn, work 6 d c in next 2 rows, with ch 1 between. *Row* 4: ch 4, yarn over needle, insert needle in first d c of row below, draw through, then in 2nd d c draw through, now yarn over needle, draw through 3 loops, then 2 loops. (This is a decrease). Make 1 decrease in this manner at the beginning of the next 3 rows. Work 3 more rows with 3 d c in each row, including the ch 4 (10 rows from beginning). Break thread. Work 3 more pieces spacing equal distances apart. Work piece in center front, 3 rows longer, after your decreasing. *Center Ring*—Ch 3, join, ch 4, work 20 tr cr in ring. Sew each piece to this ring. *Brim*—Skip 10 rows from center back, fasten yarn in 11th row. Ch 1, work 4 d c between next 2 d c, skip 1 d c and work 1 d c between next 2 d c. Continue in this manner, working 4 d c and 1 d c, until you have 20 patterns, ch 1 and fasten in 10th d c on left side of center back. Break thread. *Row* 2: Start 2nd row on same side as first row. Skip first shell and fasten yarn in first single d c. Ch 1, and work 6 d c in center of 4 d c, ch 1 and work 1 d c in 1 d c, continue in this manner around row, ending with ch 1 and fasten in last single d c. Work 3 more rows starting and ending rows in same manner as row 2. Work last row of patterns starting at 9th row on band at center back, work 1 row following patterns to 9th row from center back. Work over wire with s c enough to keep wire covered. Start crocheting over wire at beginning of patterns and have it closed at center back. Adjust on head before closing, if possible. Put ribbon velvet through first row of band as shown on illustration.

INFANT'S FOUR-PIECE SET
STYLE No. 614
Size—Infant

Material—3 fold Saxony Sacque—2, 1 ounce balls; Cap—1, 1 ounce ball; Shoes—1, 1 ounce ball; Booties—1, 1 ounce ball.
1 Bone Crochet Hook, size 3.
Gauge—7 sts to 1 inch for single cr.

SACQUE

Ch 63 sts (ch should measure approximately 11 inches). Work 2 d c in 4th st from hook, * skip 1 ch and work 2 d c in next ch, repeat from * across row ending with 3 d c in last pattern (30 patterns in row). *Row* 2: * Ch 2, turn, work 2 d c between first and 2nd d c of row below (this is an increase), count this increase as one pattern. Work 2 d c between first and 2nd pattern, work 2 d c between next patterns, continue in this manner until you have 7 patterns (this is one half of front). Work 4 d c between next patterns (this is an increase). Work 7 more patterns (this is first half of back). Work 4 d c between next patterns (this is an increase). Work 7 more patterns (this is 2nd half of back). Work 4 d c between next patterns (this is in increase), and work 7 more patterns for other half of front, ending with 3 d c between last d c

Illustration 163. Style No. 614, Infant's four-piece set. *Juvenile Styles,* Volume 2, Page 23.

and ch 3 of row below. *Row* 3: Repeat from * adding one more pattern in each front and one more pattern in each half of back. Work 4 d c in center of 4 d c of row below. (35 patterns in row). Work even for 14 more rows. On next row, work 13 patterns and ch 11 sts, skip 19 patterns (include the increased patterns as one pattern). Work 27 patterns, ch 11 sts (underarm) and skip 19 patterns, work 13 patterns. Ch 2, turn, work even to ch sts and work 2 d c in first ch, * skip 1 ch and work 2 d c in next ch, repeat from * to end of ch (6 patterns for underarm), work even to ch st at other underarm and work 6 more patterns over ch. Work 6 more rows even.

Edging—With contrasting shade, hold right side of work toward you, starting at neck, work scallop as follows: Fasten yarn in first ch 3 of first row and work * 1 h d c in next ch 3, 3 d c in same st, 1 h d c in same st, s c into following ch 3, of 3rd row. Repeat from * around entire sacque to other side of neck. Break thread. With white, ch 2 and sl st into each d c of scallop omitting one s c between each scallop. Finish armholes in same manner.

Collar—Work 4 rows of pattern around neck, increasing at beginning and end of every row and working 4 d c above 4 d c of sacque at back and shoulders. Work scallops in same manner around collar.

CAP

Crown—Ch 3, join in ring and work 7 s c in ring. Then work 2 s c in each st until there are 24 sts around. * Work 1 s c in each of the next 4 sts, 2 s c in next st, repeat from * (thus increasing in every 5th st) until there are 50 sts around; then increase in every 15th st until there are 100 sts around. Work even until crown measures 4½ inches from center to edge. Ch 1 and turn, skip 1 st and work 1 s c in each s c of previous row to within 4 inches of ch 1 (back of cap). * Ch 1 and turn, skip first st, work 1 s c in each st across row, repeat from * for 8 rows, decreasing 1 st in each row, but do not have decrease at same place as previous row. Work 1 row completely around cap, skipping 3 sts at back, spaced a few sts apart.

Brim—Fold front of cap in half and place marker. Hold wrong side of work toward you, ch 2 and work 1 d c in first st, * skip 1 s c and work 2 d c in next st, repeat from * to marker then work 4 d c in center of cap. Continue from * to * to end of row. Row 2: Ch 2, turn, work 2 d c between the 2 patterns of previous row. Continue to work 2 d c between 2 d c of previous row to 4 d c, then work 4 d c in center of 4 d c of previous row. Work 2 d c between 2 d c of previous row. Repeat row 2 twice.

Edging—With contrasting shade, starting at beginning of brim work scallops as follows: Fasten yarn in first pattern, (right side of band), work 1 h d c in 2nd row, 3 d c in same st, 1 h d c in same st, s c in next row. Work scallops in this manner between each pattern, s c between next pattern. Work 1 s c between each d c across front of cap, break thread. With white, ch 2 and sl st into each d c of scallop omitting 1 s c between each scallop.

Reprinted from *Juvenile Styles,* Volume 2, Page 23.

INFANT'S THREE PIECE SET
STYLE No. 606
Size 6 Months

Material—Saxony 3 Fold, 2 1-oz. balls. 1 Bone Crochet Hook, size 3.

SACQUE

Yoke—Ch 83 sts (ch should measure approximately 11 inches long) and work 1 d c in 4th ch from hook, d c in each st across row. *Row 2*: ch 3, turn (this ch 3 forms first st of following row) d c in next 11 sts, (1 d c, ch 1, 1 d c) in next st (1 d c, ch 1, 1 d c will be referred to as a seam st). Work 1 d c in next 16 sts (sleeve), work seam st in next st, d c in next 20 sts (back) work seam st in next st, d c in next 16 sts (sleeve), work seam st in next st, d c in last 12 sts. *Row 3*: ch 3, turn, * d c in each st to seam st and work (1 d c, ch 1, 1 d c in seam st), repeat from * to last seam st, d c in each st to end of row, ch 3, turn. Repeat 3rd row, 8 times.

Lace Pattern—Ch 4, skip 1 st and * work 4 d c in next st, ch 1, skip 1 st and work 1 d c in next st, ch 1, repeat from * ending with 4 d c in first seam st. Skip sleeve sts and ch 3, start patterns in back with 4 d c in next seam st. Continue patterns across back to next seam st, ending with 4 d c in seam st. Ch 3 and skip sleeve, work 4 d c in next seam st. Continue in same manner, ending with 1 d c in last st. *Row 2*: ch 4, turn, * work 4 d c in center of 4 d c of row below. Ch 1, work 1 d c in d c of row below, ch 1, repeat from * to ch 3, joining sleeve, work 1 d c in center st of ch 3, work patterns in this manner to end of row. Ch 4, turn. Repeat 2nd row, 12 times.

Sleeves—Join wool at underarm, ch 4, skip 1 st and * work 4 d c in next st, ch 1, skip 1 st and work 1 d c in next st, repeat from * around armhole ending with 4 d c, join with sl st in 3rd ch at beginning of row. Ch 4 and follow patterns for 10 rows, joining each row with a sl st and ch 4 at beginning of each row. Ch 3, work 1 row of d c skipping every alternate st. Join with a sl st, ch 2, work 1 d c in each st for 2 more rows. Break thread.

Edge—With baby pink or blue, work 1 s c around entire sacque and cuffs. with ch 3, between each s c.

CAP

Crown—Ch 3, join, ch 3, work 13 d c in ring, join with a sl st in ch 3 of first row. Ch 3, work 3 d c in first st, * skip 1 st and work 4 d c in next st, repeat from * around row (7 patterns). Join with a sl st.

Row 3: Sl st in first 2 sts, ch 3, work 3 d c in center of first pattern of row below. Skip 2 d c and work 4 d c and between first and 2nd patterns, work 4 d c in center of next pattern, work in this manner, 4 d c in center of each pattern and 4 d c between each pattern around row (14 patterns in row).

Row 4: Sl st first 2 sts, ch 3, work 3 d c in center of first pattern of row below, 4 d c in center of next pattern. Continue in this manner working 4 d c in center of each pattern of row below (14 patterns).

Row 5: Repeat row 4.
Row 6: Repeat row 3.

Work even for 8 rows after last increased row. On 9th row, work to with-

Illustration 164. Style No. 606, Infant's three-piece set. *Juvenile Styles*, Volume 2, Page 27.

in 5 patterns of beginning of last row. Ch 3, turn, work 4 d c in center of first pattern, * work 1 d c in center of next pattern, 4 d c in center of next pattern, repeat from * to end of first short row. Ch 3, turn, work 4 d c in center of first pattern, 1 d c in 1 d c, repeat from * to end of row. Work 4 more rows in same manner. Work 2 more rows with 6 d c in shell, instead of 4 d c. Break thread. Holding edge of last row toward you, work picot as follows: With baby pink or blue, starting at end in last pattern, ch 2, sl st into first st, * ch 2, sl st into next st, repeat from * to end of last row of shells. Do not break thread, fold last 4 rows of patterns back and s c side of band to side of cap, s c in each d c across front of cap, continue around back of cap and other side. Fasten ribbon as shown on illustration.

BOOTIES

Starting at instep, ch 13 sts, work 1 d c 3rd st from hook and work 1 d c to end of chain. Ch 2, turn, work 1 d c in each st for 5 more rows. Ch 30 sts, and sl st to other corner. Ch 2 and d c in each st around instep and each st of ch, for 2 rows. Work 3 more rows decreasing 4 sts to each round; do not have decreases come over those of previous row. Break thread and sew seam at sole. Work 1 row of d c around top of bootie, decreasing 5 sts, skip these sts equal distances apart. Work beading as follows: Ch 4, skip 1 st and work 1 d c in next st, * ch 1, skip 1 st, d c in next st, repeat from * around row, ch 1 and join with a sl st.

Pattern—Ch 3, * work 4 d c between next 2 d c of row below, work 1 d c between next 2 d c, repeat from * around row, ending with 4 d c. Join with a sl st, ch 3 and * work 4 d c between 4 d c of row below. Work 1 d c in 1 d c of row below, repeat from * for 1 row. Join with a sl st and ch 3. Work 5 more rows in same manner. With baby pink or blue, work scallops as follows: * Work (1 h d c, 3 d c, 1 h d c), between 4 d c of row below, s c into next d c, repeat from * around row. With white, * ch 1, sl st into next s c, repeat from * around row.

Reprinted from *Juvenile Styles,* Volume 2, Page 27.

Maybelle
No. 711
Three-Piece Crocheted Set

Size—Infant
Material—Saxony 3 fold—2 One Ounce Balls, Sacque; One 1 Ounce Ball, Cap; ½ One Ounce Ball, Shoes.
One Bone Crochet Hook, Size 3.

SACQUE

Starting at neck, ch 85 sts (to measure approximately 11 inches). Work 1 d c in 4th ch from hook, 1 d c in each ch to end of row (83 d c), including ch 3 at beginning of row. Row 2—Ch 3, turn, work 1 d c in first d c, 3 d c in next st, 1 d c in each of the next 2 d c, * skip 1 d c, 1 d c in each of the next 2 d c, 3 d c in next st, 1 d c in each of the next 2 d c, repeat from * across (14 patterns in row). Row 3—Ch 3, turn, skip 1 st, 1 d c in next d c (picking up back st), 5 d c in next st (picking up both threads). Remainder of sacque is worked in this manner. Work 1 d c in each of the next 2 sts, * skip 2 sts, 1 d c in each of the next 2 d c, 5 d c in next st, 1 d c in each of the next 2 d c, repeat from * across. Row 4—Ch 3, turn, skip 1 st, 1 d c in each of the next 2 d c, 3 d c in next st, 1 d c in each of the next 3 d c, * skip 2 sts, 1 d c in each of the next 3 sts, 3 d c in next st, 1 d c in each of the next 3 d c, repeat from * across. Row 5—Ch 3, turn, skip 1 st, d c in each of the next 2 sts, 5 d c in next st, 1 d c in each of the next 3 sts, * skip 2 sts, 1 d c in each of the next 3 sts, 5 d c in next st, 1 d c in each of the next 3 d c, repeat from * across. Row 6—Ch 3, skip 1 st, 1 d c in each of the next 3 sts, 3 d c in next st, 1 d c in each of the next 4 d c, * skip 2 sts, 1 d c in each of the next 4 sts, 3 d c in next st, 1 d c in each of the next 4 d c, repeat from * across. Continue in this manner adding 2 d c in each pattern every other row, until you have 11 rows from beginning. Work over 2 patterns (front), skip 3 patterns (sleeve), continue over 4 patterns (back), skip 3 patterns (sleeve), continue over 2 patterns (front), ch 3, turn, continue around sacque increasing in same manner for 8 more rows. Break thread. Attach yarn at armhole, ch 2, work over 3 patterns, working 3 d c in center of each pattern instead of making every other row an increase. At end of first row, ch 3, turn, sleeve is worked back and forth. Work 10 rows from underarm. Break thread. Sew up sleeves.

Edging—With baby pink or blue, attach yarn on right side of bottom of sleeve, * skip 1 st, work (1 h d c, ch 2, 1 d c, ch 1, 1 h d c) in next st, skip 1 st, s c in next st, repeat from * around bottom of cuff. Work edging around entire sacque in same manner.

CAP

Ch 4, join, ch 3, work 11 d c in ring, join with a sl st. Row 2—Ch 3, 2 d c in each st (24 d c) including the ch 3 at beginning of row, join with a sl st. Row 3—Ch 3, 2 d c in next st, * 1 d c in next st, 2 d c in next st, repeat from * around row (36 d c), join with a sl st. Row 4—Ch 3, 1 d c in next st, 2 d c in next st, * 1 d c in each of the next 2 sts, 2 d c in next st, repeat from * around (48 d c), join with a sl st. Row 5—Ch 3, 1 d c in next 2 sts, 2 d c in next st, * 1 d c in each of the next 3 sts, 2 d c in next st, repeat from * around (60 d c), join with a sl st. Inc in this manner, having 1 more d c between each increase, thus adding 12 more sts in each row, until you have 9 increased rows (108 sts). Work without increasing for 5 more rows. Ch 3, turn, skip first st, work 1 d c in each st to within 26 sts of ch 3 at beginning of row (back of cap). * Ch 3, turn, skip first st, 1 d c in each st across, repeat from * for 6 more rows, decreasing 2 sts in each

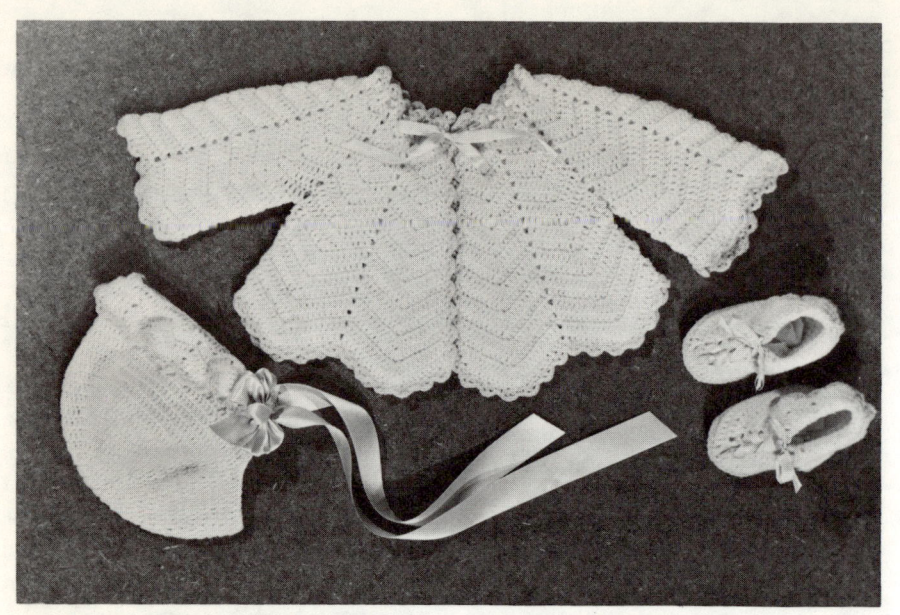

Illustration 165. Maybelle, No. 711; three-piece crocheted set. *Juvenile Styles*, Volume 3, Page 20.

row, but do not have decreases at same place as previous row.

Band—Row 1—Ch 3, turn, work 1 d c in first d c, 3 d c in next st, 1 d c in each of the next 2 d c, * skip 1 d c, 1 d c in each of the next 2 d c, 3 d c in next st, 1 d c in each of the next 2 sts, repeat from * across (11 patterns in row). Row 2—Ch 3, turn, skip 1 st, 1 d c in next d c (picking up back st), 5 d c in next st (picking up both threads). Remainder of band is worked in this manner. Work 1 d c in each of the next 2 sts, * skip 2 sts, 1 d c in each of the next 2 d c, 5 d c in next st, 1 d c in each of the next 2 sts, repeat from * across. Row 3—Ch 3, turn, skip 1 st, 1 d c in each of the next 2 d c, 3 d c in next st, 1 d c in each of the next 3 sts, * skip 2 sts, 1 d c in each of the next 3 sts, 3 d c in next st, 1 d c in each of the next 3 d c, repeat from * across. Row 4—Ch 3, turn, skip 1 st, d c in each of the next 2 sts, 5 d c in next st, 1 d c in each of the next 3 sts, * skip 2 sts, 1 d c in each of the next 3 sts, 5 d c in next st, 1 d c in each of the next 3 d c, repeat from * across. Break thread.

Edging—With baby pink or blue, attach yarn on right side on top of band, * skip 1 st, work (1 h d c, ch 2, 1 d c, ch 1, 1 h d c) in next st, skip 1 st, s c in next st, repeat from * across, break thread. Fold band back, with pink or blue, s c in each st across front of cap. Fold back brim, with white, s c around sides and back of cap, crocheting sides of band to cap. Skip 3 sts across back, thread thread.

SHOES

Sole—Ch 17 sts, work 1 d c in 4th ch from hook, work 1 d c in next 12 ch, 3 d c in last st, 12 d c on other side of ch, 3 d c in last st. Join with a sl st, in 3rd ch of turning cr, ch 3. Row 2—Work 1 d c in next 2 d c, 2 d c in next st, 1 d c in next 7 d c, 2 d c in next st, 3 d c in next 3 sts, 3 d c in end st. D c in each of the next 3 sts, 2 d c in next st, 1 d c in each of the next 7 d c, 2 d c in next st, 3 d c in next 3 d c, 3 d c in end st, 1 d c in next st. Join, ch 3. Work 1 more row in same manner increasing 8 sts to a round. Fasten thread at center end of sole. Ch 3, dec 1 st as follows: * Yarn over needle, insert needle in first d c (picking up back loop only), draw yarn thru, then in 2nd d c draw thru, Yarn over needle draw thru 3 loops, then 2 loops (this is a dec), work 2 d c in next 2 sts, make a dec in same manner. Work around sole to within 4 d c of ch 3 at beg of row. Make a dec, work 2 d c in next 2 sts, ch 3, turn, repeat from * (picking up both threads), until you have 7 rows.

Cuff—Row 1—Ch 3, turn, work 1 d c in first d c, 3 d c in next st, 1 d c in each of the next 2 d c, * skip 1 d c, 1 d c in each of the next 2 d c, 3 d c in next st, 1 d c in each of the next 2 sts, repeat from * 2 more times (4 patterns). Row 2—Ch 3, turn, skip 1 st, 1 d c in next d c (picking up back st), 5 d c in next st (picking up both threads). Work 1 d c in each of the next 2 sts, * skip 2 sts, 1 d c in each of the next 2 d c, 5 d c in next st, 2 d c in next 2 sts, repeat from * across. Repeat Row 2, once. With contrasting shade, work 1 row of s c around opening at front and sides of cuff, working 2 s c in each row. Work scallop around top as follows: * Skip 1 st, work (1 h d c, ch 2, 1 d c, ch 1, 1 h d c) in next st, skip 1 st, s c in next st, repeat from * around bottom of cuff. Work 1 row of s c around bottom of sole.

Reprinted from *Juvenile Styles*, Volume 3, Page 20.

Shoulderette
No. 714
Three-Piece Infant's Set

Material—Saxony 3 fold. Shoulderette—2 one ounce balls. Cap—1 one ounce ball. Booties—1 one ounce ball.

SACQUE

Ch 100 sts, to measure 18 inches.

Row 1—3 tr cr in 4th ch from hook, ch 1, 3 tr cr in same st. *Skip 2 sts, sl st in next st, skip 2 sts; 3 tr cr in next st, ch 1, 3 tr cr (shell). Repeat from *, ending with 3 tr cr in last st (½ shell). Ch 1, turn.

Row 2—*Work a shell in back loop of next sl st, sl st in ch 1 of next shell. Repeat from *, ending with ½ shell in last tr cr of last shell. Ch 1, turn. Repeat Row 2, for 8 inches. Fold piece in half having last row of shells meet first row of shells. Work cuffs around narrow ends as follows: Join with a sl st, ch 3, work 2 d c in each shell across (30 d c). Work 1 s c in each st for 8 rows. Work edge around entire sacque as follows: *Ch 3, sl st in next st, repeat from *around cuff. Work around shells in same manner, skip 1 st between shells on last row (this is top of shoulderette). Fold about 4 rows back for collar. Block as shown on illustration.

CAP

Ch 3, join in ring and work 7 s c in ring. Then work 2 s c in each st until there are 24 sts around. Inc in every 5th st until there are 56 sts around, sl st in next st. Shell st. Row 1—*Skip 1 s c, 3

Illustration 166. Shoulderette, No. 714; three-piece infant's set. *Juvenile Styles,* Volume 3, Page 24.

tr cr in next st, ch 1, 3 tr cr in same st, skip 1 st, sl st in next st, repeat from *around (14 shells). Ch 4, sl st in ch 1 of first shell at beginning of row. Row 2—*Work a shell in back loop of next sl st, sl st in ch 1 of next shell. Repeat from *, ending with shell in back loop of sl st at beginning of ch 4. Sl st in ch 1 of first shell of row below. Ch 4, sl st in center of first shell at beginning of row. Repeat Row 2, until you have 8 shell rows. From now on cap is worked back and forth. When you ch the 4 sts at end of last row, turn and sl st in ch 1 of last shell made (front of cap). Work 10 shell across and ½ shell in next sl st (10½ shells). Ch 1, turn, Row 2—*Work a shell in back loop of next sl st, sl st in ch 1 of next shell. Repeat from *ending with a ½ shell in last tr cr of last shell, ch 1 turn. Repeat Row 2 for 14 rows from beginning. Edging—*Ch 3, sl st in next st, repeat from *across front of cap; skip 1 st between shells. Fold last 3 rows of shells back. S c across front of cap, around sides (cr sides of band to cap) and back of cap. Attach ribbons as shown on illustration.

BOOTIES

Starting at instep, ch 13 sts, work 1 s c in 2nd st from hook and work 1 s c in each st to end of chain. Ch 1, turn, work 1 s c in each st for 12 more rows. Ch 28 sts and sl st to other corner. S c in each st around instep and each st of ch, for 5 rows. Work 5 more rows decreasing 3 sts to each round, do not have decreases come over those of previous row. Break thread and sew seam at sole. Work 2 rows of s c around top of bootie, decreasing 2 sts in each row, skip these sts equal distances apart. Work beading as follows: Ch 4, skip 1 st and work 1 d c in next st, *ch 1, skip 1 st, d c in next st, repeat from *around row, ch 1 and join with a sl st. Shell st. Row 1— *Skip 2 d c and 3 tr cr in next space, ch 1, 3 tr cr in same st, skip 1 d c, sl st in next space, repeat from *around row (6 shells). Ch 4, sl st in ch 1 of first shell at beginning of row. Row 2— *Work a shell in back loop of next sl st, sl st in ch 1 of next shell repeat from *around ending with shell in back loop of sl st at beginning of ch 4, sl st in ch 1 of first shell of row below. Ch 4, sl st in center of first shell at beginning of row. Repeat Row 2 until you have 7 shell rows. On last row do not ch 4 sts. Edging—*Ch 3, sl st in next st, repeat from * around row; skip 1 st between shells.

Reprinted from Juvenile Styles, Volume 3, Page 24.

Crocheted Blanket

No. 715

1¼ Yards in Length—1 Yard Width.

1 Bone Crochet Hook, size 4.

Material—Zephyr Paradise, variegated Germantown, 4 Four-Ounce Skeins, 1 Four-Ounce Skein, plain color.

Gauge—5½ sts to 1 inch.

Make a ch 1¼ yards long or desired length of cover.

Row 1—Work a s c in each st to end of ch, ch 1, turn.

Row 2—S c in back loop of each st across, ch 2, turn.

Row 3—* Skip 1 st, d c in next st (picking up front loop), d c in st just skipped, repeat from * across, ch 1, turn.

Row 4—S c in back loop of each st across, ch 2, turn.

Row 5—Repeat Row 3 and Row 4 until cover measures 1 yard wide. Work 7 rows of s c around entire cover, working 3 s c in each corner.

Reprinted from Juvenile Styles, Volume 3, Page 26.

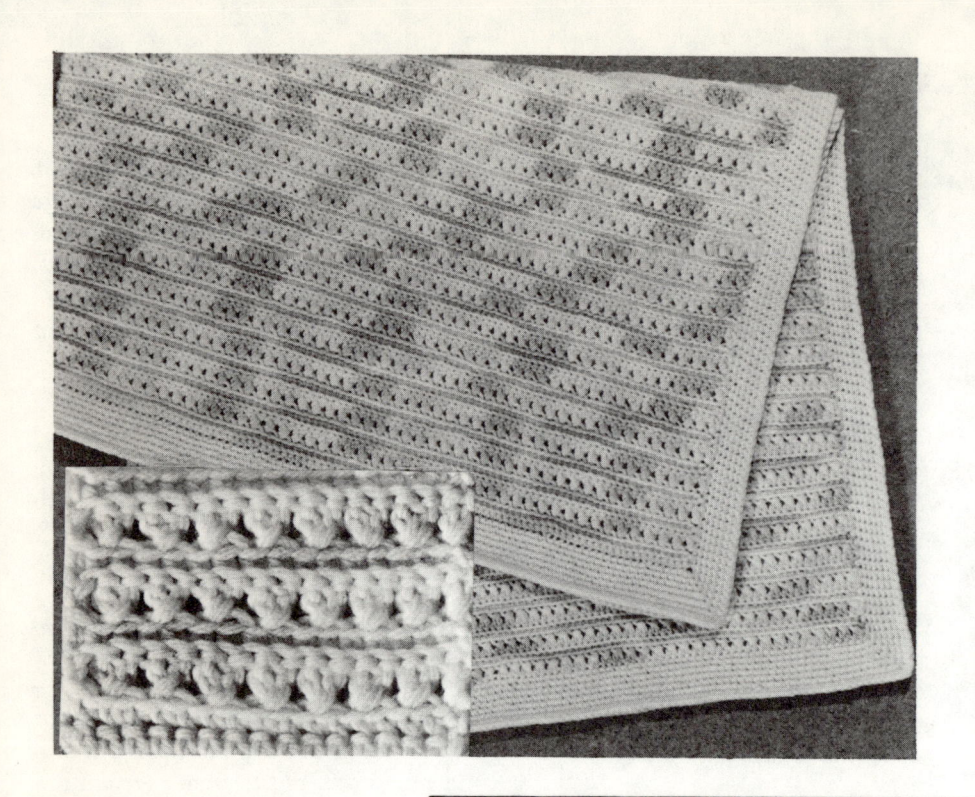

Illustration 167. Crocheted Blanket, No. 715; *Juvenile Styles*, Volume 3, Page 26.

Knitted Blanket
No. 716

Illustration 168. Knitted Blanket, No. 716; *Juvenile Styles*, Volume 3, Page 27.

1 Pair Needles, American Standard, No. 5.
1 Bone Crochet Hook, size 3.
Material—Variegated Germantown or Zephyr Paradise, 4 Four Ounce Skeins of Varigated. 1 Four Ounce Skein Plain color.
Finished Size 36 inches Width—42 inches Length.
Gauge—6 sts to 1 inch.

Pattern—Multiple of 3 plus 1 st.

Swatch—Cast on 16 sts.

Row 1—K 1, * yarn over, K 3 pass first st of the K 3 over last 2 (leaving 2 sts on needle), repeat from * across.

Row 2—K back.

Row 3—* K 3 pass first st over last 2 sts, yarn over, repeat from * ending row, K 1.

Row 4—K back.

Cast on 193 sts—to measure about 32 inches. Work in pattern until piece measures 38 inches or desired length of cover. Work 2 inches of s c around piece, working 3 s c in corners. Block lightly on wrong side.

Reprinted from *Juvenile Styles*, Volume 3, Page 27.

A Convalescing Jacket Ensemble
No. 800

Needles—1 Pair Bone Nos. 3 and 7 American Standard.

Material—8 one ounce balls, pink Saxony, Mother's. 2—one ounce balls, pink Saxony, Baby's. One-half ounce contrasting shade, Saxony.

Scale—13 sts to 2 inches, No. 7 needles. Size 34 mother's, 3 months, baby's.

MOTHER'S JACKET

Back—With No. 7 needles, cast on 135 sts, *K 3, sl 1 st, repeat from *across row, ending with K 3, P back. Repeat these 2 rows for 8 inches. Bind off 4 sts at beg of the next 2 rows for underarm (127 sts). K 2 tog at beg of the next 8 rows (119 sts). Continue in pattern for 2 more inches. Change to No. 3 needles, on right side, *P 2, K 1, repeat from *across row, ending with P 2. On next row, K 2, P 1 across row. Repeat these 2 rows, for 5 inches. Bind off 7 sts at beg of the next 10 rows, bind off remaining 49 sts for back of neck.

Right Front—With No. 7 needles, cast on 71 sts, work in pattern for 8½ inches. Bind off 4 sts at beg of the next row at underarm, P 2 tog at beg of the next 4 rows at underarm. Work even for 2 more inches. At beg of the next row at front, bind off 4 sts. Change to No. 3 needles and repeat yoke pattern (P 2, K 1) for 3 inches, bind off 10 sts at beg of the next row at neck edge. Now K 2 tog at beg of every row at neck edge, until 39 sts remain. Bind off 7 sts at beg of every row at shoulder, 5 times and continue to K 2 tog at neck edge, until all sts are bound off. Work left front to correspond.

Sleeves—With No. 3 needles, cast on 65 sts, work in pattern, P 2, K 1, ending with P 2. Next row, K 2, P 1, ending row with K 2, repeat these 2 rows for 3 inches. Work 1 more row and inc 1 st at beg and end of row. Change to No. 7 needles and work in pattern, K 3, slip 1 st, end row with K 3. P back. Continue to work in pattern and inc 1 st at beg and end of every 6th row until you have 107 sts. Work even until sleeve measures 20 inches from cuff or desired length to underarm. Bind off 3 sts at beg of the next 2 rows, then bind off 2 sts at beg of the next 2 rows. Now K 2 tog at beg and end of every K row until 53 sts remain, bind off. Sew up seams at underarm and shoulder, sew up sleeves and insert into armhole gathering at top a little. Hem the 4 bound off sts at front. Work 2 rows of s c around yoke and neck working 3 loops for buttonholes on right side of yoke, on first row. With contrasting shade start smocking on right hand side at bottom of yoke. Sew the first 2 K sts tog, then the next 2 K sts, leave the thread loose between the 2 smocked sts. Repeat across row. Start 2nd row, turn, skip first K st and work back in same manner. Work fronts and 5 rows of smocking on cuffs in same manner. Sew on buttons.

BABY'S JACKET

Back—With No. 7 needles, cast on 91 sts, *K 3, sl 1 st, repeat from *across row, ending with K 3, P back. Repeat these 2 rows for 4 inches. Bind off 4 sts at beg of the next 2 rows (83 sts). Work in pattern for ¾ inch more. With No. 3 needles, *P 2, K 1 (right side), repeat from *across row, ending with P 2. Next row, K 2, P 1, repeat these 2 rows for 2¼ inches. Bind off 6 sts at beg of the next 8 rows, bind off remaining 35 sts for back of neck.

Right Front—With No. 7 needles, cast on 47 sts, work in pattern for 4 inches, bind off 4 sts at beg of the next row at underarm, K back. Purl 2 sts tog at underarm, work pattern for ¾ inch more. Bind off 4 sts at beg of the next row at front edge (hem). With No. 3 needles, *P 2, K 1, repeat from *across row, next row K 2, P 1, across row. Repeat these 2 rows for 1½ inches. At beg of next row at front edge, bind off 6 sts, then K 2 tog at beg of every row at neck edge, until you have 27 sts left. Bind off 6 sts at beg of the next 4 rows at shoulder edge and continue to K 2 tog at neck edge, until all sts are bound off. Work left front to correspond.

Sleeves—With No. 3 needles, cast on 44 sts, P 2, K 1, across row. Next row, K 2, P 1, repeat these 2 rows for 1 inch. With No. 7 needles, K 3, slip 1 st, ending with K 3 (K last 2 sts tog), P back. Work in pattern, increasing 1 st at each end, every inch, until sleeve measures 4 inches (51 sts). Work 1 inch even. Bind off 3 sts at beg of the next 2 rows. K 2 tog at beg of every row, until you have 35 sts left, bind off. Sew up seams at underarm and shoulder, sew up sleeves and insert into armhole gathering at top a little. Hem the 4 bound off sts at front. Work 2 rows of s c around yoke and neck working 2 loops for buttonholes on right side of yoke, on first row. With contrasting shade start smocking on right hand side at bottom of yoke. Sew the first 2 K sts tog, then the next 2 K sts, leave the thread loose between the 2 smocked sts. Repeat across row. Start 2nd row turn, skip first K st and work back in same manner. Work fronts and 3 rows of smocking on cuffs in same manner. Sew on buttons.

BOOTIES

With No. 3 needles, cast on 47 sts, *K 3, sl 1 st, repeat from *across row, ending with K 3, P back. Repeat these 2 rows for 4 inches. On right side, K 1, *Y O, K 2 tog, repeat from *across row, P back. K 15, then P 2, K 1, for 17 sts, turn, K 2, P 1 for 17 sts. Repeat these 2 rows on 17 sts for 26 rows, break thread. Holding right side toward you, pick up 12 sts on side of instep, K across front of instep, pick up 12 sts on other side of instep, K on last 15 sts. K 7 rows even. *On next row dec 1 st at each end and 4 sts spaced at equal distances apart. K 3 rows even, repeat from *2 times, bind off. Sew seam at sole and back. With 2 strands of yarn, ch 90 sts. Tape thru beading. Sew ½ inch hem in top of bootie.

Reprinted from *Juvenile Styles*, Volume 4, Page 2.

Illustration 169. A convalescing jacket ensemble for mother and baby, No. 800. *Juvenile Styles,* Volume 4, Page 2.

Illustration 170. Royal Highness, a cape and hood, No. 803. *Juvenile Styles,* Volume 4, Page 7.

Royal Highness

No. 803

CAPE AND HOOD IN "SUMMER SKY BLUE"

Size—6 months to 1 year
Needles—1 pair American Standard No. 2. 1 Circular No. 4.
Material—Paradise Zephyr 10 ounces.
Gauge—6 sts to 1 inch.

CAPE

Starting at neck, with No. 2 needles, cast on 76 sts K 1, P 1, for 3 rows. Beading: K 1, *Y O, K 2 tog, repeat from *across row. K 1, P 1 for 3 rows, cast on 2 sts. Change to No. 4 circular needle.

Yoke—Work in garter st (K each row). Row 1—K 8, *inc 1 st, K 5, repeat from *across row to within last 8 sts, K 8. Do not inc in first and last 8 sts thruout yoke. Cast on 2 sts. Row 2—K 1 row. Row 3—On next row, K back to within last 4 sts, bind off 2 sts for buttonhole, K 2. On next row, cast on 2 sts over those bound off, K across row. *Repeat Row 1 (but do not cast on the 2 sts). K 3 rows even. Repeat from *until you have 182 sts, working 2 more buttonholes, 1 inch apart. On next row, K 24 sts, *slip 1 st, K 18 sts, repeat from *to within 25 sts, slip 1 st, K 24. On next row, K 3, P to within last 3 sts (Purling the sl st), K 3, repeat these 2 rows for 1 inch. On next K row, K 3, inc 1 st, K 9, inc 1 st, K 10, sl 1 st, continuing pattern across row, making an inc in center of each gore. Inc in 4th to last st same as beg of row. Work even for 1 inch. Inc in same manner every inch, until cape measures 11 inches from end of yoke. K 12 rows, 6 ribs, bind off loosely on wrong side.

Cord—Ch 3, join, work 5 s c in ring. Work 2 s c in each st, until you have 12 s c. Work even until you have 5 rows. Fill with cotton. S c around decreasing a few sts in each row to close opening. Ch 24 inches. Make another ball in same manner and attach to 2nd end.

HOOD

Starting at first half of neck edge, with

212

No. 2 needles, cast on 42 sts, K 1, P 1 for 4 rows. Change to No. 4 needles. *K 1 row, P 1 row for 1 inch always knitting first 4 sts on Purled rows for border at front. Now K 2 sts tog at back edge, repeat from *until piece measures 5 inches, 37 sts. (measuring after the K 1, P 1 edge). Work 1 inch even. To start peak at top: *Row* 1—K 30 sts, turn. *Row* 2 and all even rows, P back, slipping first st. *Row* 3—K 24, turn. *Row* 5—K 18, turn. *Row* 7—K 12, turn. *Row* 9—K 6, turn.

All sts are now on left hand needle (this completes half of hood). On next row starting at back, K 9 turn. Following row: K 15, turn. Next row K 21, turn. Continue in this manner, increasing 6 sts every other row, until you have 33 sts on right hand needle, turn. P back and on next row, K 37. Work other half to correspond increasing 1 st every inch at back edge. Fold in half and sew seam. Sew hood to cape, starting about 2 inches from beading at beg of cape, gathering across leaving 2 inches at end.

Reprinted from *Juvenile Styles*, Volume 4, Page 7.

A Sailor's Sweetheart
No. 808
CROCHETED JACKET

Size 4 to 6 years

1 *Bone Crochet Hook, size 3.*
Material—Cashmere Sports, 4 two ounce balls. One-half ounce ball white and red. 6 gold buttons.

Back—Ch 68 (to measure about 12 inches). (72 chs, size 6). Work 1 s c in 2nd ch from hook, s c in each ch. Ch 1, turn, work 12 rows of s c. On 13th row, inc in every 7th st across row (76 s c). Next row, ch 2, turn, insert hook in 2nd ch from hook, draw yarn thru, insert needle in first s c, wrap draw thru 2 loops, wrap thru 2 more (same as d c). *Insert needle in large loop of st, draw thru, insert needle in next s c, complete same as d c, repeat from *across row (right side). Ch 1, turn, s c in each st across row. Repeat these 2 rows for 8 inches. On next s c row, s c to within last 3 sts, ch 2, turn, follow pattern across row to within last 3 sts. Ch 1, turn, s c across row do not s c in last 2 sts, ch 2, follow pattern across row, do not work in last 2 sts. Follow pattern across for the next 6 rows and do not work in last st of each row (8 sts off on each side). Work in pattern for 5½ inches, or desired length to shoulder. On next s c row, *s c to within last 6 sts, ch 1, turn, s c to within last 6 sts at other end, (remainder of back is worked in s c rows), repeat from *2 more times, break thread.

Left Front—Ch 34, (36 chs, size 6) work 1 s c in 2nd ch from hook, work 1 s c in each ch across row. Ch 1, turn, work 12 rows of s c. On 13th row, inc in every 7th st across row. Work same as back to underarm. On next s c row, work to within last 3 sts of underarm. Ch 2, follow pattern across row. On next row, s c to within last 2 sts, *ch 2 follow pattern across row, on next row, s c to within last st, repeat from *3 times. (9 sts off at underarm). When piece measures about 1½ inches from underarm work pocket as follows: Work over 6 sts from underarm side. Pocket: With another strand of yarn, ch 17 sts loosely, work in pattern for 2 inches, break thread, insert pocket. Continue pattern on pocket for 16 sts and skip 16 on sweater; continue across front. Follow pattern until front measures 10½ inches from bottom at front edge, dec 2 sts at front edge (by not working in last s c and the turning cr). Work even at armhole edge, and do not work in last st of every row at neck edge, until you have 20 sts. When piece measures same as back to shoulder, s c to within last 6 sts at shoulder edge, 2 times (same as back), and continue to dec at neck 2 more times. Work right front to correspond, omitting pocket.

Sleeves—Ch 41 sts (to measure about 6 inches), (45 chs, size 6). Work 1 s c in 2nd ch from hook, s c in each ch to end of row. Ch 1, turn, work 10 rows of s c. On 11th row inc 4 sts across row at equal distances apart. Work in pattern same as for back for 1 inch. On next row, inc 1 st on each side. Continue to inc 1 st on each side every inch until you have 60 sts across row. Work even until sleeve measures 10 inches from bottom of cuff or desired length to underarm. *On next row work to within 3 sts at end of row, repeat from *once. On next row work to within 2 sts at end of row, repeat from *once (50 sts). Now work to within 1 st of each row until you have 28 sts left. Sew shoulder seams and sides. Sew sleeves and insert into armholes making a small inverted pleat at top.

Starting at right front, work 1 row of s c completely around fronts and neck. Work 3 more rows of s c on left front, break thread. Work 1 row of s c on right front making ch 3 loops for buttonholes about 2 inches apart. Work 2 more rows of s c over chains. Work 2 rows of s c of red on pocket, 2 rows of white, sew ends.

Collar—Ch 49 sts, work 1 s c in 2nd ch from hook, s c in each ch across row. Work in pattern for 3 inches. Work over 12 sts. Dec 1 st (by not working in last st) at end of every s c row on outer edge of collar until you have 2 sts. Work other side of collar to correspond. Work 1 row of s c around outside edge of collar, increasing 2 sts in each corner. Work 2 rows of blue, 2 rows of red. Sew to jacket.

Reprinted from *Juvenile Styles*,
Volume 4, Page 14.

Illustration 171. A Sailor's Sweetheart, a crocheted jacket, No. 808. *Juvenile Styles*, Volume 4, Page 14.

Goldilocks

No. 810

LITTLE PRINCESS AND HER DOLLY

Size 4-6 years
Needles—1 Circular Needle, No. 3.
1 *Pair American Standard No. 1.*
Material—*Kashmire Sports Yarn; 8 ounces, size 4; 10 ounces, size 6. 22-inch zipper.*
Gauge—*7½ sts to 1 inch.*

DRESS

Starting at bottom, with No. 3 circular needle, cast on 375 sts, size 4 (427 sts, size 6), do not join. K in garter st for 9 rows, 5 ribs.

Size 4—Work as follows: P 31, *K 3, P 59, repeat from *4 times, K 3, P 31. K back. Repeat these 2 rows for 1 inch. First dec: K 13, K 2 tog, K 12, K 2 tog, K 7, *K 2 tog, K 16, K 2 tog, K 15, K 2 tog, K 16, K 2 tog, K 7, repeat from *4 times, dec last panel same as first panel. *Work 1 inch even. Make another dec in same manner having decreases come directly above previous decreases. (24 sts less after each decreased row). Repeat from *until you have 159 sts. Work even until piece measures 12 inches or desired length to waist line.

Size 6—K 9 rows for border same as size 4. P 37, *K 3, P 67, repeat from * 4 times, K 3, P 37. K back, repeat these 2 rows for 1 inch. First dec: K 16, K 2 tog, K 15, K 2 tog, K 7, *K 2 tog, K 18, K 2 tog, K 19, K 2 tog, K 18, K 2 tog, K 7, repeat from *4 times, dec last panel same as first panel. Work 1 inch even. Make another dec in same manner every inch, until you have 163 sts. Work even until piece measures 14 inches or desired length to waist line. *K 16 (size 6, K 18) (including 3 K sts), with No. 1 needles, K 1, P 1, for 49 sts, continue with circular 3 needle, K 29 (back gore), with No. 1 needles, K 1, P 1, for 49 sts. Continue with No. 3 circular needle, K 16 (size 6, K 18). P back following pattern, repeat from * for 1½ inches. On right side of work continue on No. 3 circular needle same as before without ribbing for 2¾ inches. (3¼ inches, size 6). Size 4 and 6—From now on continue fronts and back for size 6 same as size 4 only you will have 1 more st on each front and 2 more sts in back. K 37 to underarm, put on st holder. Bind off 7. K 71 sts for back, put other front on st holder, P 2 sts tog at beg of the next 4 rows (67 sts). Work even following pattern for 4½ inches (5 inches size 6). Bind off 5 sts at beg of the next 8 rows, bind off remaining 27 sts for back of neck. Continue on left front, bind off 7 sts for underarm, following pattern, K 2 tog at underarm 3 more times (34 sts) work even for 1 inch more (1½ inches, size 6). On wrong side, P 13, K 15 (border for top of pocket), P 6 across. K back, repeat these 2 rows for 4 more rows. On next row, P 13, bind off 15 sts for pocket edge, P across. With separate yarn, cast on 15 sts, K 1 row, P 1 row for 2½ inches, put on st holder. K 6 sts, K the 15 sts from st holder for pocket, K across. P 1 row, K 1 row for 1 inch. Now P 2 tog at beg of every row at neck edge until 23 sts remain. Bind off 5 sts at beg of the next 4 rows at shoulder and continue to P 2 tog at neck edge, until all sts are bound off. Work Right Front to correspond.

Sleeves—With No. 1 needles, cast on 48 sts (size 6, 52 sts), K 1, P 1, for ¾ inch. Change to No. 3 needles, K 1 row, next row, P 16, K 3, P 10, K 3, P 16. K back. K these last 2 rows and inc 1 st at each end every 4th row, until sleeve measures 2 inches from beginning, 54 sts. Now inc 2 sts in center gore as follows: *K to first gore and K 4 sts after gore, inc 1 st, K to within 5 sts of 2nd gore, inc 1 st, K across. Continue to inc at seam ends every 4th row and 2 sts between gores every 6th row, repeat from * until piece measures 3 inches, 62 sts. Bind off 3 sts at beg of the next 2 rows, then K 2 tog at beg and end of next K row, now K 2 tog at beg and end of every 4th row (continue to inc 2 sts between gores every 6th row) until you have 50 sts. Now K 2 tog at beg and end of every K row (do not inc in center gores), until you have 44 sts. Now K 1, P 1 ribbing between gores and continue to K 2 tog at beg and end of every K row, until ribbing measures ¾ inch, bind off.

Collar—With white, cast on 56 sts, K 4 rows, 3 ribs. K 1 row, P 1 row, always knitting first and last 3 sts on purled rows (border). Continue these 2 rows for 4 inches. K 16, bind off 24 sts, K 16. Work 3 rows even on last 16 sts, keeping K 3 border on outer edge. Now dec 1 st every 4th row on neck edge and dec 1 st on outer edge (by knitting 4th and 5th st tog) every 8th row, until you have 2 sts, bind off. With red and royal blue, embroider 2 rows around collar as illustrated. Sew shoulder seams. Sew up sleeve seams, sew into armhole having fullness at top of sleeve. Sew pockets on inside of dress (do not stitch thru on right side). Sew on collar. Insert Zipper.

Instructions for the knitted doll dress and beret to match Goldilocks' dress shown here can be found on page 54.

Reprinted from *Juvenile Styles*, Volume 4, Page 16.

Colleen
No. 814
JERKIN, SOCKS AND BEANIE IN RED SPORTS YARN

Size 12

Needles—1 pair American Standard No. 4.

Material—Kashmir Sports—4 two ounce balls. Beanie—one ounce. 7 buttons.

Gauge—7 sts to 1 inch.

JERKIN

Back—Starting at bottom, cast on 104 sts, *K 2, P 4, repeat from *across, ending row with K 2. Next row, right side, K back. *Repeat these 2 rows for 1 inch. Dec 1 st at each end, repeat from *5 times, 6 inches (92 sts). Work 2 inches even. *Inc 1 st at each end, work 1 inch even, repeat from *for 5 times, 13 inches, 104 sts. Work ½ inch even. Bind off 7 sts at beg of the next 2 rows for underarm (90 sts). K 2 sts tog at beg of the next 12 rows (78 sts). Work even until armhole measures 8 inches, measuring straight up from where the 7 sts were bound off. On next K row, K 13 sts, K 1, P 1 ribbing to within last 13 sts. Bind off 5 sts at beg of the next 8 rows, continue to follow K 1, P 1 sts for back of neck, bind off remaining 38 sts.

Front—Work same as for back until piece measures 5 inches (having decreases and increases same on sides as back). On next row on right side, K 3, K 1, P 1 for 30 sts (border for pocket), K 28, P 1, K 1, for 30 sts (border for pocket), K 3. Follow pattern across row and, K 1, P 1, for pocket borders, for 1 inch. On next row, follow pattern to pocket borders, bind off K 1, P 1 borders, loosely in K 1, P 1.

Pockets—Cast on 30 sts. K 2, P 4 across row, ending P 4. K back. Continue pattern for 5 inches, put sts on st holder. Make another pocket with K 2 border, on opposite edge. Put on st holder also. On wrong side, follow pattern for 2 sts, insert 30 sts for pocket (following pattern), continue across row, inserting 2nd pocket. Continue same as for back, until piece measures 3 inches above armhole. Now work in pattern on first 13 sts for 5 inches, bind off 5 sts at armhole edge, 2 times, then bind off 3 remaining sts. Work last 13 sts in same manner.

Band at neck—Holding right side of work toward you, pick up 55 sts along left side of neck, K across 52 sts (center front), pick up 55 sts along right side. K 1, P 1, decreasing 2 sts at each corner, every row (always have decreases over previous decreases). On 4th row, inc 1 st at beg and end of row. When border measures 1 inch, bind off in K 1, P 1. Sew shoulder seams. Pick up 116 sts around armholes, K 1, P 1 for 1 inch, bind off K 1, P 1. Sew up right side seams. On left front, pick up 122 sts, K 1, P 1 for 3 rows. On next row, K 8, *bind off 4 sts for buttonhole, K 13, repeat from *5 times, bind off 4 for buttonhole, K 8. On next row, cast on 4 sts over those bound off. Work 4 more rows, bind off K 1, P 1 loosely. Work left back to correspond omitting buttonholes. Work 1 row of s c around bottom or turn under ½ inch. Sew pockets; do not have sts showing on right side. Sew on buttons.

BEANIE

With No. 4 needles, cast on 8 sts, P back. Row 2—Inc in each st (16 sts), P back. Row 4—*Inc 1 st, K 1 st, repeat from *across row (24 sts). P back, Row 6—*Inc 1 st, K 2 sts, repeat from *across row. Continue in this manner, having 1 more st between each increase, until you have 18 sts between each increase. K 1 row, P 1 row without increasing, for 6 rows. Now decrease in same manner as you increased. *K 2 sts tog, K 18, K 2 tog, repeat from *across row, P back. Decrease in this manner having 1 st less between each decrease for 5 more K rows. K 1 row on purled side (hem), then K 1 row, P 1 row for ½ inch, bind off loosely. Turn back ½ inch hem and sew.

SOCKS—No. 814

Needles—1 set No. 12 steel.

Material—Kashmer Sports—4 ounces.

Gauge—9 sts to 1 inch. Size 9.

Cast on 84 sts (30-30-24), K 1, P 1 for 1½ inches. K in pattern (K 4, P 2 for 1 rnd. K next rnd), until work measures 6½ inches from beg. K first 2 sts of first needle on 3rd needle. Dec 1 st at beg of first needle and 1 st at end of 3rd needle. Continue decreasing in this manner every ½ inch, 8 more times (66 sts). K even until work measures 11½ inches from beg or desired length.

Heel—K 15, slip last 15 sts of rnd on same needle (30 sts). Divide remaining sts evenly on 2 needles for instep. Work 2½ inches in stockenette st (K) on 30 heel sts, knitting the first and last st of every row, end with purled row.

To shape Heel—K 19, sl 1 st, K 1, p.s.s.o., turn, P 9, P 2 tog, turn. *K 9, sl 1 st, K 1, p.s.s.o., turn, P 9, P 2 tog, turn. Repeat from *until all sts are worked. K back 5 sts, this completes heel. Slip all instep sts on 1 needle. With another needle, K remaining 5 heel sts and pick up 16 sts along side of heel. With another needle, pick up 16 sts along other side of heel and K 5 remaining heel sts. Work 1 rnd even, keeping instep sts in pattern.

Instep—First needle: K to last 3 sts. K 2 tog, K 1. 2nd needle, work in pattern. 3rd needle, K 1, P 2 tog thru back of sts. K to end of needle. K 3 rnds even. Continue to dec in this manner every 4th rnd 3 more times (17 sts remaining on each of the first and 3rd needles). Continue to work even until foot measures 5½ inches from where sts were picked up at heel.

To shape Toe—First rnd: (K 8, K 2 tog) 7 times. K 2 rnds even. 4th rnd: (K 7, K 2 tog) 7 times; continue decreasing 7 sts every 3rd rnd in above manner, until there are 14 sts remaining, break thread, draw thru remaining sts, fasten securely. Weave elastic thread into wrong side of cuff with a tapestry needle.

Illustration 172. Colleen, a jerkin, socks and beanie, No. 814. *Juvenile Styles*, Volume 4, Page 23.

Slumber Time "Florella" Knitted Infants Set

FLORELLA KNITTED INFANT SET

Size 6 months

Needles—1 Pair American Standard No. 1 and No. 3.

Material—Saxony—3 fold. Sacque 2 one ounce balls. Cap—1 one ounce ball. Booties—one-half ounce.

Gauge—8 sts to 1 inch.

SACQUE

Starting at bottom, with No. 3 needles, cast on 191 sts, K 7 rows (4 ribs). P 1 row, K 1 row, for ½ inch, end with a purled row, K first and last 4 sts on purled rows for border. The following 13 rows form pattern: Row 1—K 5 *Y O, K 2 tog, repeat from * to last 4 sts, K 4. Row 2—And all even rows, K 4, P to last 4 sts, K 4. Row 3—K. Row 5—K 7, *Y O, K 2 tog, K 6, repeat from * to last 6 sts, K 6. Row 7—K 5, *K 2 tog, Y O, K 1, Y O, K 2 tog, K 3, repeat from * to last 5 sts, K 5. Row 9—Same as Row 5. Row 11—K. Row 13—Same as Row 1. P 1 row, K 1 row, until work measures 6 inches, ending with a purled row. Next row, K 52 sts, slip remaining sts on st holder, turn, P back, keeping border on edge. K 50 sts, K last 2 sts tog. Continue to dec in this manner on each K row, 4 more times, 47 sts, end with a purled row. Put these 47 sts on st holder, place 87 sts from st holder on needle for back, K 1 row, P 1 row. Now K first 2 sts and last 2 sts tog on each K row, 5 times, 77 sts. Slip these 77 sts on st holder with first 47 sts. Work on remaining 52 sts to correspond to other front. Put on st holder.

Sleeves—With No. 1 needles, cast on 56 sts, K 2, P 2 for 1¼ inches. With No. 3 needles, K 1 row P 1 row for ½ inch. Row 1—K 1, *Y O, K 2 tog, repeat from *ending row, K 1. Row 2 and all even rows P. Row 3—K. Row 5—K 3, *Y O, K 2 tog, K 6, repeat from * to last 3 sts, K 3. Row 7—K 1, *K 2 tog, Y O, K 1, Y O, K 2 tog, K 3, repeat from * to last 2 sts, K 2. Rows 9, 11, and 13, same as rows 5, 3, and 1. K 1 row, P 1 row until sleeve measures 5½ inches from beg. K 2 sts tog at beg and end of next 5 K rows, 46 sts. Work 2 rows even, end with a purled row, put on st holder. K other sleeve to correspond. Place sts of first front, then sleeves, back, 2nd sleeve and other front on one needle (263 sts).

Yoke—Holding right side of work toward you, K 5, *K 2 tog, K 1, K 2 tog, K 1, K 2 tog, K 1, K 2 tog, repeat from *11 times, K 2 tog, K 1, (K 2 tog, 13 times), *K 1, K 2 tog, K 1, K 2 tog, K 2, K 2 tog, repeat from *11 times, K 1, K 2 tog, K 6, 182 sts. First and alternate rows, K 4, P to last 4 sts, K 4. Row 2—K 2, Y O, K 2 tog (buttonhole), K 2, *Y O, K 3 tog, K 11, repeat from *12 times, Y O, K 2 tog, K 6. Row 4—K 6, *Y O, K 2 tog, K 11 repeat from *12 times, Y O, K 2 tog, K 6. Row 6—K 6, *Y O, K 3 tog, K 10, repeat from *12 times, Y O, K 2 tog, K 6. Row 8—K 6, *Y O, K 2 tog, K 4, Y O, K 2 tog, K 4, repeat from *12 times, Y O, K 2 tog, K 6. Row 10—K 2, Y O, K 2 tog (buttonhole), K 2 *Y O, K 3 tog, K 1, K 2 tog, Y O, K 1, Y O, K 2 tog, K 3, repeat from *12 times, Y O, K 2 tog, K 6. Row 12—K 6, *Y O, K 2 tog, K 3, Y O, K 2 tog, K 4, repeat from *12 times, Y O, K 2 tog, K 6. This row finishes flower pattern in yoke. Continue decreasing in this manner, knitting 3 tog instead of 2 tog every 4th row, making 1 st less between eyelets every 4th row. Work 1 more buttonhole in 18th row, work 2 more rows after buttonhole. Row 22—K 2, *Y O, K 2 tog, Y O, K 3 tog, repeat from *to last 3 sts, K 2 tog, K 1, (98 sts). P back. Change to No. 1 needles, work in K 2, P 2, ribbing for 5 rows, bind off. Sew sleeve seams at beg of decreased rows to body of sweater. With 2 strands of yarn, crochet a chain about 150 sts, tape thru beading, at neck or tape may be omitted, if desired.

CAP

With No. 1 needles, cast on 100 sts. Work in ribbing of K 2, P 2, for 1 inch. Change to No. 3 needles, K 1 row, P 1 row for ½ inch. Follow pattern as given for bottom of sacque to 5th row. Start 5th row with K 6 instead of K 7. On 7th row, start with K 4 instead of K 5, then K 1 row, P 1 row, until work measures 4 inches. Cast on 6 sts at end of next row; cast on 7 sts at end of next row. K 2 tog, K 11, *Y O, K 3 tog, K 11, repeat from *7 times, Y O, K 2 tog. Alternating rows, P. Now K 2 tog, K 10, *Y O, K 3 tog, K 10, repeat from *7 times, Y O, K 2 tog. Continue to dec this manner, having one st less on each K row between eyelets until 25 sts remain. K 2 tog across row. Break yarn and thread thru remaining sts. Draw tog and sew seam of crown to where sts were added. With No. 1 needles, pick up 88 sts across bottom of cap and K 2 sts, P 2 sts, for 4 rows. Next row, K 2, *Y O, K 2 tog, repeat from *across row. K 2, P 2 for 4 rows, Bind off. Make tape same as sacque.

LONG BOOTIES

With No. 1 needles, cast on 40 sts, K 2, P 2, for 1 inch. Change to No. 3 needles, follow pattern as given for sleeve of sacque. K 1 row, P 1 row, until work measures 4 inches.

Beading—K 1, *Y O, K 2 tog, repeat from *to last st, K 1. P back. K 1 row, P 1 row for 6 rows.

Instep—K 27, turn, P 14, turn. On these 14 sts, K 1 row, P 1 row for 6 rows. Pattern: Row 1—K 7, Y O, K 2 tog, K 5. P back. Row 3—K 5, K 2 tog, Y O, K 1, Y O, K 2 tog, K 4. P back. Row 5—Same as Row 1. Continue to P 1 row, K 1 row, for 7 more rows, (18 rows) for instep, end with a purled row, break thread. Holding right side toward you, join yarn to side of instep, pick up 15 sts on side of instep, knit across instep sts, and pick up 15 sts on other side of instep, K last 13 sts (70 sts). K 7 rows even. On next row, *dec 1 st at each edge and 4 sts spaced at equal distances apart. K 5 rows even. Repeat from *2 times (10 ribs), weave or bind off and sew seam at sole and back. With 2 strands of yarn, ch 90 sts, tape thru beading.

SHORT BOOTIES

With No. 3 needles, cast on 40 sts. K 8 rows. K 1 row, P 1 row for 3 rows. Follow pattern as given for sleeve of sacque. P 1 row, K 1 row for 3 rows. Follow directions given for long bootie beginning with beading.

Illustration 173. Florella knitted infant set, No. 900. *Juvenile Styles*, Volume 7, Page 4.

Snow Time Is Fun Time for Brother, Sister and Dolly...

SNOW SET

Size 1 year to 2 years

Needles—1 pair American Standard No. 3 and 5. 1 set double point Nos. 3 and 5 (for Mitts).

Material—Jacket—6 ounces Knitting Worsted—4 ply. Leggins—6 ounces. Caps—2 ounces each. Mittens—1 ounce. Buttons—12 Pearl. Angora—½ ball.

Gauge—5½ sts to 1 inch.

JACKET

Back—With No. 5 needles, cast on 58 sts (62 sts, size 2). K 5 rows, K 1 row, P 1 row until back measures 7 inches (7½ inches, size 2). Bind off 3 sts at beg of next 2 rows, then K 2 sts tog at beg of next 6 rows (46 sts). Work even for 4½ inches (5 inches, size 2), measuring straight up from where the 3 sts were bound off. Bind off 4 sts at beg of the next 6 rows, bind off remaining sts for back of neck.

Right Front—Cast on 46 sts (48 sts, size 2), K 6 rows. Row 1—K 3, P 2, K 6, (cable), P 2, K 10, (K 12 sts, size 2), P 2, K 6 (cable), P 2, K 13. Row 2—P 13, K 2, P 6, K 2, P 10, K 2, P 6, K 5. Repeat rows 1 and 2, once. On next row and every 8th row thereafter, twist cable on K 6 pattern in this manner, slip first 3 sts, as if purling onto double, pointed needle and hold in back of work, K next 3 sts then bring the slipped sts forward and K them. On next K row and every 8th row, work buttonhole as follows: K 2, bind off 1 st; cast on 1 st on next row over 1 st bound off. Work even until piece measures 2¾ inches from start. On next K row, K 3, P 2, K 6, P 2, inc in next st, K 8, inc in next st, P 2, K 6, P 2 dec 1 st. K 10, inc in last st. Continue increasing every 10th row (inc in first K st after first cable and last K st before 2nd cable) decreasing first K st after 2nd cable and inc in last st, until you have 4 center increases (54 sts). Work even until piece measures 7 inches from beg. (7½ inches, size 2). On next P row, bind off 4 sts for underarm, then P 2 tog at beg of every row at underarm, 3 times (47 sts). Work even for 3 inches, (3½ inches, size 2), measuring straight up from where the 4 sts were bound off. On next K row, K 3, P 2, K 6, P 2, K 5, bind off 8 sts, K 5, P 2, K 6, P 2, K 6. Dec 1 st at beg of every row at neck edge, until you have 15 sts. Bind off 7 sts at beg of next 2 rows at shoulder and continue to dec 1 st at neck edge. Work 2nd shoulder, decreasing same as first shoulder until 12 sts remain, bind off 6 sts at beg of next 2 rows at border edge. Pick up these 12 sts on right side, K back. Next row, K 2, bind off 1 st, on next row, cast on 1 st over 1 bound off. K 1 row, bind off.

Left Front—Cast on 13 sts (15 sts, size 2), K 5 rows. K 1 row, next row, K 3, P to end of row. Repeat these 2 rows, until piece measures 2¾ inches. On next K row, inc in first st, K 7, K 2 tog, K 3. Continue to inc and dec, every 10th row, until you have 4 increases and 4 decreases. Work even until piece measures 7 inches (7½ inches, size 2). Bind off 4 sts at beg of next row at underarm, then K 2 tog at beg of every row at underarm, 3 times (6 sts left). Work even for 4½ inches, (5 inches, size 2). Bind off 6 sts.

Sleeve—With No. 3 needles, cast on 38 sts (42 sts, size 2). K 1 st, P 1 st for 1¼ inches. Change to No. 5 needles, next row, K 14, P 2, K 6 (cable) P 2, K 14. Next row P 14, K 2, P 6, K 2, P 14. Repeat these 2 rows, twisting cable on 5th row and every 8th row thereafter thru-out sleeve and inc every 8th row until sleeve measures 7 inches, 48 sts (8 inches, size 2). Bind off 3 sts at beg of next 2 rows, then K 2 tog at beg and end of every 4th row, until you have 30 sts, K 2 tog at beg and end of every row until 24 sts remain, bind off. Sew shoulder seams.

Band at Neck—Pick up 58 sts, K 1 st P 1 st for 6 rows, making buttonhole on 2nd row: K 1, P 1, K 1 bind off 1 st, cast on 1 st over 1 bound off on next row. Bind off K 1, P 1.

Finishing—Sew up seams at underarm. Sew sleeves tog, insert sleeves into armholes. With Angora, work 1 row of s c around right front and neck. On side of band at neck and the shoulder at back, pick up 12 sts, K 4 rows, bind off.

LEGGINS

Cuff—With No. 3 needles, cast on 40 sts (46 sts, size 2), K 1 st, P 1 st for 14 rows. Change to No. 5 needles, K 1, P 1 for 3 more rows. K next row, increasing every 6th st across row. P 1 row, K 1 row, increasing every 6th row at beg and end, until you have 62 sts. Now inc in every 4th row, until you have 69 sts. Inc in every 2nd row until you have 78 sts (87 sts, size 2), or desired length to crotch. Work 2 rows even. *On next K row, bind off 2 sts, K to end of row. On next purled row, P 2 sts tog (place marker for back) repeat from *once. Work 2 rows even, dec 1 st at beg and end of next 2 K rows. Now dec 1 st every 6th row at front edge, 6 times, meanwhile dec every 8th row at back edge, 2 times. Work 6 rows even (10 rows, size 2). On next purled row, P 28, turn, slip first st, K to back edge, P 22, K back, P 16, K back, P 10, K back. P 5, K back. P across all sts. Change to No. 3 needles, K 1, P 1 for 4 rows. On next row, K 2, *Y O, K 2 tog, repeat from *across row, K 1, P 1 for 4 more rows, bind off loosely, K 1, P 1. Work other leg to correspond. Sew each leg tog up to crotch; sew front and back seams. With 2 strands of yarn, ch 160 sts, insert thru beading.

With No. 5 needles, cast on 28 sts.
Row 1—P 2, K 6 (cable), P 2, K 8, P 2, K 6 (cable), P 2. Next row, K 2, P 6, K 2, P 8, K 2, P 6, K 2. Repeat these 2 rows and twist cable on 5th row, then every 8th row thereafter. Now inc 1 st in first and last sts of center panel, every inch until you have 5 inches (38 sts). Work ½ inch even. Now cast on 5 sts at end of the next 8 rows and 7 sts at end of next 2 rows, continuing cable (92 sts). Working these sts, stockenette. *Now dec 1 st on each side of center panel and 1 st at beg and end of next row, work 1 inch even repeat from * once. (84 sts). Work even until piece measures 4 inches measuring from where the first 5 sts were cast on. With No. 3 needles, work in ribbing K 1, P 1 for 6 rows, with angora and No. 5 needles, P 1 row on right side of work. Now P 1 row on wrong side. K 1 row, P 1 row (this will turn back with Purling for right side) until angora piece measures 1½ inches, bind off on wrong side of band. Leave an end of Angora long enough to sew to beginning of the K 1, P 1 band. Sew sides to back piece.

With No. 3 needle, pick up 52 sts on bottom of cap, including the K 1, P 1 along sides. K 1 st, P 1 st for 4 rows, bind off K 1, P 1. Pick up 4 sts for chin band on side of front ribbing and K in garter sts on these 4 sts for 4½ inches, K 1, bind off 1, K 2. Next row K 2 and cast on 1 st over 1 bound off, K 1. Work 2 more rows, bind off.

BOY'S KNIT CAP

With No. 3 needles, cast on 7 sts, P back. Row 2—Inc in every st (14 sts), P back. Row 4—*Inc 1 st, K 1 st, repeat from *across row (21 sts), P back. Row 6—*Inc 1 st, K 2 sts, repeat from *across row. Continue in this manner having 1 more st between each inc, until you have 9 sts between each inc (77 sts). With No. 5 needles, K in garter st for 6 rows (3 ribs). Bind off 11 sts loosely at beg of the next 2 rows, continuing in garter st. Cast on 9 sts at beg of the next 2 rows. Next row K 8, P 1, right side K across to within last 9 sts, P 1, K 8. K next row. Repeat these last 2 rows in this manner until you have 3 inches from bound off sts. Bind off 9 sts for turn back at beg of next 2 rows, cast on 11 sts at end of next 2 rows. K in garter st for 6 more rows. Now dec same as you increased. With No. 3 needle, *K 9, K 2 tog, repeat from *across row, P back. *K 8, K 2 tog, repeat from *across row. P back. Continue decreasing in this manner until you have 7 sts, draw yarn thru sts and sew wheel tog. With Angora work 1 row of s c around bound off sts on wheel and turn-back. Tack turn-back to cap. Skip 1 inch on wheel at back, pick up 4 sts, K in garter st for 4½ inches, K 1, bind off 1, K 2. Next row, K 1 and cast on 1 st over 1 bound off. Work 2 more rows, bind off.

MITTENS

Left Mitten—With No. 3 needles, cast on 8 sts on first needle, 14 sts on second needle, 10 sts on third needle, with 4th needle, K 1, P 1, for 6 rnds. Next rnd, *Y O, K 2 tog, repeat from * for 1 rnd. K 1, P 1, for 6 rnds. Change to No. 5 needles. First needle K, second needle K 2, P 2, K 6, P 2, K 2, third needle K. Work 3 more rnds.

Thumb Gore—First needle, K first 4 sts and slip them to third needle, K 1, K 1, inc 1, K 1, work to end of rnd, twisting cable on 5th rnd, then every 8th rnd. Work 1 rnd even. Next rnd, inc 1, K 3, inc 1, K 3, P 2, K 6, P 2, K 2 to end of rnd. Work 1 rnd even. K 1, K 5, inc 1, work to end of rnd. Work 1 rnd even. Slip 10 sts from first needle to st holder. On first needle, cast on 4 sts, work over second needle, K 9 sts from third needle, slip remaining sts from third needle to first needle, and work until piece measures 2¾ inches from end of ribbing. Slip 1 st from end of first needle to second needle, slip 1 st from beg of third needle to end of second needle. First needle, K to within 3 sts of end, sl 1 st, K 1 st, psso, K 1, second needle, K 1, K 2 tog, work to within 3 sts of end, sl 1, K 1, psso, K 1, third needle, K 1, K 2 tog, K to end of needle. Work 1 rnd even. Repeat these 2 rnds until 12 sts remain. Weave tog, or bind off and sew.

Thumb—Divide 10 thumb sts on 3 needles. Join yarn and pick up 4 sts over 4 cast on sts. On first row, dec 2 sts over 4 picked up sts, then work even for 1 inch. K 2 tog for 1 rnd. Break yarn and thread through remaining sts. Fasten securely.

Right Mitten—Work same as for left hand until beg of thumb gore. Work over first and second needles, third needle, inc 1, K 1, inc 1, K 1, slip remaining sts from third needle to first needle. Finish same as left mitten increasing on the third needle instead of the first needle. Ch 80 sts, tape thru beading of cuff.

DOLLY'S SNOW SUIT

Needles—1 set No. 3 double pointed, American Standard.

Material—1 two-ounce ball, sports Yarn, Baby Blue. 12 yards of White Angora. 7 small pearl buttons.

Gauge—7 sts to 1 inch.

These instructions may be used for the 14″ MARY HOYER Doll.

Jacket—Cast on 20 sts (tightly) for back. K 3 rows, P 1 row, K 1 row, for 1½ inches, increasing 2 sts on each side. Bind off 2 sts on each side, for underarm (20 sts), work even for 1¼ inches. Bind off 3 sts at beg of next 4 rows, bind off remaining 8 sts for back of neck.

Right Front—Cast on 21 sts, K 3 rows. Row 1—P 4, K 1, P 4, K 1, P 3, K 1, P 4, K 1, K 2 (border). Row 2—

Right side, K 2 (border), P 1, K 4 (cable), P 1, K 3, P 1, K 4 (cable), P 1, K 4. Repeat Row 1. Always keep 2 border sts K on purled rows. Next row, 4th row, twist cable, (and every 8th row thereafter). To twist cable, sl first 2 cable sts on double pointed needle, then K next 2 sts, K 2 sts from cable needle. On 3 K sts between cable inc 1 st after the P st, and before the next P st, every 6th row twice (25 sts). When piece measures 1½ inches, bind off 2 sts for underarm. Work even for 1 inch. On right side work in pattern for 8 sts, bind off center 7 sts between cable, on last 8 sts, work in pattern for 4 rows, K 2 tog at neck edge once. Bind off 3 sts at beg of the next 2 rows at shoulder, dec 1 more st at neck edge. Work other shoulder to correspond, do not bind off 6 sts for shoulder but K 3 rows for border, bind off.

Left Front—Cast on 6 sts, K 3 rows, P 1 row, K 1 row for 1½ inches, always keeping first 2 sts K on purled rows for border. Bind off 2 sts for underarm, work even for 1¼ inches, bind off. Sew shoulders together.

Sleeves—Pick up center 6 sts, P back, pick up 2 sts, turn, K across inc in every other st, pick up 2 sts. P back. Next row K 6, P 1, K 4, P 1, K 4. Pick up 2 sts. Continue following pattern picking up 2 sts at end of every row, until you have 26 sts. Now K 1 row, P 1 row, following pattern for ½ inch, dec 1 st on each side. Work cable on center K 4 sts, same as for front. *Work 1 inch even, dec 1 st on each side, repeat from *once. Work until sleeve measures 3½ inches from underarm (20 sts). K 1, P 1, for 5 rows, bind off. Work other sleeve to correspond.

Band—Pick up 28 sts on right side starting at border and ending on shoulder. K 1 st, P 1 st for 4 rows, bind off and work 6 s c along this side of shoulder to sew on buttons, for 2 rows.

Finishing—With Angora, work 1 row s c making ch 2 loops for buttonholes, 4 up the side and 2 over shoulder, continue around neck band. Sew up side seams and sleeve seams.

Ski Pants—Cast on 40 sts, 12 sts on 1st needle, 12 sts on 2nd needle, 16 sts on 3rd needle. K 2, P 2 for 1 inch. Inc 8 sts, about every 5th st, 48 sts. K plain for 1¾ inches. Put 24 sts on st holder, cast on 8 sts for crotch: on these 32 sts, K 5½ inches. Cuff: K 2 sts tog until you have 16 sts. K 2, P 2 for 1 inch. Put 24 sts on 3 needles, pick up 8 sts on crotch, work to correspond to other leg.

Cap—Cast on 17 sts, K 1, P 1, K 4 (cable), P 1, K 3, P 1, K 4 (cable), P 1, K 1. Next row, P 1, K 1, P 4, K 1, P 3, K 1, P 1, P 4, K 1, P 1. Repeat these 2 rows once. Next row, twist cable and twist cable every 8th row thereafter. Work in pattern for 1 inch. Inc 2 sts on center K 3 sts. Work 1 inch even. Inc 2 more sts. Work 4 rows even. Now cast on 4 sts at beg of the next 8 rows (53 sts) working these sts in stockinette st. Work 1 inch even make 4 decreases same manner as you increased (49 sts). When piece measures 2¼ inches dec 5 sts across row.

On right side. P back with angora. Now P on wrong side. Now K 1 row, P 1 row (the purling will be on the right side when turned back), for 6 more rows, bind off. Sew on right side to beg of angora. Pick up 40 sts around bottom, K 1 st, P 1 st, for 3 rows, bind off K 1, P 1. Do not break thread. Pick up 3 sts for chin strap on end of K 1, P 1. K in garter sts for 2 inches, bind off, leaving an end to make a ch 2 for buttonhole.

Reprinted from *Juvenile Styles*, Volume 7, Page 12.

Illustration 174. Snow set, No. 904. Note the doll on the little sled. *Juvenile Styles*, Volume 7, Page 12.

Little Mama...
Little Dolly Lace Baby Dresses

Size 3 *years*

1 *Steel Crochet hook, size* 7.

Materials—4 *balls*—400 *yds. Mercerized Cotton or Pearl Cotton.*

Gauge—10 *d c to* 1 *inch.*

Starting at bottom, ch 483, work 1 d c in 4th ch from hook, 1 d c in each ch to end of row, join with a sl st (do not twist), ch 3. Row 2—Work 1 d c in each of the next 18 d c, *ch 3, skip 2 d c, sl st in next st, ch 3, sl st in same st (a pico made), ch 4, skip 2 d c, 1 d c in each of the next 19 d c, repeat from *around row, ending row with an open pattern, sl st in ch 3 at beg of row. Row 3—Ch 3, make a dec as follows: wrap Y O needle, insert needle in next d c, draw thru, draw thru next d c, draw thru 3 loops, draw thru 2 loops, 1 d c in each of the next 14 d c, make a dec. *Ch 3, sl st in center of ch 3 of row below, ch 5, sl st in 2nd ch of next ch 4, ch 4, make a dec, d c in next 15 d c, make a dec, repeat from *ending row with an open pattern, sl st in ch 3 at beg of row. Row 4—Ch 3, work 5 d c in next 5 d c, ch 3, skip 2 d c, pico in next st, ch 4, skip 2 d c, work 6 d c in next 6 d c. *Ch 3, pico in center of ch 5, ch 4, 6 d c in next 6 d c, ch 3, skip 2 d c, pico in next st, ch 4, skip 2 d c, 6 d c in next 6 d c, repeat from *around row, join. Row 5—Ch 3, work 5 d c in next 5 d c, *ch 3, sl st in center of ch 3 of row below, ch 5, sl st in 2nd ch of next ch 4, ch 4, 6 d c in next 6 d c, repeat from *around row, join. Row 6—Ch 3, 5 d c in next 5 d c, ch 2, s c in center of ch 5, of row below, ch 2, work 6 d c in next 6 d c. Ch 3, pico in center of ch 5 of row below, ch 4, *6 d c in next 6 d c, ch 2, s c in center of ch 5, ch 2, 6 d c in next 6 d c. Ch 3, pico in center of ch 5, ch 4, repeat from *around row,

join. Row 7—Ch 3, work 16 d c in next 16 sts, *ch 3, sl st in center of ch 3, ch 5, sl st in 2nd ch of ch 4, ch 4, work 17 d c, repeat from *around row, join with a sl st, ch 3. Rows 8 to 18—Follow pattern decreasing 1 d c at beg and end of every d c group on the 9th, 15th, 21st, 27th, 33rd and 39th rows. Work 4 more rows even, join with a sl st. On 44th row, sl st over 3 d c, ch 3, work 2 d c in next 2 d c, follow pattern around row, ending row with 3 d c, ch 3, turn. Row 45—Follow pattern and make 1 dec in center of d c group. Remainder of dress is made with 4 d c between open patterns. Work back and forth following pattern until you have 50 rows from beg, or desired length to underarm. Work over 5 d c groups and 4 open patterns for back, for 12 rows, decreasing 1 d c at armhole edge at end of 2 rows. Work 2 d c on armhole edge and 2 open patterns, 2 d c groups, continue in pattern for 7 rows. On 8th row work over 1 d c group, 1 open pattern, 2 d c, 2 s c, fasten off for slanting shoulder. Fasten thread at 5th d c group at underarm and work to correspond to other side of back. Skip 2 open patterns and 1 d c group for underarm and work over 9 d c groups and 8 open patterns for front for 10 rows. Work shoulder same as for back for 9 rows, work ½ row same as back. Sew shoulder seams.

Sleeves—Ch 62 (to measure 7 inches). Work 1 d c in 4th ch, work 1 d c in each ch to end of row, (59 d c). Ch 3, turn, work 1 d c in each st, ch 3, turn. Row 3—Work 1 d c in each of the next 7 d c, *ch 3, skip 2 d c, pico in next st, ch 4, skip 2 d c, 8 d c in next 8 sts, repeat from *across row. Work 4 more rows following open pattern same as for dress and inc 1 d c in each d c group on every row. Row 8—Inc 2 extra d c on end d c groups, thus increasing 3 sts. Row

218

9—Ch 1, turn, sl st over 5 d c for underarm, ch 2, follow pattern across but do not inc in the first and last d c group, working only to within last 6 d c. Rows 10, 11, 12 and 13 and 14—Ch 2, turn, dec 1 st at beg of every row and dec 1 st in last 2 d c, do not d c in last ch (thus decreasing 2 sts at end of row), following pattern as before. Row 15—Ch 3, sl st in center of ch 5, ch 3, work 7 d c, ch 3, skip 2 d c, pico in next st, ch 4, follow pattern across row, do not inc for remainder of sleeve, end row with ch 3, sl st in ch 5, ch 2, d c in last d c. Row 16—Ch 3, d c in first d c, turn, follow pattern across row, end row with d c in last ch. 3. Row 17—Ch 2, turn, make a dec, follow pattern across row and (ch 2, s c, ch 2). Over 3 center patterns, end row with a dec in last 2 d c. Work 3 more rows making decreases in same d c group at beg and end as before. Work 1 more row, Ch 1, s c in next st, 2 h d c in next 2 sts. D c across row to within last 5 d c, 2 h d c 2 s c, sl st in last st. Break thread. Insert sleeves into armholes.

Reprinted from *Juvenile Styles,* Volume 7, Page 16.

Illustration 175. Lace dress, No. 906. Dolly is dressed in a miniature version of the same dress. *Juvenile Styles,* Volume 7, Page 16.

Illustration 176. Detail of the sleeve of the lace dress. *Juvenile Styles,* Volume 7, Page 16.

Instructions for the matching lace doll dress can be found on page 68.

"Love at first sight"

SLIP-OVER AND JERKIN

Size 4 to 6 years
Needles—1 Pair American Standard No. 2 and 4.
Material—Kashmir Sports, 2 two ounce balls each for Slip Over and Jerkin.
Gauge—7 sts to 1 inch.

SLIP-OVER

Back—With No. 2 needles, starting at bottom, cast on 74 sts (78 sts, size 6), K 1 st, P 1 st, for 2½ inches.

Size 4—Change to No. 4 needles, work pattern as follows: (on wrong side). Row 1—P 2 tog to make 73 sts for pattern for size 4 only. P 3, *sl 1, P 1, sl 1, P 1, sl 1, P 7, repeat from *across row, ending, P 4. Next row, (right side) K 3, *P 7, K 5, repeat from *across row, ending P 7, K 3. Next row, P 4, *sl 1, P 1, sl 1, P 1, sl 1, P 7, repeat from *across row, end row, P 4.

Size 6—P 4, *sl 1, P 1, sl 1, P 1, sl 1, P 8, repeat from *across row ending, P 4. Next row, right side, K 3, *P 7, K 6, repeat from *across row ending K 3. Repeat these last 2 rows of each pattern, until piece measures 7 inches from start (7½ inches, size 6). Bind off 3 sts at beg of the next 2 rows, for underarm, then bind off 2, at beg of the next 2 rows. Now K 2 tog at beg of the next 16 rows, 47 sts. Work even until armhole measures 6 inches from where the 3 sts were bound off (6½ inches, size 6). Bind off 4 sts at beg of the next 6 rows, bind off remaining 23 sts for back of neck.

Front—Work same as for back to end of armhole shaping. On next row, work pattern over 23 sts, follow pattern to end of row (dividing for V neck). K 2 tog and follow pattern over last 22 sts only, K 2 tog at beg of every 6th row at neck edge, until you have 14 sts, when armhole measures same as for back, bind off 4 sts at beg of the next 3 rows and K 2 tog at beg of every row at neck edge. Work other side to correspond.

Band at Neck—With No. 2 needles, pick up 24 sts across back of neck, K 1 st, P 1 st, for ¾ inch, bind off loosely, K 1, P 1. Pick up 108 sts on front, K 1, P 1, for ¾ inch, decreasing 2 sts at center front on every row. Sew shoulder seams.

Armbands—Pick up 136 sts, K 1, P 1, for ¾ inch. Sew side seams.

JERKIN

Back—With No. 2 needles, starting at bottom, cast on 78 sts (83 sts, size 6), K 1 st, P 1 st for 2½ inches.

Size 4—Change to No. 4 needles, work in pattern as follows: K 1, st, P 1 st, for 8 sts, P 1, *sl 1, P 1, sl 1, P 1, sl 1, P 7, repeat from *across row, ending P 4. Next row, K 3, *P 7, K 5, repeat from *across row ending P 7, K 1, P 1 over 8 sts.

Size 6—K 1 st, P 1 st, for 8 sts, P 1, *sl 1, P 1, sl 1, P 1, sl 1, P 8, repeat from *across row, ending P 4. Next row, K 3, *P 7, K 6, repeat from *across row, end row P 7, K 1, P 1 for 8 sts. Repeat these last 2 rows for pattern to underarm, 8 inches from start (8½ inches, size 6) bind off the 8, K 1, P 1, sts, follow pattern to end of row. Bind off 3 sts at beg of next row. Now bind off 2 sts at the beginning of the next 2 rows. K 2 sts tog at beg of the next 16 rows, 49 sts. Work even until piece measures 6 inches (6½ inches, size 6). Then bind off 5 sts at the beg of the next 6 rows, bind off remaining 19 sts for back of neck.

Front—Work front same as for back to 1 inch above armhole shaping (work K 1, P 1 sts on opposite side to correspond to back). Work 6 buttonholes (K 1, P 1, K 1 bind off 3, K 1, P 1. Next row, cast on 3 sts over those bound off), about every 15th and 16th rows apart, the first one about 11th and 12th rows. The 7th buttonhole is worked in 5th and 6th row of ribbing on armhole. work in pattern for 15 sts, bind off 19, work last 15 sts until armhole measures 6 inches (6½ inches, size 6) bind off 5 sts, 3 times. Work other side to correspond. Sew shoulder seams.

Band at Neck—With No. 2 needles, pick up 20 sts for back of neck, K 1 st, P 1 st for ¾ inch, bind off. Pick up 84 sts, 32 side, 20 front, 32 side. K 1, P 1, decreasing 2 sts at each corner, every row (always have decreases over previous decreases). On 4th row, inc 1 st at beg and end of row. When border measures ¾ inch, bind off, K 1, P 1.

Armbands—Pick up 136 sts, K 1, P 1, for ¾ inch. Sew right side seams.

Reprinted from *Juvenile Styles,* Volume 7, Page 19.

Illustration 177. Slip-over and jerkin, No. 907. *Juvenile Styles,* Volume 7, Page 18.

Illustration 178. Cable turtle neck and cable jacket, No. 913. *Juvenile Styles,* Volume 7, Page 27.

"My Sister and I" Are Two-of-A-Kind...

CABLE TURTLE NECK
Size 8 to 10 years

Needles—American Standard No. 3 and 5.

Material—Knitting Worsted, 4 four ounce skeins.

Scale—6 sts to 1 inch (after cable is twisted).

Back—Starting at bottom, with No. 3 needles, cast on 76 (size 10, 80 sts). K 2 sts, P 2 sts, for 3 inches. Change to No. 5 needles, on next row, inc 1 st, K across, inc last st. Next row, K 6, P 6, repeat from *across row, end row, K 6. Repeat these 2 rows, 4 more times. On right side, make cable as follows: *K 6, sl next 3 sts on cable needle, place needle at back of work, K next 3 sts, then K sts from cable needle, repeat from *across row. Cable is twisted every 12th row thru-out sweater. Work even until piece measures 12 inches, or desired length to underarm. Bind off 3 sts at beg of the next 2 rows, K 2 tog at beg of the next 4 rows (68 sts). Work even until armhole measures 6 inches (6½ inches, size 10), K 20, bind off 28, K 20, on the last 20 sts, bind off 6 sts at beg of the next 3 rows at armhole edge and K 2 tog at neck edge. Work other side to correspond.

Front—Work same as for back until armhole measures 4 inches from underarm. K 26, bind off 16, K 26. K 2 tog at beg of every row at neck edge, until 20 sts remain. Bind off 6 sts at beg of the next 3 rows at shoulder and dec 1 st at neck edge until all sts are bound off. Work other 26 sts to correspond.

Sleeves—With No. 3 needles, cast on 40 sts, K 2, P 2 ribbing for 2 inches. Change to No. 5 needles and inc 1 st, K across, inc in last st. K 6, P 6 across row, end with K 6. K across. Now follow pattern increasing 1 st at both ends every inch, until sleeve measures 12 inches, 62 sts, work 1 inch even or desired length to underarm. Bind off 3 sts at beg of the next 2 rows, K 2 tog at beg and end of every 4th row until you have 42 sts. K 2 tog at beg and end of the next 8 rows (26 sts), bind off. Sew shoulder seams.

Turtle Neck Band—With No. 3 needles, pick up 52 sts at front, K 2, P 2, ribbing, for 4 inches. Pick up 40 sts at back and K 2, P 2 for 4 inches. Sew ends together and shoulders. Sew up seams at underarm, sew up sleeve seams, insert into armhole.

CABLE JACKET
Size 8 to 10 years

Needles—American Standard No. 5.

Material—Knitting Worsted, 4 four ounce skeins. 7 buttons.

Scale—6 sts to 1 inch (After Cable is twisted).

Starting at bottom, cast on 162 sts (Size 10, 174 sts), K 7 rows (4 ribs). K 6, P 6 across row, end row, K 6. K 1 row. Repeat these 2 rows, 5 more times. On right side, make cable as follows: *K 6, slip next 3 sts on cable needle, place needle at back of work, K next 3 sts, then K sts on cable needle, repeat from *across row. When work measures 2½ inches or every 21st and 22nd rows (22nd and 23rd rows, size 10), from bottom, make buttonhole as follows: On right side of work K 3, bind off 2, K 1, follow pattern. Work buttonhole every 2½ inches 5 more times, last buttonhole is made in neck band. Cable is twisted every 12th row thru-out sweater. Work even until you have 4 cables and work 6 more rows in pattern. Now work ribbing and cable for wastline as follows: On wrong side, K 6, *P 6, K 2, P 2, K 2, repeat from *across row. Next row, K 12, *P 2, K 2, P 2, K 6, repeat from *across, ending with K 12. Repeat these 2 rows 4 more times, then cable, work 6 more rows. Now continue as before until piece measures 12 inches, from bottom (12½ inches, size 10), K 40 (44, size 10), (front), bind off 6, K 70 (74 st, size 10) (back), bind off 6, K 40 (44, size 10), (front). Work even on these 40 sts front and K 2 tog at armhole edge, 3 times. When piece measures 16 inches, (16½ inches, size 10), bind off 8 sts at neck edge and dec 1 st at neck edge at beg of every row, until 21 sts remain. Now bind off 6 sts at armhole edge 3 times and continue to dec at neck until all sts are bound off. Attach yarn on wrong side of back, follow pattern for 1 row, now dec 1 st at beg of the next 4 rows. Work even until back measures 6 inches (6½ inches, size 10). Bind off 6 sts at beg of the next 6 rows, bind off remaining 30 sts for back of neck. Work other front to correspond.

Sleeves—Cast on 40 sts, K 2, P 2, ribbing for 2 inches. Next row, inc 1 st, K across, inc in last st. K 6, P 6 across row, end with K 6. K back. Now follow pattern increasing 1 st at both ends every inch until sleeve measures 12 inches (62 sts). Work 1 inch even or desired length to underarm. Bind off 3 sts at beg of the next 2 rows, then bind off 2 sts at beg of the next 2 rows. Now K 2 tog at beg and end of every 4th row until 32 sts remain. (30 sts, size 10). K 2 tog at beg and end of every row, until you have 22 sts, bind off. Sew shoulder seams.

Neck Band—Pick up 25 sts on each front, 26 across back, (76 sts). K 6, K 2, P 2 across, K last 6 sts. On next row, K 3, bind off 2, follow pattern across and work 5 more rows, bind off. Sew sleeve seams and insert into armhole having a little fullness at top of sleeve.

Illustration 179. Boy's and girl's vests, No. 914. Juvenile Styles, Volume 7, Page 28.

'TEEN TEAM -

BOY'S AND GIRL'S VESTS
Size 14 to 16

Needles—1 pair American Standard No. 3 and 5.
Materials—Knitting Worsted, 4 ply, 10 ounces. 4 leather or wooden buttons.
Gauge—5½ sts to 1 inch.

BOY'S VEST

Back—With No. 3 needles, cast on 86 sts (90 sts, size 16). K 1 st, P 1 st, for 3 inches. Change to No. 5 needles, P 2 (P 4, size 16), *K 4, P 2, repeat from *across row, ending row with P 2 (P 4, size 16). Next row, K 2, (K 4, size 16) *P 4, K 2, repeat from *across row, end with K2 (K 4, size 16). Repeat these 2 rows for 12 inches from beg (12½ size 16). Bind off 5 sts at beg of the next 2 rows, bind off 2 sts at beg of the next 2 rows. Now K 2 tog at beg of every row, until you have 12 sts off on each side, 62 sts. Work even for 10 inches (10½ inches, size 16), measuring straight up from where the 5 sts were bound off. Bind off 6 sts at beg of the next 6 rows, bind off remaining 26 sts for back of neck.

Left Front—With No. 3 needles, cast on 54 sts (56 sts, size 16), K 1 st, P 1 st for 3 inches. Put first 10 sts on st holder (to be worked later for ribbing). With No. 5 needles, K 2, *P 4, K 2, repeat from *across row ending row K 2 (K 4, size 16). Next row, P 2 (P 4, size 16), *K 4, P 2, repeat from *across row, end row, P 2. Repeat these 2 rows until you have 7 rows, on 8th row, work cable over first and every other K 4 rib as follows: Sl first 2 sts to double pointed needle, hold in back of work, then K 2 sts, K 2 sts from double pointed needle. Work 7 rows even then work another cable, twist over 2nd and every other rib of K 4 across row. Work 7 rows even. Work even in this manner to underarm. Dec at armhole edge same as for back and K 2 tog at beg of every 3rd row at neck edge, until you have 18 sts. Work even on 18 sts until armhole measures same as for back. Bind off 6 sts at beg of every row at shoulder edge 3 times. Work Right Front to correspond.

Border—With No. 3 needles, continue with 10 K 1, P 1 sts from st holder and work buttonholes as follows: Starting yarn at inside of border, P 1, K 1, P 1, bind off 3, K 1, P 1, K 1, P 1. On next row, cast on 3 sts over those bound off. Work buttonhole every 2½ inches, 3 more times. Continue border until piece measures around sweater after sewing shoulder seams. When sewing on border, stretch slightly. Weave or bind off and sew to border sts at front.

Armholes—With No. 3 needles, pick up 120 sts, K 1, P 1 for ¾ inches, bind off K 1, P 1.

GIRL'S VEST

Back—With No. 3 needles, cast on 86 sts, K 5 rows. Change to No. 5 needles, work same as for back of Boy's Sweater.

Right Front—With No. 3 needles, cast on 50 sts, (52 sts, size 16), K 5 rows in garter st, K first 6 sts, put on st holder (to be K later). With No. 5 needles, P 2, *K 4, P 2, repeat from *across row ending P 2 (P 4, size 16). Next row, K 2, *P 4, K 2, repeat from *across row, ending K 2. Repeat these 2 rows and work pattern same as for boy's. Work Left Front to correspond, casting on 6 sts less, the border will be continued from right front.

Border—With No. 3 needles, continue with the 6 K sts from st holder and work buttonhole 1½ inches from bottom as follows: K 2, bind off 2, K 2. On next row, cast on 2 sts over those bound off. Work buttonhole every 2½ inches, 3 more times. Finish sweater same as boy's.

Reprinted from *Juvenile Styles*, Volume 7, Page 28.

"watch the birdie, *Honey*

SMOCKED DRESS

1 Pair Needles, American Standard, 14 inch, Nos. 2 & 4.
Material—Light Weight 3 ply or Baby Yarn — 4 one ounce balls. 10 yards of Angora. 4 small pearl buttons.
Gauge—7½ sts to 1 inch.
Pattern—Multiple of 3 plus 2.

Size	1 Yr.	3 Yrs.

Starting at neck, with No. 2 needles, cast on 122 sts 122 sts *P 2, K 1, repeat from * across row, ending row, P 2 (right side). Next row, *K 2, P 1, repeat from * across row, ending row K 2. Repeat these 2 rows for ¾". On wrong side, *inc 1 st, K 1, P 1, repeat from * across row, ending row, inc 1 st, K 1. 163 sts 163 sts On next row, *P 3, K 1, repeat from * across row, ending row, P 3. Next row, *K 3, P 1, repeat from * across, ending row, K 3, repeat these last 2 rows until yoke measures 2½" 3"
Change to No. 4 needles, on right side, K 27 back, inc 1 st, place marker, inc 1 st, K 26 sleeve, inc 1 st, place marker, inc 1 st, K 49 front, inc 1 st, place marker, inc 1 st, K 26 sleeve, inc 1 st, place marker, inc 1 st, K 27, back. P back. Inc in this manner on K rows, before and after each marker (on this row only, inc in every 3rd st on sleeves only) on every K row, until raglan sleeve below yoke measures 3" 3½" K to end of first sleeve, P back between sleeve markers and K 1 row, P 1 row, on sleeve, until sleeve measures 1" 1¼" from underarm. K 3, K 2 tog across row. Change to No. 2 needles, on right side, P 2, K 1. On next row, follow pattern same as yoke for 1½", bind off. K across front and 2nd sleeve, (put front on st holder.) Work 2nd sleeve to correspond to first. K over 2nd half of back, joining backs. On next K row, *K 2, inc 1 st, repeat from *3 more times. K across row to within 12 sts, *inc 1 st, K 2, repeat from *3 more times. *Work 1 inch even, inc 1 st at beg and end of next row, work ¾" even, inc 1 st at beg and end of next row, repeat from *until skirt measures 12" 13" or desired length. On next row on right side, K 1, *Y O, K 2 tog, repeat from * across row. P 1 row, K 1 row for 5 rows, bind off. Work front to correspond.

Pockets—Cast on 14 sts 16 sts P 1 row, K 1 row, increasing 1 st at beg and end of every K row until you have 20 sts 22 sts Work even until pocket measures 2" 2½" Change to No. 2 needles, P 2, K 1 in pattern for ¾" ¾" bind off in pattern.

Finishing—Sew up side seams and sleeves. Work 2 rows of s c around vent at back, making 4, ch 3 loops for buttonholes on last row.

Smocking—On right side of dress, at left back, with contrasting shade of Angora, sew the first 2 K sts tog (about 4th row from top), then the next 2 K sts, leaving the thread loose underneath the 2 smocked sts. Repeat across row. Turn, start 2nd row, working in same manner, skipping first K st (thus forming a diamond). Work 2 more rows. Work 2 rows of smocking on top of pocket. Work 2 rows of smocking on cuffs.

Reprinted from *Juvenile Styles*, Volume 8, Page 11.

Illustration 180. Smocked dress trimmed with angora, No. 954. *Juvenile Styles,* Volume 8, Page 11.

Illustration 181. Jacket, cap, gloves and mittens, No. 961. *Juvenile Styles,* Volume 8, Page 22.

Million Dollar Baby ...on a budget!

JACKET

Needles—1 pair American Standard No. 4. 1 blunt embroidering Needle.
Material—Knitting Worsted 10 oz. Blue. Angora Trim, 22 Yards contrasting shade. Cap—3 ozs. 6 Pearl Buttons.
Gauge—5½ sts to 1 inch.

Size	4 Yrs.	6 Yrs.

Back—Cast on 61 sts 65 sts work in Moss st (Moss st is K 1, P 1 on an uneven amount of sts), until back measures 8" 9"
Bind off 3 sts at beg of the next 2 rows, K 2 tog at beg of the next 4 rows 51 sts 55 sts
Work even until armhole measures 5" 5½"
measuring straight up from where the 3 sts were bound off. Bind off 6 sts at beg of the next 6 rows, bind off for back of neck remaining 15 sts 19 sts

Left Front—Cast on 35 sts 37 sts
Row 1—K 1, P 1 for 12 sts, K 6, P 1, K 1 for remaining 17 sts 19 sts
Row 2—P 1, K 1 for 14 sts 16 sts K 1, P 1, K 1, P 6, K 1, P 1, K 1; K 1, P 1, for 9 sts. Repeat these 2 rows, until front measures same as for back to underarm. Bind off 4 sts at beg of the next row that begins at underarm, then K 2 tog at beg of every row at underarm 2 more times. Work even until armhole measures 3½" 4"
Bind off 5 sts at neck edge, then K 2 tog at beg of every row at neck edge, until you have 20 sts left. Now bind off 6 sts at shoulder edge, 3 times and continue to K 2 tog at neck edge.

Right Front—Work to correspond to Left Front, working buttonhole 1" from bottom as follows: K 2, bind off 2, follow pattern across, on next row, cast on 2 sts over bound off sts. Work buttonholes about 1½" apart (place pins on left front).

Sleeves—Cast on 31 sts 35 sts work in moss st for 2" 3"
*inc 1 st at each end, work 1 inch even, repeat from * until sleeve measures. 9" 10"
47 sts 51 sts
Work ½" even or desired length to underarm. Bind off 4 sts at beg of the next 2 rows, then K 2 tog at beg of the next 8 rows 31 sts 35 sts
Now K 2 tog at beg and end of every 4th row, until there remain 21 sts 23 sts
K 2 tog at beg and end of every row, until 13 sts 15 sts remain, bind off.

Finishing—Sew back to fronts, sew sleeve seams. Sew shoulders and insert sleeves into armholes, having a little fullness at top.

Collar—With wrong side toward you, skip 2 sts at end and pick up to within 2 sts at opposite end, 54 sts 58 sts K 1, P 1, K 1, P across to within last 3 sts, K 1, P 1, K 1. K next row, keeping first and last 3 sts in moss st and inc 1 st at beg and end of every K row on the 4th st, work these 2 rows in this manner until collar measures 2" 2¼"
Work 3 rows in moss st, bind off loosely.

Embroidering—With Angora fasten and insert needle thru the K 1 st, *skip 4 sts, downward, insert needle thru the next st, repeat from * to bottom of sweater, turn, insert needle thru same st at opposite side, continue to top of sweater. Work 3 more (K 1 st panels) to correspond. Embroider design as shown on illustration. Sew on buttons.

CAP

Cast on 18 sts, *K in garter st (K each row), for ¾". Inc 1 st at beg and end of next row, repeat from *, until you have 30 sts, 4½". Work ¾" even. K 2 tog at beg of every row, until you have 20 sts, bind off. Cast on 28 sts, work in garter st for 1 inch. *K 2, inc 1 st, K to end of row, K back, repeat from * until you have 38 sts. K 5 rows even. On same edge, *K 2, dec 1 st, K to end of row, K back, repeat from * until you have 28 sts. Work even until piece measures 8½", 48 ribs. Now inc and dec in same manner as before until you have 28 sts. Work 1" even, Bind off.

Finishing—Sew straight piece to back, starting at narrow end of back. Stretch front band a little as you sew. Steam the seam. (With Angora over-whip around seam about ½" apart, do not break thread and work back in same manner working thru same st on opposite side). With yarn, work 1 row s c across front of cap, being careful not to draw over points. With Angora over-whip in same manner as back of cap.

Ties—Fold brim back about 1½" on each end, pin. With Yarn, ch 12" now s c around sides and back of cap, decreasing to fit nape of neck. Ch 12", at end. Work 1 row s c over chs and back of cap.

GLOVES

Needles—1 Set each Nos. 1 and 3 double pointed.
Materials—2 oz. 3 ply yarn.
Gauge—7½ sts to 1 inch.

Size	4 Yrs.	6 Yrs.

Left Glove—With No. 1 needles, cast on 40 sts (12-12-16) and work in K 1, P 1 ribbing for 2" 2½"
K 8, P 1, K 1, P 1, *K 2, P 1, K 1, P 1 repeat from * once, K to end of rnd. Continue in pattern for ½" ½"

Change to No. 3 needles, inc 1, K 1, inc 1, K 1 (thumb gore) work to end of rnd, work 2 rnds even. Continue in this manner, having 2 more sts in thumb gore every 3rd rnd, until there are 4 inc in thumb gore, work 2 rnds even. Next rnd, slip first 12 sts on a thread, cast on 4 sts on 3rd needle, work to end of rnd. Work even 10 rnds 14 rnds

First Finger—K first 8 sts, cast on 2 sts, slip all but the last 4 sts on a thread, K last 4 sts. Divide these 14 sts on 3 needles, join in rnd, and K 1¾" 2"
K 2 tog for 1 rnd, break yarn, thread through remaining sts, draw tight and fasten securely. Finish all fingers and thumb in same manner.

Second Finger—K next 5 sts of rnd. (back of glove), cast on 2 sts, K last 5 sts of rnd, pick up 2 sts at base of first finger. Divide these 14 sts on 3 needles, K 2" 2¼"
K 2 tog for 1 rnd.

Third Finger—K next 4 sts, cast on 2 sts, K last 5 sts of rnd, pick up 3 sts at base of 2nd finger. Divide these 14 sts on 3 needles, K 1¾" 2"
K 2 tog for 1 rnd.

Fourth Finger—K remaining 9 sts, pick up 3 sts at base of 3rd finger. Divide these 12 sts on 3 needles, K 1½" 1¾"
K 2 tog for 1 rnd.

Thumb—K 12 sts from thread, pick up 4 sts at base of thumb. Divide these 16 sts on 3 needles, K 1½" 1¾"
K 2 tog for 1 rnd.

Right Glove—Work same as left glove for 2" 2½"
To Start Pattern—K 23, P 1, K 1, P 1, K 2) twice, P 1, K 1, P 1, K 4. Work same as left glove to first finger.

First Finger—K 4, cast on 2 sts, slip the last 8 sts on a thread, K last 8 sts, divide these 14 sts on 3 needles, K 1¾" 2"
K 2 tog for 1 rnd. K remainder of glove

same as left glove, beginning at front of glove to K up sts for remaining fingers.

MITTENS

Needles—1 set each, double pointed, Nos. 3 and 5.
Material—2 oz. Knitting Worsted.
Gauge—6 sts to 1 inch.

Sizes	4 Yrs.	6 Yrs.
With No. 3 needles, cast on	34 sts	36 sts
K 1, P 1 for	10-12-12 2"	12-12-12 2½"

K even for ½".

Thumb Gore—Change to No. 5 needles, inc 1, K 1, inc 1, K to end of rnd. K 1 rnd even after each increased rnd. Inc 1, K 3, inc 1, K to end of rnd. Inc in this manner until you have in thumb gore 4 inc. Slip first 12 sts to a st holder, cast on 4 sts, K even until piece measures from end of ribbing

	3½"	3¾"
Slip from first needle to 3rd needle	2 sts	2 sts
Slip from first needle to 2nd needle	—	1 st
Slip from 2nd needle to 3rd needle	3 sts	4 sts

First needle, K 1, K 2 tog, K to within last 3 sts of 2nd needle, sl 1, K 1, psso, K 1; 3rd needle, K 1, K 2 tog, K to within 3 sts of end, sl 1, K 1, psso, K 1. K 1 rnd even. Repeat these last 2 rnds until there remain 14 sts / 16 sts. Weave tog or bind off and sew.

Thumb—Divide 12 sts on 3 needles. Join yarn and pick up 4 sts over 4 cast on sts. On first row, dec over 4 picked up sts — 2 sts / 1 st — work even for 1¾" / 2". K 2 tog for 1 rnd, break yarn and thread through remaining sts, fasten securely. Work other mitten in same manner.

Reprinted from *Juvenile Styles*, Volume 8, Page 23.

Instructions for doll's dress can be found on page 80.

Illustration 182. Lace dress and Dutch cap, No. 965. *Juvenile Styles*, Volume 8, Page 30.

LACE DRESS AND DUTCH CAP
ILLUSTRATED ON COVER
No. 965

LACE DRESS

Needles—1 Steel Crochet hook, size 9.
Materials—4 balls, 400 yds. mercerized cotton. 4 small pearl buttons. 1 yd., ¼" velvet.
Size 3

Skirt—Starting at waist line, ch 164 sts, to measure 21". Work 1 d c in 4th ch from hook, *ch 1, skip 1 ch, d c in next ch, repeat from * across until you have 83 d c including ch 3 at beg of row. Work 1 more d c in last ch, ch 3, turn. Row 2—D c in next d c, *ch 2, s c in next d c, ch 4, sl st in 3rd ch (picot), ch 2, s c in next d c, ch 2, d c in next d c, repeat from * across row, ending row, 2 d c, ch 3, turn. Row 3—D c in next d c, *ch 2, s c in 2nd ch (next to picot), ch 5, sl st in 3rd ch, from hook, ch 3, s c in first ch from picot, ch 2, d c in next d c, repeat from * across, ending row, 2 d c, ch 3, turn. Row 4—D c in next d c, *ch 2, s c in center of ch 3, ch 5, sl st in 3rd ch, ch 3, s c in first ch from picot, ch 2, 1 d c in next d c, repeat from * across, ending row, 2 d c, ch 3, turn. Row 5—Repeat Row 4. Row 6—D c in next d c, *ch 2, s c in center of ch 3, ch 5, sl st in 3rd ch, ch 3, s c in first ch from picot, ch 2, 2 d c in next d c, repeat from * across, ending row, 2 d c, ch 3, turn. Rows 7 and 8—Work even. Row 9—Inc in each d c group. Rows 10 and 11—Work even, join, ch 3, turn, (remainder of skirt is joined at end of each row). Row 12—Inc in each d c group. Rows 13 to 17 inclusive—work even. Row 18—Inc in each d c group. Rows 19 to 23 inclusive—Work even. Row 24—Inc in each d c group. Rows 25 to 35 inclusive—Work even. Row 36—Inc in each d c group and work (ch 3 instead of ch 2 before and after d c groups for remainder of skirt). Rows 37 to 51 inclusive—Work even, join, ch 7.

Scallop—*Work 13 tr cr in every d c group with ch 1 between each tr cr, ch 1, s c in center of picot, ch 1, repeat from * around row, join, break thread.

Top of Dress—Back—Join thread to left side of vent, ch 3, work row 2 of skirt, following pattern above beading. Follow pattern of skirt for 4 more rows, break thread. Join thread at vent edge of left back, ch 3, work over 5 picot patterns, ending 2 d c in next d c, ch 3, turn. Work even until there are 13 rows from beading, having 2 d c at beg and end of each row. Work over 2 picot patterns at shoulder edge, having 2 d c at beg and end of each row for 4 rows. To shape shoulder, s c half way across next row, complete row with 3 d c with ch 1 between each d c, break thread. Work right back to correspond.

Front—Skip 4 picot patterns for underarm, fasten thread in next d c, ch 3, 1 d c in same st, follow pattern across front for 9 picot patterns, ending 2 d c in next d c. Follow pattern across front, having 2 d c at beg and end of rows, until there are 14 rows from beading. Work over 2 picot patterns for shoulder for 8 rows, slope shoulder same as back. Work other shoulder to correspond. Sew shoulders.

Frill at Sleeve—Fasten thread at underarm, and work 2 s c in each row around sleeve, ch 3, turn, work 1 d c in next s c, *ch 2, skip 1 s c, s c in next st, ch 4, sl st in 2nd ch (picot), ch 1, skip 1 s c, s c in next st, ch 2, skip 1 s c, 3 d c in next st, repeat from * across row, ending 2 d c in last 2 s c, ch 3, turn. Now work in pattern increasing 2 d c in each d c group, and having 2 d c at beg and end of rows, following picots same as for dress, until there are 4 pattern rows. *Work 10 tr cr in every d c group with ch 1 between each tr cr, ch 1, s c in picot, repeat from * around row, break thread. Sew edge of frill to underarm.

DUTCH CAP—4 blocks

With 2 strands of thread, starting at center, ch 3, join with a slip st to form ring. 1st rnd. Ch 3 (to count as d c), 2 d c in ring, ch 3, *3 d c in ring, ch 3, repeat from *2 more times. Join with a sl st to 3rd st of starting ch. 2nd rnd. Sl st in each st to first ch loop, ch 3, 2 d c in loop, ch 3, 3 d c in same loop, ch 3 *(3 d c, ch 3, 3 d c) in next loop, ch 3 repeat from *2 more times. Join as before. 3rd rnd. Sl st in each st to first ch loop, ch 3, 2 d c in loop, ch 3, 3 d c in same loop, ch 3, 3 d c in next loop, ch 3, *(3 d c, ch 3, 3 d c) in next loop, ch 3, 3 d c in next loop, ch 3, repeat from *2 more times, join. 4th rnd. Sl st in each st to first ch loop, ch 3, 2 d c in loop, ch 3, 3 d c in same loop, ch 3, 3 d c in next loop, ch 3, 3 d c in next loop, ch 3 *(3 d c, ch 3, 3 d c) in next loop, ch 3, 3 d c in next loop, ch 3, 3 d c in next loop, ch 3, repeat from *2 more times, join. Continue in this manner, increasing 2 sts at d c groups in each rnd, until there are 11 sts in each group, join, break thread.

Join two blocks with 1 row of s c across one side. Join third block to side of block one and one side of block two. Join fourth block to opposite sides of blocks two and one. Keep s c loose enough to prevent drawing. Work 2 rows of s c completely around hat decreasing 2 s c in back and front, spaced a few sts apart.

Scallop: *ch 5, sl st in 3rd ch from hook, ch 3, skip 3 sts, s c in each of the next 3 sts, repeat from *around.

Reprinted from *Juvenile Styles*, Volume 8, Page 30.

INDEX

A

Alabama, Miss: See Miss Alabama
Alaska, Miss: See Miss Alaska
Alfred, Meyer and Weissman: 201
Alice Blue Dress and Pinafore: See Patterns/Instructions, Sewing, Dress and Pinafore, Alice Blue
Alice in Wonderland: See Fashion Shows
Allentown, Pennsylvania: 45
Anita - Skiing Costume: See Patterns/Instructions, Knitting, Skiing Costume, Anita
Annabelle: See Patterns/Instructions, Knitting, Sport Suit, Annabelle
Apeda Studios: 200
Arizona, Miss: See Miss Arizona
Arkansas, Miss: See Miss Arkansas
Arlene - Bathing Ensemble: See Patterns/Instructions, Knitting, Bathing Ensemble, Arlene
Arlene - Crocheted Hat: See Patterns/Instructions, Crocheting, Hat, Arlene
Art Needlework: 33

B

Ballerina: See Patterns/Instructions, Sewing, Ballerina
Ballet Costume: See McCall Printed Pattern 1564; Patterns/Instructions, Sewing
Barbie: 35
Beaumont, Heller and Sperling Advertising Agency: 45
Becky: See Mary Hoyer Dolls
Ber-Mel Yarn Company: 200, 201
Berkshire Knitting Mills: 10
Billie Riding Habit: See Patterns/Instructions, Crocheting, Riding Habit, Billie
Blanket: See Patterns/Instructions, Crocheting, Blanket; Patterns/Instructions, Knitting, Blanket
Blouse and Jumper: See Patterns/Instructions, Sewing
Borelli, Bonnie: 37, 41
Bridal Party: See Fashion Shows
Bride: See Fashion Shows
Bride Dress and Veil: See Patterns/Instructions, Sewing
Bridesmaid Dress and Hat: See Patterns/Instructions, Sewing
Bridesmaids: See Fashion Shows
Brown, Alice: 2

C

California, Miss: See Miss California
Canada, Miss: See Miss Canada
Cape: See McCall Printed Pattern 1564; Patterns/Instructions, Sewing
Cape, Headband and Muff: See McCall's Printed Pattern 1891; Patterns/Instructions, Knitting
Carol - Suit and Hat: See Patterns/Instructions, Crocheting, Suit and Hat, Carol
Cathy: See Mary Hoyer Dolls; Unique Doll Company
Christian Science Monitor: 33, 34
Cinderella: See Fashion Shows
Clemenson, Kathleen: 41
Clemenson, Maybelle: 36, 41, 44
Clemenson, Sharon: 41
Colleen - Jerkin, Socks and Beanie: See Patterns/Instructions, Knitting, Jerkin, Socks and Beanie, Colleen
Colorado, Miss: See Miss Colorado
Connecticut, Miss: See Miss Connecticut
Connie - Short and Sweet (Coat and Beret): See Patterns/Instructions, Knitting, Coat and Beret, Connie - Short and Sweet
Convalescing Jacket Ensemble, A: See Patterns/Instructions, Knitting, Jacket Ensemble, A Convalescing
Corine - Queen of the Jungles (Long Dress and Cap): See Patterns/Instructions, Knitting, Long Dress and Cap, Corine - Queen of the Jungles
Crocheted hats Styled by BER-MEL: 201

D

Delaware, Miss: See Miss Delaware
District of Columbia, Miss: See Miss District of Columbia
Dolly Madison: See Patterns/Instructions, Sewing
Dolores - Skating Costume: See Patterns/Instructions, Crocheting, Skating Costume, Dolores
Dress: See McCall's Printed Pattern 1891; Patterns/Instructions, Sewing
Dress and Parasol Cover: See McCall's Printed Pattern 1891; Patterns/Instructions, Sewing

E

Earth, Miss: See Miss Earth
Edmonds, Debby: 43, 44
Ellis Mills Department Store: 2
Evening Dress and Cap: See McCall Printed Pattern 1564; Patterns/Instructions, Sewing

F

Fairy Godmother: See Fashion Shows
Fairy Princess: See Fashion Shows
Fashion Shows:
  Alice in Wonderland, 42
  Bridal Party, 34
  Bride, 43
  Bridesmaids, 43
  Cinderella, 34, 41
  Fairy Godmother, 41, 42
  Fairy Princess, 42, 44
  Gretel, 42
  Groom, 43
  Hansel, 42
  Jupiter's Darling, 42, 44; See also Miss Bo-Peep
  Little Bo-Peep, 34; See also Miss Bo-Peep
  Little Red Riding Hood, 42
  Maid of Honor, 43
  Miss Alabama, 37
  Miss Alaska, 37, 41
  Miss Arizona, 37, 38
  Miss Arkansas, 38
  Miss Bo-Peep, 42; See also Little Bo-Peep
  Miss California, 38
  Miss Canada, 38
  Miss Colorado, 39
  Miss Connecticut, 39
  Miss Delaware, 39
  Miss District of Columbia, 39
  Miss Earth, 43, 44
  Miss Florida, 39
  Miss Georgia, 39
  Miss Hawaii, 39
  Miss Idaho, 39
  Miss Illinois, 39
  Miss Indiana, 39
  Miss Iowa, 39
  Miss Kansas, 30
  Miss Kentucky, 39
  Miss Louisiana, 39
  Miss Maine, 39
  Miss Mars, 34, 42, 44
  Miss Maryland, 39
  Miss Massachusetts, 39
  Miss Michigan, 39
  Miss Minnesota, 39
  Miss Mississippi, 39
  Miss Missouri, 39
  Miss Montana, 39
  Miss Muffet, 34, 42
  Miss Nebraska, 39
  Miss Neptune, 42, 44
  Miss Nevada, 39, 40
  Miss New Hampshire, 40
  Miss New Jersey, 40
  Miss New Mexico, 40
  Miss New York, 40
  Miss North Carolina, 40
  Miss North Dakota, 40
  Miss Ohio, 40
  Miss Oklahoma, 40
  Miss Oregon, 40
  Miss Pennsylvania, 40
  Miss Pluto, 34, 43, 44
  Miss Rhode Island, 40
  Miss Saturn, 42, 44
  Miss South Carolina, 40
  Miss South Dakota, 40
  Miss Tennessee, 40
  Miss Texas, 40
  Miss Uranus, 42, 44
  Miss Utah, 40
  Miss Venus, 42, 44
  Miss Vermont, 40
  Miss Virginia, 40
  Miss Washington, 40
  Miss West Virginia, 40
  Miss Wisconsin, 40
  Miss Wyoming, 40, 41
  Prince Charming, 41, 42
  Queen, 34, 38
  Seven Dwarfs, 34
  Snow White, 34, 42
Fiberoid Doll Company: 8, 10
Florella Infants Set: See Patterns/Instructions, Infants Set, Florella
Florida, Miss: See Miss Florida
Frisch Doll Company: 10
  Gigi: 9, 10, 16, 25, 28, 29; See also Mary Hoyer Dolls

G

Gardner, Margaret: 41
Georgia, Miss: See Miss Georgia
Gigi: See Frisch Doll Company; Mary Hoyer Dolls
Goldilocks - Little Princess and Her Dolly: See Patterns/Instructions, Knitting, Princess Dress, Goldilocks - Little Princess and Her Dolly
Goldilocks - Princess Dress and Beret: See Patterns/Instructions, Knitting, Princess Dress and Beret, Goldilocks
Greta - Dutch Treat (Dutch Costume): See Patterns/Instructions, Crocheting, Dutch Costume, Greta - Dutch Treat
Gretel: See Fashion Shows
Groom: See Fashion Shows

H

Hans and Tina - "The Pond's Sweethearts" (Skating Costume): See Patterns/Instructions, Knitting, Skating Costume, Hans and Tina - "The Pond's Sweethearts"
Hansel: See Fashion Shows
Hawaii, Miss: See Miss Hawaii
Hess, Arlene: 4, 5; See also Hoyer, Arlene; Price, Arlene; Price, Jean B. Mrs.
Hoyer, Arlene: viii, 2, 3, 8, 36, 41, 201; See also Hess, Arlene; Price, Arlene; Price, Jean B. Mrs.
Hoyer, Mary: 1, 3, 8, 10, 19, 20, 33, 34, 35, 36, 41, 43, 139, 200, 201
Hoyer, William: viii, 1, 3, 9, 10, 33, 34, 35, 200

I

Idaho, Miss: See Miss Idaho
Ideal Novelty and Toy Company: 8, 10
  Vicky: 10; See also Mary Hoyer Dolls
Illinois, Miss: See Miss Illinois
Indiana, Miss: See Miss Indiana
Infant's Four-Piece Set: See Patterns/Instructions, Crocheting
Infant's Three Piece Set: See Patterns/Instructions, Crocheting
Iowa, Miss: See Miss Iowa
Isabelle - Skating Costume: See Patterns/Instructions, Knitting, Skating Costume, Isabelle

J

Jackie - Bare Back Rider: See Patterns/Instructions, Crocheting, Bare Back Rider, Jackie
Janette - . . . in the Spotlight (Skating Outfit): See Patterns/Instructions, Knitting, Skating Outfit, Janette - . . . in the Spotlight
Janie: See Mary Hoyer Dolls
Janie - "Miss Victory" is a Modern Cinderella (Evening Gown, Jacket and Fascinator): See Patterns/Instructions, Knitting, Evening Jacket and Fascinator, Janie - "Miss Victory" is a Modern Cinderella; Patterns/Instructions, Sewing, Evening Gown, Janie - "Miss Victory" is a Modern Cinderella
Jo-Ann - Swimming Suit: See Patterns/Instructions, Knitting, Swimming Suit, Jo-Ann
Judy - Lace Party Dress: See Patterns/Instructions, Crocheting, Lace Party Dress, Judy
Julianna, - Ski Suit: See Patterns/Instructions, Knitting, Ski Suit, Julianna
Jupiter's Darling: See Fashion Show
Juvenile Styles: viii, 1, 8, 19, 21, 33, 36, 200, 201-223
Juvenile Styles Publishing Company: 21, 36

K

Kansas, Miss: See Miss Kansas
Kathleen - Another Dance . . . Another Date . . . Another Gown for "Miss Victory" (Evening Gown, Jacket and Snood): See Patterns/Instructions, Knitting, Jacket and Snood, Kathleen - Another Dance . . . Another Date . . . Another Gown for "Miss Victory;" Patterns/Instructions, Sewing, Evening Gown, Kathleen - Another Dance . . . Another Date . . . Another Gown for "Miss Victory"
Kelly, J. Bayard Mrs.: 35
Kelly, Robin: 35, 43
Kentucky, Miss: See Miss Kentucky

L

Lace Dress and Dutch Cap: See Patterns/Instructions, Crocheting
Lace Dress and Hat: See Patterns/Instructions, Crocheting
Lancaster County, Pennsylvania: 2
Lenstrohm, Lois Ann: 33
Lightcap, Sharon: 41, 43, 44
Lingerie: See McCall's Printed Pattern 1891; Patterns/Instructions, Sewing
Little Bo-Peep: See Fashion Shows; Miss Bo-Peep
Little Mama . . . Little Dolly Lace Baby Dresses: See Patterns/Instructions, Crocheting, Lace Baby Dresses, Little Mama . . . Little Dolly
Little Red Riding Hood: See Fashion Shows
Lipfert, Bernard: 1, 8
Louise - Travel in the Best Circles (Dress): See Patterns/Instructions, Crocheting, Dress, Louise - Travel in the Best Circles
Louisiana, Miss: See Miss Louisiana
"Love at first sight" - Slip-Over and Jerkin: See Patterns/Instructions, Knitting, Jerkin, "Love at first sight;" Patterns/Instructions, Knitting, Slip-Over, "Love at first sight"
Lucille - Roller Skating Outfit: See Patterns/Instructions, Knitting, Roller Skating Outfit, Lucille
Lucretta - Skating Costume: See Patterns/Instructions, Crocheting, Skating Costume, Lucretta

M

McCall Pattern Company: 139
McCall Printed Pattern 1564: 166-179
  Ballet Costume: 173, 174, 176, 177, 179, 185; See also Patterns/Instructions, Sewing
  Cape: 173, 174, 175; See also Patterns/Instructions, Sewing
  Evening Dress and Cap: 170, 171, 173, 174, 185; See also Patterns/Instructions, Sewing
  Skating Suit: 167; See also Patterns/Instructions, Crocheting
  Slip and Panties: 172, 174, 175, 176, 178; See also Patterns/Instructions, Sewing
  Sunsuit and Bonnet: 172, 175, 176, 177, 178, 179, 185; See also Patterns/Instructions, Sewing
McCall's Art Needlework magazine: 36; See also McCall's Needlework and Crafts magazine
McCall's Needlework and Crafts magazine: 10, 12, 13, 14, 15, 16, 17, 18
McCall's Printed Pattern 1891: 180-199
  Cape, Headband and Muff: 183; See also Patterns/Instructions, Knitting
  Dress: 186, 189, 190; See also Patterns/Instructions, Sewing
  Dress and Parasol Cover: 186, 197, 198, 199; See also Patterns/Instructions, Sewing
  Lingerie: 187, 191, 192; See also Patterns/Instructions, Sewing
  Peignoir with Nightgown: 185, 186, 187, 188, 189, 192, 193, 194, 195, 196; See also Patterns/Instructions, Sewing
McCanns Business School: 2
Maid of Honor: See Fashion Shows
Maine, Miss: See Miss Maine
Margie: See Mary Hoyer Dolls; Unique Doll Company
Mars, Miss: See Miss Mars
Mary Hoyer Dolls:
  Becky: 10, 18, 30, 31, 164
  Cathy: 10, 17, 18, 30, 31, 32, 43; See also Unique Doll Company
  composition: 8, 9, 11, 12, 19, 20, 21

Gigi: 9, 10, 16, 25, 28, 29; See also Frisch Doll Company
  hard plastic: 8, 9, 11, 13, 14, 15, 16, 17, 18, 19, 20, 35, 38, 43
  Janie: 10, 30, 32
  Margie: 10, 16, 17, 18, 30, 32, 43; See also Unique Doll Company
  Vicky: 10, 16, 18, 43; See also Ideal Novelty and Toy Company
  vinyl: 10, 11, 16, 17, 18, 28, 30, 31, 32, 35
Mary Hoyer Doll Manufacturing Company: 10, 12, 13, 162, 164
Mary Hoyer Twins, Bobby and Betty - School Outfits: See Patterns/Instructions, Knitting, School Outfits, Mary Hoyer Twins, Bobby and Betty
Maryland, Miss: See Miss Maryland
Mary's Dollies: 1, 8, 9, 10, 19, 20, 21, 33, 36, 45-139, 145, 148, 150, 152, 156, 159
Massachusetts, Miss: See Miss Massachusetts
May-Belle - The Majorette: See Patterns/Instructions, Crocheting, The Majorette, May-Belle
Maybelle - Three-Piece Set: See Patterns/Instructions, Crocheting, Three-Piece Set, Maybelle
Mayree (Party Frock): See Patterns/Instructions, Crocheting, Party Frock, Mayree
Michigan, Miss: See Miss Michigan
Million Dollar Baby - Jacket, Cap, Gloves and Mittens: See Patterns/Instructions, Knitting, Jacket, Cap, Gloves and Mittens, Million Dollar Baby
Minnesota, Miss: See Miss Minnesota
Miss Alabama: See Fashion Shows
Miss Alaska: See Fashion Shows
Miss Arizona: See Fashion Shows
Miss Arkansas: See Fashions Shows
Miss Bo-Peep: See Fashion Shows; Little Bo-Peep
Miss California: See Fashion Shows
Miss Canada: See Fashion Shows
Miss Colorado: See Fashion Shows
Miss Connecticut: See Fashion Shows
Miss Delaware: See Fashion Shows
Miss District of Columbia: See Fashion Shows
Miss Earth: See Fashion Shows
Miss Florida: See Fashion Shows
Miss Georgia: See Fashion Shows
Miss Hawaii: See Fashion Shows
Miss Idaho: See Fashion Shows
Miss Illinois: See Fashion Shows
Miss Indiana: See Fashion Shows
Miss Iowa: See Fashion Shows
Miss Kansas: See Fashion Shows
Miss Kentucky: See Fashion Shows
Miss Louisiana: See Fashion Shows
Miss Maine: See Fashion Shows
Miss Mars: See Fashion Shows
Miss Maryland: See Fashion Shows
Miss Massachusetts: See Fashion Shows
Miss Michigan: See Fashion Shows
Miss Minnesota: See Fashion Shows
Miss Mississippi: See Fashion Shows
Miss Missouri: See Fashion Shows
Miss Montana: See Fashion Shows
Miss Muffet: See Fashion Shows
Miss Nebraska: See Fashion Shows
Miss Neptune: See Fashion Shows
Miss Nevada: See Fashion Shows
Miss New Hampshire: See Fashion Shows
Miss New Jersey: See Fashion Shows
Miss New Mexico: See Fashion Shows
Miss New York: See Fashion Shows
Miss North Carolina: See Fashion Shows
Miss North Dakota: See Fashion Shows
Miss Ohio: See Fashion Shows
Miss Oklahoma: See Fashion Shows
Miss Oregon: See Fashion Shows
Miss Pennsylvania: See Fashion Shows
Miss Pluto: See Fashion Shows
Miss Rhode Island: See Fashion Shows
Miss Saturn: See Fashion Shows
Miss South Carolina: See Fashion Shows
Miss South Dakota: See Fashion Shows
Miss Tennessee: See Fashion Shows
Miss Texas: See Fashion Shows
Miss Uranus: See Fashion Shows
Miss Utah: See Fashion Shows
Miss Venus: See Fashion Shows
Miss Vermont: See Fashion Shows
Miss Virginia: See Fashion Shows
Miss Washington: See Fashion Shows
Miss West Virginia: See Fashion Shows
Miss Wisconsin: See Fashion Shows
Miss Wyoming: See Fashion Shows
Mississippi, Miss: See Miss Mississippi
Missouri, Miss: See Miss Missouri
Mohnton, Pennsylvania: 2
Montana, Miss: Miss Montana
"My Sister and I" Are Two-of-A-Kind - Turtle Neck and Jacket: See Patterns/Instructions, Knitting, Jacket, "My Sister and I" Are Two-of-A-Kind; Patterns/Instructions, Knitting, Turtle Neck, "My Sister and I" Are Two-of-A-Kind

N

Nadine - Red Cross Nurse: See Patterns/Instructions, Knitting, Red Cross Nurse, Nadine
Nan and Jack - The Ship's In (Sailor Costume): See Patterns/Instructions, Knitting, Sailor Costume, Nan and Jack - The Ship's In
Nancy and Dick - The Cow Boy and Girl: See Patterns/Instructions, Knitting, The Cow Boy and Girl, Nancy and Dick
Nebraska, Miss: See Miss Nebraska

Neptune, Miss: See Miss Neptune
Nevada, Miss: See Miss Nevada
New Hampshire, Miss: See Miss New Hampshire
New Jersey, Miss: See Miss New Jersey
New Mexico, Miss: See Miss New Mexico
New York, Miss: See Miss New York
North Carolina, Miss: See Miss North Carolina
North Dakota, Miss: See Miss North Dakota

O

Ocean City, New Jersey: 10, 34, 35
Ohio, Miss: See Miss Ohio
Oklahoma, Miss: See Miss Oklahoma
Olga - Skating Outfit: See Patterns/Instructions, Skating Outfit, Olga
Oregon, Miss: See Miss Oregon

P

Paintings:
  Arlene: 4
  Bootsie Siamese cat: 5
  Flowers: 4
  Heron in the Swamp: 5
  House on the Hill: 4
  Karen, 6 years old: 5
  Karen, 13 years old: 5
  The Pond: 4
Patsy - Coat, Hat and Bag: See Patterns/Instructions, Crocheting, Coat, Hat and Bag, Patsy
Patterns/Instructions:
  Crocheting:
    Bare Back Rider, Jackie: 100, 101
    Bathing Ensemble, Paula: 96, 97
    Blanket: 209, 210
    Coat, Hat and Bag, Patsy: 92, 93
    Coat, Hat and Muff, Zorina - "Miss Victory" dressed as a Charming Ally: 78, 79
    Dress, Louise - Travel in the Best Circles: 125, 126
    Dress and Hat, Susanna - "Miss Victory" Sends V mail to her V male: 90, 91
    Dutch Costume, Greta - Dutch Treat: 113, 114
    Hat, Arlene: 201
    Infant's Four-Piece Set: 204, 205
    Infant's Three Piece Set: 206, 207
    Jacket, A Sailor's Sweetheart: 213
    Lace Baby Dresses, Little Mama . . . Little Dolly: 218, 219
    Lace Dress, Terry - Little "Miss Victory" and her little Mommy: 80, 81
    Lace Dress and Dutch Cap: 223
    Lace Dress and Hat: 203, 204
    Lace Party Dress, Judy: 68, 69
    Majorette, The, May-Belle: 70, 71
    Party Frock, Mayree: 64, 65
    Riding Habit, Billie: 98, 99
    Sailor Costumes, Nan and Jack - The Ship's In: 129, 130, 131
    Shoulderette, Three-Piece Infant's Set: 208, 209
    Skating Costume, Dolores: 105, 106
    Skating Costume, Lucretta: 76, 77
    Skating Outfit, Olga: 53, 62, 63
    Skating Suit: 167; See also McCall Printed Pattern 1564
    Suit and Hat, Carol: 123, 124
    Sun Dress and Cape, Renée: 135, 136
    Three-Piece Set, Maybelle: 207, 208
    Travel Costume, Peggy: 111, 112
  Knitting:
    Bathing Ensemble, Arlene: 58, 59
    Blanket: 210
    Cape, Headband and Muff: 183; See also McCall's Printed Pattern 1891
    Cape and Hood, Royal Highness: 212, 213
    Coat and Beret, Connie - Short and Sweet: 127, 128
    Coat and Hat, A Yoke Coat for Dolly and Her Mamma: 202, 203
    The Cow Boy and Girl, Nancy and Dick: 119, 120
    Evening Jacket and Fascinator, Janie - "Miss Victory" is a Modern Cinderella: 84; See also Patterns/Instructions, Sewing, Evening Gown, Janie - "Miss Victory" is a Modern Cinderella
    Infants Set, Florella: 216
    Jacket, "My Sister and I" Are Two-of-A-Kind: 220
    Jacket, Cap, Gloves and Mittens, Million Dollar Baby: 222, 223
    Jacket Ensemble, A Convalescing: 211, 212
    Jacket and Snood, Kathleen - Another Dance . . . Another Date . . . Another Gown for "Miss Victory:" 89; See also Patterns/Instructions, Sewing, Evening Gown, Kathleen . . . Another Dance . . . Another Date . . . Another Gown for "Miss Victory"
    Jerkin, "Love at first sight:" 219
    Jerkin, Socks and Beanie, Colleen: 215, 216
    Long Dress and Cap, Corine - Queen of the Jungles: 94, 95
    Princess Dress, Goldilocks - Little Princess and Her Dolly: 214
    Princess Dress and Beret, Goldilocks: 54, 55
    Red Cross Nurse, Nadine: 72, 73
    Roller Skating Outfit, Lucille: 107, 108
    Sailor Costume, Nan and Jack - The Ship's In: 129, 130, 131
    School Outfits, Mary Hoyer Twins, Bobby and Betty: 117, 118
    Skating Costumes, Hans and Tina - "The Pond's Sweethearts:" 121, 122, 123
    Skating Costume, Isabelle: 137, 138
    Skating Outfit, Janette . . . in the Spotlight: 132, 133
    Ski Suit, Julianna: 56, 57

Skiing Costume, Anita: Frontispiece, 102, 103, 104
Skiing Costume, Sonja: 74, 75
Slip-Over, "Love at first sight:" 219
Smocked Dress: 221, 222
Snow Suit: 217, 218
Sport Suit, Annabelle: 60, 61
Swimming Suit, Jo-Ann: 115, 116
Tennis Dress, Sunny - "Miss Victory" is Queen of the Courts: 82, 83
Turtle Neck, "My Sister and I" Are Two-of-A-Kind: 220
Vests, Boys' and Girls', Teen Team: 221
The Wavette: 66, 67
The Westerner: 109, 110
Sewing:
  Ballet Costume: 173, 174, 176, 177, 179, 185; See also McCall Printed Pattern 1564
  Ballerina: vii, 145, 146, 147
  Blouse and Jumper: 7, 164, 165
  Bride and Dress and Veil: 139, 140, 141, 142, 143, 144
  Bridesmaid Dress and Hat: 7, 140, 141, 142, 143, 144
  Cape: 173, 174, 175; See also McCall Printed Pattern 1564
  Dolly Madison: 20, 41, 134, 159, 160, 161
  Dress: 186, 189, 190; See also McCall's Printed Pattern 1891
  Dress and Parasol Cover: 186, 197, 198, 199; See also McCall's Printed Pattern 1891
  Dress and Pinafore, Alice Blue: 7, 150, 151
  Evening Dress and Cap: 170, 171, 173, 174, 185; See also McCall Printed Pattern 1564
  Evening Gown, Janie - "Miss Victory" is a Modern Cinderella: 85, 86; See Patterns/Instructions, Knitting, Evening Jacket and Fascinator, Janie - "Miss Victory" is a Modern Cinderella
  Evening Gown, Kathleen - Another Dance . . . Another Date . . . Another Gown for "Miss Victory:" 86, 87, 89; See also Patterns/Instructions, Knitting, Jacket and Snood, Kathleen - Another Dance . . . Another Date . . . Another Gown for "Miss Victory"
  Lingerie: 187, 191, 192; See also McCall's Printed Pattern 1891
  Peignoir with Nightgown: 185, 186, 187, 188, 189, 192, 193, 194, 195, 196; See also McCall's Printed Pattern 1891
  Scotch Plaid Jumper and Blousette: 6, 162, 163, 164
  Shorts and Halter: 152, 153, 155
  Slacks and Shirt: 152, 154, 155
  Slip and Panties: 172, 174, 175, 176, 178; See also McCall Printed Pattern 1564
  Southern Belle: 6, 148, 149
  Sun Bonnet Sue: 156, 157, 158
  Sunsuit and Bonnet: 172, 175, 176, 177, 178, 179, 185; See also McCall Printed Pattern 1564
  Terry Cloth Beach Robe: 152, 154
Paula - Bathing Ensemble: See Patterns/Instructions, Crocheting, Bathing Ensemble, Paula
Peggy - Travel Costume: See Patterns/Instructions, Crocheting, Travel Costume, Peggy
Pehlman, Grace: 36, 41
Peignoir with Nightgown: See McCall's Printed Pattern 1891; Patterns/Instructions, Sewing
Pennsylvania, Miss: See Miss Pennsylvania
Pluto, Miss: See Miss Pluto
Price: Arlene: 44; See also Hess, Arlene; Hoyer, Arlene; Price, Jean B. Mrs.
Price, Jean B. Mrs.: 35; See also Hess, Arlene; Hoyer, Arlene; Price, Arlene
Price, Karen: 3, 5, 35
Price, Kevin: 3
Price, Kim: 3
Price, Lynne: 3, 43, 44
Prince Charming: See Fashion Shows

Q

Queen: See Fashion Shows

R

Reading Automobile Club Magazine: 34
Reading Eagle: 35
Reading, Pennsylvania: 2, 3, 10, 19, 20, 33, 34, 45, 200, 201
Reading Times: 33, 35
Renée - Sun Dress and Cape: See Patterns/Instructions, Crocheting, Sun Dress and Cape, Renée
Rhode Island, Miss: See Miss Rhode Island
Ritter Advertising Agency: 45
Royal Highness - Cape and Hood: See Patterns/Instructions, Knitting, Cape and Hood, Royal Highness

S

Sailor's Sweetheart, A - Jacket: See Patterns/Instructions, Crocheting, Jacket, A Sailor's Sweetheart
Saturn, Miss: See Miss Saturn
S. B. Novelty Company: 19
Scotch Plaid Jumper and Blousette: See Patterns/Instructions, Sewing
Sensenig, Daniel: 2
Sensenig, Jane: 2
Sensenig, Mary: See Hoyer, Mary
Seven Dwarfs: See Fashion Shows
Shirley Temple: 8
Shober, Jan: 4
Shorts and Halter: See Patterns/Instructions, Sewing
Shoulderette - Three-Piece Infant's Set: See Patterns/Instructions, Crocheting
Skating Suit: See McCall Printed Pattern 1564; Patterns/Instructions, Crocheting

Slacks and Shirt: See Patterns/Instructions, Sewing
Slip and Panties: See McCall Printed Pattern 1564; Patterns/Instructions, Sewing
Smocked Dress: See Patterns/Instructions, Knitting
Snow Set: See Patterns/Instructions, Knitting
Snow White: See Fashion Show
Sonja - Skiing Costume: See Patterns/Instructions, Knitting, Skiing Costume, Sonja
South Carolina, Miss: See Miss South Carolina
South Dakota, Miss: See Miss South Dakota
Southern Belle: See Patterns/Instructions, Sewing
Spool Cotton Company: 201
Steiff: 35
Sun Bonnet Sue: See Patterns/Instructions, Sewing
Sunny - "Miss Victory" is Queen of the Courts (Tennis Dress): See Patterns/Instructions, Knitting, Tennis Dress, Sunny - "Miss Victory" is Queen of the Courts
Sunsuit and Bonnet: See McCall Printed Pattern 1564; Patterns/Instructions, Sewing
Susanna - "Miss Victory" Send V mail to her V male (Dress and Hat): See Patterns and Patterns/Instructions, Crocheting, Dress and Hat, Susanna - "Miss Victory" Sends V mail to her V male

T

Teen Team - Boy's and Girl's Vests: See Patterns/Instructions, Knitting, Vests, Boy's and Girl's, Teen Team

Temple, Shirley: See *Shirley Temple*
Tennessee, Miss: See Miss Tennessee
Terry Cloth Beach Robe: See Patterns/Instructions, Sewing
Terry - Little "Miss Victory" and her little Mommy (Lace Dress): See Patterns/Instructions, Crocheting, Lace Dress, Terry - Little "Miss Victory" and her little Mommy
Texas, Miss: See Miss Texas
This Month In Reading: 36

U

Unique Doll Company: 9
 Cathy: 10, 17, 18, 30, 31, 32, 43; See also Mary Hoyer Dolls
 Margie: 10, 16, 17, 18, 30, 32, 43; See also Mary Hoyer Dolls
Uranus, Miss: See Miss Uranus
Utah, Miss: See Miss Utah

V

Venus, Miss: See Miss Venus
Vermont, Miss: See Miss Vermont
Vicky: See Ideal Novelty and Toy Company; Mary Hoyer Dolls
Virginia, Miss: See Miss Virginia

W

Washington, Miss: See Miss Washington
Wavette, The: See Patterns/Instructions, Knitting

Wertz, Kathleen: 41
West Virginia, Miss: See Miss West Virginia
Westerner, The: See Patterns/Instructions, Knitting
Whitman, Sallie: 2
Wisconsin, Miss: See Miss Wisconsin
Wyoming, Miss: See Miss Wyoming
Wyomissing, Pennsylvania: 10,

Y

Yeich, Cliff: 34
Yoke Coat for Dolly and Her Momma, A - Coat and Hat: See Patterns/Instructions, Knitting, Coat and Hat, A Yoke Coat for Dolly and Her Momma

Z

Zorina - "Miss Victory" dressed as a Charming Ally (Coat, Hat and Muff): See Patterns/Instructions, Crocheting, Coat, Hat and Muff, Zorina - "Miss Victory" dressed as a Charming Ally
Zug, Elizabeth: 4

About the Author

Mary Hoyer, the originator of the famous Mary Hoyer Doll, has spent the greater part of her life creating the playthings of which little girls' dreams are made.

She began her career as a fashion designer in the early 1930s designing children's knitwear for several major yarn manufacturers. Her husband, William, formed a publishing company known as "Juvenile Styles" under which name six volumes of patterns for clothing to fit infants and children, all designed by Mary Hoyer, were published. In 1937 she conceived the idea of creating a slim bodied doll for which she would design knit and crochet patterns. The Mary Hoyer Doll, sculpted by Mr. Bernard Lipfert and manufactured by the Fiberoid Doll Company, was born and proved successful beyond her dreams. Nine volumes of *Mary's Dollies,* containing over 40 patterns and instructions for knit and crochet garments to fit the Mary Hoyer Doll, were published. Mary Hoyer also designed commercial patterns which were published by the McCall Pattern Company. Numerous kits for making additional clothes as well as a myriad of accessories to go with the doll were made available through the Mary Hoyer Doll Manufacturing Company which the Hoyers formed to handle the business.

Upon retirement this multi-talented lady turned to oil painting for a hobby and has nearly 100 paintings to her credit. Occasionally one of her granddaughters can talk her into sewing a specially designed gown for one of their Mary Hoyer Dolls.

A resident of Reading, Pennsylvania, for almost all of her life, Mary Hoyer and her husband now divide their time between Reading and Florida. Their daughter, Arlene, operates a women's apparel store at the Mary Hoyer Shop in Reading.